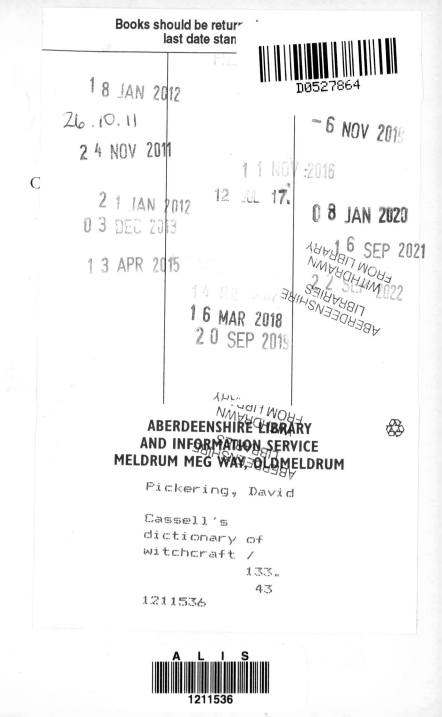

Cassell's
Dictionary of Witchcraft

David Pickering

CASSELL

This edition first published in the UK 1996 by
Cassell
Wellington House, 125 Strand, London WC2R 0BB
First paperback edition 1998
This edition 2002

Distributed in the US by
Sterling Publishing Co. Inc.
387 Park Avenue South, New York, NY 10016, USA

British Library Cataloguing-in-Data
A catalogue record for this book is available from the British Library

ISBN 0-304-36562-9

Printed and bound in Great Britain by
Bookmarque Ltd, Croydon, Surrey

Contents

Notable Outbreaks of Witchcraft 1320–1775

←NORTH AMERICA: *Salem 1692*

Mora 1669

Auldearn 1662

Aberdeen 1597

Renfrew 1697

Perth 1623

Stockholm 1675

Pittenweem 1704

North Berwick 1590

Edinburgh 1670

Kilkenny 1324

Pendle 1612, 1634

Burton 1596

Bury St Edmunds 1645, 1662, 1694

Bilson 1620

Warboys 1593

Somerset 1664

St Osyth 1582

Rheinbach 1631, 1636

Cologne 1625–6, 1630–6

SAXONY

Newbury 1643

Chelmsford 1566, 1579, 1589, 1645

Wapping 1652

Arras 1459–60

Würzburg 1623–33

Bamberg 1609–33

Channel Islands 1562–1736

Louviers 1647

Treves 1582–94

Eichstätt 1637

BOHEMIA

NORMANDY *1589–94, 1600–45*

Paris 1079–82

LORRAINE

Bavaria 1590–1631

Loudun 1634

BURGUNDY

HOLY ROMAN EMPIRE/GERMANY **1400–1775**

AUSTRIA 1570

Luxeuil 1529

FRANCHE-COMTÉ

Auxonne 1660–1

SALZBURG

Bordeaux

TYROL

SOUTHERN FRANCE *1320–1682*

Como 1514

Brescia 1510

BASQUE COUNTRY *1576–1609*

Toulouse

Avignon

Aix-en-Provence

Carcassonne

Preface

The paraphernalia of witchcraft, with its old hags, broomsticks, black cats, cauldrons and spells, is central to the cultural iconography of contemporary Europe and America. Tales of witches and demons are imbibed throughout the Western world at the earliest age through the media of children's books, television, fairytales and films (not least the cartoon classics of the Disney Studios). Teenagers and adults, meanwhile, accept without hesitation the archetypal witch as a standard character in horror films, novels and computer games.

Depictions of witches on broomsticks are to be found everywhere – on packaging, in advertising, as logos and in countless other contexts. Even our language reflects the influence of witchcraft: a beautiful face is described as 'bewitching' or 'enchanting'; a vindictive woman is called 'an old witch'; people admit to having fallen 'under a spell'; investigations into corruption or underhand dealing are commonly dubbed 'witch-hunts'. At Hallowe'en, the most important date in the witches' calendar, millions of people attend parties, chaperon their children on 'trick or treat' visits to the neighbours, decorate their homes with images of pumpkins, skeletons and witches, or curl up in front of a late-night horror movie that might very well present scenes of sabbats and black masses among other supernatural goings-on.

In an increasingly secular age, popular interest in all matters relating to the supernatural seems to have redoubled as enquiring minds seek evidence of something beyond materialist preoccupations. Few people believe seriously in the rather confused 'black magic' philosophy associated with witchcraft, as developed by Christian demonologists, but many recognise in the subject not only an opportunity to see history from a different viewpoint but also a chance to admit the exhilarating possibility of there being other ways of interpreting their own lives. Among other reasons, witches were persecuted not so much because of the evil deeds they were said to commit but because it was thought that through their supposed allegiance with the Devil they rejected conventional Christian thinking and thus represented a challenge to established society.

In this book I have attempted to shed light on the historical reality behind the myth of witchcraft and to show how the stereotypes were close to the truth in some cases and wildly inaccurate in others. In many instances it is difficult to be precise about what happened in a particular case – whether torture was employed or whether accused witches really believed in the claims they made, for example – but in others first-hand or second-hand accounts bring the reader vividly close to the events themselves. Witchcraft is history in the raw, an obsession that traumatised much of civilised society for a period of some two hundred years or more and which left an indelible mark upon the European psyche.

Entries are arranged alphabetically and include generic articles on such topics as demons, familiars, the Inquisition, sabbats, shape-shifting, spells and torture that serve to bring together a host of disparate but related entries. Other articles explore the witchcraft tradition of certain countries or regions or confine themselves to describing the most significant trials and the personages involved. Also included are a number of entries detailing the folk beliefs that evolved as part of witchlore and others summarising the theories of the most influential demonologists and other authorities on the subject. Copious cross-references throughout provide links with related articles that may be of interest to the reader.

Once again, my thanks go to the editors and production staff at Cassell for their assistance and to Jan, Edward and Charles for the familiar spirit.

David Pickering

Introduction

Witchcraft defined

Although the word 'witchcraft' comes from Old English *wiccian*, meaning to practise sorcery, witchcraft is considered by most authorities to be quite distinct from the much broader category of sorcery. Witchcraft is a reflection of Christian religious philosophy and culture, while sorcery, expressed in the common language of superstition, curses and spells, is a generic characteristic of folklore worldwide.

Sorcery denotes the pursuit of a certain end through magic, which might be harnessed through such varied means as simple herbalism, the use of waxen images or more elaborate spell-making. Common to all folklore traditions and to virtually all eras, sorcery relies upon the intervention of good and bad spirits but does not necessarily involve any deeper specifically anti-Christian purpose. A sorcerer might call on the assistance of demons, but in so doing there is no automatic presumption that he or she thereby denies the supremacy of God.

A witch, however, necessarily renounces the rites of baptism in order to make a pact with the Devil, with the aim of enjoying inherent magical gifts and gaining direct access to occult power. In the words of the Puritan William Perkins, 'the very thing that maketh a witch to be a witch, is the yielding of consent upon covenant'. In signing such a pact a witch lines up against everything that the Christian Church represents and is presumed to intend the repudiation and destruction of God Himself. It is witchcraft in this specific, historical, anti-Christian sense that is discussed in this book, rather than the broader science of sorcery, which belongs more properly to the realm of folklore.

The roots of witchcraft

Mankind has always called on the mysterious powers of nature to intervene in everyday life – to cure disease, promote harvests, drive off enemies and so forth. The underlying concepts of spell-casting, cursing and even the business of flying through the air on bewitched animals or demons are millennia old and in some respects are of pre-Christian pagan origins (although medieval and post-medieval witchcraft probably did not represent a continuous thread of belief going back to before the time of Christ).

The medieval mind was not unduly troubled by the activities of sorcerers, prophets and healers, all of whom claimed knowledge of various types of folk magic without posing a threat to the Christian Establishment with which they coexisted. The boundaries between conventional religious practice and folklore were frequently blurred and the common populace relied upon a wide array of charms, amulets and other superstitious beliefs as well as upon the power of prayer both to protect themselves and, on occasion, to bring harm to an enemy. In an age when medicine was still in its infancy every community boasted its 'Wise Women', whose roles combined those of midwife, doctor, vet, herbalist, psychiatrist, seer and confessor.

The anonymous *Canon Episcopi* of the tenth century AD emphasised the relatively unconcerned attitude of the Church towards allegations of sorcery. It was admitted that some people made outrageous claims about their powers, such as flying through the air and casting spells, but it was self-evident, according to the *Canon*, that these people were deluded – as no one could possibly perform such feats. Self-proclaimed witches should be chastised, therefore, for allowing themselves to be thus deluded, rather than for actually doing the things they claimed. The *Canon Episcopi* presented a considerable intellectual obstacle to the demonologists of later centuries who wished to see the persecution of witches officially sanctioned. The authority of the *Canon* could not be overruled, and it denied that witchcraft was a possibility in reality: if witchcraft was not a reality, then its practice could not be punished and its adherents subjected to the authority of the courts.

If a local 'Wise Woman' was actually brought to trial the case usually arose out of actual harm that had transpired, such as murder by poisoning – that sorcery might be alleged was merely incidental: it was the crime itself that mattered. Suspects accused of employing magic were routinely sentenced to such light punishments as the payment of fines or a series of appearances in the pillory.

Medieval society was relatively stable, but the collapse of the feudal system, coupled with famines, warfare and splits within the Roman Catholic Church in the early fourteenth century, signalled a fundamental change in the European psyche. The arrival of the Black Death in Europe in 1347, leading to the death of some twenty-five million people (one-third of the population), led to increased socio-economic turmoil and intense anxiety throughout the continent. Suddenly, it seemed that civilisation itself was tottering on the brink of chaos. With this increase in tension, which threatened the hierarchy of both Church and State, came a need for scapegoats to blame for this apocalyptic state of affairs. Mystic forces of evil, it was claimed, surely lay behind these disasters and the guilty parties needed to be rooted out.

Almost any nonconformist group would do. Among the groups that were consequently singled out for persecution were the Jews and various heretical sects, which were suspected of conspiring with Satan to overturn the Christian order. Satan, the enemy within, was recast as the personification of chaos and the demonologists of the Catholic Church were soon hard at work providing an intellectual basis for the persecution of those deemed to be the Church's opponents. Crimes laid at the door of the Knights Templar, for instance, included child sacrifice, sexual perversity and veneration of the Devil.

With these sects destroyed, the demonologists cast about for a new scapegoat group (regardless of whether or not such a group really existed). The coincidence between the charges that had been trumped up against the Knights Templar and others and the accusations that had been made against sorcerers over the centuries made them natural candidates for suspicion. Traditional sorcery was now combined with Satanism to create a new heresy: witchcraft.

The early development of European witchcraft

The Inquisition, the office of the Roman Catholic Church whose job it was to identify and exterminate heresy in all its forms, played a key role in the early persecution of Europe's witches. Having stamped out such heretics as the Cathars, the Waldensians and the Knights Templar with ruthless efficiency, the Inquisition – which had enriched itself and the mother Church by confiscating the wealth of its victims – eagerly latched on to the possibility of having witches declared heretics and thus brought within its sphere of influence.

The theory evolved that a new, and much more dangerous, generation of sorcerers dedicated to worshipping the Devil and to overthrowing Christ's Church on Earth had sprung up and was even now launching a concerted full-scale invasion of the civilised world. It was not so much the damage that such witches did that mattered but the fact that they had denied Christ. Such denials were, it was argued, treason against God – and no crime could be more serious than that. The fact that a deranged old hag might be suspected of denying her baptism was itself deserving of punishment, but the notion that, though perhaps weak and confused as an individual, she could be part of a vast international conspiracy against the established order made her infinitely more threatening.

The demonologists pointed to the Bible as the supreme authority for the reality of witchcraft, quoting, for instance, the story of the Witch of Endor, through whom Saul attempted to communicate with the spirit of the deceased Samuel, and the legends surrounding Simon Magus, a rival of the Apostle Peter who was alleged to have attempted to learn to fly. Many notable Christian thinkers, including St Augustine, had expressed a belief in divination and allied magic and their names were now quoted as 'proofs' of the witchcraft threat.

To those who objected on the grounds that God was all-powerful and therefore demons could not wield magical powers at the behest of witches, the demonologists answered that God permitted the Devil certain powers to do evil as a means of testing mankind.

Some authorities attempted a distinction between good and bad, or 'white' and 'black', witchcraft. White witchcraft was harmless sorcery and so no threat to the Church; only 'black' magicians derived their powers from the Devil. This subtlety was lost on most witch-hunters, however, and it was more generally accepted that anyone who claimed, or was suspected of, magic powers of any sort had consorted with demons and was therefore guilty of heresy, for which the only possible punishment could be death. In view of the alleged emergence of this new, more powerful sect of witches the relatively lenient terms of the *Canon Episcopi* were irrelevant, and the inquisitors stressed the need for far more stringent measures to be put in place. As early as 1258 Pope Alexander IV had sanctioned the prosecution of suspects accused of practising magic, but it was some time before witchcraft became legitimate territory for the Inquisition. In 1320, after much pressure from his minions, Pope John XXII finally accepted the theory that witchcraft was a heresy because it necessarily involved a pact with the Devil. Accordingly, he instructed the Inquisition to destroy all those incriminated in such Devil worship:

> [Pope John,] desiring fervently that all evildoers, infecting the flock of Christ, be put to flight from the house of God, wishes, orders, and commissions you, by his authority, to seek out and otherwise proceed against those who sacrifice to devils or worship them, or render homage to them, by giving them a charter or something else signed with their name; those who make an open avowed pact with the devils; those who fashion or cause to be fashioned any waxen image, or anything else to bind the devil, or by invocation of devils to commit any kind of *maleficium*; those who, by misusing the sacrament of baptism, baptise a figurine of wax or one made of something else, or cause it to be baptised, or by invocation of devils make or cause anything similar to be done

... and also those sorcerers and witches who use the sacrament of the mass or the consecrated host as well as other sacraments of the church, or any one of them, in form or matter, for sorcery or witchcraft.

The first steps in a systematic campaign against witchcraft were made with a series of witch-hunts in southern France in the 1320s. The inquisitors, evidently anxious to establish heretical intent and thus to confirm their right to hear the accusations, took care to probe into the motives of suspects brought before them. Through the extraction of confessions by torture the Inquisition successfully gathered 'evidence' for the whole paraphernalia of witchcraft, including sabbats, cannibalism, intercourse with demons and veneration of the Devil in the form of a goat. These 'discoveries', which supported the notion of a huge and highly malevolent subversive pan-European organisation devoted to Satan, served to whip up panic throughout southern France, Switzerland, northern Italy and the southern German states, with thousands being sent to the stake for such offences.

Records suggest that some two hundred convicted witches were burned at Carcassonne and another four hundred at Toulouse between the years 1320 and 1350. In these early stages the Church handled all witch trials, passing convicted witches to the secular authorities for punishment with a hypocritical plea for clemency to be shown to them. The first secular trial for witchcraft took place in Paris in 1390, and subsequently most suspects were examined by secular or episcopal courts. The Church, however, continued to gather information against suspects and to play a leading role in securing convictions (the spoils being divided between the various parties concerned).

By the end of the fifteenth century the mythology of witchcraft was well developed and various stereotypes were firmly established. Although in reality, especially on the Continent of Europe, witches might be of any age, sex or class, the popular imagination depicted the archetypal witch as an aged, poverty-stricken old crone who as likely as not had a reputation for eccentric and unfriendly behaviour.

Usually she lived apart from 'normal' civilised society, often in company with certain animals (cats, blackbirds, mice and the like), which were likely to be identified as her familiars. Her guilt could be proved by discovery of the Devil's mark about her person, and further established by searching for the witch's marks at which she fed her imps. Allegations that might be brought against her included the casting of various spells to cause illness, damage to property and even death, riding to sabbats on a broomstick, consorting with demons and paying homage to the Devil.

Evidence of a pact with the Devil was decisive, as this was the offence at the heart of the heresy of witchcraft. The Protestant George Gifford noted: 'A witch by the word of God ought to die the death not because she killeth men – for that she cannot, unless it be those witches which kill by poison, which either they receive from the devil or he teacheth them to make – but because she dealeth with devils.'

In 1484 Pope Innocent VIII's bull *Summis Desiderantes* sanctioned the Inquisition's use of the severest measures against accused witches. Because of the unique nature of the crime suspects were presumed guilty until proved otherwise and were deprived of the usual safeguards of the law, frequently being denied knowledge of the charges against them and being prohibited from calling witnesses for their own defence or from hiring a lawyer to act on their behalf. The issuing of the 1484 bull effectively marked the start of the main period of persecution.

The witchcraft hysteria

Christian western Europe was gripped by widespread paranoia about the supposed activities of witches for a period of some three hundred years, roughly from the middle of the fifteenth century to the middle of the eighteenth century. What happened between 1450 and 1750 constituted a veritable holocaust and a puzzling refutation of the civilised values of post-Reformation Europe. The normal ideals of humanity, legality and tolerance were almost casually set aside in order to root out many of the most defenceless people in society, and to have them brutally exterminated on charges that were preposterous even to the most bigoted and superstitious minds.

During this period countless suspects were hauled before the authorities on the flimsiest evidence, viciously tortured or otherwise pressured into making a confession and then summarily put to death, usually by burning or, in England and later in colonial America, by hanging. Details of sabbats and the names of others attending them were routinely extorted during torture so that further trials could be set in motion, leading to a rash of trials that might result in the decimation of the population of certain villages and towns. The small German town of Quedlinburg, for instance, saw 163 of its inhabitants executed as witches in a single day. The fact that torture was not permitted in England under the common law meant that English society was spared the epidemics of witchcraft hysteria that blighted the German states, but even here there were a number of notable mass trials that culminated in the execution of several members of alleged covens.

The split between the Catholic and newly emergent Protestant worlds in the fifteenth century had relatively little effect upon the spread of the hysteria. The Protestant authorities adopted the procedures of their Catholic counterparts and proved just as ruthless in their suppression of Devil-worship, often quoting Catholic authorities as justification for their witch-hunts. Perhaps the most influential publication on the subject was the infamous *Malleus Maleficarum*, which was issued in 1486 as a guide to judges in witchcraft cases. It codified for the first time a host of myths concerning witches and suggested how best to set about obtaining convictions. The distinction between black and white witchcraft, the authors alleged, was illusory and all witches should be exterminated wherever they were found.

It seems that the hysteria was worst in states where power was decentralised and the judges involved were in close contact with the communities from which came the accusations – typically born out of petty jealousy or trivial quarrels. In the tiny prince-bishoprics of Germany, for instance, the witch judges were much influenced by local prejudice and all too often proved both unwilling and unable to resist the hysteria that gripped their courts. In countries where judges were able to think about the evidence in a more detached and sober fashion victims were far fewer in number. The use of torture was a crucial factor. The demonologist Jean Bodin expressed the orthodox view regarding the application of torture in witchcraft cases in his *De la Démonomanie des Sorciers* of 1580:

> Now, if there is any means to appease the wrath of God, to gain his blessing, to strike awe into some by the punishment of others, to preserve some from being infected by others, to diminish the number of evil-doers, to make secure the life of the well-disposed, and to punish the most detestable crimes of which the human mind can conceive, it is to punish with the utmost rigour the witches.

Suspects had little hope of escape if they were accused in states where torture was accepted as a means of extracting confessions of guilt. Once an allegation of witchcraft was made, the fate of the accused was sealed. Unsupported accusations were readily accepted by many courts, and if any corroborating evidence was needed the authorities had only to torture the suspect into giving the required confession or to identify upon their body the incriminating Devil's mark. The discovery of a single mole, wart, scar or other imperfection on the skin would suffice to indicate guilt (one famous lawyer of Cologne roundly declared that no one with such a flaw on their skin could be entirely innocent).

In countries where torture was prohibited, courts faced greater difficulty in obtaining convictions. In England and Scandinavia, for instance, there was less reliance upon the obtaining of confessions and more emphasis upon accusations of actual *maleficia* committed by suspects, together with such physical evidence as witch's marks and the possession of familiars (a peculiarity of English witches given relatively little attention elsewhere). Because of the bar on torture – though certain forms of duress were allowed – witch-finders in these countries were able to gather very little evidence of covens or sabbats and so were rarely able to turn an isolated case into an epidemic of trials.

There were, none the less, various ingenious ways in which a suspected witch might be tested even in countries where overt torture was prohibited. Before an alleged witch was brought before the authorities he or she might have been subjected to the ordeal of swimming (tossing into a pond or river to see if the suspect floated or not) or weighing against a church Bible. The prisoner might also have been pricked for discovery of the Devil's mark, which was supposed to be insensitive to pain and could not bleed.

The worst atrocities were witnessed in the German states, then part of the Holy Roman Empire: for every witch put to death in England, where witchcraft became a felony in 1542 and a capital offence in 1563, perhaps as many as a hundred German witches were killed. Church and State united in Germany in using witchcraft to seize the assets of rich and poor alike, preying on the gullibility of both the prince-bishops and the general public to execute thousands of alleged witches and acquire their property. It was reported in 1600 by one witchcraft judge that 'Germany is almost entirely occupied with building fires for the witches'. The diocese of Bamberg in particular is remembered for the spate of trials that was conducted there with the utmost savagery in the late 1620s, when something like a hundred witches were put to death each year between 1626 and 1629. Other areas that suffered more than most included the states of Lorraine, Trèves (Trier) and Würzburg. In the Silesian town of Neisse the executioner constructed an iron oven in which he roasted approximately a thousand convicted witches.

Another centre of the hysteria was Scotland. The crucial figure in the case of Scotland was James VI (later James I of England), the well-educated but superstitious king who was tainted by the witchcraft hysteria raging elsewhere in Europe when he visited Denmark to meet his intended bride. On his return home James interested himself in the trial of the so-called North Berwick Witches, whose crimes were said to have included the attempted murder of James himself through shipwreck, image magic and poisoning. One of the witches, Agnes Sampson, had a reputation as a healer – but it would appear from the surviving records that most of the accused had nothing to do with witchcraft and there was probably no plot.

The trial had strong political overtones because James's cousin, the Earl of Bothwell, was implicated, but, whatever the machinations at work, James was clearly much affected by the episode. In 1597 he published his infamous *Daemonologie*, written partly in refutation of the sceptical Sir Reginald Scot's *A Discoverie of Witchcraft*, in which James stressed the reality of the witchcraft threat and called for much more stringent action to be taken. As king of a united England and Scotland James wasted little time in putting his ideas into practice, and it was under his Witchcraft Act of 1604 that the majority of famous British witches were tried. It was for James, incidentally, that William Shakespeare wrote his play *Macbeth*, with its three 'weird sisters'.

The malevolent activity of self-styled 'witchfinders' served to intensify the hysteria wherever they operated. Among the most notorious of these was the Englishman Matthew Hopkins, the self-appointed 'Witchfinder-General' who instituted a reign of terror over a period of eighteen months or so in the eastern counties of England in the 1640s. Like witchfinders elsewhere in Europe, he traded on the climate of fear and suspicion and amassed considerable earnings from the employment of his services before public revulsion drove him into premature retirement.

For the most part the witchcraft hysteria never extended beyond the borders of Christian western Europe, but it did occasionally lead to outbreaks elsewhere in the world where European influence was pronounced. Most notable of these regions was Puritan New England, which was then still under English rule. Colonial America in the late seventeenth century faced many pressures, including conflict with the Indians and continuing new arrivals. Several witchcraft trials culminated in executions, and the hysteria reached a climax in 1692 with the notorious case of the Salem Witches. The trauma of the Salem case had a profound effect upon the colonies and effectively marked the end of witchcraft belief in the Americas.

By the time the hysteria finally petered out tens of thousands of accused persons had been put to death on charges of witchcraft throughout Europe and colonial America. Historical estimates of the number of dead went as high as nine million, but more realistic modern estimates have suggested a total of between twenty thousand and one hundred thousand victims (a figure of around fifty thousand is cautiously accepted by many authorities).

The decline of witchcraft

The witchcraft panic began to subside in most parts of Europe from the mid-seventeenth century (although there were late flare-ups in such countries as Poland and Hungary well into the succeeding century). Society was now more stable than it had been in the previous two or three centuries, and the need for scapegoats receded. The fractured states of Germany, in which the hysteria had reached its height, were slowly consolidated into a larger country and Church and State felt immune to the witchcraft threat. A new rationality led to the rejection by courts of spectral evidence and the testimony of young children.

The last English witchcraft trial was staged in 1712, while the last one in Scotland took place in 1722. The laws against witchcraft in England and Scotland were repealed in 1736 and in most countries the hysteria was defunct by 1750. The last Dutch trial was held as early as 1610, the last French trial took place in 1745, the last German case was heard in 1775, the last Swiss case in 1782 and the last Polish case in 1793. With the removal of legal prohibition and a new reluctance to accept the actual interference of Satan in earthly affairs, the practice of witchcraft was once again reduced to the level of mere superstition and sorcery as it had originally been in the years before the thirteenth century.

The word 'witchcraft' is now commonly assumed to cover magic practices of all kinds, including voodoo and other rites better described as 'folk religions'. Cases that have captured the headlines over the years since the mid-eighteenth century have on the whole referred to instances of common or garden sorcery rather than witchcraft, and only rarely has a suspect been accused of having made a pact with the Devil. In most of these cases, a person has been accused of some *maleficia* achieved through magic without regard to the origins of his or her powers.

The very occasional exception has been recorded, however. In 1928 the London *Sunday Chronicle* reported the case of an old woman of Horseheath, Sussex:

> One day a black man called, produced a book, and asked her to sign her name in it. The woman signed the book, and the mysterious stranger then told her she would be the mistress of five imps who would carry out her orders. Shortly afterwards the woman was seen out accompanied by a rat, a cat, a toad, a ferret, and a mouse. Everybody believed she was a witch, and many people visited her to obtain cures.

The link between post-Reformation witchcraft and modern Satanism is faint. Occultists such as Aleister Crowley were much more concerned to develop their own personal intellectual creeds through the language of demonology and Devil-worship than they were to establish themselves as latter-day witches. None the less, the terminology has become confused and it is all too easy now to accept Crowley, Gerald Gardner and others as the direct descendants of historical witches, rather than as the precocious aspiring sorcerers they properly are.

The theories of Margaret Murray, published in the 1920s, are often quoted by those anxious to forge a link between contemporary witchcraft and the historical variety, which may in turn (according to Murray's theory) be traced back to pre-Christian pagan religion. This linkage is highly artificial and most modern scholars reject it, although practitioners of 'Wicca' in its various modern forms continue to argue the case, seeing themselves as the heirs of some lost nature religion long since obscured by the development of more sophisticated religious codes such as Christianity.

Aberdeen Witches The city of Aberdeen was gripped by the witchcraft hysteria in 1596 and consequently witnessed one of the most notorious series of TRIALS in Scottish legal history. In response to growing public alarm at the witchcraft threat, ministers and elders of the Reformed Church busied themselves in collecting evidence against a host of suspects in the Aberdeen area, mainly elderly women.

In the flurry of accusations that were exchanged all manner of supernatural evil-doing was alleged. It was claimed that the numerous culprits had worked magic to cause death by the power of the EVIL EYE, to make husbands become adulterers, to harm livestock, to turn milk sour, to raise storms, to cause NIGHTMARES and to make love CHARMS, among other malpractices. Such was the sensitivity to witchcraft at the time that concocting even the most harmless herbal remedy was sufficient grounds for an arrest. Under pressure, which included subjection to the ordeal of SWIMMING, many of the accused confessed in some detail about their practices. In addition to the above they claimed that they had danced with demons round the market cross of Aberdeen at the hour of midnight on HALLOWE'EN, and that they had also cavorted around an ancient grey stone situated at the bottom of the hill at Craigleuch to the music of the DEVIL himself.

It emerged that the Aberdeen witches met in COVENS of thirteen members under the direction of the Devil, disguised as a grey stag, a BOAR or a DOG and calling himself Christsonday. He was often accompanied by his consort, the Queen of ELPHEN. Members of the covens were required to KISS their master and mistress on the buttocks as a gesture of obeisance, and sexual intercourse with them frequently took place at their meetings.

Janet Wishart, a crone among the many accused, was typical. She was suspected of murdering one Andrew Webster by magic and causing the ague in another man, Alexander Thomson, and was further accused of taking body parts from a corpse, while still on the gallows, for her own nefarious purposes. Another woman, Isobel Cockie, was accused of bewitching mills and livestock, while Margaret Ogg allegedly devoted her attentions to poisoning meat. Helen Rogie made waxen images of her victims to cause them harm, Isobel Strachan misled young men, Isobel Ritchie made magical foods for expectant mothers and Isobel Ogg raised storms. Many of those arraigned before the authorities in Aberdeen had been identified by one of their number, who claimed to have been present at a huge gathering of two thousand witches at Atholl. Andrew Mann, himself a confessed witch, had agreed to turn King's Evidence and was appointed WITCHFINDER for the court, testing suspects by PRICKING them for the DEVIL'S MARK.

At the close of proceedings in April 1597 no fewer than twenty-three women and one man were found guilty of the crimes with which they were charged. The hapless victims were tied to stakes, strangled by the public executioner and then burned to ashes at a site in the vicinity of modern Commerce Street to prevent the evil in their bodies being passed on to others. Legend has it that the stench from the fires lingered over Aberdeen for weeks. Several of those arraigned before the court escaped this grim fate by committing suicide while confined in the Tolbooth or in Our Lady's Pity-vault. The bodies of these wretches were dragged through the streets until they were torn to shreds. Those whose guilt was found 'not proven' were branded on the cheek and banished from the city.

Among the grisliest mementoes of the trials are the surviving accounts showing how much it cost to burn Janet Wishart and one of her alleged confederates. Including the stake, the fuel, the executioner's rope and his fee, the cost of taking their two lives was £5 8s 4d. The official accounts ran as follows:

For 20 loads of peat to burn them: 40 shillings
For a boll [6 bushels] of coal: 24 shillings
For four tar barrels: 26 shillings, 8 pence
For fir and iron barrels: 16 shillings, 8 pence
For a stake and dressing of it: 16 shillings
For four fathoms [24 feet] of tows [hangman's rope]: 4 shillings
For carrying the peat, coals and barrels to the hill: 8 shillings, 4 pence
To one justice for their execution: 13 shillings, 4 pence

Not long after the end of the Aberdeen trials King JAMES I published his *Daemonologie*, which did much to whip up further witch hysteria throughout Scottish society.

See also SCOTLAND.

Adam, Isobel *see* PITTENWEEM WITCHES.

Agar, Margaret *see* SOMERSET WITCHES.

Agrippa von Nettesheim, Heinrich Cornelius 1486–1535. Also known as Heinrich Cornelis, this German writer, adventurer, alchemist, physician and scholar was famed for his interest in the black arts and only narrowly escaped condemnation as a witch himself.

The life of Cornelius Agrippa is cloaked in mystery, but it seems he pursued his interest in witchcraft and related matters with zeal. He devoted himself to the study of the complex CABALA system of magic, and legend has it that on one occasion in 1525 he was visited in his laboratory in Florence by the Wandering Jew, the unfortunate soul who insulted Christ on his way to Calvary and was sentenced to roam the Earth until Judgement Day. Several of the stories surrounding his name were developed by the eighteenth-century German dramatist Johann Wolfgang von Goethe when he came to write *Faust*. Agrippa's writings include a massive treatise, *De Occulta*

Philosophia in which he set out a defence of magic practice, claiming that such knowledge illuminated man's understanding of God and the natural world.

Aix-en-Provence Nuns A group of nuns who in 1611 were at the heart of a sensational witchcraft trial in the city of Aix-en-Provence in FRANCE. The case revolved around Sister Madeleine de Demandolx de la Palud, a nun who had a history of depressive illness. She came from a wealthy background and had been admitted to an Ursuline convent in 1605 at the age of nine, but was later sent home because of her nervous instability. When she was thirteen she came under the influence of a handsome thirty-four-year-old priest from Marseilles, Father Louis Gaufridi, a friend of the family who was soon spending a great deal of time alone with her. It became evident that Madeleine was in love with the priest and, after a visit that lasted an hour and a half, rumours began to spread about the couple.

Gaufridi was warned by his superiors against further visits, and in 1607 Madeleine was sent to the Ursuline convent in Marseilles as a novice. Here she confessed to the Mother Superior that she had indeed had an affair with the priest – but the matter was at this stage taken no further, beyond Madeleine's removal to the convent at Aix-en-Provence where it would be more difficult for the pair to meet.

The enforced separation seems to have been too much for Madeleine. She began to suffer fits and shocked her superiors at the convent when, at Christmas 1609, she seized a crucifix during confession and destroyed it. She also complained of being tormented by DEMONS and declared that she had been bewitched by Gaufridi by means of a CHARM hidden in a WALNUT. It was decided that she was indeed possessed and an EXORCISM was attempted, though without success. In a climate of gathering hysteria in the convent, three more nuns began to succumb to similar fits.

When questioned, Gaufridi denied any immorality with Madeleine, but her allegations about his conduct became more detailed as time passed. She claimed that he had first seduced her at the age of thirteen (later revised to nine) and had continued to have sex with her ever since. According to Madeleine, he had also repudiated God and had presented her with a FAMILIAR in the form of a green devil.

Five more nuns developed symptoms of hysteria interpreted as the result of demoniacal POSSESSION, of whom Louise Capeau (or Capelle) seemed to suffer the worst. Madeleine and Louise were now brought before Sebastian Michaëlis, the Grand Inquisitor in Avignon, who had presided over the burning of eighteen witches in the city back in 1582. Further exorcism failed to improve the situation, though the girls furnished their interrogators with additional details of the spirits that possessed them. According to Louise, Madeleine was possessed by 6666 devils, including the mighty BEELZEBUB, and this bewitchment was directly attributable to Gaufridi. Louise herself was possessed by three powerful devils named Grésil, Sonnillon and Vérin.

Father Michaëlis next took the imaginative step of requesting Gaufridi himself to exorcise the girls. The priest was inexperienced in such procedures, however, and the girls only mocked him. He was flung into gaol, but Michaëlis, failing to find any real evidence to convict the priest on the grounds of witchcraft, soon had to release him. Gaufridi now appealed to the Pope to condemn the girls for their 'fooling', and Madeleine in her turn was placed under close supervision. Her condition worsened: she spoke of visions, sang bawdy love songs, disrupted services and neighed like a horse. She also told shocking stories about SABBATS, complete with details of sodomy and cannibalism.

In February 1611, in response to the interest that the affair was attracting throughout France, the case was brought before the civil courts in Aix-en-Provence. The trial caused a sensation. Madeleine's erratic behaviour in court, switching without warning from pleading for forgiveness from the luckless Gaufridi to violent condemnations of his sexual perversions and cannibalism, interrupted from time to time by uncontrollable seizures of lust, made a deep impression. On two occasions she was reported to have attempted suicide.

Gaufridi, weakened by months in a dank, rat-infested dungeon, was inspected for the DEVIL'S MARK, which was duly found. Under torture, he admitted all the charges laid against him, conceding that he had agreed a pact with Satan (*see* PACT WITH THE DEVIL), duly signed in his own blood, in order to enjoy intercourse with any woman that he desired (over a thousand, he claimed, had succumbed to his lust in this way). Madeleine, he explained, had become particularly obsessed by him and had surrendered herself to him both in the sabbat and outside. He desperately revoked these confessions in court, but a guilty verdict was inevitable and he was sentenced to death; the court gave instructions that he should be burned over a pyre of bushes rather than logs so that his agony would be prolonged.

On the day of execution Gaufridi was repeatedly subjected to the tortures of STRAPPADO and SQUASSATION until his limbs were severely dislocated, in the hope that he would reveal the names of his accomplices. He was then dragged through the streets on a hurdle for five hours before being strangled (an unexpected mercy considering the original sentence: *see* BURNING OF WITCHES) and his body burned to ashes.

The death of Gaufridi seemed to release Madeleine instantly from her devils, though Louise Capeau showed no sign of improvement and remained in similar torment for the rest of her days. Neither did Louise Capeau cease to make allegations of witchcraft: a few weeks after Gaufridi's execution a blind girl was burned on the strength of her testimony. Further troubles were visited upon Madeleine thirty years later, in 1642, when she herself was charged with being a witch. Another accusation of witchcraft followed in 1652 and, after the Devil's mark was found on her, she was fined and imprisoned for life. She died in 1670, at the age of seventy-seven, shortly after being released into the custody of a relative.

All Hallows' Eve *see* HALLOWE'EN.

Allier, Elisabeth b.1602. French nun who was at the centre of one of the most celebrated cases of demoniacal POSSESSION of novices and nuns that were reported throughout FRANCE in the seventeenth century. According to the Dominican friar François Farconnet of Grenoble, who wrote an account of the case, Elisabeth Allier was possessed at the age of seven, when two devils, named Bonifarce and Orgeuil, slipped into her body on a crust of bread. When Farconnet made his first attempt at EXORCISM, some twenty years later, he heard the DEMONS in her body speaking to him in gruff voices, though Allier's lips did not appear to him to move at all. Five further attempts at exorcism failed to have the desired effect, while Allier herself was contorted by violent fits and convulsions. In his *True Relation* of the case Farconnet described how he saw her tongue protrude from her mouth by a length of more than four fingers before the demons were finally expelled.

Alphonsus de Spina d.1491. Spanish Franciscan cleric, author of the earliest book to be published on the subject of witchcraft. De Spina was converted from Judaism to Catholicism by the Franciscans, and much of his writing had a marked anti-Semitic flavour. He served as Confessor to King John of Castile and subsequently became a professor at Salamanca and ultimately Bishop of Thermopolis. His *Fortalicium Fidei* (*Fortress of the Faith*), written around 1459, took in several subjects but culminated in a discussion of demonology and those unfortunates who fell into the worship of evil. The author lamented that many old women were easily deceived by demons into imagining that they could fly and could work evil through magic. He identified Dauphiné and Gascony in FRANCE as particular hotbeds of such nefarious activity, describing how witches there venerated a BOAR with the obscene KISS. He noted with approval that many suspected witches had been slaughtered by the Inquisition based at Toulouse.

America *see* UNITED STATES OF AMERICA.

amulet Magical object that was worn or carried about the person in order to fend off the threat of witchcraft, or otherwise to benefit from its supernatural properties. The most popular modern amulets include agates and gemstones, to which various qualities such as good health may be ascribed. Amulets that were formerly valued over the centuries for their effectiveness in countering witchcraft and other evils included miniature horseshoes, teeth, bits of ROWAN wood, anything made of IRON, lengths of red thread, crosses and CHARM bracelets among a host of other objects.

Some were commonplace objects easily obtainable by all, but others were more bizarre and included soil taken from a fresh grave, which was deemed highly effective against tuberculosis, and water collected from the tops of three waves. Yet others, such as lucky stones and coins, were unique and became nationally famous for their protective powers, being handed down in particular families over the centuries (they were sometimes rented out, for a fee, to others in need). These latter amulets included the chemise of the pious Hungarian-born wife of the Scottish king Malcolm Canmore, Queen Margaret, who died in 1093. This chemise, carefully preserved through the years, was considered a powerful safeguard against the threat of enchantment and was used as swaddling clothes for the infant future King James III of Scotland in 1452 and again for James V in 1512.

The carrying of amulets was once much recommended in countries where the populace went in daily fear of falling victim to the EVIL EYE. At one time many people fearful of witchcraft carried about them amulets comprising small pieces of paper upon which were written various holy words, such as the Paternoster or the Ave Maria or the Gospel of St John, as these were widely believed to deter evil. Others slipped into their shoe a piece of paper on which was written the LORD'S PRAYER. Although approved by the Catholic theologian Thomas AQUINAS, such practices never caught on in Protestant countries.

Amulets – or more properly 'talismans', as they sought to induce magic powers rather than merely to deflect evil – were also used for healing purposes in white magic. These traditionally included prehistoric flint arrowheads and holed stones (*see* HAG-STONE), which might also be kept in the bedroom or cattle byre to ward off malevolent spirits.

See also PROTECTION AGAINST WITCHCRAFT.

angelica Aromatic plant that was formerly valued for its protective properties in relation to witchcraft. Associated with St Michael the Archangel and sometimes called the 'Root of the Holy Ghost', angelica was said to provide protection against witches, rabies and the plague, among other threats. It was also recommended to dispel thoughts of lust in the young.

Anti-Christ *see* GREAT BEAST.

aphrodisiac *see* LOVE POTION.

apple The apple had a number of uses in witchcraft and superstition as a whole, being widely used for DIVINATION (especially in affairs of love) and as an ingredient in certain SPELLS. The link between the apple and witchcraft is commemorated annually in the custom of 'ducking' for apples at HALLOWE'EN.

Aquinas, Thomas 1225–74. Dominican theologian, prominent among the religious philosophers who defined the theological basis of the Roman Catholic Church. Among Aquinas's important and highly influential writings were several passages that were to have a fundamental effect upon the development of European witchcraft in the centuries after his death. His writings were frequently quoted by the writers of the *Malleus Maleficarum* and other principal treatises on witchcraft, lending intellectual weight to the theories of later demonologists and thus contributing to the gathering panic that culminated in the witchcraft hysteria of the sixteenth and seventeenth centuries.

The writings of Aquinas lent support to five main areas of witchcraft theory. Firstly, he appeared to believe that men were capable of having sexual intercourse with SUCCUBI, which might then change sex and become INCUBI in order to impregnate mortal women. On the strength of this proposition sexual relations with demons became a standard charge in subsequent witchcraft trials. Secondly, Aquinas drew on biblical authority for the notion that the minions of Satan could fly through the air (*see* TRANSVECTION).

Thirdly, he agreed that the Devil could deceive men into thinking that they could change shape; it was but a short step from this for later demonologists to quote Aquinas as support for the idea that the Devil's cohorts really did change their shape. Fourthly, Aquinas confirmed that demons could raise storms and perform other spells, and, lastly, he asserted that they could interfere in human relationships through the magic of LIGATURE.

The fact that Aquinas agreed to the possibility of pacts being made with the Devil paved the way for this becoming the grounds for conviction of suspected witches as heretics. This in turn meant that convicted witches were deemed to deserve the same severity of punishment that was imposed upon other varieties of heretic.

Armstrong, Anne *see* FORSTER, ANNE.

Arras Witches The victims of one of the first organised witch-hunts to take place in northern FRANCE, carried out by the INQUISITION in the years 1459–60. At a time when notions of what a witch was were still ill defined, the Inquisition established links between the alleged practices of certain locals and the recognised HERESY of the Waldensians or Vaudois. Pierre le Broussart, the Inquisitor for the Arras region, was moved to act by the confessions of Robinet de Vaulx, a condemned prisoner who named Deniselle Grenières as a witch. Grenières in turn implicated, under torture, five more people, who were also subjected to physical ill treatment. In desperation one of them, Jehan la Vitte, attempted to cut out his own tongue in order to make torture futile, but he only cut his mouth and was in any case required to write down his answers.

Typical of the charges facing the Arras Witches were allegations that they had met with the DEVIL, had performed the homage of the obscene KISS (of the Devil's backside), had shared a banquet with him and had indulged in promiscuous sex with one another. Despite advice from the church authorities, who recommended leniency since no murder or misuse of the host had been suggested, the Inquisition insisted on capital punishment. Five of the accused were paraded in public in the shameful robes of convicted heretics before being burned alive.

More suspects were rounded up and tortured in the weeks that followed. Many of them were tricked into making confessions by promises that they would be allowed to go free if they co-operated in this way. Despite the 'confessions' that the Inquisitor obtained by such means, the secular authorities refused to sanction his activities and eventually insisted on the release of some of the accused. The rest were freed on the return from Rome of the Bishop of Arras. In 1491 the Parlement of Paris went so far as to issue a public condemnation of the Inquisition's conduct in the affair and to invite survivors to offer prayers for those who had been put to death.

arthame *see* ATHAME.

Ashtaroth Powerful demon who was believed to know all secrets and could allegedly be summoned to make revelations about the past and future. Ashtaroth (or Astaroth) appeared in the form of a half-white, half-black human male, though he began life as the nature goddess Astarte. Worshipped by Solomon after persuasion from the women in his harem, Astarte represented love and fruitfulness and was celebrated in orgiastic rites, until, according to the Old Testament, she was transformed into a demon as punishment for opposing the Christian God.

Reputed to have revolting foul-smelling breath, Ashtaroth had command of forty legions in Hell and was one of the demons to which Madame de MONTESPAN was reputed to have made human sacrifices in her attempts to obtain magical influence over Louis XIV of France (*see* CHAMBRE ARDENTE AFFAIR).

Tradition has it that he could only be summoned successfully on Wednesdays, and then only between the hours of ten and eleven at night.

See also GREAT GODDESS.

Asmodeus Demon who personified lust and lechery. It is thought that this demon was descended ultimately from the Persian deity

Aeshma Daeva, the God of Anger, who moved men to thoughts of revenge. Adopted by the Jews, he was frequently depicted causing trouble between husbands and wives by preventing intercourse between them and by promoting adultery, and it was but a short step from this to his eventual status as the God of Lust. Solomon acquired power over Asmodeus by means of a magic ring, and obliged the demon to help in the building of the Temple; Asmodeus, however, deceived Solomon into giving him the ring, which he then flung into the sea (only to see a fish return it to Solomon in its belly).

When summoned by witchcraft, Asmodeus was reputed to manifest on the back of a dragon and to have three heads, those of a bull, a man and a ram. If treated with due respect (the person who summoned him had to do so bareheaded) he might grant the power of INVISIBILITY and might also reveal the whereabouts of hidden treasure.

Astaroth *see* ASHTAROTH.

athame Black-hilted knife traditionally carried by witches for ceremonial purposes. Supposedly possessing magical properties of its own, the athame (or arthame) always had a black handle and often bore magic symbols on the blade. According to widely accepted practice, as described in *The Key of Solomon* and other textbooks on rituals, the knife was supposed always to remain on a witch's person and was to be used in INITIATION ceremonies and in the drawing of MAGIC CIRCLES as well as in the mixing of herbs and other ingredients in spell-making.

Auldearn Witches COVEN of thirteen Scottish witches at Auldearn, Morayshire, that was exposed to the world when Isobel GOWDIE made her startling and voluntary confession of witchcraft in 1662. The detailed account with which she furnished the authorities threw light on what were believed to be the practices of typical Scottish covens of the seventeenth century.

According to Gowdie's testimony the coven, led by a woman named Jean Marten, comprised thirteen members, who met regularly at a prehistoric stone circle together with the DEVIL and their FAMILIARS to make mischief through a variety of magical rituals. There they indulged in wild DANCING, drinking and sexual orgies. Feasts shared by the coven began with the following grace:

> We eat this meat in the Devil's name,
> With sorrow and sighs and mickle shame;
> We shall destroy both house and hold;
> Both sheep and cattle in the fold,
> Little good shall come to the fore,
> Of all the rest of the little store.

A typical ruse practised by the coven was the raising of storms, which was achieved by slapping a rock repeatedly with a wet rag while intoning:

> I knock this rag upon this stone
> To raise the wind in the Devil's name;
> It shall not lie, until I please again.

On one occasion the coven descended upon a dye-works at Auldearn and bewitched the vats so that in future the cloth would always come out dyed in the Devil's colour, black. Another trip took them into the world of the FAIRIES, where they were terrified by the sight of 'elf-bulls', as Isobel Gowdie recalled: 'The hill opened, and we came to a fair and large braw room, in the daytime. There are great bulls routing and skoyling there, at the entry, which feared me.'

All the members of the coven were adept at transforming themselves into the shapes of various animals. Gowdie recalled how on one escapade, while turned into a HARE, she had only narrowly evaded the jaws of some dogs by running straight through her own house and into someone else's. By a complicated ritual involving the making of a miniature plough drawn by TOADS the witches of Auldearn allegedly had the power to render a farmer's land sterile and thus to present the 'stolen' crop to the Devil. They also learned to shoot 'elf arrows' fashioned by the fairies: Gowdie herself boasted of having shot and killed a woman with one. Other victims of the coven included the young sons of the Laird of Park, allegedly killed by the destruction of clay images made in their likenesses (*see* IMAGE MAGIC).

Each member of the coven had his or her own personal imp, who went by such unusual names as Swein, Pikle nearest the Wind and Rorie. The Devil (whose identity was not otherwise revealed) apparently kept his witches in close check, however, and would beat anyone who incurred his displeasure. Gowdie, who named fellow members of the coven, described how one of their number, Margaret Wilson, was brave enough to fight back when the Devil chastised her and how another, Bessie Wilson, would swear foully at him. But most of the others bowed meekly to such abuse.

The records of the Auldearn court concerning the trial of the coven members are incomplete, but it is generally assumed that most if not all those named joined Gowdie herself on the gallows. Also tried at Auldearn at much the same time were witches variously identified as Katherine Sowter, the Witch of Bandon and Janet Breadheid.

See also SCOTLAND.

Austria In common with the states of GERMANY, Austria suffered heavily during the witchcraft hysteria of the sixteenth and seventeenth centuries. In Austria, the persecution reached a peak during the reign (1576–1612) of Emperor Rudolf II, who was much influenced by his witch-hating Jesuit advisers, and it ignited once more towards the end of the seventeenth century, when many victims were put to death in the provinces of Styria and the Tyrol.

The witchcraft panic was at first slow to gather momentum in Austria, with few cases before 1570. Under Emperor Maximilian II (reigned 1564–76) sentences meted out to convicted witches were rarely worse than a fine. More severe punishments were ordained by the CAROLINA CODE of 1532, which insisted upon death by burning in cases involving HERESY or ill-intentioned sorcery, but the Code was largely ignored by the Austrian courts.

Rudolf II, convinced that he personally was the victim of witchcraft plots, saw to it that the climate changed dramatically after he came to power in 1576. Those who would have been dismissed as mad under Maximilian II were now hauled before the courts and sentenced to be burned at the stake. Changes in the law meant that it became easier to secure convictions on charges of witchcraft, and over the next 150 years many suspects were executed on little more evidence than a few suspicious items – bones, pots of ointment and the like – being found among their belongings. Others were sent for trial on the strength of accusations made by young children or simply because they were themselves the children of known witches.

Suspects brought before the courts in the German-speaking parts of the Tyrol were denied any knowledge of the accusations made against them, and were automatically returned to the torturer if an initial confession was retracted. The normal legal safeguards designed to protect the innocent were routinely set aside in view of the unique nature of the crime. Only those below the age of seven were safe from legal retribution.

A witchcraft scare in Salzburg in 1677–81 cost a hundred lives, the condemned being tortured into confessing and then beheaded, strangled or burned. The passing of strict new witchcraft laws in 1707 under Emperor Joseph I led to another flaring up of witchcraft hysteria and, though there were few further cases, legal torture of witchcraft suspects was not prohibited until 1776. The remaining witchcraft laws were repealed in 1787.

Auxonne Nuns   A case of mass possession that led to a widely reported witchcraft investigation in Auxonne, FRANCE, in 1660.

The allegations sprang up around the figure of Father Nouvelet, the young father confessor to an Ursuline convent, with whom eight of the nuns had apparently fallen in love (though he was by all accounts not a good-looking man). The erotic dreams of which the sex-starved nuns complained were considered the work of DEMONS, and the automatic assumption was that Father Nouvelet himself must have had a hand in this. The priest adroitly diverted the threat posed by such thinking by claiming that he too had been bewitched, and suspicion passed instead to two local peasant women. The two suspects were accordingly brought before the courts, but nothing could be proved against them and they were sentenced merely to banishment (unfortunately for them, an angry mob set upon them as they left the building and put them to death).

Father Nouvelet, meanwhile, set about driving out the devils said to be in possession of his eight charges by somewhat unconventional means: he lay in the same bed with them and got them to adopt sexually provocative poses at the altar during special services of EXORCISM. The Mother Superior, Sister St Colombe (Barbara Buvée), expressed her opposition to such methods. However she succeeded only in attracting the enmity of her nuns, who claimed she was a witch and a lesbian and the real source of the possessions. Already no favourite with the authorities, she now found herself in chains awaiting trial as a witch.

Barbara Buvée's trial opened in Dijon on 5 January 1661 and all France revelled in the evidence that was presented, much of it concerning physical intimacies between Buvée and the other nuns. One nun, Sister Gabrielle de Malo, referred to 'mutual touchings' and another described how the Mother Superior had kissed her and fondled her breasts. Others reported visions in which the Mother Superior had committed obscene acts. The judges, however, found no grounds for believing that any crime had been committed and the accused woman, supported by the evidence of several physicians (who doubted that the POSSESSIONS were real), was acquitted. This was a reflection of the more tolerant and sceptical atmosphere that characterised much of European society in the wake of the witchcraft mania of the early seventeenth century. Barbara Buvée moved to a different convent, and the hysteria that had threatened the nuns at Auxonne was eventually forgotten.

Baites, Anne *see* FORSTER, Anne.

B

Bamberg Witches The principality of Bamberg was the scene of some of the most brutal witchcraft trials in German history. Under the rule of Prince-Bishop Gottfried Johann Georg II Fuchs von Dornheim, at least six hundred people were burned as witches in the years 1623–33. The persecution began under Bishop Johann Gottfried von Aschhausen, the 'Witch-Bishop' who ruled Bamberg between 1609 and 1622 and was responsible for sending some three hundred alleged witches to their deaths. Johann Georg II stepped up the campaign, establishing a witch-hunting organisation under the Suffragan Bishop Friedrich Förner and building special prisons to house suspects. He also rode roughshod over legal niceties: the details of accusations against suspected witches were often left undisclosed and many suspects were denied a lawyer to act in their defence. Once arrested, a suspect had little chance of escaping the death penalty.

Trials were often perfunctory and records exist of one victim, Anna Hansen, being brought to the block for execution only three weeks after she was arrested. Numerous prominent citizens fled the principality or died in the witch-hunts, their estates being used to pay for their trial, torture and execution and anything left over being forfeited to the Bishop himself (a powerful incentive to him to pursue the campaign with vigour and to concentrate on wealthy suspects). Dr Georg Hahn, Vice-Chancellor of Bamberg, was one of the few who dared to question the policy – in 1628 he was tortured and burned at the stake with his wife and his daughter for his trouble. Moreover, the confession extracted from the Vice-Chancellor under torture implicated five burgomasters, sealing their fate with accusations that they had committed such offences as sexual intercourse with DEMONS and riding to SABBATS on BLACK DOGS (see JUNIUS, JOHANNES). Appeals by refugees from Bamberg to Emperor Ferdinand II to overrule the Prince Bishop's courts were of no avail, as the Bishop ignored all pleas for moderation.

The most hideous aspect of the Bamberg witch trials was the extensive use of torture. The interrogators employed a wide range of procedures to extract confessions, including the use of the BOOTS, cold baths, forced feeding with salted herring (which provoked a raging thirst), immersion in baths of scalding water laced with lime, laceration of the neck using a rope, the prayer stool (a spiked board on which the accused was forced to kneel), roasting on an iron chair, scorching the skin of the armpits or groin with burning feathers dipped in sulphur, scourging, the stocks (which were specially fitted with iron spikes to intensify the agony), the LADDER, STRAPPADO and THUMBSCREWS. Convicted witches were sometimes subjected to further agonies on the way to execution, their right hands being severed or, in the case of women, their breasts being torn by red-hot pincers.

Eventually, the outcry against the campaign became so great that in 1630 the Emperor was obliged to take sterner action against the Prince-Bishop. Records of the proceedings were examined and the Bamberg courts were instructed to make accusations public and to allow the defendants legal counsel. Confiscation of property was also forbidden, but the use of torture was not curtailed and the climate of terror in the region did not recede until the following year, when Bishop Förner died. There were no executions for witchcraft in Bamberg in 1631, and in 1632 the death of the witch-hating Bishop of Bamberg finally brought the persecution to an end.

See also GERMANY.

Baphomet Evil-working demon who was allegedly worshipped by the KNIGHTS TEMPLAR and was subsequently identified with the DEVIL venerated by practitioners of black magic. Named through a corruption of 'Mahomet' or else derived from two Greek words meaning 'absorption into knowledge', Baphomet was described as the idol revered by the Knights Templar when the Order was accused of heresy and other crimes in 1307. According to the confessions extracted from twelve of the knights, the idol comprised a human SKULL or a stuffed human head, or some kind of carved head with three faces. The knights were supposed to consider the idol the fount of all their riches and also a powerful fertility CHARM.

Later authorities claimed that Baphomet was identical with the cloven-footed goat-headed winged deity worshipped by witches at their SABBATS. Representing fertility, lust and wisdom, this entity was said to have descended ultimately from the male goat worshipped by cults in ancient Egypt. The notorious Aleister CROWLEY adopted the name Baphomet as one of his titles.

baptism *see* INITIATION.

Barclay, Margaret d.1618. Scottish gentlewoman who was tried as a witch at Irvine, Ayrshire, in 1618. The wife of a respected burgess of Irvine, Margaret Barclay was, in contrast to conventional victims of the witchcraft mania of those times, young and spirited. She had, however, fallen out with her brother-in-law, John Deans, and his wife, Janet Lyal, after she had been falsely accused by them of theft. The rift was mended after recourse to the church courts, but the affair still rankled with Margaret Barclay and, when John Deans was about to set sail as captain of a merchant vessel, she was heard to voice the wish that the ship and its captain might sink to the bottom of the sea. Witnesses claimed that she was seen dropping hot coals into the water to cause the ship to run on to the rocks.

Unfortunately, the ship failed to return on the due date and a beggar by the name of John Stewart, claiming powers of clairvoyance, stated it to be lost. When it emerged that the ship had indeed sunk off Padstow in Cornwall, Stewart was promptly arrested, upon which he alleged that Margaret Barclay, who was already under suspicion for the ship's loss, had asked him for a curse to use against the vessel. According to Stewart, Barclay and two accomplices, accompanied by the DEVIL in the form of a BLACK DOG, had met at a deserted house to fashion clay figures which they had then hurled into the sea to ensure that the vessel foundered. The sea itself had frothed wildly and turned red.

Next to be arrested was one of the accomplices, a woman named Isobel Insh, who was further implicated by evidence obtained from her eight-year-old daughter. In a desperate attempt to escape confinement in the belfry of the kirk in Irvine, Insh fell and died from her injuries five days later.

Stewart and Barclay herself were then subjected to torture under the direction of the Earl of Eglington. Stewart managed to free himself from his chains and avoided further agony by hanging himself from the door of his cell, using the ribbons from his hat. Margaret Barclay, denied any such escape, was subjected to the 'most safe and gentle torture' of having heavy iron bars placed on her bare legs until she could bear the pain no more and made a full confession. Every word of this she later retracted in court, but the jury declined to accept her retraction and found her guilty, upon which she was strangled and then burned to ashes at the stake.

The final victim of the case was one Isobel Crawford. She had been named as an accomplice in Barclay's forced confession and, after bravely enduring much torture, also died at the stake – though steadfastly insisting on her innocence and refusing to forgive the executioner.

The last word on the tragic case went to the nineteenth-century novelist Sir Walter Scott, who after reading an account of the trial wrote: 'It is scarce possible that, after reading such a story, a man of sense can listen for an instant to the evidence founded on confession thus obtained, which has been almost the sole reason by which a few individuals, even in modern times, have endeavoured to justify a belief in the existence of witchcraft.'

See also SCOTLAND.

Bargarran Impostor An eleven-year-old girl, Christine (or Christian) Shaw, whose allegations resulted in the trial of twenty-one alleged witches in Renfrewshire, Scotland, in 1697. Often considered the Scottish equivalent of the 1593 trial of the WARBOYS WITCHES in England, the case – depending as it did on the most unreliable testimony of young children – revealed how the witch hysteria still gripped people north of the border at this relatively late date.

Christine Shaw was the daughter of a gentleman of Bargarran near Paisley. She instigated the dreadful chain of events when, in August 1696, she began to suffer fits, which she was quick to blame on two local women, Katherine Campbell and Agnes Naismith (with both of whom she had recently fallen out). She complained that she was being tormented by the two women in spectral form, and witnesses reported that when confined in her bedroom she frequently vomited pins, animal hair, bones, feathers, egg-shells and other items. Some said that they had even seen the girl flying around the house in the course of her fits.

The doctors failed to find a medical cause for Christine's hysteria, and in 1697 the Privy Council sanctioned an investigation into her allegations. By now the accusations encompassed another seven people, including the high-born Margaret Lang and her daughter Martha Semple, who were inclined to regard the whole affair with contempt. But some of the victims took the allegations badly and in their desperation responded by naming other witches in the area: the list grew to twenty-one persons.

Constantly attended by ministers of the Church, who did little to dissuade Christine from her delusions and even arranged a day of fasting on her behalf, the plaintiff was joined in her accusations by the three grandchildren of one of the accused, Jean Fulton. These children complained of being forced to attend SABBATS and being obliged to participate in spells designed to procure the deaths of a minister, two other children and two passengers on a ferryboat that was capsized by magic.

The case, now involving twenty-six defendants, was brought before an official commission on 13 April 1697. After the various confessions were heard, the jury was warned that to acquit the accused, upon some of whom the DEVIL'S MARK had been found, would make them accessories to their crimes. Not surprisingly, the jurors found guilty three of the men, including the fourteen-year-old James Lindsay, and four of the women: Katherine Campbell, Agnes Naismith, and Margaret Lang and her daughter. The seven 'Paisley Witches' thus condemned were hanged and then burned (some of them still alive) in Paisley on 10 June 1697. The site of the atrocity is still indicated by a horseshoe at Gallo Green, George Street.

Christine Shaw seems to have been cured of her fits by the deaths of her alleged tormentors. She went on to marry a minister and to acquire local fame by bringing to Paisley machinery for the manufacture of fine sewing thread, thus making the town a centre of the linen thread trade.

In 1839 two writers visiting the Shaw household, which remained unchanged from Christine's day, reported discovering a small hole concealed close to her bed. By this means an accomplice could easily have introduced the pins and other debris that she was said to vomit.

Barton, Elizabeth *c.*1506–34. English domestic servant, dubbed the 'Maid of Kent', who attracted considerable fame as a prophetess and witch.

Elizabeth Barton claimed that her prophetic powers were granted to her by the Virgin Mary after she was miraculously cured of fits at a certain priest's chapel in Aldington, Kent. Her recovery from violent fits (which, it transpired, were faked at the priest's instructions) and her newly discovered skills as a seer turned the chapel into a popular place of pilgrimage, and many distinguished persons sought the girl's advice regarding the future.

All went well enough until, apparently with prompting from various quarters, the 'Maid of Kent' delivered a series of prophecies that warned of dire consequences as a result of Henry VIII's divorce from Anne BOLEYN. Prophesying death and disaster for a monarch was always taken very seriously, and the King's supporters quickly set about discrediting the prophetess. Rumours were spread to the effect that Barton was a witch; she was duly arrested on charges of treason and ultimately condemned to death.

Before being hanged at Tyburn Barton admitted her deception and confessed how she had allowed herself to be manipulated by others. She recognised that pride had caused her downfall 'because the thing which I feigned was profitable to them, therefore they much praised me'.

Basque Witches For a long time the Basque region of the Pyrenees had a reputation as a hotbed of witchcraft, largely because its geography kept it remote from the cultures of France and Spain and made the authorities in both countries suspicious of the area's inhabitants. The Basque peoples were left relatively untouched by the Celtic cultures of Spain and France three thousand years ago and the region remained similarly secure from the Roman invasions of Julius Caesar, retaining its own language and folk customs. When Christianity arrived the Basques combined the new beliefs with the old ones, and it was not unheard of for priests to conduct Christian services on Sundays and to preside over the worship of older gods at other times in the week.

The region was officially noted as a centre of witchcraft practices as early as the fourteenth century, by which time local sorcerers had a widespread reputation for using magic to express their malevolent intent towards others, destroying property, livestock and crops. Ostensibly Catholic congregations were known to insist that their priests kept mistresses, apparently to divert them from dallying with local women, and in some areas where cults worshipping the dead thrived no Christian bishop was allowed passage. Others venerated a mysterious goddess called 'la Dama' (the lady), a mountain deity who is thought to have survived from an earlier religion.

It was inevitable, then, that the INQUISITION should single out the Spanish Basques for special attention. Infiltrating spies and sending in ruthless investigators, the Inquisitors had little trouble in furnishing evidence to support the initial premise that the area was dominated by Satan's hordes, with countless suspects providing detailed confessions of relations with devils and demons and so forth. In most accounts, the DEVIL was described as appearing in the shape of a GOAT or sometimes a mule, though he occasionally took the form of a man.

Early in the seventeenth century the French followed suit with the Basques living on their side of the border, sending the lawyer Pierre de LANCRE to the Pays de Labourd, Béarn, in 1608 to root out and destroy those who worshipped 'pagan' gods. This he did with terrifying zeal, claiming to have executed as many as six hundred Labourd witches in a four-month period. Best known among de Lancre's victims was the young priest Pierre Bocal, who was rumoured to preside over both Christian and non-Christian rites. The fact that Bocal donned a goat's-head mask when officiating in the worship of the Basque region's old gods was more than enough to prove his guilt as a witch and in 1609 he was burned alive, aged just twenty-seven.

It was alleged by the witch-hunters that the region had become a hiding-place for demons expelled by missionaries in the Far East. As many as twelve thousand witches were reported to have gathered for a SABBAT in Bordeaux, while attendances at other sabbats were rumoured to have reached as much as a hundred thousand. Confessions were obtained in many cases from children, who implicated hundreds of people with allegations that they had attended sabbats, celebrated BLACK MASSES, flown through the air, eaten dead bodies, murdered enemies, made magical ointments and had sexual relations with the Devil.

In the end the slaughter in the Basque region, particularly under de Lancre, proved too much for the local population. When five thousand fishermen returned from voyages to Newfoundland to find that many of their loved ones had perished they went on the rampage, and there was further discontent when de Lancre had three priests burned. He was driven to the conclusion that the entire population of the region was infected by the witchcraft contagion, but even he could not sustain genocide on such a scale.

See also FRANCE.

Bast *see* CAT.

bat An animal that has long been associated with the darker side of superstition, especially with witchcraft and the Devil. With their nocturnal flight and habit of roosting in lonely places such as ruins and caves, bats have always inspired dread. In many cultures they are linked with evil and death, and protective charms were once recited automatically if a bat flew overhead.

It was once widely believed that witches had the power to transform themselves into bats. It was thus very unlucky to discover that a bat had found its way into one's home, or for a bat to fly round a house or into a windowpane, as this foretold the death of someone within. If bats were seen to fly vertically upwards and then down to earth this was also an ominous sign – it meant that witches would soon be gathering in the locality. In some parts of Europe the superstitious carried a bat's bone in the belief that this would protect them from the ill magic that was associated with the animal. Alternatively a household might be protected from witchcraft by carrying a live bat three times round the outside of the house and then nailing its dead body beside a window or to the door of an outhouse.

Bats were also useful in witchlore as ingredients in various potions. A few drops of bat's blood were supposedly included in some recipes for LOVE POTIONS and FLYING OINTMENT, so that a witch intending to fly on her broomstick would enjoy a bat's mastery of the air and avoid colliding with anything. Bat's blood might also be used in celebrations of the BLACK MASS and in drawing MAGIC CIRCLES. Witchlore also claimed that washing one's face in bat's blood bestowed the ability to see in the dark.

The use of bats in a variety of occult rites has continued into modern times: in 1962 the authorities in New York felt it necessary to outlaw the sale of 'voodoo' drugs that included bat's blood as an ingredient. The modern mythology of the vampire has also served to consolidate the association of the bat with black magic, though this appears to have been a relatively recent invention by the cinema. The older European legends never linked the bat with the vampire myth, and Bram Stoker himself, author of the original Dracula story, did not make a particular point of suggesting such a link.

Bateman, Mary 1768–1809. English sorceress who was tried for her crimes in 1808. Born in Topcliffe, Yorkshire, Mary Bateman fell into a life of petty crime and made her living as a confidence trickster.

Reputedly a fortune-teller, abortionist and procurer of CHARMS of various kinds, she was widely known as a witch but, in an age in which the witchcraft mania of previous times was already history, she was never prosecuted as such. Instead, she met her end on the gallows on more prosaic charges – for the murder of one Rebecca Perigo.

Bavaria In common with other German states, Bavaria suffered considerably from the witchcraft hysteria that swept Europe in the early seventeenth century. Under Duke William V and his son Maximilian I, influenced by their Jesuit advisers, the state was convulsed by a long succession of bloody witch-hunts from about 1590, when William V called for an investigation into witchcraft in the region and, with the approval of the Jesuit University of Ingolstadt, sanctioned the first trials.

Prosecutions were modelled on earlier trials reported from elsewhere in Germany. The approach to evidence in witchcraft cases was also much influenced by consultation with BINSFELD'S newly published *Malleus Maleficarum*. Torture was routinely used to extract confessions, and records remain of at least one suspect in Munich who was tortured indefinitely and without interruption until she gave an admission of guilt to her interrogators. Those found guilty as witches were encouraged to name accomplices and so the hysteria continued to spread, claiming more and more victims.

Some towns and villages lost more inhabitants to the panic than others. Among the most badly hit was the town of Werdenfels in the Alps, where forty-nine out of a population of 4700 were burned as witches in the years 1590–1. In Schongau in 1598–9, meanwhile, all other trials were set aside so that the judges could devote themselves to the business of prosecuting alleged witches and sentencing them to death.

Many victims were identified by professional witch-hunters who, for a fee, examined suspects for WITCH'S MARKS. Public executioners were able to amass considerable fortunes from the increasing number of burnings and emerged as among the most powerful and influential members of their local communities, often doubling as witch-hunters (as did the notorious Jörg Abriel of Trèves, for example: *see* TRÈVES WITCHES).

After 1597, when on William's abdication Maximilian I succeeded his father, the hysteria intensified. Maximilian believed that witchcraft was responsible for his own wife's sterility and, having personally witnessed the torture of witches as a young man, he pursued the campaign with new vigour, aided and abetted by the Jesuits. New laws threatened the death penalty to anyone found guilty of making a PACT WITH THE DEVIL and permitted those who retracted their confessions to be returned immediately to the torturer for further ill treatment. Such was the intensity of the hysteria that court officials subsequently disallowed retractions altogether, and would take signs of fear in the accused at the time of arrest as proof positive of their guilt. In 1619, when a judge in Ingolstadt dropped charges of witchcraft against a woman and three children, Maximilian intervened personally to ensure that the case went ahead. He also issued a set of *Instructions on Witchcraft* in 1622 in an effort to inspire judges to harsher measures against suspected witches.

A degree of moderation was finally introduced around 1631, when various humanitarian advisers persuaded Maximilian I to relax the witch-hunting campaign that had claimed so many lives. The arrival of an invading Swedish army a year later effectively brought the mania to an end. Sporadic outbreaks of the witch hysteria did, however, continue to occur for a hundred years or more. In 1722, for instance, a man named Georg Pröls was accused of witchcraft by some children and, after savage torture, was beheaded and burned in Moosburg, near Freising. Others implicated by the dead man's confession were released by the authorities, who feared that a series of witchcraft trials might ignite a serious panic recalling the worst atrocities of the previous century.

The last witchcraft cases witnessed in Bavaria included the mass trial of about twenty suspects at Augsburg in 1728–34, which resulted in several executions, and the trial and execution of Anna Maria SCHWÄGEL in Kempten in Swabia in 1775 (thought to be the last execution for witchcraft in the whole of Germany).

See also EICHSTÄTT WITCH; GERMANY.

Bavent, Madeleine c. 1607–47. French nun who was tried as a witch in Rouen in 1647, during the reign of Louis XIV. An orphan brought up by her uncle and aunt, from the age of twelve Bavent worked as assistant to a woman who made habits for a local convent, and was noted for her deeply religious nature. When she was in her teens her beauty attracted the attention of a Franciscan friar, Father Bontemps, who visited to hear the confessions of Madeleine and her fellow workers and became her lover.

A short time afterwards Madeleine entered the Franciscan convent of Louviers, a few miles from Rouen, where she came under the charge of the supervising priest, Father Pierre David. Father David had some unusual ideas about how a convent should be run. In imitation, he claimed, of the innocence of Adam and Eve he insisted that the nuns went naked to their prayers in the chapel, and according to Bavent he encouraged lesbian relationships between the women, asserting that any act was excusable if the soul was illuminated by the Holy Spirit.

Father David, who never actually seduced Madeleine though he did indulge in what she called 'certain indecent caresses and mutual masturbation' with her, died in 1628. His place was taken by Father Mathurin Picard, who furthered David's ideas and made the celebration of sexuality the central theme of the nuns' worship. As the prettiest, Madeleine was appointed queen of this unorthodox coven and – addressed as ASHTAROTH – played the chief role in the various orgiastic rituals devised by Picard, who was disguised as a god called Dagon. Typical ceremonies culminated in Madeleine being laid naked on the chapel altar with her legs parted; Picard then offered a 'mass' on her belly before seducing her – though in her own account she complained that this was against her will.

Madeleine bore a baby as a result of her involvement in Picard's ceremonials, though it is uncertain what became of it (the child may have been brought up in Madeleine's old orphanage). Picard and other select individuals also seduced several of the other nuns, allegedly beguiling them through the use of love philtres, the ingredients of which were said to include the limbs of corpses and menstrual BLOOD. SABBATS were held once or twice a week, attended by Picard, his fellow chaplain Father Thomas Boullé, a few of the nuns and an assortment of lay people and demons. During the rituals human flesh would sometimes be consumed and Madeleine would be raped or otherwise seduced. She was also sexually violated by a demon in the shape of a black CAT, which often lay in wait for her in her cell. When Picard died in 1642, Boullé took his place and further elaborated the coven's activities along similar lines, but the nuns began to display symptoms of demonic possession in public and to attract unwanted attention outside the convent walls. Among other manifestations of abnormal activity, the sisters startled observers by delivering long streams of obscenities and blasphemies, demonstrating a loathing for sacred objects and sacraments, cursing violently during prayers and exposing their private parts in the most lewd manner. Others displayed almost superhuman strength, but disclaimed all knowledge of what transpired during these 'fits' once they had recovered from them.

The extraordinary life of the Louviers nuns came under serious threat when one of the nuns, Sister Anne, became jealous of Madeleine and in 1643 made public accusations that she had consorted with the DEVIL. Of the fifty-four nuns, fourteen or more, in a wave of psycho-sexual hysteria, claimed they had been possessed by the Devil (*see* POSSESSION) and all put the blame on Bavent for bewitching them. Madeleine herself retorted that, if she was guilty, then Sister Anne and, for good measure, the Mother Superior were equally so.

Public services of EXORCISM were held and the nuns were quick to rise to the occasion, exhibiting symptoms of hysteria and falling into fits. The remains of Father Picard were disinterred and excommunicated (when relatives found the body on a rubbish heap they demanded satisfaction, and a royal commission had to intervene).

The Bishop of Evreux, appreciating the severity of the scandal, had Madeleine arrested and examined for WITCH'S MARKS. Visual examination failed to locate any and she was subjected to PRICKING for the DEVIL'S MARK, a point on her body where she was insensitive to pain. Again, none was found. Despite the lack of such 'evidence',

Madeleine was charged with being a witch and sentenced to life imprisonment.

Perhaps to prevent her making further damaging allegations, Madeleine was incarcerated in a dank underground cell at the Ursuline convent in Rouen. Here she was fed an inadequate diet of bread and water and was sexually abused on a regular basis by her gaolers and by servants of the Bishop. Her attempts at suicide failed and in the end Madeleine made a full confession to the Bishop (although she later asserted that much of it had been concocted on the strength of what was being suggested to her by her interrogators).

As a result of Madeleine's confession Father Boullé, who had been arrested on witchcraft charges in 1644, was sentenced to death for bewitching the nuns. After torture, he was drawn through the streets of Rouen on a hurdle and then burned alive on 21 August 1647. His ashes were scattered in the wind. The remains of Father Picard were publicly burned, as was another priest by the name of Duval after he too was implicated by Bavent in the affair. The convent itself was closed and the nuns sent elsewhere.

Madeleine Bavent's confession did little to ease her situation. Although one witness admitted that he had lied about the black masses, the authorities continued to keep her in solitary confinement and she died before the year was out, aged forty.

See also FRANCE.

bay The bay tree was sacred to the ancient Romans and centuries later retained its reputation as a magical plant, capable of deterring witches and evil spirits among other properties. Bay trees were formerly often planted close to houses because they were believed to safeguard the inhabitants from evil spirits and the plague and also to ward off lightning. Many people carried bay leaves on the person in the belief that they gave protection against numerous diseases.

Witchlore suggested that the bay had many uses in medicine, and it was a common ingredient in the spells cast by WHITE WITCHES. Bay leaves were also used for the purposes of DIVINATION, as they were in classical times. The time-honoured procedure involved burning the leaves and discerning from the way they were consumed by the flames what lay in store. If the leaves burned without a sound misfortune would follow, but if they crackled noisily all would go well. Aspiring lovers were advised to sleep with bay leaves pinned to their pillow on St Valentine's Eve, to enjoy visions of their future partner.

Bedford, Duchess of *see* WOODVILLE, ELIZABETH.

Beelzebub The prince of DEMONS, who was regarded as second only to SATAN himself in the hierarchy of Christian demonology. Beelzebub was the god of the Philistine city of Ekron, being dubbed 'Lord of the Flies' (from *baal*, meaning lord, and *zebub*, meaning flies) reputedly because of the clouds of flies that gathered around his blood-soaked idol; alternatively the name might have meant 'lord of the high house'. He was identified in the Bible as the most powerful of the false gods.

Medieval authorities, who sometimes ranked Beelzebub above even Satan, described him as a huge figure with two large horns and vast bat-like wings, duck's feet, a lion's tail and thick black hair. In later centuries demons that materialised at SABBATS were often identified as Beelzebub, especially if they took the form of a huge fly, and he was reputed to demand sexual intercourse with all the females present. When the demonologist Peter BINSFELD drew up a hierarchy of Hell in 1589 he identified Beelzebub as the demon of gluttony, and several witches confessed that at their banquets they blessed the food in the name of Beelzebub, the 'creator and preserver of all things'.

It was through Beelzebub, it was claimed, that other lesser demons might be summoned – but care had to be taken in calling him up. If a MAGIC CIRCLE was not properly prepared beforehand, the death of those invoking him might result. Aleister CROWLEY said he had successfully raised up Beelzebub and had sent him, with forty-nine attendant demons, to attack his rival, Samuel MATHERS.

Bekker, Balthasar 1634–98. Dutch clergyman who was among the most important opponents of the witch-hunters of the seventeenth century. Holland was fortunate to escape the worst of the witchcraft delusion through the energetic efforts of a long succession of scholars who committed themselves to intellectual argument against belief in such supernatural activities. To Bekker, whose most influential publication was *De Betoverde Weereld* (*The World Bewitched*) in 1691, it was a mistake to attribute anything not readily understandable to witchcraft and other paranormal activity. Spirits might well exist, he argued, but they had no influence over the affairs of ordinary mortals. Neither could spirits take POSSESSION of a person, nor forge pacts in exchange for a person's soul. He blamed the papacy for encouraging the witchcraft delusion in order to line the pockets of the clergy.

Bekker himself was accused of atheism, thrown out of his ministry and ultimately expelled from the Dutch Reformed Church, but his writings contributed significantly to keeping the witch-hunters out of Holland.

Belial The demon of lies, who was identified in the Bible as a source of great evil and even as the lord of all demons. Deceitful and evil-hearted, Belial was reputedly one of the demons that Gilles de RAIS attempted to raise in the pursuit of his ill doing. Once considered the equal of BEELZEBUB, by medieval times Belial had been relegated to one of the lesser demons of Hell.

bells A superstition of ancient origins claimed that witches and other evil spirits could not abide the sound of church bells. According to tradition, if the church bells were rung when witches were gathering for a SABBAT the sound would cause them and their BROOMSTICKS to crash to earth.

Snakes and mice would also be driven away by the noise. In extension of this belief, bells were often rung on occasions when evil was to be confronted, notably during the service of EXORCISM.

By way of contrast, it was once believed that bells could also be used to summon the dead. If a bell was correctly forged using a certain combination of special metals, and buried in a churchyard grave for a week, its tolling would oblige the dead to leave their resting places at the command of the sorcerer (*see* NECROMANCY).

Benet, Johanna *see* CANDLE MAGIC.

Bennet, Elizabeth *see* ST OSYTH WITCHES.

Bergson, Moina 1865–1928. French occultist, sister of the Nobel Prize-winning philosopher Henri Bergson, who was one of the first members of the Hermetic Order of the GOLDEN DAWN. Born in Paris, she studied art in London and joined the Theosophical Society and then the Golden Dawn shortly after its foundation in 1888. A keen student of the occult, she married Samuel MATHERS, head of the Golden Dawn group, in 1890 and moved to Paris with him two years later, where she continued her investigations into ancient religions, especially those of Egypt. In particular, she explored the extinct beliefs surrounding the GREAT GODDESS and the HORNED GOD, identified by many as the precursor of Christianity's DEVIL.

Bergson and her husband sought to communicate their ideas by performing 'Rites of Isis' ceremonies both in public at the Théâtre Bodinière and, in a rather more explicit fashion, in private at their home. In these peculiar shows, which incorporated music, dance and invocations to the gods, Bergson herself played the Egyptian goddess Isis, while her husband impersonated Osiris. Such activities were frowned upon by other members of the Golden Dawn back in Britain: the couple were accused of dabbling in black magic and Mathers was expelled. After he died in 1918 Bergson established a new lodge of the Golden Dawn in London, concentrating once again upon the mythology surrounding the Horned God.

That others believed that Bergson's investigations had brought her into contact with black magic is illustrated by the allegations of a former colleague, Violet Firth, who claimed that she was being persecuted by demons after quarrelling with her former friend in 1920. According to Firth, she was pursued by black tomcats and on one occasion actually attacked by one the size of a tiger (the Great Goddess of Egyptian myth was often portrayed in the form of a lioness or CAT).

Berkeley, Witch of Unnamed English witch who, according to legend, lived at Berkeley in Gloucestershire in the early Middle Ages. The cautionary tale of the Witch of Berkeley, told by William of Malmesbury and much repeated over the centuries, possibly dates as far back as 1065.

The tale concerns an old witch who had a married son and two other children, one a monk and the other a nun. Tragedy struck when the old woman was brought news by her FAMILIAR (variously identified as a chough or a jackdaw) to the effect that her married son and his family had died in an accident. Fearing that she too was doomed to die and worried that her soul would be claimed by the Devil, the witch gave careful instructions to her surviving children about the disposal of her body. In the hope of keeping her soul out of Hell they were to sew her corpse up in a stag's skin, lay her on her back in a stone coffin, place a heavy stone on the lid and bind the coffin with chains. Psalms would have to be said on her behalf for fifty nights without interruption, and masses on fifty mornings in succession. If, at the end of all this, her body was left unmolested in its grave for three days they could rest assured that her soul was saved.

When the old woman died some time later the children followed her instructions to the letter. It was, however, apparently to no avail, for on the night that she was laid in her stone coffin a terrible demon broke into the church and snatched her away. The last that anyone saw of the old woman was her being forcibly carried off on a black horse.

Bible The Bible has long been quoted as the ultimate authority backing the persecution of witches in Christian society. Most infamous of all is the exhortation from Exodus, chapter 22, verse 18: 'Thou shalt not suffer a witch to live.' The English rendition of this verse is, however, inaccurate, as the Hebrew original singles out not witches, but poisoners. Despite the fact that this error was recognised as far back as the sixteenth century, the intent behind the verse was almost universally accepted in the misinterpreted form when the persecution of witches became widespread.

Similarly, the verse damning any 'woman with a FAMILIAR spirit' was nothing to do with witchcraft but a mistranslation of the Hebrew for 'pythoness' (*see* ENDOR, WITCH OF). Another passage adopted as justification for the witch-hunters was Deuteronomy, chapter 18, verses 10–12, which identified diviners, soothsayers, augurs, sorcerers, charmers, mediums, wizards and necromancers as 'an abomination to the Lord', but once again the topic of witchcraft as it was later recognised is not singled out. In *Letters on Demonology and Witchcraft*, the nineteenth-century writer Sir Walter Scott commented of the Old Testament: 'It cannot be said that, in any part of that sacred volume, a text occurs indicating the existence of a system of witchcraft ... In the four Gospels, the word, under any sense, does not occur.'

Somewhat perversely, the Bible is often identified as the original source of the Western witchcraft tradition, for it introduced the figure of SATAN (at first simply an official in the court of Heaven) and enumerated the DEMONS who were destined to become the deities of the alleged witch cult. The Bible makes no link between sorcerers of Christ's time and Satan, however, and certainly makes no judgement on witchcraft in the sense that it was understood in the seventeenth century.

On a more prosaic level, at one time weighing suspected witches against the big Bible kept in the local church was a favourite way of determining their guilt. If the accused witch proved heavier than the Bible, he or she was innocent. If the Bible proved heavier, he or she was deemed guilty – although there is no evidence that any court accepted such a test as evidence (*see* WEIGHING AGAINST THE BIBLE).

The physical presence of a Bible in a household was reputed to be a considerable deterrent against witches and other evil spirits. In times gone by it was not uncommon for mothers to leave their babies unattended for long periods with just an open Bible beside the cradle to keep roaming witches and demons at bay.

Bideford Witches *see* EXETER WITCHES.

bier right A test of witchcraft, which was based on the ancient folk belief that the body of a murder victim would bleed if brought into the presence of the murderer. Bier right was revived as a last resort in difficult cases in the twelfth century. The procedure was recommended by JAMES I in his *Daemonologie* in 1597, and the notable Presbyterian scholar and writer Richard Baxter was just one of many distinguished authorities convinced of its efficacy in murder cases, as he made clear in his discussion of bier right in *The Certainty of the World of Spirits* (1691):

> What shall we say to the many certain histories of the fresh bleeding of murdered bodies, when the murderer is brought to it, or at least, when he toucheth it, whether it be by the soul of the dead, or by a good spirit that hateth murder, or by the devil appointed for revenge, it seems plainly to be an invisible spirit's operation.

The method came to be associated particularly with witchcraft cases. One of the most celebrated uses of bier right in testing for witchcraft occurred in the trial of Jennet Preston, who was indicted for murder by sorcery alongside other PENDLE WITCHES. She was required to touch the corpse of Thomas Lister, her alleged victim, upon which it immediately began to bleed. Although she denied any blame, Preston was tried for the murder at York on 27 July 1612 and was hanged soon afterwards.

A later example of the use of bier right in such investigations was the trial of the 'Dalkeith Witch' Christine Wilson in SCOTLAND in 1661. Ordered by the authorities to touch the corpse of her supposed victim, Wilson laid her finger upon the fatal wound – which 'to the great admiration of all the beholders' began to bleed profusely as 'proof' of the woman's culpability.

Bilson Boy Case of witchcraft that turned out to be among the most widely reported hoaxes of the early seventeenth century. In 1620 William Perry of Bilson near Stafford, in the English Midlands, alleged that an elderly crone, Jane Clark, had bewitched him and caused him to suffer fits. The court, however, was inclined to scepticism, especially in the light of the fraudulent LEICESTER BOY case four years earlier. In the end the trial was abandoned and Perry – the so-called 'Bilson Boy' – admitted that the fits had been faked.

Remarkably, not long after the trial Perry tried the same ruse again. This time the affair came to the attention of Thomas Morton, Bishop of Lichfield. Morton examined the boy and reluctantly conceded (for he realised that his reputation was at stake) that the symptoms, which included the throwing up of various odd objects, must be genuine when Perry passed blue urine. As a last test, a spy was set to watch Perry secretly in his chamber. This proved the boy's undoing: thinking he was unobserved, Perry revealed the means by which he had made his urine blue – an inkpot under the bed. Similarly, the boy's claims that devils sent him into fits whenever the first words of St John's Gospel were read were disproved when he failed to respond in the promised way when the offending verse was read in Greek (a language he did not understand).

It eventually transpired that Perry had been taught to feign POSSESSION by a Roman Catholic priest, who had shown him how to perform such tricks as vomiting pins, rags and straw. The priest had hoped to fake a successful EXORCISM in collaboration with the boy, and thus to win favour with his superiors.

Binsfeld, Peter c.1540–1603. German demonologist and author of the highly influential *Tractatus de Confessionibus Maleficorum et Sagarum* (*Treatise on Confessions by Evildoers and Witches*) in 1589. Having studied under the Jesuits in Rome, Binsfeld became convinced of the reality of the threat posed by witchcraft and wrote his treatise in an attempt to encourage the persecution of suspected witches throughout Europe. Although he questioned the validity of the DEVIL'S MARK, he warned judges against accepting recantations of confessions, gave tacit approval of their attempts to extract the names of accomplices from confirmed witches, and generally added his support to the notion that witchcraft, being a crime quite different from all others, could be prosecuted in a way that set aside the usual safeguards designed to protect the innocent.

Binsfeld also made an attempt to produce a new list of the hierarchy of Hell, for the elucidation of judges in witchcraft cases. According to Binsfeld there were seven chief DEMONS, each presiding over one of the deadly sins. These were Lucifer (pride),

Mammon (avarice), Asmodeus (lechery), Satan (anger), Beelzebub (gluttony), Leviathan (envy) and Belphegor (sloth).

Binsfeld's book, despite its obviously bigoted viewpoint, was much quoted by legal authorities in both Catholic and Protestant states and was used to justify the persecution of suspected witches by courts throughout Europe for a hundred years or more.

See also TRÈVES WITCHES.

birds *see* BLACKBIRD; CROW; RAVEN.

Bishop, Ann *see* SOMERSET WITCHES.

Bishop, Bridget *see* SALEM WITCHES.

Bithner, Jakob *see* WITCHFINDER.

Black Assizes *see* CANDLE MAGIC.

black book *see* GRIMOIRE.

black dog Spectral DOG, described in numerous English legends and folktales, in which form the DEVIL was once thought to roam the Earth. Various surviving confessions by accused witches had the Devil manifesting himself at SABBATS in the form of a black dog, often with huge burning eyes. Some witches actually confessed to having intercourse with the Devil while he was in this form, though the 'dog' often walked on its hind legs and seemed to have a man's hands.

black mass Parody of the Catholic mass, which was often depicted as a central feature of the SABBAT of European witchcraft. According to popular imagination, such masses were celebrated in honour of (and even in the presence of) SATAN himself, using a naked woman as the altar for the ritual defiling of the sacred host in a conscious refutation of the Christian rite. In reality, however, there never was a single such rite pursued by witches throughout history around the globe, but rather a confusion of ceremonies of a somewhat irreligious nature sharing both similar and dissimilar features.

Although the black mass of popular mythology, with its blasphemous anti-Christian character and strong sexual content, is essentially a relatively recent invention promoted by popular fiction and the cinema, its roots may be traced back over a thousand years. There are few surviving records of confessions describing celebrations of black masses before the nineteenth century, and the term itself was not used until late in that century. However, many 'confessed' witches hinted that the alleged COVENS to which they belonged performed altered versions of Christian rituals at their meetings and certainly indulged in sexual perversity of one kind or another. Whether or not these events really took place is very debatable, as confessions were routinely based on 'leading' questions, often after the suspect had suffered prolonged torture. It has been cogently argued that the real inventors of the black mass were the interrogators themselves, who created such ideas in order to justify their own actions and to profit by them.

As far back as the seventh century the Church Council of Toledo condemned the observance of a mysterious semi-religious ceremony dubbed the 'Mass of the Dead', which was designed to cause the death of a named victim through magic. Essentially, this involved reciting the mass for the dead and inserting the name of a still-living enemy, who would assuredly die in a matter of days. In Gascony in south-western France, meanwhile, priests were reported to conduct the 'Mass of St Secaire', in which they secured the death of an enemy by magic. In these rites, the priest had sexual intercourse with a woman who then served as the altar while the priest consecrated a black triangular host and blessed water from a well in which a child had been drowned. Similar masses were celebrated elsewhere to secure lovers, to oblige loved ones to return and to grant a variety of other wishes. The curious Gascon 'Mass of the Holy Spirit' was almost faithful to the Christian original, except that it allegedly had the effect of obliging God to grant any wish that might be requested.

It would appear that at some ceremonies the presiding witch would offer celebrants a chalice of water (replacing the usual wine) or would consecrate a turnip black with rot or even an old black boot in the place of the Christian host. Prayers might be voiced to the Devil to save his 'congregation'; this is significant in the eyes of some sociologists, who are tempted to interpret such appeals as expressions of political dissent against an oppressive ruling class. This reading, however, hardly explains the well-known story of the black mass that was celebrated in 1580 on the orders of Queen Catherine de' MEDICI, the most powerful woman in France. According to the account given in Jean Bodin's *De la Démonomanie des Sorciers*, a priest fed a white host to a young boy, whose throat was then cut so that his BLOOD might be used in a black mass to restore the health of the Queen's son.

Francesco-Maria GUAZZO reported a young witch's description of a black mass celebrated in Aquitaine in south-west France in 1594:

> They also performed a travesty of the mass, celebrated by one clothed in a black cope with no cross woven into it. At the time of the holy sacrifice and the elevation of the host, he lifted a segment or round of turnip stained black, upon which they all with one voice cried out, 'Master, help us!' The chalice contained water instead of wine; and they made their holy water as follows: the goat pissed into a hole dug in the ground, and with this undiluted water the celebrant sprinkled them all with a black aspergillum.

On other occasions witches were reported to have tried orthodox Christian rites before resorting to black masses to achieve their aims. In 1680, as part of the revelations that were made public during the extraordinary CHAMBRE ARDENTE AFFAIR which involved some of the highest-placed aristocrats in France, a French witch identified as 'La Voisin' was alleged to have celebrated a conventional mass but, when this did not work, to have performed another ceremony of a more obscene occult nature: a naked woman was used as an altar and celebrants were offered the blood of a sacrificed child to drink and a host comprising mixed blood and flour.

Other witches apparently arranged to have the instruments they used in their spells covertly blessed in Christian masses in order to endow them with greater power. This was usually effected by slipping the object in question under the altar cloth or by approaching a member of the clergy who was known to be a practising witch.

Desecration of the sacred host was commonly included in confessions extracted from suspected witches. Some witches were alleged to purloin the host from churches in order to defile it in their own ceremonies, urinating upon it or thrusting it into the vagina of the female who was acting as the human altar. Such accusations were, of course, likely to inspire loathing in even those doubtful about the reality of witchcraft, and to add further ammunition to the arsenal of the witch-hunters who argued for harsher persecution of such 'enemies' of Christian society. Garbled prayers based on Christian originals might also be mouthed in a deliberately nonsensical fashion. Thus, 'hoc est corpus' from the conventional mass became 'hocus-pocus', a phrase that subsequently passed into everyday language to signify any form of gobbledegook.

The fragmentary accounts of black masses before the nineteenth century suggest that the ritual denunciation of Christ and the Church was of only secondary importance to Europe's witches in the post-medieval era, but with the development of SATANISM from the 1890s a more elaborate and deliberately anti-Christian conception of such rituals was devised. The prime purpose of the black mass was now established to be the honouring of Satan and all that was opposed to Christianity – a celebration of the triumph of the flesh over the spirit. The Christian rites were now deliberately turned on their head, prayers being said backwards, crosses being turned upside down and everything carefully done in reverse. The traditional use of naked women as altars and the blasphemous consecration of black hosts, meanwhile, became indispensable elements of redefined modern convention.

blackbird In common with other birds that have black plumage, the blackbird was sometimes identified as a favourite form for witches' FAMILIARS. According to ancient British superstition the blackbird had had ominous associations even earlier, reputedly being a messenger from the world of the dead.

Blackmore, Anne *see* HORSE-CHARMING.

Blanchu, Etienette *see* RAIS, GILLES DE.

Blanckenstein, Chatrina 1610–*c*.1680. Elderly German woman who was tried as a witch in Naumburg, Saxony, in 1676. The case of Chatrina Blanckenstein, a widow from a respectable background, illustrates the extent to which, during the hysteria of the seventeenth century, accusations of witchcraft could on the slightest evidence blight the lives of even the most respected citizens, and could also extend to touch the lives of their offspring years later.

The case began when a neighbour's baby died four days after eating some jam that Chatrina Blanckenstein's daughter had exchanged for some fuel, having no money with her at the time. The baby's death was blamed on witchcraft and suspicion immediately fell on the Blanckenstein household. Other neighbours reported chasing HARES in the vicinity of the Blanckenstein home, and a town watchman said he had seen three CATS with red eyes nearby. On this and other equally trivial evidence, the courts ordered Chatrina Blanckenstein's trial for murder by witchcraft.

Despite strenuous efforts by her sons to obtain her release, she was thrown into prison and, after all appeals were rejected, subjected to torture with the BOOTS, the THUMBSCREWS and the LADDER. Further pain was inflicted by twisting her neck with ropes, to the point where it was feared that she would be killed. Remarkably, the elderly widow refused to confirm any of the allegations put to her and, when the interrogators failed to locate the DEVIL'S MARK upon her, she was released.

The case was dropped after she had reimbursed the court for the cost of her own torture, but the suspicions connected with the family name were not dispelled. In 1689, some years after the widow had died, her daughter (whose name is not recorded) was accused of employing witchcraft to secure the death of another baby. The court, doubtless recalling the accusations made against Chatrina Blanckenstein, pursued the case with vigour. Unable to find a lawyer for her defence, the daughter was sent for torture. On sight of the instruments that were to be used on her she agreed at once to make a full confession, admitting that she had killed the child as charged and, further, that she had enjoyed sexual relations with a devil named Heinrich, that she had killed various livestock and that she had denied the Holy Trinity. After naming her accomplices she attempted suicide by hanging herself with her belt, but she was resuscitated and, in due course, burned alive.

Blocula *see* MORA WITCHES.

blood A witch's blood was long considered the vehicle of his or her magic. The evil power that a witch enjoyed was held to be passed from a witch to his or her offspring 'in the blood', and it was therefore thought essential that when a witch was put to death the body was thoroughly destroyed, so that all trace of the witch's evil was safely eradicated. (This belief is thought to have lain at the root of the Continental custom of burning heretics and witches, rather than having them hanged as they were in England.) A witch was also believed to sign the all-important PACT WITH THE DEVIL in his or her own blood, and also to feed any FAMILIAR with blood from special teats.

A witch's power could be broken, according to widely held superstition, by the procedure of SCORING ABOVE THE BREATH – that is, causing a witch to bleed from cuts or scratches inflicted anywhere above the mouth and nose. Another countermeasure concerning blood involved the preparation of a WITCH BOTTLE containing the HAIR, blood and URINE of a suspected victim of witchcraft: this was boiled over a fire at midnight, causing the culprit terrible agony and even death.

Because the essence of a person's life force was supposed to reside in their blood, it was common for blood to be included as an ingredient in spells of various kinds. The magic of blood could be used to subdue demons, to release victims from demonic possession, to prevent disease, to forestall bad luck and to draw MAGIC CIRCLES. Sometimes, in order for a spell to work, it was necessary for a sample of an intended victim's blood (or hair, skin and so forth) to be procured. This could then be incorporated in a wax image in order to direct the malevolent influence at the right person.

The accusation that in the course of their SABBATS witches drank the blood of young children and babies specially murdered for this purpose was regularly levelled at hapless suspects. It was rumoured that no less a person than Catherine de' MEDICI ordered that a young boy's blood be drunk at a BLACK MASS in order to restore the health of her own ailing son.

Superstition formerly had it that witches shared with blacksmiths a unique influence over the blood, and could stop its flow in both humans and animals at will. Persons from both callings used to set themselves up as blood-charmers, offering to use their magical powers to staunch haemorrhages in exchange for a small sum. The blood of a newly hanged man was widely reputed to be particularly efficacious at healing a range of ailments. It had to be allowed to drip on to the sufferer while the deceased felon was still on the gallows.

See also BIER RIGHT.

boar A favourite animal disguise of the DEVIL, in which, according to the confessions of tortured witches, he was reported to have manifested himself at numerous SABBATS. The pig was originally identified as a representative of evil in the New Testament, primarily through the story of the Gadarene swine, the DEMONS who fled from Christ in the form of pigs. Centuries later, witches in IRELAND and New England (*see* UNITED STATES OF AMERICA) frequently described the Devil appearing to them in the form of a large black boar. Elsewhere there was a strong tradition that pigs were highly susceptible to demoniacal POSSESSION, and it was not unheard of for ailing pigs to be sacrificially burned in order to prevent the demons inhabiting them from harming other pigs. Records survive of a pig being ritually burned alive at Huntingdon in eastern England as late as 1833.

Bocal, Pierre *see* BASQUE WITCHES.

Bodenham, Anne *see* DR LAMB'S DARLING.

Bodin, Jean 1529–96. French lawyer and political philosopher who was the author of a number of early and highly influential books on the subject of witchcraft. The publication of Bodin's *De la Démonomanie des Sorciers* in 1580 was a landmark in the development of the witchcraft hysteria of the sixteenth and seventeenth centuries, arguing as it did for much more strenuous action against suspected witches who, Bodin claimed, were staging an invasion of the Christian world under their master the Devil.

Among other things, the author criticised the burning of witches over slow fires, on the grounds that the condemned prisoner usually died after only half an hour and therefore escaped further punishment. He also added his support to the theories that witches could turn themselves into wolves and that they could cause harm through the magic of LIGATURE. Faced with the apparent impossibility of the idea that witches could fly, Bodin offered his own ingenious explanation. According to him, witches flew on their BROOMSTICKS in spirit only, while their bodies remained at home to deceive those who suspected them.

In Bodin's view, the nature of witchcraft was such that proving the crime was much more difficult than in other offences. Therefore, the usual legal safeguards should not be allowed and the investigator should feel free to adopt such irregular procedures as taking into account the evidence of young children, encouraging informants by assuring them of confidentiality and never acquitting a person once he or she was accused. A judge who allowed a convicted witch to live should, the author claimed, be put to death himself. Bodin also attempted one of the first legal definitions of a witch: 'one who knowing God's law tries to bring about some act through an agreement with the Devil'.

Some authorities chose to scorn Bodin for his gullibility and to condemn him for his part in whipping up fear of witchcraft throughout Europe. Others, however, impressed by the author's qualifications (Bodin boasted an extensive education in the classics, law, philosophy and economics and presided as judge over many witchcraft trials), accepted his claims and quoted his book in justifying the atrocities committed in the name of Church and State against accused witches. A substantial portion of his most famous work was dedicated to detailing the means by which suspects might be interrogated, tortured, prosecuted and put to death, and the records indicate that he personally approved the torture of even children and invalids in cases in which he was professionally involved.

Bodin died of plague in his native city of Angers, but his book continued to exercise a pernicious influence for years to come, the author's prestige and learning bolstering his calls for the harshest persecution of witches wherever they were found.

bodkins *see* PRICKING.

Böffgen, Christine d.1631. German widow who was tortured to death as a witch in the Rhineland village of Rheinbach under the instructions of the notorious witch judge Franz BUIRMANN. The case of Böffgen, a respected local matriarch, was among the most scandalous trials connected with Buirmann's name and continued to be remembered well into the twentieth century as one of the most regrettable episodes in the village's history.

Arrested by the authorities after accusations of witchcraft were made against her by two people already in gaol, Böffgen was allowed only a perfunctory hearing before being handed over to the torturers. Blindfolded and shaved, she was subjected first to the ordeal of PRICKING and then placed upon the torture stool, with vices tightened on her legs (*see* BOOTS). A confession extracted by these means was recanted by the prisoner as soon as the vices were removed, but the authorities ordered further physical abuse and, after four days of such ill treatment, the old woman died. Masses for her soul were still being conducted in the village church of St George in the 1920s.

Boguet, Henri *c.*1550–1619. French lawyer and writer, who as one of Burgundy's most notorious witch judges was responsible for sending some six hundred accused witches to their deaths. His activities marked one of the worst localised outbreaks of the witch hysteria of the late sixteenth century, and his publication in 1602 of the *Discours des Sorciers*, in which he discussed many of the cases in which he had been involved, compounded his misdeeds by contributing substantially to the climate in which fear of witchcraft intensified in decades to come. As chief judge at St Claude in Burgundy, Boguet launched his witch-hunt by mercilessly torturing an accused witch called Françoise Secretain into naming numerous accomplices. Virtually everyone, including very young children, who was subsequently brought before Boguet's court was condemned to death, and many were burned alive without the benefit of being first strangled by the executioner. In one of the most horrifying cases, a man named Claude Janguillaume managed to free himself from the ropes that bound him to the stake and was thrust back into the flames three times before he finally died.

Boguet's book arising from his experience in Burgundy went through twelve editions in a scant twenty years and became one of the most trusted authorities on the conduct of witch trials. Through case histories he built up a strong argument for belief in such phenomena as TRANSVECTION, WITCH'S MARKS and the bewitching of livestock. Of particular interest to other witch judges was an appendix in which the author codified the legal articles of relevance to witchcraft, and described the procedure that should be followed in court in the prosecution of such cases.

See also FRANCE.

Boleyn, Anne *c.*1507–36. English woman who became Henry VIII's second wife in 1533 but was soon rumoured to be a witch. Secretly married while negotiations were still in progress to have Henry's marriage to Catherine of Aragon dissolved, Anne Boleyn lost the King's favour within three months of the ceremony and it was not long before he was seeking ways of extricating himself from the union. The fact that Anne had a rudimentary sixth finger on her left hand was seized upon by the King's supporters as a sign of her involvement in sorcery, and the word rapidly spread that the Queen had ensnared the sovereign by bewitching him. Henry was not best pleased when she gave birth to a daughter (destined to be Elizabeth I) rather than a son and then lost a male child during pregnancy. He now voiced his own suspicions about his wife's dabbling in sorcery and, in combination with rumours about her infidelities to the King, her fate was sealed. Anne Boleyn was executed on a charge of treason on Tower Green in London on 19 May 1536.

Bolingbroke, Roger *see* COBHAM, ELEANOR, DUCHESS OF GLOUCESTER.

boots Instrument of TORTURE kept for use in cases specifically involving witchcraft or treason. The boots, or 'Spanish boots' ('bootikins' in Scotland), comprised two vices shaped to enclose the legs of the victim – or, in simpler form, four strong lengths of wood bound together lengthwise with the top and bottom left open. These could be tightened cruelly by hand or by knocking in wedges with blows from a mallet in order to crush the bones and flesh of the accused with excruciating pain. Records exist of the boots being employed in many countries, including Scotland (*see* FIAN, JOHN), Germany and France (*see* CHAMBRE ARDENTE AFFAIR).

Bosse, Marie *see* CHAMBRE ARDENTE AFFAIR.

Bostock, Bridget *see* WHITE WITCH.

Bothwell, Francis Stewart, Fifth Earl of *see* FIAN, JOHN; JAMES I; NORTH BERWICK WITCHES.

Bouillon, Duchess of *see* CHAMBRE ARDENTE AFFAIR.

Boullan, Joseph-Antoine 1824–93. French occultist, who led the notorious Church of Carmel in Lyons in the late nineteenth century. An educated man, Boullan was a Catholic priest until he was defrocked because of a sexual liaison with a nun, Adèle Chevalier, who became pregnant by him. The couple subsequently set up their own religious community and then joined the Church of Carmel, which had already been condemned by the Pope in 1848. Boullan inherited the leadership of the group in 1876 and, with his new lover Julie Thibault, made sex central to the so-called 'Union of Life' and other rites that were practised by the cult, which was run more or less as a witches' COVEN.

After several years pursuing sexual gratification with his disciples Boullan attracted the enmity of the Marquis de GUAITA, who engaged in 'psychic warfare' with the Church of Carmel's leader. According to his supporters, Boullan eventually fell victim to the curses directed at him by Guaita and his followers, being struck down without warning while apparently in good health. Deprived of his leadership, the organisation quickly disintegrated. A sympathetic account of the Church's activities and principles was published by the writer Joris-Karl HUYSMANS in 1891.

Boullé, Thomas *see* BAVENT, MADELEINE.

Boy of Nottingham *see* DARRELL, JOHN.

Brandon, Witch of Unnamed English witch who, in the eleventh century, was recruited by the Norman invader William the Conqueror in his campaign against the Saxon rebel Hereward the Wake in the fens of East Anglia. According to Ivo Taillebois in his *De Gestis Herwardi Saxonis*, William was prevailed upon to consult the witch at her home in Brandon; together they plotted how to use her magic against the Saxon enemy. Unfortunately for William, Hereward was in the room disguised as a simple potter, so he heard everything that passed. When the next attack was mounted by the Normans, the Witch of Brandon was placed upon a high wooden tower from which she shouted curses and cast spells against the Saxon rebels. In response, Hereward instructed his men to set fire to the reeds surrounding the Normans and the army was soon in headlong flight from the flames and smoke. Many perished in the panic, but William was among those lucky to escape. The Witch of Brandon herself fell from her tower in the general confusion and broke her neck.

Breadheid, Janet *see* AULDEARN WITCHES.

Brewham Witches *see* SOMERSET WITCHES.

bridle *see* WITCH BRIDLE.

Brinvilliers, Marie-Madeleine d'Aubray, Marquise de 1639–76. French aristocrat who was tried as a witch in a sensational trial in Paris in 1676. Marie-Madeleine d'Aubray developed an early interest in both witchcraft and sex, having regular intercourse with her two older brothers from the age of twelve and quickly exhausting the sexual prowess of her husband, Antoine Gobelin, Marquis de Brinvilliers. Subsequently she took numerous lovers and further explored sexual matters, while also experimenting with poisons and other black arts.

Having established which poisons worked best by the expedient of trying them out on patients in the Paris hospitals while ostensibly visiting them with food and broth, the Marquise murdered her father and her two brothers and then directed her attentions towards her husband. Success in this latter case was forestalled by her current lover, who dosed the Marquis with antidote as a safeguard against falling victim himself, in his turn, to his mistress's lethal habits.

The Marquise's interest in witchcraft was publicly revealed in 1676 when various poisons and other incriminating evidence were found among her belongings. She was arrested and subjected to vicious torture in order to obtain a confession, which was soon forthcoming. As an aristocrat, the Marquise was spared being burned alive and was instead beheaded before her body was burned to ashes in front of virtually the entire French court. Before she died, she complained that she was only one of many in French high society who had interested themselves in black magic – a claim that led to Nicholas de la Reynie, chief of police, carrying out an investigation with wide repercussions (*see* CHAMBRE ARDENTE AFFAIR).

Briqueville, Roger de *see* RAIS, GILLES DE.

Brocken *see* WALPURGIS NIGHT.

broomstick The traditional means of flight with which witches have been associated since the fifteenth century. Originally the broomstick was only one of several everyday implements that were alleged to serve in this way. Historical accounts give details of witches flying on cleft sticks, distaffs and even shovels as well as on the now conventional broomstick, while some witches were credited with achieving flight mounted on DEMONS, animals or such unlikely things as eggshells and wisps of grass – or indeed without a vehicle of any kind. Most intriguing is the suggestion that the broomstick only became associated with the business of flying through the confusion of the word 'cat', an old dialect term for a broomstick, with the animal of that name, which was reputed to be one of the creatures which carried witches to their SABBATS.

According to the *Errores Gazariorum*, published in 1450, apprentice witches were presented on their INITIATION with a stick smeared with FLYING OINTMENT. The earliest recorded confession to flying on a broomstick dates from 1453, when Guillaume Edelin of St Germain-en-Laye, near Paris, claimed that he had performed this feat. Some later accounts suggested that only those unable to attend sabbats due to infirmity were granted such flying sticks. Surviving documents from the early seventeenth century list GOATS, black rams, wolves, oxen and other animals as vehicles for flight commonly used by witches, but subsequently the broomstick (a traditional symbol of womanhood, while a pitchfork signifies maleness) was recognised as more usual. Indeed, it was claimed by some that any broomstick left out of doors on the night that a sabbat was held would take itself off to the gathering, whether carrying a witch or not.

Having smeared their broomsticks and themselves with flying ointment, witches uttered 'Go, in the Devil's name, go!' or something similar and left their houses by means of the CHIMNEY (perhaps an extension of the old custom of leaving a broom showing at the chimney to indicate that the woman of the house was not at home). Alternatively, a witch secretly planning to join a COVEN might leave a broomstick in her bed in order to conceal her absence from her husband. However, a broomstick laid across the threshold was once widely considered a sure way of deterring a witch from entering.

In reality few witches ever confessed to flying on broomsticks, although many admitted performing ritual dances at covens while straddling a length of stick (a likely source of the tradition). The broomstick retains its mystic associations, however, and its powers are still celebrated in Mummers' plays and other ancient folk customs. For many years couples in Wales could celebrate a 'broomstick wedding', in which they confirmed their union by jumping over a broomstick laid in the doorway of their new home. There was also a superstition that a virgin stepping over a broomstick would experience the consequence of becoming a mother before she became a wife.

In the popular imagination the broomstick now occupies a prominent place in the iconography of witchcraft and ranks alongside the pointed HAT and the black CAT as one of the essential accoutrements of any bona fide witch.

See also TRANSVECTION.

Brown, Thomas *see* PITTENWEEM WITCHES.

bryony Herbaceous climbing plant that was allegedly used in many witches' potions when MANDRAKE was not available. Black bryony was identified with mandrake, while white bryony was dubbed 'womandrake'. Among other properties useful to the practitioner of witchcraft the plant was reputed to be highly effective as a purgative, to promote fertility in humans and in horses, to act as an aphrodisiac (*see* LOVE POTION), to ease various gynaecological problems and also to reduce bruising (hence the French name for the plant, which translates as 'herb of beaten wives').

Buckingham, George Villiers, First Duke of 1592–1628. English statesman who became a favourite of JAMES I and is also said to have been adept in the black arts. James I was renowned for his severe attitude towards proven witches but seems to have cast a blind eye over the interest of his favourite, who was raised to the peerage and became the second richest nobleman in England. Educated in France, George Villiers married Katherine Manners, who was also rumoured to be a witch, and attended closely upon the King throughout his last years.

When James lay dying in 1625 it is said that he allowed the Duke and his wife to perform a bizarre ceremony in the hope of prolonging his life. In the strictest privacy of the royal bedroom, the couple, playing godfather and midwife while James looked on, dressed a piglet in christening robes and then held a ritual baptism, naming the pig James and then chasing it out of the room in the belief that the pig would take the King's illness away with it. Unfortunately, the spell failed and the King died.

The Duke was virtually ruler of England during the minority of Charles I, but no recourse to witchcraft could save him from an early death. He was stabbed by a discharged naval officer, John Felton, while inspecting the navy at Portsmouth dockyards.

George Villiers, Second Duke of Buckingham (1627–87), succeeded his father as a notable statesman and had a similar reputation as an exponent of witchcraft. Brought up with the royal family, he lived in exile after the Civil War but reclaimed his estates by marrying Mary Fairfax, daughter of the Parliamentarian general, and became one of the most dissolute of Charles II's courtiers as well as his chief minister and a successful playwright. In 1670, as ambassador to France, the Duke met the notorious coven leader Catherine Deshayes and may well have attended one of her sabbats, at which naked women served as the altar (*see* CHAMBRE ARDENTE AFFAIR). He made a second visit to Paris and returned to the Deshayes coven in 1672. Subsequently he fell out with the King after being dismissed from office due to pressure from his political rivals.

Buirmann, Franz fl.1630s. German lawyer who presided as judge over numerous witchcraft trials and sent hundreds of suspected witches to the stake. Prominent among the most ruthless of the witch judges during the witchcraft hysteria that traumatised

GERMANY in the seventeenth century, Buirmann was given special powers as a travelling judge by the Prince-Archbishop of Cologne, who allowed him precedence over all local authorities. Free of interference from lesser justices, Buirmann ranged throughout Cologne and neighbouring areas, striking chiefly at wealthy suspects whose property was subsequently confiscated.

A man of little education, Buirmann had suspects tortured with the utmost severity in order to obtain confessions and the names of accomplices. Surviving records indicate that under his direction suspects were routinely tortured by means of the BOOTS, or strapped to a metal witch's chair beneath which a fire was lit. Other suspects were raped, had their bones broken or were jerked violently about the room while wearing a spiked iron collar that lacerated the neck. Many suspects died in the course of such abuse (see BÖFFGEN, CHRISTINE), while those who confessed were burned alive, often in huts of straw.

Even Buirmann's own associates were not safe from his murderous attention: in 1636, at Siegburg, he had his own executioner burned as a witch. Other victims included the sister of a woman who had refused the witch judge's amorous advances and no less a personage than the mayor of the village of Rheinbach, which witnessed some of the worst atrocities during visits by Buirmann in 1631 and 1636. In response to Buirmann's first visit, in 1631, the terrified population of Rheinbach clubbed together to offer a substantial bribe to the witch judge to move on to another locality, which he agreed to do. Five years later, however, he returned, and in that one village alone it has been estimated that one person in every two families was put to death on Buirmann's orders.

Bulcock, John and Jane *see* PENDLE WITCHES.

Burning Court *see* CHAMBRE ARDENTE AFFAIR.

burning of witches With the exception of ENGLAND and New England (*see* UNITED STATES OF AMERICA), where witches were usually hanged (see below), the conventional method of disposing of condemned witches was death by burning at the stake. This punishment was the traditional means of execution for heretics and was particularly appropriate in the case of witchcraft: experts upon the subject consistently stressed the need to destroy the victims' bodies completely, lest their magic powers be passed on. Angela, Lady of Labarthe, who was executed in Toulouse in 1275, is sometimes quoted as the first woman to be burned as a witch, and burnings continued into the eighteenth century.

Generally speaking, witches were burned alive unless they had secured the court's sympathy in some way and were granted the mercy of being strangled at the stake or hanged prior to burning. Condemned witches who recanted their confessions just before the death sentence was carried out lost the right to be dispatched in this fashion and were surrendered to the flames while still alive. All witches were burned alive in Italy and Spain, regardless of whether they had recanted or not.

The usual procedure for burning a witch was to tie the condemned prisoner to a stake surrounded by straw, wood and other flammable materials, which were then set alight. Travellers on the Continent left descriptions of certain towns that boasted a forest of stakes outside the town gates, and some localities witnessed hundreds of burnings in a single year. It was suggested by one contemporary that in the town of Como in Italy, for instance, around a thousand witches were burned to death in 1523. The smoke usually killed the victims before the flames reached them, but many people suffered terrible burns before dying. In some parts of Europe the condemned person was placed within a small hut of dry straw or in a barrel of pitch, which was then set alight. In all cases, the fire would be kept going until the body of the deceased was reduced to ashes, which might then be scattered in the wind. If a witch's FAMILIARS had been identified and captured, these too would be thrown on to the pyre.

In cases where the condemned witch had refused throughout the proceedings to cooperate with the court he or she might, as a punishment, be burned over a fire of brush or green wood, which took longer to turn into a blaze and so prolonged the death agony.

Even this cruelty was insufficient for some witch-haters. Jean BODIN, for instance, wrote:

> Whatever punishment one can order against witches by roasting and cooking them over a slow fire is not really very much, and not as bad as the torment which Satan has made for them in this world, to say nothing of the eternal agonies which are prepared for them in Hell, for the fire here cannot last more than an hour or so until the witches have died.

In England witches were always hanged, unless they were also guilty of murdering their husbands or their masters or of plotting the death of the monarch, in which cases they were guilty of treason and would be sentenced to die at the stake. Rare examples of English witches who died at the stake included Mother Lakeland, who was burned at Ipswich on 9 September 1645 after being found guilty of using witchcraft to murder her husband and others, and May Oliver, who was burned for similar crimes at Norwich in 1659.

Burnings were the preferred method of execution north of the border and memories of the burning of witches in SCOTLAND lingered into relatively recent times. Perhaps the most notable illustration of this was the curious ritual of 'burning the witch', which was observed on the royal estate of Balmoral in Kincardine and Deeside until at least the end of the nineteenth century, with Queen Victoria herself in attendance. Alexander Macdonald described this arcane ceremony in *Scottish Notes and Queries*:

> A huge fire was kindled in front of the Castle opposite the main doorway. The Clansmen were mustered, arrayed in highland garb. At a signal, headed by a band, they marched toward the palace. The bonfire was kindled so as to be in full blaze when the procession reached it. The interest of the promenade was centred on a trolley on which there sat the effigy of a hideous old woman or witch called the Shandy Dann. Beside her crouched one of the party holding her erect while the march went forward to the bagpipes' strain. As the building came in sight, the pace was quickened to a run, then a sudden halt was made a dozen yards or so

from the blaze. Here, amid breathless silence, an indictment is made why this witch should be burned to ashes, and with no one to appear on her behalf – only this *advocatus diaboli*, paper in hand – she is condemned to the flames. With a rush and a shout and the skirling of bagpipes, the sledge and its occupants are hurled topsy-turvy into the fire, whilst the mountaineer springs from the car at the latest safe instant. There follow cheers and hoots of derisive laughter, as the inflammable wrappings of the Shandy Dann crackle and splutter out. All the while the residents at the castle stand enjoying this curious rite, and no one there entered more heartily into it than the head of the Empire herself.

It is said that anyone walking on Gallows Hill two miles outside Scalloway on the island of Shetland, where the last witch was burned in 1700, will be able to discern the ashes still visible in the soil, from the island's many witch burnings.

See also EXECUTIONS.

Burroughs, George *see* SALEM WITCHES.

Burton Boy Thomas Darling (b.1582), a young English boy whose testimony led to the trial of several elderly women as witches in 1596. The lamentable affair began in Burton-on-Trent on 27 February 1596, when the fourteen-year-old Thomas fell ill after a walk in the woods. Subsequently he complained of visions of the DEVIL and other demons, including one in the form of a green cat, and people suspected that he had been bewitched. When asked who might be responsible, Darling recalled that an ancient crone he had met in the woods had taken exception when he had broken wind in her presence and had responded with the words:

> Gyp with a mischief and fart with a bell, I will go to heaven and thou shalt go to Hell.

The suspect, described as wearing a grey gown and a broad-brimmed hat and having three WARTS on her face, was confidently identified by the boy's relatives as the sixty-year-old Alice (or Alse) Gooderidge of Stapenhill. Gooderidge confessed to being in the woods on the day in question but denied the boy's version of events, saying that Thomas had instead abused her as a witch. The boy's fits became more frequent when Gooderidge was brought near him and she was searched for WITCH'S MARKS. Gooderidge submitted to the ordeal of SCORING ABOVE THE BREATH in the hope that the boy would drop the charges, but Darling persisted in his accusations. Her failure to recite the LORD'S PRAYER correctly was deemed telling evidence of her guilt, and a local man added to the weight of proof against her when he alleged that she had bewitched his cow.

In a bid to obtain a full confession, Alice Gooderidge was fitted with a pair of shoes and her feet placed so close to the fire that the shoes grew intensely hot. Despite the pain, she refused at first to confess any misdeeds, but was eventually forced to admit to keeping a FAMILIAR in the shape of a DOG named Minny. This dog had been given to her by her mother, which was in keeping with witchcraft tradition and so the mother, Elizabeth Wright, was also charged as a witch. Thomas Darling confirmed the mother's involvement when he went into further frenzies at the sight of her.

At this point in proceedings the infamous exorcist John DARRELL, who was convinced that Gooderidge was a witch, entered the case, performing a bizarre service over Darling that seemed to lead to a marked improvement in the boy's condition (Darrell was later obliged to admit that he had faked much of the ritual). At the ensuing trial, Alice Gooderidge was found guilty of witchcraft, but she died shortly afterwards in Derby gaol before the death sentence could be carried out. The fate of her mother is not recorded.

In 1599 Thomas Darling admitted that he had invented the affair 'to get myself a glory thereby'. Four years later his tongue got him into further trouble when he fell foul of the authorities at Oxford University, being sentenced to have his ears cropped after he libelled the Vice-Chancellor.

Bury St Edmunds Witches The town of Bury St Edmunds in Suffolk in eastern ENGLAND was the scene of two notorious witch trials. The first took place in 1645, at the instigation of the self-styled

Witchfinder-General Matthew HOPKINS, and the second, which was well documented, in 1662, before the future Lord Chief Justice Sir Matthew HALE.

The trial of August 1645 culminated in the arrest of nearly two hundred suspects, of whom the most notable was an elderly clergyman named John Lowes from the village of Brandeston. Lowes was disliked by his parishioners, who enthusiastically provided Hopkins with grounds for indicting the unlucky parson, who, perhaps significantly, was suspected of having unpopular Royalist sympathies. Hopkins subjected Lowes to SWIMMING in the moat of Framlingham Castle and then to the torture of being forced to walk backwards and forwards with barely a pause for several days and nights (an ordeal known as WALKING A WITCH) until the accused was in such a state of delirium that he was ready to confess to all manner of forbidden practices.

It emerged from these confessions that Lowes had made a PACT WITH THE DEVIL, had kept several FAMILIARS and had sunk a ship off Harwich (with the loss of fourteen lives) by the use of magic, as well as committing other misdeeds such as destroying cattle. Proof that a ship had been lost at the time in question was not considered necessary and although Lowes quickly withdrew the confession when he had recovered from his ill treatment the clergyman was one of eighteen who died on the scaffold before Hopkins turned his attention elsewhere. Refused a clergyman to read the burial service over him, Lowes was obliged to speak the words himself on his way to the gallows. Other victims of Hopkins's activities in Bury St Edmunds included a woman who was burned for the treasonable murder of her husband by witchcraft (*see* BURNING OF WITCHES).

The second trial of Bury St Edmunds witches took place in 1662 and was destined to have considerable influence upon the decisions of the judges in the later trial of the SALEM WITCHES. The case concerned two widows, Rose Cullender and Amy Duny of Lowestoft, who were charged with numerous acts of witchcraft including the bewitching of several children, one of whom had died. The two women had allegedly caused infestations of lice, children to fall ill or to suffer fits, farm carts to overturn and chimneys to fall. Further damning evidence concerned a TOAD that had been found in a baby's bedding – on the advice of a Dr Jacob of Yarmouth the toad had been thrown into the fire and shortly afterwards, so it was alleged, Amy Duny had been seen to have scorched arms.

The evidence of the children, who complained that the women were appearing to them as ghosts even during the proceedings and had caused them to experience paralysis and to vomit pins and nails, was particularly damaging. As additional proof of the presence of witchcraft the court noted that, under the baleful influence of Duny and Cullender, the children stumbled over the name of Christ when asked to read from the Bible and screamed when touched by one of the two women. It was also claimed that examination of Amy Duny – remarkably, by the mother of one of the children involved – had revealed teats for the feeding of her familiars (*see* WITCH'S MARK).

In the face of such a wealth of 'evidence', supported by Hale's remarks at the end of the trial to the effect that if so many countries had laws against witchcraft then it must exist, the jurors had no hesitation in finding the two women guilty. They were hanged, though protesting their innocence, four days later. In reality, probably the only crime of the two unfortunate women – who were known to have hot tempers – was to have uttered vague threats against their neighbours after, for instance, being refused the opportunity to buy a few herrings.

Hale, who readily accepted witchcraft as a proven reality, professed himself satisfied with the outcome. Later legal authorities lamented the credence that had been given to unsupported accusations and the manner in which the clearly fraudulent evidence of some witnesses was none the less allowed. Even during the trial, some of those present suggested imposture when one of the girls failed a test designed to prove how the touch of Amy Duny caused her to scream: blindfolded, she screamed just as loudly and fell into a fit when touched by someone else. The conclusion of the trial remains an indelible stain on the reputation of Sir Matthew Hale, one of England's most celebrated legal figures.

Bury St Edmunds was, however, the scene of another landmark case in the history of English witchcraft in 1694, when Chief Justice

Sir John HOLT determinedly acquitted another accused witch, Mother Munnings, of causing death by witchcraft.

Bute, John Stuart, Third Earl of *see* HELL-FIRE CLUB.

butter-spoiling Among the many calumnies routinely directed at witches was the relatively petty but oft-repeated allegation that they would exact revenge on their enemies by interfering with the process of churning and making butter. If butter failed to 'turn' in the churning process it was once inevitable that witchcraft would be suspected. Many witches brought to trial were charged with spoiling butter, and some accused persons confessed to committing, or attempting to commit, such misdemeanours.

Farmers and dairymaids could protect their butter against witchcraft through a wide variety of magical countermeasures. Reciting certain charms while the churning was in progress was recommended, as was tossing a pinch of SALT into the fire before commencing work. A SILVER coin or three hairs from the tail of a black CAT might be dropped into the cream to ward off malevolent magical interference, while in Ireland dipping the hand of a dead man into the mixture was said to be similarly effective. Using a churn made of ROWAN wood was reputed to assist in the churning, and if witchcraft was seriously suspected plunging a red-hot poker or a red-hot horseshoe into the cream would break the spell (and leave the culprit with a nasty burn).

See also PROTECTION AGAINST WITCHCRAFT; SPELL.

Buvée, Barbara, Sister St Colombe *see* AUXONNE NUNS.

buying wind *see* STORM-RAISING.

cabala Obscure philosophical system, originally of Jewish origins, which has exerted considerable influence over occultists of many nationalities over the centuries. This body of secret lore, allegedly first revealed by God to Abraham, suggests that man's existence is but the lowest of ten planes of being through which the spirit may progress, guided by an understanding of this highly complex and often mystifying system, which is passed down from one generation of wise men to the next.

Combining astrology with sophisticated concepts about the principles of unity and divinity, the cabala appealed to such occult practitioners as Eliphas LEVI and Aleister CROWLEY, who absorbed many cabalist doctrines into their own philosophical systems. Not the least of the system's attractions was its promise that if a man developed his potential in the right way he could ultimately come to rule the universe.

On a more practical level, the names of philosophical deities revered by the cabalists were assumed to have magical power in themselves; and consequently these were often incorporated into the elaborate rituals observed by practising occultists in the nineteenth and twentieth centuries. Examples include Hokhmah and Reshith, male Gods of Wisdom, Hesed, God of Love and Mercy, Netsah, the God of Endurance, Binah, the Goddess of Understanding and Intelligence, Din or Geburah, the Goddess of Power, Hod, the Goddess of Majesty, and Tifereth, the Goddess of Beauty.

Cadière, Marie-Catherine b.1709. French girl who in 1731 was one of the central protagonists in what became recognised as the last great witchcraft trial to be argued in the French courts. The deeply religious daughter of a widow of Toulon, Catherine Cadière was a very beautiful young woman but by the age of eighteen seemed set on a life of religious devotion, joining a group of like-minded women in her home city for prayer and meditation under the directorship of a respected Jesuit, Father Jean-Baptiste Girard. Catherine's ambition was evidently to become a saint through her devotions and this, she claimed, led her to seek a special relationship with the priest. Others speculated that she had in fact fallen in love with the fifty-year-old cleric – and, further, that this could only be the result of witchcraft on his part.

For a year Father Girard encouraged Catherine in her hopes of achieving sainthood, but he eventually came to doubt that she would ever achieve such holy status and in 1730 he recommended her to enter the convent of Ste Claire-d'Ollioules. This disappointment went hard with Catherine and soon she was suffering violent fits, hallucinations and hysteria. Attempts to exorcise the girl of the demons that seemed to be tormenting her failed, and now she alleged that her agonies were the consequence of being bewitched by Girard, who, she revealed, had seduced her. Her brother and her lawyers, meanwhile, located four more pupils of Girard and four nuns who were willing to repeat similar accusations against the priest.

The scandal quickly escalated and soon the matter was brought before the courts, with great publicity. The trial opened on 10 January 1731 amid scenes of almost hysterical excitement. On the eve of the trial Catherine, supported by her brother (who clearly hoped to see his sister canonised), staged midnight EXORCISMS before vast crowds, who were rewarded with 'proof' of the girl's POSSESSION by devils when she fell into a motionless trance.

The evidence that was unearthed in the trial proved sensational. Catherine, it seemed, had claimed 'intimate communion with God' but had, allegedly, been bewitched by Girard into allowing him to indulge in a variety of sexual perversions. The crucial moment had occurred when Girard had bent over her and breathed on her face, so that she was magically consumed by love for him: 'Then stooping down and putting his mouth close to hers, he breathed upon her, which had such a powerful effect upon the young lady's mind that she was immediately transported with love and consented to give herself up to him. Thus did he bewitch the mind and inclinations of his unhappy penitent.'

The priest, Catherine claimed, had then set about a systematic campaign to rob her of her honour. At first he had kissed her and fondled her body, explaining that he could promise her 'holy freedom'; when he caressed her breasts he explained that she would acquire greater strength of soul through such physical humiliation. Girard eventually completed his conquest and from then on fell into the habit of making love to her on a regular basis, sometimes for several hours at a time. To the titillation of those in the court, Catherine went on to describe how Father Girard had indulged in various sadistic practices, thrashing her naked buttocks with a whip to purge her of her unsaintly scruples.

Girard, for his part, protested strenuously at such allegations. If he had been seen to put his head close to hers, it was because he was hard of hearing. If he had expressed love for her in his letters, this was but the love that any priest should show his charges. He also blackened his former devotee's reputation with revelations that she had bribed various witnesses to give evidence supporting her story. She had, he added, also faked the 'miracles' that she claimed – on one occasion smearing her face with her own menstrual blood when alleging to have been magically besmirched when celebrating the passion of Christ.

With accusation and counter-accusation being hurled across the courtroom the trial threatened to descend into farce, and after many months of such exchanges the judges were unable to decide who, if anyone, to execute. In the end, Father Girard was sent back to the Church to be reprimanded for dubious conduct, while Catherine Cadière was sent home to live quietly with her mother. An angry mob tried to inflict their own punishment on the priest, but he got away and was subsequently cleared of any blame by the ecclesiastical authorities. He died in 1733.

The case obsessed countless observers both in France and beyond, and inspired numerous books which delighted in the lascivious details of the affair. Critics claimed that the authors of such volumes were interested only in the salacious aspects of the case, but this was itself telling, for no one at this late date seemed prepared to take the allegations of witchcraft very seriously. Indeed, the case only reached the courts in the first place because the charge of witchcraft brought with it the more damaging accusation of fornication.

Cagliostro, Count Alessandro 1743–95. Originally known as Giuseppe Balsamo, this Italian adventurer, charlatan and magician was among the most famous occultists of the eighteenth century. Dubbed the 'King of Liars' by the British writer Thomas Carlyle, Cagliostro, who was born into poverty in the slums of Palermo in Sicily, became famous throughout Europe for his exaggerated claims of success in alchemy and magic. Travelling from one country to another before settling in Paris, he impressed many gullible people at all levels of society with his apparent knowledge of astrology and of a range of occult arts. He made a fortune selling an elixir of eternal youth to the often well-heeled clients who sought his advice, though he was unmasked on various occasions for fraud and forgery of his results. None the less, he persisted in his claims that he could perform spells to raise the dead, could provide highly effective LOVE POTIONS (notably the sometimes dangerous cantharides) and could prophesy the future by crystal ball-gazing.

Ultimately, Cagliostro was obliged to leave France after he was implicated in a confidence trick concerning a valuable diamond necklace supposedly ordered for, but never delivered to, Queen Marie Antoinette. Back in Italy, having set up as a sorcerer in a house in the Piazza Farnese in Rome, where he received many notable dignitaries, he was denounced to the Inquisition by his wife and thrown into gaol. He died after serving five years of a life sentence at the fortress of San Leo in the mountains of northern Italy. According to some accounts he was strangled by his gaoler; others claim he died of the syphilis he had contracted on his travels in Spain as a young man.

cakes and wine *see* ESBAT.

Cambrai Nuns This early instance of the phenomenon of hysterical POSSESSION concerned the nuns of the convent at Cambrai, FRANCE, in 1491. Perhaps the first recorded outbreak of such hysteria, the case began with a nun who suffered a series of fits that were quickly blamed on witchcraft. The nun at the centre of the case then named others around her as witches, and they too began to show signs of demonic possession, barking like dogs, prophesying the future and allegedly performing feats of superhuman strength. Ultimately the nun who had initiated the whole scare was herself accused of being a witch, completing a cycle of accusation and counter-accusation that was to be echoed in many later cases.

It may well be significant that the case of the Cambrai Nuns, which set the model for many later instances, followed almost immediately on the papal bull issued by Pope INNOCENT VII, which was intended to alert Church authorities everywhere to the ever-present and indeed growing threat of witchcraft.

candle magic The use of wax candles in casting spells over intended victims of black magic. This variation upon IMAGE MAGIC employed the latent magic of fire as a means of bringing harm to a witch's enemies. The customary procedure involved the formal identification of a candle with a specific person. Once thus dedicated, the candle might be stuck with pins and set alight in the belief that the enemy concerned would suffer extreme pain and even death.

Candle magic had a long history: early examples date back to the fifteenth century and beyond. In 1490, for instance, Johanna Benet appeared before the Commissary of London charged with lighting a wax candle with the intention of causing a certain man a lingering death as the wax slowly melted. A remarkably late example of candle magic was recorded in a case for assault that was heard in Norwich in 1843. According to the evidence given in court, a Mrs Bell had lit a candle, stuck pins in it and then mixed some dragon's blood and water with some nail parings in an oyster shell – upon which a certain Mr Curtis had found himself unable to move his arms and legs. Unfortunately for Mrs Bell, Mrs Curtis had witnessed the preparation of the spell, which she genuinely believed had caused her husband's paralysis.

Among the most notorious cases involving the alleged use of candle magic was that of Roland Jenks and the 'Black Assizes' that were held in Oxford in 1577. Jenks, a Catholic bookseller, had been imprisoned and condemned on charges of selling seditious literature, though he was also suspected as having knowledge of the black arts. When a sudden epidemic of typhus gripped the prison and consequently the judge, jury, witnesses and lawyers assembled for the Assizes, many people assumed that Jenks had caused it. According to rumour, on being condemned Jenks had fashioned and lit a magical candle to raise the plague, which went on to claim the lives of many townspeople.

More cheerfully, candles might also be used in the business of procuring partners in love by means of magic. A lover might summon the object of his or her desire by piercing a lit candle wick with two pins and then intoning the following rhyme:

'Tis not the candle alone I stick,
But (lover's name)'s heart I mean to prick.
Whether he/she be asleep or awake,
I'll have him/her come to me and speak.

If the spell was correctly performed, the desired person was expected to appear before the flame reached the pins.

See also HAND OF GLORY.

Candlemas Christian festival celebrated on 2 February in honour of the Virgin Mary, and also a significant date in witchlore. In the Christian calendar, Candlemas commemorates Christ's first visit to the Temple with his mother. In the pagan calendar it marked the beginning of spring. Candles blessed during the rituals of Candlemas were reputed to ward off witches, as well as to keep illness and thunderstorms at bay. Such protection was deemed especially desirable as Candlemas also marked one of the most important festivals in the witches' calendar, being one of the dates upon which major SABBATS were supposedly held.

Canewdon Witches The village of Canewdon in Essex has long had a reputation as one of the oldest strongholds of witchcraft in English folk history, and the area of south-eastern England in which it lies is often called the 'Witch Country'. According to legend, as long as the church tower in Canewdon stands there will be seven witches in the village, 'three in silk and three in cotton, one being the parson's wife, one the butcher's wife and one the baker's wife'. Tales of an active COVEN thereabouts persisted well into the twentieth century.

Time-honoured tradition has it that the local coven meets at Canewdon CROSSROADS, which has a dread reputation and is said to be haunted by a witch executed for her activities many years ago. A patch of bare grass by the river, called the 'Witches' Field', is another place where they are supposed to convene.

A farm labourer named George Pickingale, who died in 1909, is reputed to have been the last of the 'master witches' in the village. Surviving tales credit him with the power to assemble his coven with a wooden whistle, with the gift of the EVIL EYE and with the ability to charm WARTS. He was also known to threaten to use his magic for harmful ends in order to extort free beer from neighbours, among other favours. His FAMILIARS manifested in the form of wizened little white mice, which were supposedly passed down from one master witch to another and which continued to infest Pickingale's cottage long after his demise.

Earlier generations of Canewdon witches were renowned for their power to halt machinery and wagons by a single penetrating look or by turning themselves into wheels, and at various times were accused of sending plagues of lice and other unpleasant creatures against their enemies. All, it seems, kept familiars in the form of white mice, which were sometimes buried with their masters and mistresses.

Many houses in the village were protected with WITCH BOTTLES and other precautions, and over the years a good many local women were ducked in the village pond in an attempt to prove or disprove their innocence.

Canon Episcopi Religious document of obscure origins that was for many centuries respected as the official view of the Catholic Church on the subject of witchcraft. According to the canon, which was formerly attributed to the Council of Ancyra around AD 314 (though this has now been discounted), witchcraft was nothing more than delusion and therefore anyone who believed that it could actually take place was guilty of HERESY:

> It is also not to be omitted that certain abandoned women per-
> verted by Satan, seduced by illusions and phantasms of demons,
> believe and openly profess that, in the dead of night, they ride
> upon certain beasts with the pagan goddess Diana, with a count-
> less horde of women, and in the silence of the dead of night fly
> over vast tracts of country, and obey her commands as their mis-
> tress, while they are summoned to her service on other nights.
> But it were well if they alone perished in their infidelity and did
> not draw so many others along with them into the pit of their
> faithlessness. For an innumerable multitude, deceived by this false
> opinion, believe this to be true and, so believing, wander from the
> right faith and relapse into pagan errors when they think that
> there is any divinity or power except the one God ... It is therefore
> to be publicly proclaimed to all, that whoever believes such things
> or similar things loses the faith, and he who has not the right faith
> in God is not of God, but of him in whom he believed, that is, the
> devil. For of our Lord it is written, 'All things were made by him.'
> Whoever therefore believes that anything can be made, or that
> any creature can be changed to better or worse or be transformed
> into another species of likeness, except by God himself who made
> everything and through whom all things were made, is beyond
> doubt an infidel.

The *Canon Episcopi* was incorporated into the *Corpus Juris Canonici* in the twelfth century and became an established part of canon law, having a profound impact upon attitudes to witchcraft in medieval times. Witchcraft was, on the highest authority, a fiction, and anyone who believed in it was openly condemned by the Church. As all supernatural power was possessed by God alone, such things as night rides and shape-shifting from one animal disguise to another were clearly impossible.

Opposition to the Church's stance on witchcraft grew steadily over the centuries, however, and such scholars as Thomas AQUINAS argued that Satan did indeed interfere in human affairs through witches, who were thus deemed to deserve officially sanctioned persecution. Because the Church would not admit that anyone could perform the supernatural acts that the followers of Diana and their successors were alleged to indulge in, suspects could not be punished for doing them, but only for believing that they did them. Sentences were therefore relatively lenient, to the frustration of those who perceived in witchcraft a real threat to Christian civilisation. Typical sentences on charges of witchcraft practices included the observance of periods of penance and fasting, although some suspects were also subjected to trial by ordeal.

Among the arguments put forward by activists pressing for reform of ecclesiastical law was the notion that a new sect of witches had sprung up since the original canon had been drafted, rendering it inappropriate in changed times. This new generation of witches was, it was argued, much more powerful (and therefore more threatening) than its predecessors, having the ability to perform all the supernatural feats of which the Church had decided that its forebears were incapable.

Ultimately the INQUISITION, which had a vested financial interest in getting witchcraft condemned as a real and existing evil, persuaded the Pope to change the Church's attitude on the matter. In 1484 INNOCENT VIII finally decided that witchcraft was a reality, that witches really flew, that they really had sex with the Devil, changed shape and so forth – and the official position was reversed. It now became heretical for anyone to deny the existence of witchcraft as a real and functioning evil, thus greatly facilitating the development of the witchcraft hysteria that swept the Christian world over the next two centuries.

Capeau, Louise *see* AIX-EN-PROVENCE NUNS.

captoptromancy *see* SCRYING.

Carolina Code   The criminal code of the Holy Roman Empire, under which countless witchcraft suspects were prosecuted in Continental Europe in the sixteenth century. Introduced in 1532, the Code sanctioned the use of torture in examinations of suspects:

> If anyone teaches others witchcraft; or if he misleads people into bewitching and in addition brings those he has deceived to effect bewitchment; also if he has associated with witches, either male or female; or with such suspected things, actions, words and ways as imply witchcraft; and, moreover, if he is defamed by these same witches; these indications give just proof of witchcraft and sufficient grounds for torture.

Those who confessed were to be questioned about how they first became witches, about their procedures and also about their accomplices. Anyone who caused harm through witchcraft was subject to the death penalty:

> If someone did injury or damage to people through witchcraft, she must be punished from life to death, and this punishment must be done by burning. But where someone uses witchcraft without causing injury, she should be punished in another way, according to the magnitude of the crime ...

Continental witch judges diverged increasingly from the Code towards the end of the sixteenth century and calls were made to the Emperor to see that it was observed more strictly.

Carpzov, Benedict 1595–1666. Judge who systematised German law and is usually remembered as the founder of legal science in Germany, but who is also supposed to have signed death warrants for some twenty thousand convicted witches. A Lutheran, Carpzov delivered verdicts on witchcraft cases from all over Saxony after they were referred to the Leipzig Supreme Court, on which he sat.

A devout churchgoer who claimed to have read the Bible fifty-three times, he was all too ready to interpret witchcraft as a real and direct challenge to religious faith; as a result he pursued suspects with ruthless determination and blind prejudice. He accepted that the SABBATS and obscene rituals described by suspects under torture actually took place, and never questioned the idea that witches possessed the power of flight and had sexual intercourse with DEMONS on a regular basis, often giving birth to elves in consequence.

Carpzov held that practitioners of witchcraft should be hounded with maximum force and local judges were allowed special licence in such cases, which were considered beyond the ordinary scope of the law. Accused persons, for instance, were not to be allowed to question witnesses about their evidence, because they might seek to confuse them. He also sanctioned the extensive employment of TORTURE against the accused in order to obtain the all-important confessions. Carpzov himself recommended no fewer than seventeen different varieties of torture, which ranged from slowly roasting the suspect over candles to driving wedges under their nails and then setting fire to these. The bodies of executed witches were to be left unburied to deter others from falling into similar ways.

Dubbed the 'Lawgiver of Saxony', Carpzov published his opinions on witchcraft in the *Practica Rerum Criminalum* of 1635, which became a standard source of reference for others committed to the persecution of witches in Protestant Germany. Although this work added little new to the understanding of witchcraft as it was then perceived, it did make an attempt to legitimise systematic persecution by giving it a legal basis. Decisions recorded by Carpzov in his book were still being used as authority to have witches put to death a hundred years later.

In his defence, Carpzov did act humanely in easing the plight of condemned victims. He ruled that suspects should not be kept in underground dungeons where they might fall prey to venomous snakes, and also dictated that the condemned be given three days' warning of their execution and be fed properly in the intervening period. Conscious that many local courts were presided over by ill-trained and even slow-witted men, he also attempted to ensure that only intelligent, educated men sat as judges in such cases.

Carr, Robert, Earl of Somerset *see* OVERBURY, SIR THOMAS.

cat The most commonly depicted animal companion of the conventional witch and allegedly a favourite disguise of the DEVIL and of witches themselves. Although historical records indicate that cats of all colours have been associated with witches at one time or another, it is now a convention that the archetypal witch's cat is entirely black. If the cat has so much as a single white hair, some authorities claim, it loses its potency as a vehicle of magic.

The notion that a witch's spirit FAMILIAR might favour the form of a cat probably dated back to ancient Egyptian times, when the cat was considered sacred. The Egyptian cat-goddess Bast was the patron of fertility, but the Christians redefined her as an agent of sterility, robbing people of their fertility in order to make a gift of it to the Devil. Subsequently the link between the cat and the black arts was steadily consolidated and by the time of William Shakespeare in the late sixteenth century the creature was strongly associated with the supernatural. Witches also supposedly often took feline shape themselves, although over the centuries their familiars were equally likely to take the form of CROWS, ferrets, HEDGEHOGS, mice, RABBITS, TOADS or other animals.

During the trial of the ST OSYTH WITCHES in 1582 the accused witch Ursula Kempe confessed to owning two familiars in the shape of cats, which she sent out on evil-doing errands and which were rewarded by being allowed to suck BLOOD from her left thigh. Matthew HOPKINS, in his role of Witchfinder-General in the mid-seventeenth century, reported witnessing the manifestation of familiars as cats in the course of his investigations. Such cat-familiars were allegedly inherited by one witch from another and some were said to be of considerable age, having served a succession of masters and mistresses. Elizabeth Francis, one of the CHELMSFORD WITCHES, said she had been given her cat Sathan by her grandmother and had in turn passed it on to another witch after some fifteen years.

Cats, it was claimed, could transmit information to their evil-working masters and mistresses and in some rural areas, particularly in SCOTLAND and in Continental Europe, nobody dared to discuss important family business in front of a cat for fear that it was a witch in disguise – or the Devil himself. Such animals could also perform black deeds, including murder, on behalf of their owners and could conjure up foul weather – hence the mixed feelings entertained towards the creatures by sailors, fishermen and other seafarers. During her trial for witchcraft at Lincoln in 1619, Margaret Flower admitted to attempting to kill the children of the Earl of Rutland by rubbing some of their personal belongings against the body of her cat-familiar, and to making the parents infertile by similarly rubbing feathers from the Countess's bed against the animal's belly. At a somewhat earlier date, Agnes Sampson and other confederates confessed to 'baptising' a black cat and then throwing it into the sea in order to raise a storm and thus threaten the life of the future JAMES I.

In Hungary, superstition had it that almost all cats were transformed into witches between the ages of seven and twelve years. The only precaution possible was to cut a cross in the unlucky animal's skin. Tales of other injuries being inflicted upon cats suspected of being witches, and of similar wounds then being discovered on the witches in their human form, abound in many cultures. One example was recorded in Caithness in Scotland in 1718, when a man named William Montgomery, driven to distraction by the cats that gathered around his house to talk in human voices, killed two of the animals with a hatchet and wounded several others; the next day two local women were found dead in their beds and another could not explain a deep cut in her leg.

The notorious Isobel GOWDIE claimed that she assumed the form of the cat by muttering the following spell:

I shall go into a cat,
With sorrow and sign
And a little black shot.
And I shall go in the Devil's name
Ay while I come home again.

It was, however, widely believed that a witch could take the form of a cat only nine times (reflecting the popular notion that a cat has nine lives). One test by which it could be determined if a cat was a witch in disguise was to place the animal in a bowl of HOLY WATER: if the cat tried to escape, it was undoubtedly a witch.

The link between cats and witchcraft was rarely to the creatures' advantage, and it was once customary for kittens born in May – a month when witches and the spirits of the dead were reputed to be especially active – to be drowned. It was said that they would prove useless at hunting mice and would bring snakes and other undesirable prey indoors. In France, cats were trapped in baskets and tossed alive into midsummer bonfires, while in England they were suspended in baskets and shot at with arrows. Some people showed reluctance, however, to kill a cat, believing that anyone who did so forfeited their soul to the Devil.

As recently as 1929, when a witchcraft mania swept Pennsylvania, many black cats disappeared. It was discovered that superstitious locals were scalding them in boiling water and extracting a 'lucky' bone to bring them protection against harm from the supernatural.

cauldron One of the indispensable objects that is nowadays associated with the archetypal witch of popular imagination. In centuries gone by, the high point of a SABBAT was marked by all present sitting down to partake of a ceremonial feast presided over by the DEVIL or his representative, and the cauldron had a central role to play as a cooking utensil. Accurately or not, convention prefers the picture of the ancient crone bent over a cauldron in her lowly hovel as she brews up lethal potions that may incorporate such curious ingredients as lizards, herbs, frogs, frothing phials of chemicals, and human and animal flesh.

The cauldron once represented the renewal of life and it retains its significance in contemporary occult worship, notably in the ceremony called by Gerald GARDNER 'The Cauldron of Regeneration and the Dance of the Wheel'. In this celebration of the winter solstice, the cauldron takes the place of the altar and is venerated as a sacred object in itself (recalling, perhaps, the days when the cauldron and the food it contained were of primary importance in the lives of primitive peoples). Filled with dead leaves and paraffin or brandy, the cauldron is then ignited as the members of the COVEN circle it with increasing speed, sometimes chanting prescribed verses. At the climax of the ritual the High Priest and High Priestess join hands and leap over the burning cauldron, followed by all the others present.

Sacred cauldrons bearing religious symbols have been found by archaeologists throughout Europe. No doubt this ancient tradition inspired the inclusion of the cauldron as an icon of witchcraft.

Cernunnos *see* HORNED GOD.

Chambre Ardente Affair Witchcraft scandal that shook high society in France during the reign of Louis XIV. The whole affair began over fears that members of the French nobility were being poisoned by noxious potions from a secretive international ring, which was supplying poisons to aristocrats in several countries. In 1677 the Commissioner of Police in Paris, Nicholas de la Reynie, was ordered to investigate by the King. Reynie, whose suspicions had already been alerted by the case of the Marquise de BRINVILLIERS, exposed several leaders of the ring, who included nobles, a lawyer and a banker. He also seized stockpiles of poisons hidden at various locations throughout France. Interrogation over the following year failed to reveal the names of other accomplices and the trail would have gone cold but for a chance remark by a well-connected fortune-teller named Marie Bosse, who boasted during a dinner party that after three more poisonings she would be able to retire. A lawyer who happened to be one of the guests notified the police.

Reynie set up a trap for Bosse, arranging for a female agent to pose as an unhappy wife wishing to dispose of her husband. After she had successfully obtained a bottle of poison from Bosse, the police broke into the suspect's apartment and arrested her, together with another fortune-teller known as La Dame Vigoreux (the former mistress of Bosse's two previous husbands), her daughter and her two sons – all of whom were discovered asleep in the same bed.

Bosse and La Dame Vigoreux denied all the charges made against them but went on to name several of their clients, including the highly placed Madame de Poulaillon, the first of several hundred courtiers whose identities would be disclosed to the authorities in this connection. Madame de Poulaillon had, it transpired, attempted to murder her elderly husband by poisoning him in order to acquire his fortune and to devote herself to her lover; the old man, however, had sensed danger and had fled to a monastery.

Also named by the two women were a man called Vanens, their contact with the poison ring, and the famed fortune-teller Catherine Deshayes, known as La Voisin. Deshayes, it was claimed, had poisoned her first husband, prepared aphrodisiacs, procured abortions and sold poisons to well-connected society figures, becoming in the process very rich. She had also built a chapel in her garden where she and select companions could worship the 'old gods' ASHTAROTH and ASMODEUS, with La Voisin as the head of what turned out to be a very well-connected COVEN. Guests at the BLACK MASSES celebrated at the chapel reportedly included princesses, courtiers, the public executioner and the Duke of BUCKINGHAM.

Louis XIV, realising the scandal that threatened his court, set up a secret star chamber to pursue the allegations. It became known as the 'Chambre Ardente' (the 'Burning Court'), because proceedings took place in a room draped in black and lit by candles. La Voisin and Bosse traded allegations and in the process named other clients of the coven and a third accomplice, known as La Lepère, who was renowned as an abortionist. When interrogated by the court, La Lepère protested that she never offered help to virgins or pregnant women; however another witness claimed she had procured the death of some 2500 babies, many of whom now lay buried in a garden in the Paris suburb of Villeneuve-sur-Gravois. It also emerged that La Voisin had used poison to rid herself of her own husband, and had also sold poisons to the widow of the late President of the French Parliament and to the cousin of one of the judges in the case.

In an attempt to bring the affair to an end before further damage was done, on 6 May 1678 the star chamber sentenced Bosse and La Vigoreux to death by burning and condemned one of the former's sons, François Bosse, to be hanged, while Madame de Poulaillon was sent into exile. The investigations continued, however, to uncover more highly placed suspects, including the playwright Jean Racine: a warrant for his arrest was signed, but never served.

On 23 January 1680, the scandal flared up with new intensity. The Countess of Soissons, the Marquise d'Alluye, Madame de Polignac, Madame de Tingry, the Duchess of Bouillon, the Marquise du Roure, the Duke of Luxembourg and the Marquis de Feuquières (some of them close friends of the King) were all arrested and imprisoned, or else managed to evade capture and fled the country.

The need to obtain hard evidence relating to such distinguished prisoners obliged Reynie to employ the severest measures against the suspects who had named these personages. La Voisin and the others were subjected to such hideous tortures as the BOOTS, the rack and the enforced drinking of eight pitchers of water. When La Voisin refused to talk, the Attorney-General suggested that her tongue be cut out and her hands severed, but the court restricted itself to sentencing her to be burned alive. Legend has it that she spent the night before her execution in 'scandalous debauches' with other members of the coven confined in the same cell. The death sentence was carried out on 22 February 1680, La Voisin insisting to the end that she was no witch and several times kicking away the burning wood piled around her until she was finally overcome.

Another fortune-teller, identified by the name Lesage, was tortured into confessions implicating two priests, Father Davot and the Abbé Mariette, who had apparently conducted black masses over the bellies of naked girls at La Voisin's chapel and elsewhere. Yet another fortune-teller, La Filastre, admitted that she had sacrificed her own newborn baby to the DEVIL in the course of a black mass. Madame de Lusignan was accused of cavorting naked in the woods with her priest and using a large Easter candle for obscene purposes. Father Touret was said to have had intercourse in public with a girl used as an altar at another ceremony. The Abbé Guibourg, a sixty-six-year old hunchback, was similarly accused of performing black masses with naked women serving as the altar. Under torture he confessed to having murdered a child, cutting its throat and collecting the BLOOD in a chalice. The heart and entrails from the body were used at subsequent masses, and the body plundered for ingredients for 'magic powders'. The sixteen-year-old daughter of La Voisin and one of his three mistresses confirmed this account. Details also emerged of another mass, at which Guibourg had mixed the menstrual blood of Mademoiselle des Oeillets with the semen of her companion and with dried BAT's blood to make a potion that would promote their influence over the King.

Reynie was evidently convinced by the confessions he heard, concluding that 'I have gone over and over everything that might persuade me the accusations were false, but such a conclusion is just not possible.' He disregarded the facts that incriminating evidence had been obtained by the cruellest tortures and that many of the key witnesses were of more than dubious character, contradicting themselves and, in the case of La Filastre at least, going back on their confessions when burned alive. He did, however, find compelling evidence at the homes of the accused fortune-tellers, including poisons, wax images, black candles and books giving details of black magic practices. In the face of such evidence not only Reynie but the majority of French society believed that witchcraft was proved, and the King had to act decisively to forestall a general outburst of feeling against his degenerate court.

The 'Chambre Ardente' was officially closed in August 1680, although Reynie was instructed to probe in private allegations about the King's mistress, Madame de Montespan. It was claimed that, having been initiated into La Voisin's coven, she had been through various rituals under the guidance of Deshayes and the Abbé Guibourg in an attempt to retain her special status as royal favourite.

These ceremonies had involved Madame de Montespan being draped naked over the padded altar while her requests for royal favour were repeated first to the Christian God and then to the gods of the underworld. On the third occasion, when her influence over the King was waning, she allegedly allowed Guibourg to insert the host into her vagina and then to have intercourse with her while incanting prayers on her behalf. Reynie spent the next two years building up his case against Montespan, but further action against her (as against all the other nobles implicated in the case) was eventually dropped. Louis did, however, replace her as the foremost of his mistresses, transferring his attentions to the more discreet Madame de Maintenon from 1682.

In all, 319 people had been arrested during the proceedings and thirty-six of these were executed. Another thirty-eight were sentenced to serve as slaves on the galleys or were banished. Others, like the Abbé Guibourg, were left to rot in solitary confinement in French gaols, chained to the wall and forbidden to talk to their captors. Louis subsequently had fortune-telling banned throughout France and saw to it that stricter controls were placed over the sale of poisons. Witchcraft itself was officially declared a delusion under the Edict of 1682, heralding the end of the witch mania in France. In 1709, on Louis's orders, attempts were made to destroy all written records of the Chambre Ardente Affair; nevertheless some of them survived as evidence of one of the most remarkable witchcraft scandals ever recorded.

Channel Islands   Although subject to English jurisdiction, the Channel Islands, lying so close to the coast of northern France, were greatly influenced by French cultural attitudes. Consequently the witchcraft hysteria had considerably greater impact there than on the English mainland.

Guernsey witnessed the worst of it, with fifty-eight women and twenty men being tried on charges of sorcery in the hundred years or so from the time of Elizabeth I to that of Charles I. Another sixty-six trials took place on the island of Jersey between 1562 and 1736. A notably higher percentage of trials culminated in convictions than in mainland England, where only one in five witches sent for trial was actually found guilty. Records suggest that nearly half of those accused in the Channel Islands were sentenced to death.

The means of execution also reflected Continental practice, with convicted witches often being burned instead of hanged (or burned after being hanged first). Others were banished, whipped or had their ears cut off. Among the most grisly executions that took place was that of a pregnant witch who was burned alive in Jersey's Royal Square: as she died she gave birth, and the baby was tossed into the flames by those who had come to watch.

Cases usually rested on the discovery of the DEVIL'S MARK or on evidence of MALEFICIA, which might be as trivial as a shirt being infested with lice or a cow failing to give milk. A special law passed in Jersey in 1591 effectively eradicated the distinction between 'black' and 'white' witchcraft (*see* WHITE WITCH): anyone who turned to a witch or diviner for assistance 'in their ills and afflictions' was rendered liable to a term of imprisonment. Again in imitation of French practice, the authorities in the Channel Islands had a more permissive attitude towards the use of torture in extracting confessions. Unusually, TORTURE was often employed against suspects after the death sentence had been passed, rather than before, in order to learn the names of accomplices (*see* STRAPPADO).

Among the most sensational cases heard by the authorities in the Channel Islands was that of Collette du Mont in 1617. As well as confessing to flying to a SABBAT after smearing herself with FLYING OINTMENT, the accused provided salacious details of how she had allowed the DEVIL to have intercourse with her when he came to her in the form of a BLACK DOG. Somewhat tellingly, the 'dog' stood on its hind legs and had a paw that felt just like a human hand. Other witches described Satan appearing at sabbats in the form of a CAT, among other animal disguises.

Reason eventually prevailed towards the end of the seventeenth century, and cases of alleged witchcraft became rarer, as noted by Philippe le Geyt, Lieutenant Bailiff of Jersey:

> How many innocent people have perished in the flames on the asserted testimony of supernatural circumstances? I will not say there are no witches; but ever since the difficulty of convicting them has been recognised in the island, they all seem to have

disappeared, as though the evidence of times gone by had been but an illusion.

charm An incantation or other form of words that might be recited in order to conjure up the power of magic, or an object of some description that was believed to have inherent magical power (*see* AMULET).

The speaking of charms in the course of casting spells was a central feature of the spell-making process, possibly in imitation of the prayers and chants of the Christian Church. Ranging from the simplest rhymes to elaborate passages in Latin or nonsense presumably intelligible only to the DEVIL himself, the witch's charm was part of the mythology of spells and curses. Charms would also be said over the various tools of the witch's trade, including knives and herbs, in the belief that this would strengthen their magical potency.

On the other hand, the charm was also one of the simplest and most readily available defences against the threat of witchcraft. It was commonly employed in all kinds of circumstances – on retiring for the night, in treating illnesses, on undertaking some perilous activity and so forth – in much the same way as a prayer might be recited. Very often, in fact, charms invoked the names of the saints of Christian liturgy, as in the universally known 'White Paternoster':

> Matthew, Mark, Luke and John,
> Bless the bed that I lie on.

In Scotland, sprains might be treated by binding the wound with linen thread tied with nine KNOTS and chanting the following:

> Our Saviour rade
> His forefoot slade
> Our Saviour lichtit down.
> Sinew to sinew, vein to vein.
> Joint to joint, and bane to bane,
> Mend thou in God's name.

The Church took a dim view of such charms, warning that with very few exceptions only prayers in their standard Catholic form were permissible and that the use of variations might result in the conjuring up of a demon. In Scotland, indeed, anyone found guilty of employing charms could face death by burning. According to Sir George Mackenzie's *Laws and Customs of Scotland* of 1678:

> Though charms be not able to produce the effects that are punishable in witches, yet since these effects cannot be produced without the Devil, and [since] he will not employ himself at the desire of any who have resigned themselves wholly to him, it is very just that the users of these should be punished, being guilty at least of apostasy and heresy.

Records exist of various charms designed to break spells cast by malevolent witches. One such charm to deliver a victim of a witch's spell was detailed by James Device during the trial of the PENDLE WITCHES in 1612:

> Upon Good Friday, I will fast while I may,
> Until I hear them knell
> Our Lord's own bell;
> Lord in his mass
> With his twelve apostles good,
> What hath he in his hand?
> Liking, lithe wand.
> What hath he in his other hand?
> Heaven's door key.
> Open, open, Heaven, door keys.
> Steck, steck, hell door.
> Let chrisom child
> Go to its mother mild.
> What is yonder that casts a light so farrandly?
> My own dear son that's nailed to the tree.
> He is nailed sore by the heart and hand,
> And holy harn-pan.
> Well is that man
> That Friday spell can,
> His child to learn;

A cross of blue, and another of red,
As good Lord was to the rood.
Gabriel laid him down to sleep
Upon the ground of holy weep.
Good Lord came walking by:
Sleepest thou, wakest thou, Gabriel?
No, Lord, I am sted with stick and stake,
That I can neither sleep nor wake.
Rise up, Gabriel, and go with me,
The stick nor the stake shall never deer thee.
Sweet Jesus, our Lord, Amen.

At their least exotic, charms extended to the conventional 'bless you' voiced when someone sneezed. Uttering the charm was supposed to prevent the person who had sneezed falling victim to interference by malevolent forces at a vulnerable moment, for the soul might be accidentally expelled from the body in a sneeze and saying 'bless you' assisted in its return. Others offered protection from toothache, bleeding and other bodily ills, whether of supernatural origins or not.

Typical of the charms that were recited as part of the cure for physical ailments was the following, a Scottish charm to cure hiccups:

My love's ane
The hiccup's twa;
When my love likes me,
The hiccup's awa.

An alternative to speaking the charm was to write it down and carry it about the person, usually on a string around the neck or inscribed on some form of amulet. In 1882 a charm was found scrawled on a piece of paper hidden in a crevice of a chimney joist in a cottage in Madeley, Shropshire. It was clearly intended to safeguard the household from all threat of evil and read: 'I charge all witches and ghosts to depart from this house, in the great names of Jehovah, Alpha and Omega.'

See also NIGHT SPELL; PROTECTION AGAINST WITCHCRAFT.

charm wand A glass stick, often resembling a walking stick, that may be kept in the home in order to safeguard the inhabitants from evil spirits during the night. Filled with tiny seeds or beads or bearing a myriad of hair lines in the glass, such charm wands were supposed to distract demons from their nefarious deeds. No demon, it was believed, would be able to resist the temptation to count the seeds, or hair lines, and would thus become ensnared. When morning came the wand would be wiped clean of any evil it had attracted during the night.

See also WAND.

Chattox, Old *see* PENDLE WITCHES.

Chelmsford Witches The Essex town of Chelmsford ranks high in the annals of English witchcraft. It was the scene of repeated outbreaks of the witchcraft mania that gripped the area for a hundred years from the mid-sixteenth century.

The trail of death began in July 1566, when Agnes Waterhouse, a sixty-three-year-old peasant woman from Hatfield Peverel, became the first recorded victim of the Witchcraft Act of 1563 and thus the central figure in the first important witch trial in England. Waterhouse confessed to causing the death of a man named William Fynee by sorcery, aided and abetted by her FAMILIAR, a CAT which she identified by the name Sathan. Brought before the Attorney-General, Sir Gilbert Gerard, she made a poor witness in her own defence and was consigned to the gallows, the first of all too many victims in the Chelmsford area. The fact that no less a figure than the Attorney-General had presided over the case established the trial as a precedent that many other later judges felt bound to follow. The admittance of unsupported confessions, SPECTRAL EVIDENCE, evidence from children and the acceptance of the DEVIL'S MARK as proof of guilt set the pattern for decades to come.

Agnes Waterhouse was not the only one accused. Alongside her were her daughter Joan and Elizabeth Francis, also residents of Hatfield Peverel. Francis was the first accused, charged with causing illness in the son of one William Auger, among other crimes, and subsequently with casting a spell over a woman named Mary Cocke, who experienced a similar decline in her health. Francis was relatively lucky, being sentenced on these two occasions merely to terms of imprisonment and to several appearances in the pillory. Her luck finally gave out in 1579, when she was accused of murdering Alice Poole by means of witchcraft, was found guilty and was hanged.

Elizabeth Francis confessed to having been taught the rudiments of the black arts by her grandmother when she was a child of twelve. From this long-deceased woman, called Mother Eve, she had inherited her white spotted cat-familiar, Sathan, which after many years of faithful service (given in exchange for drops of her BLOOD) she in turn passed on to Agnes Waterhouse. Through Sathan Francis had acquired a flock of eighteen sheep (which none the less 'did all wear away, she knew not how') and had nearly ensnared a rich husband by the name of Andrew Byles. When Byles eventually refused to marry her she had instructed Sathan to destroy his wealth and then to bring about his death, which quickly followed. The cat subsequently found her another husband, Christopher Francis, but the arrival of a baby proved unwelcome and Sathan obligingly killed it. Also at Elizabeth's request, the cat, turning itself into a TOAD, caused lameness in her husband by hiding in his shoe and touching his foot. After the cat had been given to Agnes Waterhouse it allegedly procured the death of her enemy, William Fynee, by causing him to contract a wasting disease. It also committed sundry other petty acts of malice, largely against the livestock of those who had caused her offence.

Joan Waterhouse, aged eighteen, stood in the dock largely as a result of the depositions of a twelve-year-old girl, Agnes Brown, who blamed her for problems with her right arm and leg. The highlight of her evidence was her detailed description of a BLACK DOG, allegedly Sathan in disguise. Joan was, however, acquitted of the charge.

Another outbreak of the witchcraft fever swept Chelmsford in 1579 when Elizabeth Francis and three others appeared before two respected justices of the Queen's Bench, John Southcote and

Sir Thomas Gawdy. The evidence again depended largely on the confessions of the accused. Accompanying Francis on the gallows at the close of proceedings was Ellen Smith, found guilty of causing the death by witchcraft of a four-year-old girl, and Alice Nokes, condemned to death on similar charges. The fourth accused, Margery Stanton, was acquitted on charges of causing livestock to perish.

Three years later Chelmsford was the scene of the infamous trial of the ST OSYTH WITCHES, which resulted in more deaths. Another mass trial followed in 1589, when nine women and one man were arraigned mostly on charges of murder by witchcraft. The 1589 trial culminated in the execution of four of the accused, of whom three – Joan Prentice, Joan Cony and Joan Upney – were hanged within two hours of the guilty verdict being reached. Perhaps in the hope of clemency at the last hour the three women confessed their crimes on the scaffold. As in many of the previous cases, much damning evidence came from children and hinged on the procurement of murder through the agency of familiars. Then in 1610 Katherine Lawrett, from Colne Wake in Essex, was charged at Chelmsford with using witchcraft to cause the demise of a valuable horse belonging to a man called Francis Plaite.

The fact that Chelmsford had already been the scene of such notoriety did much to lend credibility to the allegations that Matthew HOPKINS, the self-styled Witchfinder-General, levelled at local women in 1645, in what was fated to become one of the most appalling instances of witchcraft persecution of the seventeenth century. This fourth mass trial of witches in the Chelmsford area began with the torture of the one-legged hag Elizabeth Clarke of Manningtree, the daughter of a hanged witch, who confessed to keeping familiars and also to having intercourse with the DEVIL over some six or seven years. She went on to implicate five other women, who in turn identified others, and in all thirty-two women were brought before the county sessions on 29 July 1645.

Most of the accused were arraigned on the strength of confessions extracted by such means as SWIMMING and sleep deprivation: on Hopkins's instructions they were forced to sit cross-legged on a stool for hours without a break or were walked continuously back and forth until they were exhausted. One suspect, Rebecca West, was 'persuaded' to admit to marrying the Devil and also accused her mother, Ann West (who had been imprisoned on charges of witchcraft once before), of being a witch. Others described imps resembling cats, mice and squirrels. To add substance to the 'evidence' he had gathered, Hopkins himself claimed to have lain in wait for Clarke's familiars and reported that he saw five of them materialise in the form of a cat called Holt, a legless spaniel called Jarmara, a greyhound called Vinegar Tom, a rabbit-like creature called Sack and Sugar and a polecat called Newes.

Charged with causing death by witchcraft and/or entertaining spirits, the women had little chance against Hopkins and his detailed knowledge of the witchcraft laws. They were tried under Robert Rich, Earl of Warwick, and Sir Harbottle Grimston, who proved highly susceptible to Hopkins's suggestions. Only one of the accused was acquitted of all charges; nineteen of the others, including Elizabeth Clarke, were hanged for their crimes.

child accusers A great many witchcraft trials, among them some of the most notorious, depended almost entirely on the evidence of children. Such was the panic engendered by witchcraft that testimony that would have been rejected out of hand in any other legal context was readily believed and used to establish the guilt of countless suspects as soon as witchcraft was alleged.

The motivation of such juvenile accusers varied. Sometimes it was apparently little more than sheer delinquency, sometimes it was calculated malice designed to wreak revenge on some neighbour or family member, sometimes it was a mixture of hysteria and fear doubtless inspired by overheard adult conversations about other contemporary cases. It is noticeable that the evidence presented by many children (and, indeed, adults) often mirrored closely what had recently been published in widely available pamphlet form in connection with other trials. In some of the most lamentable cases the enthusiasm with which children detailed their accusations undoubtedly owed much to the encouragement and sympathy of their elders, who might have their own reasons for wishing to blacken the reputation of a neighbour or relation.

In some European courts, notably those in the German states in the sixteenth and seventeenth centuries, evidence of virtually any kind – including that of young children – was accepted without question in the determination to uproot witchcraft practice. As soon as a child could talk, it seemed, it was capable of being heard in court, even as a witness against its own mother (as happened in several cases) or as a defendant. In some cases, as in Navarre in France in 1527, children were purposely recruited and taken from village to village to pick out witches according to their own inclination.

In England (where evidence offered by anyone under fourteen was technically illegal) and elsewhere, children were often obliged to embroider their tales considerably in order to stand a chance of convincing a court. The fantastic evidence offered in such cases as that of William Somers, the 'Boy of Nottingham' (*see* DARRELL, JOHN) tested the credulity of judges to the limit: sometimes they refrained from accepting all that they were told, but all too often they let their gullibility sway their better judgement. The ingenuity with which some children faked demonic POSSESSION made it all the more likely that even the most outrageous claims would be believed. William Perry, otherwise known as the BILSON BOY, almost convinced the authorities that his possession was genuine when he appeared to pass blue urine (only by secret surveillance was it realised that he did it by using cotton soaked in blue ink).

Other children persuaded the authorities that they were possessed by DEMONS or were the victims of spells by vomiting on command copious amounts of pins, buttons and other extraordinary items.

JAMES I, in exposing the fraudulent evidence offered by children in several notable cases, did much to alert the judiciary to the need to examine this kind of evidence with particular care, and presumably prevented even more cases of a similar nature resulting in the deaths of innocent persons. The statistics suggest, however, that in the majority of cases in which evidence from children was heard they were cross-examined with less than the requisite vigour and many impostors remained undetected (although some confessed voluntarily in later years).

It is impossible to give an exact figure for the number of people who met their deaths directly as a result of evidence offered by children, but one case alone, the hysteria that swept Salem in Massachusetts in the late seventeenth century, accounted for no fewer than twenty-two lives (*see* SALEM WITCHES). The panic that seized the Swedish town of Mora in 1669, largely the product of accusations made by young children, resulted in some three hundred arrests and widespread fears that hundreds of children had been initiated into the service of Satan. Among those executed were fifteen children; thirty-six more between the ages of nine and fifteen were made to run the gauntlet and many more were publicly beaten for witchcraft offences (*see* MORA WITCHES).

A last sample case, recorded in the north of England in 1675, claimed only two lives but shows the appalling consequences that could stem even from the most incredible and fraudulent stories of children. The tragedy began when sixteen-year-old Mary Moor of Clayton in Yorkshire accused Susan Hinchcliffe and her daughter Anne of plotting to kill a neighbour, Martha Haigh, through witchcraft. Mary also implicated Susan's husband, Joseph, in the conspiracy. When the couple were bound over to appear at the next Assizes there was a considerable outcry from the local community, who compiled a petition stressing their belief in the innocence of the accused and hinting that Mary Moor was a less than trustworthy witness. Sadly, the stress of the whole affair proved too much for Joseph Hinchcliffe, and he hanged himself in a wood near his home. By the time his body was found, some four days later, his wife, distraught with grief and anxiety, had also died. Her last act, as she lay on her deathbed, was to utter a prayer for her accusers.

See also BARGARRAN IMPOSTOR; BURTON, ELIZABETH; BURTON BOY; BURY ST EDMUNDS WITCHES; DARLING, THOMAS; DR LAMB'S DARLING; FAIRFAX, EDWARD; GLENLUCE DEVIL; GOODWIN CHILDREN; GUNTER, ANNE; HARTLAY, EDMUND; JØRGENSDATTER, SIRI; LEICESTER BOY; LILLE NOVICES; PENDLE WITCHES; ROBINSON, EDMUND; ST OSYTH WITCHES; WARBOYS WITCHES.

chimney According to time-honoured tradition, witches always departed for their COVENS via the chimney, mounted on BROOM-STICKS or other vehicles of flight. It is unclear quite how this notion came about, but there may be a link with the archaic custom of showing a broom at the chimney to indicate that the woman of the house was not at home.

The hearth has always been revered as the spiritual centre of the home, originally because of the link with fire, which has long been considered sacred. In order to prevent witches and other evil spirits gaining access to a household by means of the chimney, in former times the hearth was often guarded by positioning the fire irons so that they formed the shape of a cross or else by scrawling various patterns, such as circles, in chalk on the hearthstones. Alternatively, old shoes (considered luck-preserving since ancient times) might be placed in the chimney or under the foundations of the house to keep witches away. Regular clearing of the chimney by a sweep was recommended: it was thought that the brushes would dislodge any witch lurking within the recesses of the chimney shaft.

See also CHARM.

Chisholm, Alexander *see* WITCHFINDER.

Cideville Witch Poltergeist case with overtones of witchcraft that led to a celebrated trial in France in 1851. The affair began in 1850, when a simple-minded forty-year-old shepherd called Felix Thorel fell out with the curé of Cideville, a small village in Normandy. The curé, Father Tinel, had discovered that one of his flock was being treated for some ailment by a WHITE WITCH (whose identity remained undisclosed) and had suggested that he go instead to the doctor. When the white witch was then arrested for practising medicine without a licence it was automatically assumed that the curé had informed on him and, seeking redress, the alleged witch recruited Thorel to exact his revenge. Thorel made public threats to bring trouble to the curé, and shortly after he touched two of the priest's young pupils the lads began to complain of unearthly happenings at the parsonage.

According to the boys' testimony, the peace in the house was disrupted by loud rappings, which, curiously enough, grew louder at command and also drummed out the rhythms of certain songs on request. When the boys were removed from the house further strange occurrences took place, with household items moving about the rooms, tables being shifted and doors becoming shut fast. Bed coverings were pulled off the occupants, candlesticks and knives were thrown and strong winds blew down the corridors.

Father Tinel demanded an apology from Thorel for causing such disruption, and one of the younger boys at the parsonage identified the man as the spectral form that had 'haunted' him for two weeks. Thorel seemed to enjoy boasting of his newly revealed supernatural ability, and after touching one of boys once more the poltergeist happenings broke out again. Thorel was less amused, however, when he was dismissed from his job and when Father Tinel struck him with his walking stick – and he went to court to charge the cleric with defamation.

No fewer than thirty-four witnesses, among them the mayor, the local seigneur, several priests and the Marquis de Mirville, a respected occultist from Paris, confirmed to the judges that the poltergeist disturbances at Cideville were real. All agreed that the boys themselves could not have caused the manifestations, and the court was left to conclude that 'whatever might be the cause of the extraordinary facts which occurred at the parsonage of Cideville, it is clear, from the sum total of the testimony adduced, that the cause of these facts remains unknown'. Thorel's case was dismissed, on the grounds that he had gone out of his way to make out that he was a witch and could hardly therefore blame the curé for repeating the idea. He may have experienced some consolation, however, when the parents of the boys in Father Tinel's charge decided to withdraw their children from his care.

circle *see* MAGIC CIRCLE.

Clarke, Elizabeth *see* CHELMSFORD WITCHES.

Clarke, Jane *see* ENGLAND.

Cleary, Bridget 1868–94. Irish peasant woman who was cruelly and unlawfully put to death after she came under suspicion of being a witch. Although few men and women were executed in IRELAND as a result of the witch mania of the sixteenth and seventeenth centuries, as late as Victorian times many people were still obsessed by fear of the supernatural and in particular of the machinations of FAIRIES and the 'little people', who were said to kidnap humans and to leave their own changelings in their place.

In 1894 when Bridget, the twenty-six-year-old wife of Michael Cleary, a labourer living a few miles north of Clonmel in Tipperary, failed to return home on time he had grave misgivings and talked about his wife being kidnapped by the fairies of nearby Kilegranach Hill, which was locally notorious as a haunt of witches. When she did finally make an appearance, her husband and other members of her family immediately accused her of being a witch and a changeling. The woman's accusers ignored her protests of innocence and determined to get a confession from her. After she refused to confess any wrongdoing Bridget was forced to sit naked on the peat fire in the kitchen, while other witnesses watched through the windows. Still she refused to confess anything that was suggested to her, even though she was repeatedly subjected to the torture until her body was terribly burned.

But at last Bridget could bear it no more and taunted her husband with the allegation that his own mother had herself consorted with the fairies more than once. This was taken as proof of Bridget's guilt, as she must, it was argued, have been present to know this information. Without further prevarication, her husband poured lamp oil over her and then set her alight where she lay on the kitchen floor.

The body of the murdered woman was buried in a shallow grave close to the house, but word of the brutal deed quickly reached the police and Michael Cleary and his accomplices were arrested. The corpse was exhumed and found to be so badly charred that considerable areas of flesh had been entirely burned away. Found guilty of manslaughter, Michael Cleary was sentenced to twenty years' hard labour. Even during the trial, he insisted that his wife had been replaced by a changeling, demanding of his neighbours: 'Did you not know that it was not my wife? She was too fine to be my wife, she was two inches taller than my wife.' The neighbours who had witnessed the death of Bridget Cleary but had done nothing to prevent it were summoned as witnesses, though no charges were brought against them.

The 'Clonmel Burning', as the atrocity became known, was widely reported. To this day, children in Clonmel may be spotted dancing in a ring while chanting the lines:

Are you a witch, are you a fairy,
Or are you the wife of Michael Cleary?

Cleworth Witch *see* DARRELL, JOHN; HARTLAY, EDMUND.

Clonmel Burning *see* CLEARY, BRIDGET.

Clophill Witches An alleged COVEN of English witches whose activities attracted widespread publicity in the 1960s. Centred on a ruined church on Dead Man's Hill at Clophill in Bedfordshire, the first incident to cause a stir took place in March 1963 when several graves in the churchyard were found to have been interfered with. The two-hundred-year-old bones resting in the grave of a young woman who had died in 1770 had been taken out and laid out in ritual fashion inside the church itself. Other incriminating evidence indicating that a BLACK MASS had taken place in the vicinity included a few scattered cockerel feathers.

The 1960s witnessed a rash of such incidents throughout the UK, though the majority of these were put down to pranks by students. In the case of Clophill, however, there seemed to be a more serious intent behind the happenings at the church, with determined efforts being made to break into well-protected tombs. When it was announced that the bones would be reburied the church was broken into a second time, though it seems that the vandals were obliged to leave empty-handed.

The suggestion that the desecration was the work of witches proved damaging to Gerald GARDNER and other leading English witches, who denied any involvement and stressed that they only practised white magic (*see* WHITE WITCH). The general conclusion was that Clophill was the meeting-place of a group of Satanists pursuing a darker brand of magic, probably attempting to raise the dead (*see* NECROMANCY).

Cobham, Eleanor, Duchess of Gloucester fl.1440. English aristocrat, wife of the all-powerful Humphrey, Duke of Gloucester, whose standing as one of the most influential women in England was destroyed by accusations of witchcraft. The roots of the scandal lay in the plotting of Gloucester's political enemies, led by Cardinal Henry Beaufort, whom the Duke – Protector during the minority of his nephew, Henry VI – had attempted to deprive of his see. Beaufort and others sought a way in which to bring Gloucester down, and in 1441 they united in allegations of witchcraft involving the Duchess (who had acquired her own enemies as Gloucester's mistress while he was still married to his first wife).

The main charge was that Eleanor Cobham had 'by sorcery and witchcraft intended to destroy the King, to the intent to advance her husband unto the crown'. Subsidiary charges included the accusation that she had won the affections of her husband by bewitching him through the use of LOVE POTIONS (a charge that was eventually dropped in favour of more serious allegations) and that she had attempted to divine her own political future by the use of magic. Accused with her as her accomplices were Canon Thomas Southwell of Westminster, Father John Hun, the respected Oxford scholar Roger Bolingbroke and Margery Jourdemain (or Jourdain), known as the Witch of Eye, all of whom had provided the Duchess with the expert knowledge of the black arts that she herself lacked. Evidence to back the charges was produced in the shape of a waxen image, said to have been fashioned on the Duchess's orders in the likeness of the King.

The trial that ensued saw the merciless pursuit of all the accused by judges who were to a man enemies of the house of

Gloucester. Bolingbroke, one of the most gifted scholars of his time, was forced under torture into supporting the allegations against the Duchess. After his arrest he was obliged to appear in public at St Paul's Cross in London wearing his sorcerer's robes and surrounded by his 'instruments of magic', which included a ceremonial sword and a chair decorated with swords and copper images, while his crimes were listed to a hostile crowd. Bolingbroke himself admitted that he had helped the Duchess to divine her future, but denied that there had been any treason in their actions. The court was not inclined to agree: bearing in mind the Duchess's high standing the judges saw in her request to Bolingbroke that she be shown the rank to which she would rise an implicit threat to the life of the King. Bolingbroke was hanged, drawn and quartered. His head was displayed on London Bridge and his limbs were sent to the cities of Oxford, Cambridge, Hereford and York as a stern warning to other scholars not to imitate his actions.

Thomas Southwell was arraigned on charges that he had taken part in black masses intended to procure the death of the King, but he died in the dungeons of the Tower of London before sentence was passed. John Hun was pardoned of his crimes, but Margery Jourdain, who had already been found guilty of a minor charge of witchcraft back in 1430, was identified as the maker of the waxen image and was burned at Smithfield for high treason and witchcraft. It was also alleged that it was Jourdain who had provided the love philtre with which Eleanor Cobham had stolen the affections of the Duke.

Because of her social connections the Duchess herself was excused torture, but she was none the less forced into admitting the charges against her (although she protested that the purpose of the waxen image had been to promote her chances of having children rather than to secure the death of the King). She escaped the death penalty but was sentenced instead to do public penance, which involved walking barefooted and bareheaded through the streets of London while carrying a heavy candle to a specified church. After she had performed three such acts of penance she spent the rest of her life in prison, first in Chester and later at Peel Castle on the Isle of Man. The Duke of Gloucester saw that her quarters were always comfortable and well staffed but in the end he too fell foul of political intrigue, dying mysteriously in prison in 1447 just a few days after he was arrested on suspicion of plotting an insurrection against Henry.

Cockie, Isobel *see* ABERDEEN WITCHES.

Cocwra, Samuel *see* WITCHFINDER.

Coggeshall Witch   English witchcraft case that culminated in the death of a woman in Coggeshall, Essex, in 1699. Widow Coman was a very old woman who had a long-standing reputation as a witch. J. Boys, the vicar of Coggeshall, was determined that she should confess her sins and hounded the poor woman into admitting various magic practices. Among other things, she confessed to signing a PACT WITH THE DEVIL and agreeing not to enter a church for five years, to keeping FAMILIARS (which she fed 'at her fundament') and to sticking pins in waxen images. Further 'proof' of her guilt was obtained when she stumbled over the words of the LORD'S PRAYER and when she refused to renounce the Devil and his imps during a service of exorcism held by the vicar.

The Reverend Boys stood aside when the local mob seized the old woman and dragged her off to the village pond. There she was subjected to the ordeal of SWIMMING – when she bobbed repeatedly to the surface this was taken as further confirmation of her guilt. To make doubly sure, the procedure was carried out twice more, each time with the same result. The vicar then instructed a midwife to search the widow for WITCH'S MARKS, and two large supernumerary 'nipples' for the feeding of imps were allegedly found.

The ill treatment that Widow Coman had received was, however, more than she could stand and a few months later she died from a chill she may have contracted during her duckings. Quite convinced of the justice of his actions, the Reverend Boys ensured that her body was buried without any of the rites that a dutiful Christian might expect.

Cole, Ann *see* CONNECTICUT WITCHES.

Cologne Witches The victims of two witch-hunts that were staged in the German city of Cologne in 1625–6 and 1630–6. Cologne escaped the worst of the witch mania that gripped GERMANY in the mid-seventeenth century by virtue of the city authorities' relatively tolerant and enlightened attitude, but the hysteria did flare up from time to time. Several witches were tried in 1625–6 in response to greater public sensitivity to the issue, but even then the authorities were reluctant to convict. The most discussed trial concerned a woman named Catherine Henot, who had been accused of bewitching the nuns of St Clare. Demonstrating the city's reputation for fair-mindedness in such cases, the church court that examined the allegations both allowed Henot her own legal counsel and refused to admit evidence from anyone who asserted the reality of demoniacal POSSESSION. Henot was consequently found not guilty – but the climate of opinion in the city was temporarily against the court and a higher ecclesiastical authority, Archbishop Ferdinand of Cologne, had the accused woman retried by a different court: she was duly condemned and burned.

The hysteria died down for a while until, in 1629, another case stirred up similar feelings in the city. This time the allegations stemmed from Christine Plum, who claimed she had been possessed by demons. Those who attempted to scorn her accusations were quickly added to her list of witches and, again on the orders of the Archbishop, the courts were soon busy with the examination of suspected persons. None the less, in contrast with events elsewhere in the German states, torture of suspects was only sanctioned by special order of the courts and property was not confiscated from the families of the condemned (though they still had to meet the costs of the trials). This liberal attitude could be credited partly to local Jesuits, who restricted the sale of books that were likely to add strength to the witch-hunting cause.

The situation worsened considerably after 1631, when dedicated witch-hunters from Leipzig fled to Cologne after their home city became engulfed in the war with Sweden. These bigots occupied themselves with seeking out and prosecuting alleged witches in large numbers and it was only through papal intervention in 1636 that Cologne, by now a hotbed for witchcraft trials, restored its reputation. The last recorded execution of a witch in Cologne was carried out in 1655.

Coman, Widow *see* COGGESHALL WITCH.

confessions   The obtaining of a confession was of paramount importance in countless witchcraft trials, a 'crime' for which there was all too often little real evidence. Many learned treatises were written on the methods that might be employed to get a suspected witch to admit his or her guilt, thus facilitating their prosecution. Whatever real evidence could be collected against a suspected witch, it remained crucial that a confession was recorded, and without it courts throughout Continental Europe often had reservations about passing the death sentence. (English law stood virtually alone in insisting upon 'real' evidence of guilt, such as the discovery of WITCH'S MARKS or proof of MALEFICIA, and, because unsubstantiated confessions were legally useless in court, relatively little effort was made to obtain them.)

Very few voluntary confessions were ever recorded (one notable exception being the startling admission of guilt made by the Scottish witch Isobel GOWDIE, which she made for unknown reasons). In the majority of cases, the use of TORTURE was crucial in getting the required statements and even in England and the American colonies, where such methods were largely prohibited, duress of various kinds (including starvation and beating) was applied in order to persuade suspects to confirm the charges made against them. One of the difficulties facing historians of witchcraft is that only rarely is it clear from surviving records whether or not torture was used in extracting a confession.

Elsewhere in Europe, where torture of the most extreme variety was sanctioned by the ecclesiastical and civil authorities, the business of obtaining confessions was relatively straightforward. Consequently a much higher percentage of witchcraft trials on the Continent resulted in a guilty verdict being brought in. Suspects who proved reluctant to admit their guilt were subjected repeatedly to the most inhumane treatment, and many of them died in the process. Virtually all who experienced such tortures as STRAPPADO and roasting in iron chairs sooner or later gave in to the demands of their interrogators, admitting all manner of implausible offences and exercising their imagination to the full in order to placate those who were persecuting them. Others were tempted by promises (often broken) that if they confessed they would be spared the death penalty.

Father Friedrich von SPEE, a Jesuit who witnessed many confessions in the German state of Würzburg, remarked in 1631 that even the most robust of those to suffer thus 'have affirmed that no crime can be imagined which they would not at once confess to if it could bring down ever so little relief and they would welcome ten deaths to escape repetition'. A confession, in Spee's eyes, was virtually inevitable in view of the means employed, and attempts at recantation of a confession were futile:

> The result is the same whether she confesses or not. If she confesses, her guilt is clear: she is executed. All recantation is in vain. If she does not confess, the torture is repeated – twice, thrice, four times. In 'exceptional' crimes, the torture is not limited in duration, severity, or frequency ... She can never clear herself. The investigating body would feel disgraced if it acquitted a woman; once arrested and in chains, she has to be guilty, by fair means or foul.

Making a full confession immediately upon being accused was no guarantee of protection against torture. Many courts would send the suspect to the torture chamber automatically on the assumption that the confession was false and made purely to avoid the physical ill treatment that would lead to 'true' revelations.

Despite the barbaric nature of the interrogations that were commonplace in witchcraft trials in Germany and elsewhere, in an attempt to give the proceedings some semblance of legality meticulous records were often kept of all that passed between suspects and their captors. Questions asked of witches when making confessions generally followed the same pattern, based on a formula derived ultimately from the trials of heretics as far back as the fourth century. In the written records of interrogation these might be listed as numbers rather than written out in full, since everyone knew what they represented. Among other things, suspects would be asked to describe their first encounter with the Devil, for details of their subsequent meetings with him and of their imps or familiars, to confirm that they had flown on broomsticks to attend sabbats and to admit such atrocities as cannibalism and bewitching to death.

Once a suspect confessed under torture he or she was allowed time to recover from the pain and was then asked again to confirm the confession, so that in court the interrogators would be able to claim that the statement was freely given. If a prisoner chose to recant, however, the chances were that he or she would be returned forthwith to the torture chamber. Attempts to withdraw confessions when brought before the courts were rarely looked upon with sympathy: this was merely a ruse, it was argued, prompted by the DEVIL to frustrate lawful proceedings against his minions. Views about what constituted a 'voluntary' confession also varied – in many regions a confession was deemed voluntary if extracted under the first of the three degrees of torture (binding and racking and similar 'mild' procedures).

Confessions made at the time of execution were encouraged and many condemned witches availed themselves of this opportunity to admit their guilt, which meant that they might be more kindly disposed of by the executioner. In most cases, witches who made a full confession when about to be burned at the stake were granted the mercy of being strangled to death before the flames reached them. The confession was customarily read aloud to the crowd which had come to see the execution, thus promoting public belief in witchcraft as a reality.

If a suspect proved particularly resilient, the confession of a fellow witch attending the same sabbat might prove sufficient evidence of guilt: if the confession was enough to condemn the person confessing, it was logically also sufficient to establish the guilt of others present at the same event. The most difficult cases to prove were those in which the suspect was alleged to have met the Devil in private, with no witnesses. In these cases a confession from the person concerned was essential and torture was routinely employed. On the Continent, at least, the interrogators would not be unduly perturbed if a prisoner was slow to cooperate in the supplying of a confession: imprisonment in dank dungeons and repeated visits to the torturer wore down the most determined will, as the Dutchman Johan Weyer made clear in his *Praestigiis Daemonum* in 1568:

> Thus these wretched women, whose minds have already been disturbed by the delusions and arts of the devil and are now upset by frequent torture, are kept in prolonged squalor and darkness of their dungeons, exposed to the hideous spectres of the devil, and constantly dragged out to undergo atrocious torment until they would gladly exchange at any moment this most bitter existence for death, are willing to confess whatever crimes are suggested to them rather than be thrust back into their hideous dungeon amid ever recurring torture.

Some deranged suspects doubtless believed in the veracity of their confessions, but the vast majority, despairing of their lives, admitted guilt to avoid further torture. Even if they had a prospect of escaping the death penalty some suspects chose to confess and to welcome death, perceiving that any future life would be intolerable – as Sir George Mackenzie, Lord Advocate to Charles II, observed in the case of some confessed witches he had questioned:

> One of them who was a silly creature told him, 'under secrecy, that she had not confessed because she was guilty, but, being a poor creature who wrought for her meat, and being defamed for a witch, she knew she would starve, for no person thereafter would either give her meat or lodgings, and that all men would beat her, and hound dogs at her, and that therefore she desired to be out of the world'.

Some condemned prisoners retracted their confessions at the last moment, braving the danger of being subjected to further torture; many more went to their deaths silent. Those who refused even to plead when brought before the court were deemed guilty of contempt, and stood to be executed for the crime of 'taciturnity' (under English law they were pressed to death).

Among the most pitiful denials of guilt made by a confessed witch was one reported by a minister visiting a woman in a German prison. According to the Reverend Michael Stapirius the woman threw herself on his mercy, explaining: 'I never dreamed that by means of the torture a person could be brought to the point of telling such lies as I have told. I am not a witch, and I have never seen the devil, and still I had to plead guilty myself and denounce others. I beseech you, for God's sake, help me to be saved!'

conjuration *see* DIVINATION.

Connecticut Witches The victims of a series of witchcraft trials in north-eastern America between the years 1647 and 1662, which culminated in at least nine, and probably eleven, deaths.

Puritan society in recently settled New England had inherited from the old world a deep-seated paranoia about witchcraft, and some authorities were inclined to adopt the severity espoused in England by such witch-hunters as Matthew HOPKINS. Legislation against witchcraft was passed in Connecticut in 1642 and the first execution of a convicted witch took place on 26 May 1647, when Alice (or Alse) Young was hanged. Subsequently several more cases came to light. Mary Johnson, of Wethersfield, confessed to intercourse with the DEVIL, and to child murder and was hanged, despite a lack of corroborating evidence, while Mary Parsons, in one of a series of trials to emanate from the town of Springfield, Massachusetts, in the late 1640s, admitted to various witchcraft practices: she was sentenced to death by a Boston court in 1651 for murdering her child, but was later reprieved. Other victims included Goodwife Bassett, found guilty of witchcraft in Stratford in 1651, two witches hanged in New Haven around 1653, and Elizabeth Garlick, who was acquitted of witchcraft charges in Easthampton, Long Island, in 1658.

In 1662 the town of Hartford, Connecticut, became obsessed with the proceedings resulting from the apparent demoniacal

POSSESSION of a girl named Ann Cole. While suffering from fits, the girl made accusations in Dutch (a language she professed not to know) about a Dutch girl and one Rebecca Greensmith, who was already being held on charges of witchcraft after being seen in the company of demons (possibly Red Indians wearing ritual head-dresses). The Dutch girl was acquitted, but under pressure Mother Greensmith confessed to intimacy with the Devil, who had first appeared to her as a deer and had later had intercourse with her. She also claimed that a COVEN met near her house, the members mani-festing there in the forms of crows and other animals. Greensmith was put to death, along with her husband Nathaniel (who denied all knowledge of the affair). The matter did not stop there, however, as the authorities attempted to track down other members of the Greensmith coven. Also arrested were Andrew Sandford and his wife and daughter, William Ayres and his wife, two married women named Grant and Palmer, Elizabeth Seager, a spinster called Judith Varlet and James Walkley: several of them are known to have been hanged. Once Rebecca Greensmith was dead, Ann Cole quickly regained her health.

There were fewer trials after 1662, but the occasional case still captured the public imagination from time to time. Another Wethersfield woman, Katherine Harrison, was sentenced to death as a witch in 1669, but the sentence was not carried out and she was banished instead. In 1671 Elizabeth Knap of Groton, Long Island, attracted attention when she started suffering fits, laughing, weep-ing and uttering strange sounds; at times it took six men to hold her down. Knap made accusations of witchcraft against a local woman, but the accused was well respected and no one was pre-pared to accept Knap's testimony. Her fits ceased and she eventually admitted that she had been tricked into making the accusations by the Devil, who had appeared to her in the form of a 'good person' and had made a pact with her to the effect that she would serve him for one year and then he would serve her for another six. As a result of this confession Knap was hanged. The pastor of Groton at the time of the incident was the Reverend Samuel Willard, who was to show commendable caution concerning the testimony of children while participating in the notorious trial of the SALEM WITCHES in 1692.

In 1697, five years after the Salem case, a group of children claiming second sight directed accusations of witchcraft at a woman named Winifred Benham and her daughter. On this occasion there was no resort to the death penalty and the alleged witches were acquitted, although they were excommunicated by the Church.

Cornfoot, Janet *see* PITTENWEEM WITCHES.

corpse-lifting *see* GRAVE-ROBBING.

Cory, Giles and Martha *see* SALEM WITCHES.

Cosyn, Edward *see* PRESTALL, JOHN.

coven A group of witches who gather together on a regular basis to work their magic, to worship the DEVIL and his minions, to call up evil spirits and to indulge in licentious revels, including intercourse with DEMONS. The word itself comes from the Latin *convenire*, meaning to assemble.

Witches of modern times certainly form small covens, but there has been much debate over the years about whether such consciously organised covens really existed in past centuries or whether they were simply a figment of superstitious imagination, an invention of demonologists backed up by unreliable confessions extracted from suspects under torture. What evidence there is, should it be accepted as real, suggests that small districts might produce one small, loosely associated coven, while more populous regions might boast several rival covens with many members.

The writer and anthropologist Margaret Murray claimed that covens have always been organised in groups of thirteen (twelve witches and the Devil himself, or his representative), but could offer little supporting evidence. None the less, the popular notion remains that witches customarily met in groups of thirteen to work their magic together, and modern practitioners of the magical arts may have learned to imitate this tradition.

The earliest reference to the word 'coven' dates only from 1662, when Isobel GOWDIE told her interrogators that in her experience witches met in covens of thirteen. Another reference to the number thirteen was made at almost the same time across the Atlantic in New England, where Rebecca Greensmith confessed to belonging to a coven comprising twelve witches and the 'man in black' (*see* CONNECTICUT WITCHES). Anne Armstrong, one of the SOMERSET WITCHES, was another witness who described her coven as consisting of thirteen members, but at least one confession from the CHANNEL ISLANDS at much the same date indicated that witches there met in groups of fifteen or sixteen, while witches elsewhere in Europe cited covens that comprised as few as three witches and others that numbered many thousands.

The notion that there should always be thirteen members probably derives, somewhat perversely, from the 'convent' of thirteen members that comprised Christ and the twelve Apostles. More speculative, and dubious, theories suggest that there may be a link between the thirteen members of the coven and the twenty-six (twice thirteen) knights of the Order of the Garter instituted by Edward III, or that thirteen is the maximum number of persons that can dance in the nine-foot circle used for black magic (thus making a very unlikely link between modern witchcraft and the ritual dances of primitive pagan religion). Other authorities argue that covens were limited to cells of thirteen members or fewer simply in order to limit the damage that might be done through enforced confessions should a participant be interrogated as a suspected witch by the authorities.

Reflecting the sexual nature of many witchcraft rites, it has always been thought desirable for each coven to achieve a rough balance between the sexes. Historically, though, many confessions related to alleged covens in which the men were apparently much outnumbered by the women.

See also ESBAT; SABBAT.

Coventry, Bishop of *see* LANGTON, WALTER.

Cox, Mrs Julian c.1593–1663. English beggarwoman who was tried for witchcraft at Taunton in Somerset in 1663. Her testimony is interesting in that it sheds light on such matters as TRANSVECTION and SHAPE-SHIFTING as understood by lay people of her time. Mrs Cox stood charged with bewitching a servant maid in revenge for the girl declining to give her money when she begged for it. The girl had been much tormented by the beggarwoman, who appeared to her in spectral form and forced her to swallow large pins. It transpired from other evidence that the old woman kept a FAMILIAR in the shape of a TOAD and was skilled at transforming herself into a HARE. According to one witness, a hare had been cornered in a large bush by his hounds: as he tried to seize the hare, to save it from his dogs, the creature changed into a woman, whom he identified confidently as Mrs Julian Cox. The transformation clearly had a profound effect on the witness, as later reported: 'He knowing her was so affrighted that his hair stood on end; and yet spake to her asked her what brought her there; but she was so far out of breath that she could not make him any answer.'

Other offences that Cox was alleged to have committed included using magic to make a neighbouring farmer's cows go mad and flying on a broomstick (she was spotted flying through her own window). The prisoner herself described how she had seen two witches and an unidentified 'black man' approaching her on broomsticks 'about a yard and a half from the ground'. When the court tried to test her guilt further by insisting that she recite the LORD'S PRAYER she endeavoured to oblige, but made the fatal mistake of leaving out the 'not' in 'And lead us not into temptation'. The accused was found guilty and executed as a proven witch.

Crew, Sir Randolph see JAMES I.

Cromwell, Lady see WARBOYS WITCHES.

crossroads The point where four roads meet has long been considered an ominous location, widely associated with witchcraft, ghosts and other evils. The roots of this tradition probably lie in primitive religion, when altars to pagan gods were sometimes placed at such intersections and might have been used for human sacrifice. The tradition was undoubtedly consolidated in later centuries by the fact that gallows were often erected at crossroads, and the corpses of executed criminals might also be hung in chains there as a warning to travellers bent on mischief. The bodies of suicides, criminals and suspected vampires were frequently buried close to crossroads, the reasoning being that the ghost of the deceased would be confused by the choice of roads and would be unable to find its way home to torment its former enemies.

Given the dread associations of such sites it was perhaps inevitable that many lonely crossroads should be identified as favourite meeting-places for witches' covens. Death and the Devil himself were supposed to lurk in the vicinity of crossroads waiting for someone to pass by, and superstition is replete with SPELLS and CHARMS that will only work if performed at a crossroads.

crow   With its legendary intelligence and ominous all-black plumage, the crow has always been regarded with misgiving and was consequently often identified as a favourite disguise of witches' FAMILIAR spirits. In ancient times the crow was the messenger of the gods, but in later centuries the popular imagination had it spying on behalf of its evil keeper and molesting victims on his or her orders. The mere sight of a crow was considered unlucky in rural superstition and was widely interpreted as a warning of death and disaster in the offing. To fend off the threat of evil that was implicit in the appearance of such a bird, children in the north of England would assail it with their own counter-threat:

> Crow, crow, get out of my sight,
> Or else I'll eat thy liver and thy lights.

Crowley, Aleister 1875–1947. British occultist, born Edward Alexander Crowley and who often referred to himself as the GREAT BEAST, who nurtured a reputation as the 'wickedest man in the world'. Born in Leamington Spa, the son of a preacher with the

Plymouth Brethren, Crowley was educated at Malvern, Tonbridge and Trinity College, Cambridge. Subsequently he indulged freely in ritual magic, drugs and orgiastic sex, organising his own covens and establishing himself as perhaps the most widely known, and condemned, practitioner of SATANISM in the twentieth century. Proclaiming that 'Do what thou wilt shall be the whole of the law', he devoted his life to occult practice, believing he was a channel for communication with the supernatural and travelling throughout the world to probe the secrets of a wide variety of mystical disciplines. Among the titles he bestowed upon himself were Earl of Boleskine, Count Syareff and Prince Chioa Khan.

After leaving Cambridge University in 1898 Crowley joined the Hermetic Order of the GOLDEN DAWN, becoming a close follower of the sect's leader, Samuel Liddell MATHERS. Two years later, however, he fell out with Mathers and, after Crowley was expelled from the group, the two squared up to each other in a campaign of 'psychic warfare'. On one occasion, Mathers reportedly despatched a SUCCUBUS against Crowley, but Crowley outwitted him by transforming it into an ugly old crone without the allurements necessary to seduce him.

Having married the sister of Gerald Kelly, an artist and Golden Dawn member destined to become the President of the Royal Academy, Crowley visited Egypt and there communicated with a spirit by the name of Aiwass, who dictated to him the various rules and laws that were to form the basis of his *Book of the Law*. According to Crowley, the year 1904 saw the advent of the third age of mankind, the age of Horus, in which the old 'slave religions' such as Christianity would be replaced by new pleasure-seeking creeds. In 1907 he formed his own coven, called the Order of the Silver Star, to put his ideas into practice. Crowley's unfettered sexual appetite, however, proved too much for his wife, who took to drink and eventually divorced him; both she and Crowley's second wife ended their lives in lunatic asylums, while at least five of his countless mistresses committed suicide.

Crowley was appointed head of a British branch of the German Order of the Temple of the Orient, loosely based on the fabled sex magic practices of the KNIGHTS TEMPLAR, in 1912. Eight years later, after transferring his activities to the USA during the First World War, he founded the Abbey of Thelema in a villa at Cefalù in Sicily. Here he and two of his many mistresses, the German-Swiss Leah Hirsig (whom he called the 'Scarlet Woman') and the French Ninette Shumway, practised drug-induced sexual magic, often in the company of visiting friends and disciples. Murals depicting the HORNED GOD and other deities were painted on the walls of the villa, which was intended to become a world centre for occult studies. Stories about the bizarre sex ceremonies performed at the house were regularly blazed in the British press, and when Crowley published a volume of autobiography the outcry intensified. Tales of Crowley's excesses both disgusted and fascinated readers in his homeland. On one occasion he was reported to have baptised a toad in the name of Christ and then crucified the creature, while gloating over its agonies.

Eventually Crowley was ordered out of Sicily by the authorities, who were quick to whitewash the infamous murals. However, the 'Great Beast' continued to pursue his studies of the occult, publishing books on the subject, including *Magick in Theory and Practice*, selling potions and presiding over new covens.

Crowley's last years saw him in decline, fighting addiction to drugs and finally dying in a boarding-house in Hastings, Sussex, at the age of seventy-two. At his funeral several of his followers sang verses in his praise, identifying him as Pan (the Greeks' name for the Horned God).

crystal-gazing *see* SCRYING.

Cullender, Rose *see* BURY ST EDMUNDS WITCHES.

culte des mortes *see* NECROMANCY.

Cunning Men *see* WHITE WITCH.

Cunningham, John *see* FIAN, JOHN.

curse The invocation of supernatural power to inflict harm upon someone or something. The ability to enact an effective curse against an enemy was considered one of the basic skills of any witch, and thousands of people were brought before the authorities across Europe on little more grounds than the alleged employment of black magic in such a way against their victims. English witchcraft trials often began with someone making the connection between some real misfortune and an old woman's curse after she had been insulted or made to suffer some inconvenience.

In some cases witches would claim their own special procedures to make their curses doubly effective (*see* IMAGE MAGIC), but in most instances a simple phrase expressing harm was sufficient. Those implicated in the scandal of the SOMERSET WITCHES, for instance, believed that the words 'A pox take it' were quite enough to cause harm to any person, animal or object that invited their enmity. The curse did not need to be actually voiced, however: simply 'ill-wishing' someone was deemed equally effective, although this usually had to be accompanied by some gesture such as spitting, pointing a finger or delivering a penetrating stare (*see* EVIL EYE).

Belief in the power of the curse, or hex, in western European society in the sixteenth and seventeenth centuries was so great that people would make considerable efforts to repair relations with any suspected witch whom they had offended. They would make good the damage done or retract the insult that had led to the curse being made, often with some gift or other favour to ensure that the curse would be lifted. It would seem likely, from the surviving evidence, that some suspected witches deliberately used to their own advantage the fear their curses could engender – although this daring ploy could prove highly dangerous if an intended victim raised the matter with the authorities.

An illustration of the credit placed by ordinary people on the power of witches' curses was the oft-repeated tale of Alice Trevisard, an alleged witch from Dartmouth in Devon. According to legend she quarrelled one evening with a sailor called William Tompson, who struck her with his musket. Muttering 'Thou shalt be better thou hadst never met with me', Alice Trevisard made good her escape – but Tompson had good reason to remember her threat in the months to come. On his next voyage he was shipwrecked when his vessel went down after a mysterious fire and he was then imprisoned for a year by the Portuguese. On his eventual return home Alice Trevisard warned his wife that his days in prison were not yet over, and sure enough he was captured by the Spanish a short time later and spent the next two years in one of their gaols. Local superstition had no hesitation in drawing the link between the woman's threat and Tompson's misfortunes.

In other widely reported cases the victims of witches' curses variously met with agonising deaths through illness or accident or suffered less serious inconveniences, usually as a result of having incurred the wrath of an old woman of the neighbourhood. Less serious consequences of these curses included the vomiting of copious amounts of strange objects, which might range from stones and pieces of coal to pins, straw and buttons. Margaret Holyday, an eighteen-year-old servant-girl from Saxmundham who was afflicted in this way in 1672, threw up bodkins, bones, egg-shells and pieces of brass among other unlikely items. Her affliction only ended after she had brought up an entire row of pins neatly stuck into a piece of blue paper.

One striking example of the entrepreneurial spirit that was sometimes applied even in such eclectic matters was the once-flourishing trade in the buying and selling of curses, a practice which dated as far back as ancient Greece. Such curses were usually sold in the form of incantations or potions and could be directed at specific individuals or at whole families, exerting their baleful influence on succeeding generations through the centuries. Typical of this phenomenon was the cursing well of St Elian at Llanelian-yn-Rhos near Colwyn Bay in Wales, where, until the late nineteenth century at least, people continued to pay a small sum to toss down the well lead boxes containing curses against their enemies. Victims of such curses could, however, bribe the keeper of the well to retrieve the box containing the relevant curse if this was thought necessary. Other areas boasted 'cursing stones', where witches repaired to utter terrible curses against their enemies (*see* STORM-RAISING).

Even in the twentieth century the concept of the curse has caused many people to spend their lives in a state of considerable trepidation – most famously in the case of the opening of the tomb of Tutankhamen in Egypt's Valley of the Kings in the 1920s. When several of those connected with the celebrated excavation died premature and mysterious deaths the tale spread that this was in punishment for breaking into the grave, as warned in a curse (now mysteriously disappeared) that was reportedly inscribed over the entrance.

In some primitive societies the power of the curse remains as strong as ever, and there are many documented cases of victims going into a permanent physical and mental decline, even to the point of death, upon learning that someone has cursed them. Even in western Europe several extraordinary cases have come to light, in relatively recent years, in which people suffering a run of bad luck have alleged psychic interference from some enemy through cursing. To cite just one of these, in 1953 a rancher in Arizona actually shot and killed a woman whom he and his neighbours believed to have put a curse on his wife.

See also EVIL EYE; MALEFICIA; SPELL; WITCH BRIDLE.

Dalkeith Witch *see* BIER RIGHT.

Dama, La *see* BASQUE WITCHES.

damnum minatum *see* MALEFICIA.

dancing Various kinds of dancing were a traditional highlight of the conventional SABBAT. The earliest surviving records of witches dancing at their revels date back to at least the thirteenth century. In 1282, for instance, a Scottish priest from Inverkeithing was accused of being a sorcerer after he admitted leading young girls of the parish in a markedly obscene phallic dance, probably of pagan origin, as part of the Easter celebrations. The priest in question escaped punishment at the hands of his superiors, who were apparently ignorant of the implications of the dance, but an outraged parishioner subsequently murdered him.

Perhaps the most notorious of the dances performed by witches at their COVENS was the 'hare and hounds' ritual dance in which the DEVIL or the leader of the coven, playing the role of the hound, furiously chased one of the female witches, impersonating the HARE. At the climax of the dance the hound caught the hare, wrestled her to the ground and had intercourse with her. According to some confessions, the participants would magically change their forms several times during the dance, adopting the forms of CATS, bees and so forth.

The Scottish witch Isobel GOWDIE gave her interrogators first-hand details of a dance performed by the coven to which she belonged. The central feature of this dance was a leap, accompanied by the words: 'Over the dyke with it!' The witches also participated in other lively dances, including 'follow-my-leader', and danced deliberately in a WIDDERSHINS direction, that is, contrary to the course of the sun. Other witches claimed that they always danced 'backwards' or with BROOMSTICKS between their legs while at their sabbats. The Devil himself often provided the music.

Pierre de LANCRE, describing the activities of the conventional coven on the Continent of Europe in the seventeenth century, included ritual dancing among the high points of sabbats. According to his account, once the banquet was over the devils present led their neighbours to a cursed tree round which the participants formed a ring, standing back to back, and proceeded to dance in the most indecent manner, often with the Devil himself at their head. Francesco-Maria GUAZZO similarly wrote that they made 'a frenzied ring with hands joined and back to back; and so they dance, throwing their heads like frantic folk, sometimes holding in their hands the candles which they have before used in worshipping the devil'. Another authority on witchcraft, Nicholas REMY, claimed that witches attending their sabbats carried on dancing like this until they were 'little short of madness' and they were found to be utterly exhausted when they finally returned home. Usually, though, the dance seems to have gone on until the participants were driven into a frenzy and then abandoned themselves to a sexual orgy in which all inhibitions were cast aside.

One Italian variant was the dance called La Volta. Like the dance that Gowdie described, this culminated in prodigious leaps in the air. The heights attained by the dancers and the complexity of the steps were proof to onlookers that only with the assistance of the Devil could the dance be mastered.

Modern witches still incorporate dancing in their rituals. Best known of these dances is the 'Dance of the Wheel', a circular dance round a bonfire performed to mark the winter solstice. At the climax of the dance the High Priest and Priestess leap through the flames hand in hand, followed by the rest of the witches in couples.

Darling, Thomas *see* BURTON BOY.

Darrell, John *c.*1562–1602. English clergyman who attempted to establish a reputation as a self-styled exorcist in witchcraft cases, but after initial success only succeeded into coming into conflict with the Church authorities. Exorcists were much employed to counter POSSESSION resulting from witchcraft on the Continent, but the notoriety that attached to Darrell's name meant that in 1603 EXORCISM by clergymen was forbidden altogether in England 'under pain of the imputation of imposture or cozenage, and deposition from the ministry' unless the person in question had a licence and the sanction of his Bishop to do so.

A graduate of Cambridge, Darrell began his career as a preacher in his home town of Mansfield, Nottinghamshire, and was subsequently ordained. The opportunity to involve himself in witchcraft cases came in 1586, when seventeen-year-old Catherine Wright was persuaded by Darrell to make accusations of witchcraft against a woman named Margaret Roper, on the grounds that Roper had ordered a demon called Middlecub to torment her. Unfortunately for Darrell, under examination Wright admitted to the authorities that she had made up the whole affair and the aspiring exorcist was lucky to escape gaol.

Darrell does not appear to have learned his lesson, for despite this setback he continued to build a reputation as an exorcist. Ten years later, in 1596, he was at it again, conducting services of exorcism in the widely reported case of Thomas Darling, the BURTON BOY (which was later revealed as a hoax). His next case was that of Nicholas Starkie and his family at Cleworth Hall, Leigh, Lancashire, during the course of which Darrell successfully exorcised no fewer than seven people allegedly possessed by demons (*see* HARTLAY, EDMUND).

The climax of Darrell's controversial career as an exorcist came in November 1597, when his assistance, and that of another priest called George More, was sought in the case of William Somers, the 'Boy of Nottingham'. Somers, a teenaged apprentice to a Nottingham musician, had begun to show symptoms of demoniacal possession and Darrell quickly confirmed this diagnosis, claiming that the boy was suffering on account of all the sins committed by the people of Nottingham. Darrell requested married couples in the city to refrain from physical intimacy and gave a sermon in which he described the boy's symptoms in graphic detail, with Somers himself obligingly demonstrating these to anyone who cared to see. Among other things, he appeared to swallow his tongue, to be seized by weeping fits and to lie on the ground as if dead. Somers was then encouraged to name those responsible for his condition and he produced the names of thirteen local witches. Whenever these women came near him he fell victim to a fit (though critics noted that this 'test' was not always infallible).

Mary Cowper, Darrell's sister-in-law, now identified one Alice Freeman as a witch. When Freeman attempted to evade questioning by claiming that she was pregnant, Darrell was quick to allege that, if she was, the child was almost certainly that of the DEVIL. Freeman's brother managed to get Somers brought before the town council, where the boy confessed that he had faked the possession. Darrell, however, refused to accept the confession and claimed that this was simply a trick by the Devil to forestall further investigation. A public inquiry followed in 1598; Somers, realising that if revealed as a fraud he risked the death penalty, now maintained the story of his possession, and Freeman and another of the accused women were brought to trial.

Proceedings in court were, however, abandoned when Somers changed tack again and admitted how he had deceived his interrogators by a variety of simple tricks. It transpired that Somers had dreamed up the whole business in order to get himself released from his apprenticeship to the musician, which he found irksome. He had discovered how to stage demoniacal possession by reading widely available pamphlets about other recent witchcraft cases, such as that of the WARBOYS WITCHES, and had gleaned further tips from Darrell himself, who had described the symptoms of the Burton Boy so that he might imitate them.

The collapse of the trial of the Nottingham Witches was a major embarrassment to Darrell and caused the exorcist to be sent to

Lambeth Palace for questioning by the Archbishop of Canterbury and other high-ranking Church officials. Although some prominent Church dignitaries sympathised with Darrell's mission against demons, he and More were censured for their conduct, defrocked and thrown into prison for a year. In 1599 one of Darrell's examiners, Samuel Harsnett, wrote a book about the affair under the title *A Discovery of the Fraudulent Practises of John Darrel, Bachelor of Arts*. Although Darrell himself wrote extensively in defence of his conduct, there is no record that he ever resumed his former activities as an exorcist.

Dashwood, Sir Francis *see* HELLFIRE CLUB.

Davies, William *see* MORGAN, NANNY.

Davot, Father *see* CHAMBRE ARDENTE AFFAIR.

de Drownestown, Eva *see* KYTELER, ALICE.

de Lancre, Pierre *see* LANCRE, PIERRE DE.

de Midia, Petronilla *see* KYTELER, ALICE.

de Rais, Gilles *see* RAIS, GILLES DE.

de Spina, Alphonsus *see* ALPHONSUS DE SPINA.

Dee, John 1527–1608. English alchemist, geographer and mathematician, who became the most celebrated sorcerer of the Elizabethan age. Author of writings on such diverse subjects as logic, astrology, natural philosophy, navigation and the calendar, Dee was one of the most inventive scholars of his time. A founding fellow of Trinity College, Cambridge, he was first accused of sorcery in 1546 when he built a mechanical beetle as a stage prop for a production of the Aristophanes play *Peace*. He then pursued the acquisition of further learning in Belgium and France under such authorities as

Cornelius AGRIPPA and became fascinated in the realm of invention that lay between science and magic.

Edward VI granted the youthful but already internationally respected Dee a pension, which he exchanged for the clerical living of Upton-upon-Severn. Subsequently Dee became astrologer to Mary I and cast horoscopes both for her and for her intended husband, Philip of Spain, but he fell foul of his royal mistress in 1555 when, probably because of his friendship with her enemy Princess Elizabeth, he was alleged to have plotted her death by magic. Other charges included the suggestions that he had procured the death of children by witchcraft and kept FAMILIARS. He managed to evade a verdict of guilty on the charge of high treason, but the court of the Star Chamber still committed him to prison, where he remained for two years. He regained royal favour, however, under Elizabeth I and was consulted by the new Queen as to the luckiest date for her coronation in 1559 (she supported him on several occasions with gifts of money to further his research into alchemy). It is, in fact, considered likely that he worked for the Queen in the capacity of spy.

In 1563 Dee published the controversial *Monas Hieroglyphia*, which discussed the mystic science of numerology. The book was written in Dee's own code and only those taken into his confidence were told how to decipher the text. In 1577 he was summoned to Windsor by the Queen in order to explain to her the natural origins of Halley's Comet, which appeared in the heavens that year.

In 1581 Dee teamed up with Edward KELLY, who shared his interest in the occult, and together they performed numerous investigations into such activities as SCRYING and NECROMANCY. Dee was particularly interested in the possibility of contacting the spirit world, if only to satisfy his intellectual curiosity. Both Dee and Kelly stated that they had been granted interviews with angels through the agency of Dee's celebrated magic crystal, which Elizabeth I herself asked to examine (it is now preserved in the British Museum in London). Dee himself was unable to see the entities summoned by this means but took down the descriptions provided by Kelly, who alone could see them. Dee often questioned the spirits himself, though he would only converse with proven good spirits.

The two scholars and their wives travelled widely, becoming at various times the guests of the King of Poland, Emperor Rudolf II of Bohemia and the Tsar of Russia. Dee and Kelly finally parted company in 1589, two years after Dee had reluctantly agreed to a wife-sharing arrangement that Kelly said had been insisted upon by his supernatural communicants. When Dee's wife Jane had expressed doubts about the arrangement, Dee had rather feebly told her: 'There is no other remedy ... so it must needs be done.'

In 1595, though no longer a favourite of Elizabeth I, Dee was given the post of Warden of Manchester College; it was while Dee was at Manchester that he was approached in the matter of the suspected possession of the children of Nicholas Starkie (*see* HARTLEY, EDMUND). Although he attempted further investigations into scrying, these were unsuccessful, as he could not find an assistant of Kelly's skill.

Dee lost the post at Manchester in 1604 and, perhaps fearing for his welfare in the witch-hunting hysteria that was then developing, he sought (but failed to obtain) a public refutation of his reputation as a magician from JAMES I. This was a disappointment for Dee, who deeply resented the description 'magician' and maintained that he had always been a dutiful Christian, despite his interest in magic. No action was threatened against the now elderly scholar, however. Despite the many extraordinary achievements of his life the eighty-one-year-old Dee died a pauper; he was buried in Mortlake, London, where he had been born.

Del Rio, Martin Antoine 1551–1608. Belgian Jesuit scholar, whose *Disquisitionum Magicarum* of 1599 was one of the most influential works on the subject of witchcraft to be published during the witch hysteria that gripped Europe between the fourteenth and eighteenth centuries. Born in Antwerp, into a wealthy family of Spanish origin, Del Rio rose to the post of Attorney-General for Brabant before entering the Jesuit order in 1580. His *Disquisitionum Magicarum* took an encyclopedic view of witchcraft and demonology, building on the conclusions of the MALLEUS MALEFICARUM and discussing everything from MALEFICIA to the best ways for judges to approach trials of accused witches. Although the author approved permission for witches to have legal counsel and discounted LYCANTHROPY, he also demonstrated determined intolerance towards those accused of witchcraft and a certain gullibility when it came to stories of their supernatural powers. He argued that judges were obliged to pass the death sentence on witches who had made a confession, and also suggested that anyone who objected to such draconian measures should be suspected of witchcraft themselves.

Del Rio's book was reprinted many times and found its way all over Europe, becoming one of the main reference authorities on the subject and in part a justification for some of the worst elements of the witch persecution. The last new edition appeared as late as 1747.

Delort, Catherine *see* FRANCE; SABBAT.

Demandolx de la Palud, Madeleine de *see* AIX-EN-PROVENCE NUNS.

Demdike, Old *see* PENDLE WITCHES.

demons and demonology The study of demons and their attributes has been pursued by both theologians and occultists for centuries. The Greek word *daimon* signifies any spirit, evil or otherwise, but Christian doctrine demanded that all spirits other than God and his angels were by definition opposed to good, and thus 'demons' came to be understood as necessarily evil entities, and servants of the DEVIL. Learned experts argued that the Devil and his minions were fallen angels and remained in the service of God, being allowed certain powers in order to test the faith of men and to punish those who veered from the path of righteousness.

In the annals of witchcraft, demons came in a range of categories. These included the imps who served witches and sorcerers and witches as FAMILIARS, carrying them to their sabbats and assisting in their spells, as well as INCUBI, SUCCUBI and poltergeists. Some showed a predilection towards tormenting priests and nuns, while others delighted in causing nightmares and other kinds of mischief. Demons might also, according to Nicolas REMY in the sixteenth century, 'so confuse the imagination of a man that he believes himself to be changed; and then the man behaves and conducts himself not as a man, but as that beast which he fancies himself to be' (a 'rational' explanation for outbreaks of LYCANTHROPY).

The conventional idea of a demon in physical form was a miniature version of the Devil, complete with horns, wings, black skin and cloven feet – although demons were widely credited with the power to change their shape at will. In order to seduce young men, for instance, they might appear to them in the form of beautiful women. Such beings were depicted in a host of paintings and engravings in medieval times and later, issuing from the mouths of those undergoing EXORCISM and lurking in the vicinity of people whom they suspected might be vulnerable to their influence. It was widely believed that they could cover vast distances, always flying at night, and that they shared an unremitting hostility towards mankind – though (at great risk to himself) a cunning magician could use his powers to make them his slaves.

According to many writers on the subject, demons shared the cunning of their master the Devil. Jean BODIN, writing in 1580, claimed that:

> It is certain that the devils have a profound knowledge of all things. No theologian can interpret the Holy Scriptures better than they can; no lawyer has a more detailed knowledge of testaments, contracts and actions; no physician or philosopher can better understand the composition of the human body, and the virtues of the heavens, the stars, birds and fishes, trees and herbs, metals and stones.

The hierarchy of demons was much discussed among theological experts in past centuries and many books were published on the subject, thus adding learned authority to the growing popular belief in such beings. Among the more notable of these were Jean BODIN's *De la Démonomanie des Sorciers* (1580), Peter BINSFELD's *Tractatus de Confessionibus Maleficorum et Sagarum* (1589), Nicolas Remy's *Demonolatreiae*

(1595), JAMES I's *Daemonologie* (1597), Martin Antoine DEL RIO's *Disquisitionum Magicarum* (1599), Henri BOGUET's *Discours des Sorciers* (1602), Francesco-Maria GUAZZO's *Compendium Maleficarum* (1608), Pierre de LANCRE's *Tableau de l'Inconstance des Mauvais Anges* (1612) and Ludovico Maria Sinistrari's *De Demonialitate* (1700). Many of these authors were also lawyers and even judges, writing from personal experience of witchcraft trials and piecing together their knowledge of the underworld from real confessions.

Demons were, according to the experts, divided into several ranks or hierarchies, presided over by Satan himself. The most fearsome of them all included ASHTAROTH, who knew all secrets, ASMODEUS, a demon of rage and lust, BAPHOMET, often identified as the GOAT of witches' sabbats, BEELZEBUB, the prince of demons identified with the sin of gluttony, BELPHEGOR, who made men slothful, LEVIATHAN, the demon of envy, LILITH, a demoness who sucked the blood of sleeping men, LUCIFER, the ruler of the underworld, otherwise known as the DEVIL or Satan and a provoker of pride and anger in men, and MAMMON, who drove men to dreams of avarice.

Besides these there was a host of minor demons, whose powers varied. Alphonsus de SPINA, writing in 1459, claimed that one-third of God's angels had become devils, and that there were precisely 133,306,668 of them. Other estimates of their numbers suggested a total of 6,660,000 demons commanded by sixty-six princes or 7,409,127 demons under the command of seventy-nine princes. An authority claimed towards the end of the sixteenth century that the number of devils then active was equivalent to more than half the population of the world.

One way of differentiating between these vast legions of demons was to categorise them according to the element that they were said to inhabit. Francesco-Maria Guazzo attempted to class demons into six types along these lines: those who inhabited the 'upper air', those who dwelt in the air nearer earth, those who had terrestrial habitats such as forests and caves, those who lived in water, those who lurked underground, and finally – and most mysteriously – those who roamed indiscriminately in the dark (the 'heliophobic' demons). Another authority divided them up into the classes of fates, poltergeists, incubi and succubi, marching hosts, familiars, nightmare demons, demons created out of human semen, deceptive demons, clean demons and demons who deluded witches into believing that they could fly.

Such scholarly study of demons was irrelevant in most witchcraft trials, however, for few judges had the learning or intellect to appreciate the fine distinctions that authorities often made between one type of demon and another. As far as the law was concerned demons belonged to one general class and were universally evil, so any dealings with them would be considered enough to confirm a suspect's guilt.

Possession by demons was conventionally tackled through EXORCISM of the victim, in the course of which the demon occupying the victim's body was asked various routine questions concerning its identity and intentions. Once the demon's name was known, many believed this gave the exorcist control over it. Each demon had its opposing saint, to whom prayers might be addressed for assistance in expelling the demon in question. Thus, according to one source, those possessed by Beelzebub might be delivered through prayers to his adversary, St Francis, while those tormented by Ashtaroth and Asmodeus might be redeemed through the intervention of St Bartholomew and St John the Baptist respectively. Demons would also be deterred by certain AMULETS and CHARMS and by anyone making the sign of the cross or the 'fig' sign (see EVIL EYE) or otherwise defending themselves with holy water, firelight, spittle, bread, salt, iron or herbs.

See also GHOST; SATANISM.

Denmark *see* NORWAY.

Derby, Earl of *see* IMAGE MAGIC.

Deshayes, Catherine *see* CHAMBRE ARDENTE AFFAIR.

Device, Alizon, Elizabeth, James, Jennett and John *see* PENDLE WITCHES.

Devil The ruler of the underworld and the prince of DEMONS, considered the arch-enemy of both God and man. Otherwise identified by the personal names of LUCIFER or SATAN, and more colloquially by such names as 'Old Nick' or 'The Prince of Darkness', the Devil was conventionally depicted as the sponsor of all evil in the world, using such agents as demons and witches to plot against mankind and to claim their souls.

According to the Bible, the Devil's role was to afflict the faithful with various misfortunes so that the true nature of their faith in God might be revealed. His role was that of the malevolent accuser, roaming the Earth looking for opportunities to expose weakness on God's behalf. Later, however, he became a more genuinely evil figure, dedicated to the destruction of man and the overthrow of God himself. The story of the fall of the angel Lucifer through pride in his own power allowed demonologists to develop the mythology of the Devil as an arch-fiend ruling over his own kingdom and seizing the souls of wicked men for his own ends. Another passage in the Bible explained how some two hundred of God's angels had lusted after mortal women and as punishment had been imprisoned in the 'valleys of the earth' – Hell. These deposed angels – the 'Watchers' – then became the nucleus of the Devil's cohorts.

The authority of the Bible was enough to convince the medieval and post-medieval mind that the Devil was an actual force to be reckoned with. The presence of paintings of the Devil, a dark figure often with horns and tail, in churches throughout the Christian world undoubtedly did much to consolidate belief in his powers. Johan WEYER, writing in 1563, stressed the Devil's capacity for evil: 'Satan possesses great courage, incredible cunning, superhuman wisdom, the most acute penetration, consummate prudence, an incomparable skill in veiling the most pernicious artifices under a specious disguise, and a malicious and infinite hatred toward the human race, implacable and incurable.'

If there was a God, it followed that by the same authority there was also a Devil. Denial of the Devil's existence was, therefore, in the eyes of the stricter Church authorities, tantamount to a denial of

God himself. (The logical extension of this, that if the Devil, the source of all evil, was created by God, then all evil in the world was ultimately attributable to God, created much difficulty for early Christian scholars.)

The Devil described by countless witches in their confessions over the centuries could manifest either in the form of a 'dark' man, dressed in black, or could appear in the shape of some animal, typically a GOAT, a BLACK DOG, a WOLF or, more rarely, a bird or a bull (perhaps echoing the bull god of ancient Mithraism). The first theological definition of the Devil, ratified by the Council of Toledo in AD 447, described him as 'a large black monstrous apparition with horns on his head, cloven hoofs ... an immense phallus and a sulphurous smell'. All confessions agreed that he was licentious and unremitting in his pursuit of evil, but a substantial body of often humorous folktales also suggested that the Devil could be slow-witted and might on occasion be outsmarted by his intended victims. This conventional picture of the Devil probably evolved in the third and fourth centuries AD, when the hermits of the Egyptian deserts, the 'desert fathers', married the biblical Satan with other older and now discarded pagan gods, such as Pan, with his cloven feet.

In return for their unqualified loyalty (expressed in the ceremonial obscene KISS) and ultimately their souls, witches were rewarded by the Devil with the gift of a FAMILIAR to serve their will and also with promises of special magical powers for the rest of their lives. In times gone by, the more superstitious genuinely thought that the Devil's disciples did indeed enjoy special powers, thus making them highly dangerous and deserving to be exterminated. More thoughtful observers, loath to admit the possibility of witches flying through the air and achieving their ends through magic, suggested that the Devil deceived his followers into believing that they had supernatural powers, when common sense insisted that they did not.

Members of covens reported their evil-doing back to the Devil when they met at their sabbats, and the Devil was reputed to bestow some extra favour upon the one who had done the most harm to his or her neighbours. According to some witches, the Devil might also join in the business of preparing wax images to use against enemies and played an active part in the revels that were a traditional high-light of important gatherings.

Devil worship reached a climax in Europe in the fifteenth cen-tury, when Gilles de RAIS and others developed their own devil-worshipping cults, sometimes celebrating their dark overlord with human sacrifices and orgiastic sex among other extreme acts. Ecclesiastical authorities claimed that the Devil was leading a cam-paign against the Christian world, recruiting witches and sorcerers to his cause and threatening to overthrow the Church itself. As memories of the 'Old Religion', with its HORNED GOD, slowly faded, the more 'modern' figure of the Devil and his cohorts took their place in the popular imagination, inheriting many of their attributes.

Although belief in a real, persistently evil Devil has fallen off in modern times (despite a papal pronouncement in 1972 that the Devil is an actual functioning power in the world today), devil wor-ship is still practised by occultists around the world (see SATANISM). The discovery of the 100-mile trail of 'Devil's hoofprints' found in the snow through south Devon in 1855 was sufficient, even at that late date, to cause widespread consternation among rural communities and to provoke rumours that 'Old Nick' himself had been abroad.

See also DEMONS AND DEMONOLOGY; DEVIL'S MARK; PACT WITH THE DEVIL.

Devil's mark A mark on a person's body that was formerly searched for by witchfinders or their agents as proof positive that the person concerned was a witch. Tradition had it that the DEVIL put his mark on every newcomer to a COVEN so as to identify the initiate as one of his own (although, according to Francesco-Maria GUAZZO, he only marked those who were considered unreliable). This he did by simply touching the skin of the apprentice witch with his finger, his tongue or a claw, by kissing the spot in question or by branding it with a hot iron.

Jacques Fontaine, physician to Henry IV of France in the early seventeenth century, elaborated on the methods used by Satan to make his mark:

> Some say that Satan makes these marks on them with a hot iron and a certain unguent which he applies under the skin of witches. Others say that the devil marks the witches with his finger, when he appears in human form or as a spirit. If it were done with a hot iron, it would necessarily follow that on the part so marked there would be a scar, but the witches testify that they have never seen a scar over the mark ... But it is not necessary to prove this, for the devil, who does not lack knowledge of medications and has the best of them, has only to mortify that place. As for the scar, the devil is such a skilful worker that he can place the hot iron on the body without causing any scar.

The mark was not always readily visible and in centuries gone by the naked body of an alleged witch – usually shaved of all hair – had to be carefully searched, frequently in public. It was widely believed that the Devil's mark or *stigmata diaboli* was insensitive to pain, and that the best way to find it was by prodding the suspect with sharp pins or lancets until a spot was located where the accused seemed to have no feeling (*see* PRICKING).

Discovery of an insensitive point, as was usually revealed in the course of such examination, was taken very seriously as evidence of a suspected witch's guilt – although it seems that in reality what the searchers found was more likely to be an old scar, a cyst, a corn, a mole, a wart, a birthmark or some other natural blemish. Medical experts who ventured to suggest that it was difficult to tell the difference between the Devil's mark and natural blemishes would be ridiculed and were likely to be dismissed as not very good doctors.

Michael Dalton, writing in *The Countrey Justice* in 1630, discussed the finding of the Devil's mark, describing it as:

> sometimes like a blue or a red spot, like a flea-biting; sometimes the flesh sunk in and hollow (all which for a time may be covered, yea taken away, but will come again, to their old form). And these

Devil's marks be insensible, and being pricked will not bleed, and be often in their secretest parts, and therefore require diligent and careful search.

Areas that had to be checked especially carefully included, in women, the breasts and the area between the legs, and, in men, the armpits, the anus and under the eyelids. In England a favourite site of the Devil's mark was the fingers; on the Continent the favoured location was the left shoulder.

Other authorities suggested that the Devil's mark might also be identified by its shape. According to one sixteenth-century source, the mark 'is not always of the same shape or figure; sometimes it is the likeness of a hare, sometimes like a toad's foot, sometimes a spider, a puppy, a dormouse'. Another tradition claimed that the mark was usually in the shape of a cloven hoof.

The notion that discovery of the Devil's mark – or even two or three of them – was conclusive physical proof of a witch's guilt was widespread, and the majority of witchcraft trials staged in Europe between the fifteenth and late seventeenth centuries included evidence of this kind. Many thousands of alleged witches went to their deaths on the strength of hearsay and subsequent discovery of the Devil's mark on their person as the only corroborating evidence against them.

See also WITCH'S MARK.

Diana Ancient Roman goddess of hunting, fertility and the moon, who in the Dark Ages was the object of veneration by a primitive witch cult that extended through much of Europe. Long before the development of the witch mania of post-medieval times Diana was identified as the leader of sorcerers (chiefly female) who accompanied her on nocturnal rides across the sky, mounted on a variety of demons and beasts – the probable origin of the notion that witches flew through the air to their SABBATS. In AD 906 the Church officially denied that such night-rides took place (*see* CANON EPIS-COPI), but the idea remained firmly entrenched in the popular imagination for many centuries and the gatherings attended by cult members doubtless provided a model for the witches' sabbat. Followers of Diana (who was also known by such names as Herodias, Hodla-Perchta, Noctiluca, Bensozia and Dame Habonde) were not identified as witches, but the link was clearly there, and in time their activities became confused with those of witches. Diana herself became identified with, and replaced by, the DEVIL. Like the Devil, the goddess was revered as the source of all evil in the world and was also credited with the power to change her shape, being commonly described in the form of a CAT.

Worship of the goddess Diana has revived in relatively recent times through the activities of various modern covens devoted to the HORNED GOD and the GREAT GODDESS, who claim to be practising a version of the long-neglected 'Old Religion'.

Dicconson, Frances *see* PENDLE WITCHES.

divination The business of using magic to learn secrets that may not be divulged by ordinary means. Men and women have consulted gods, demons and other spiritual entities for certain privileged knowledge for as long as such beings have been envisaged. Some of the very earliest laws instituted against sorcerers and witches concerned such activities, which could easily threaten the stability of the state. Consulting a diviner about the life expectancy of a monarch, for instance, could lead to the enquirer being accused of treason and being sentenced to death – as suffered by an English hermit known as Peter the Wise in 1213 after he unwisely foretold the death of King John. More usual enquiries, about the whereabouts of hidden treasure and so forth, were considered less dangerous and for many centuries practitioners of such magic were subject only to relatively mild punishment.

There has always been money to be made from offering services as a diviner, and many persons accused of witchcraft were guilty of nothing more than attempting to provide answers to questions posed by rich and poor alike, only too willing to trade such information for a few coins. Seers of various kinds were accorded some status in the ancient world (but were also subject to periodic persecution) and in later centuries kings, generals and even prominent figures in the Church thought it quite natural to consult a fortune-teller in times of crisis. Many notable scholars, such as John DEE, were famous for their skill at crystal-gazing, and would object strenuously to being labelled sorcerers or witches on these grounds alone.

None the less, some authorities considered divination as no more than an aspect of witchcraft and indistinguishable from other dealings with the spirit world that witches were supposed to pursue. William Perkins, writing in 1608, argued that any knowledge gleaned by divination was vouchsafed by the Devil himself. Protests by the accused that they communicated only with 'good' spirits were often unacceptable as a defence. In practice, however, accusations that suspects had indulged in divination rarely formed the basis for their prosecution, although they were often taken into account as supporting evidence that a person was a practising witch.

There are various means by which diviners, sorcerers and witches sought to reveal secrets about the past, present and future. These ranged from inspecting the entrails of ritually sacrificed women and children (antinopomancy) and studying the hands (chiromancy) to casting dice (astragalomancy), interpreting bird behaviour (ornithomancy), 'reading' numbers (arithmancy), gazing into basins of water (lecanomancy), noting the shapes in burning flames (pyromancy) and listening to the noises made by the belly (gastromancy). More extreme means were reputed to include raising the dead in order to quiz them about such matters (*see* NECROMANCY) and enlisting the assistance of a demon (demonomancy) – preferably from within the safety of a MAGIC CIRCLE. In times past, accusations that a witch or other person had raised the dead, however, implied something more than innocent enquiry into the future – for only those who had made a PACT WITH THE DEVIL could pretend to such expertise.

See also SHIPTON, MOTHER.

Dr Lamb's Darling The nickname that was bestowed upon Mrs Anne Bodenham, assistant to the distinguished physician and alleged sorcerer Dr John LAMB. The fact that she lived in Lamb's house rather than with her own husband was the subject of considerable scandal. Though largely unschooled, Anne Bodenham learned some of the rudiments of Lamb's magic and, after his death, sought to capitalise on this by publishing a small book of charms. Her connection with the late doctor bestowed upon her the reputation of a 'Wise Woman' and she made the most of this, settling in the village of Fisherton Anger, Wiltshire, and selling her services as a fortune-teller and herbalist. If someone sought knowledge of the future from her, for the price of three shillings she would toss various herbs into a fire set in the middle of a MAGIC CIRCLE, causing spirits to appear to answer questions put to them.

A man named Mason testified to Mrs Bodenham's abilities when he described how she had raised spirits in order to answer his queries about a lawsuit he planned against his father-in-law. According to his statement, she drew a magic circle with a staff and then laid a certain book within the circle:

> After that, she laid a green glass on the book, and placed within the circle an earthen pot of coals wherein she threw something which caused a very noisome smell ... and so calling Beelzebub, Tormentor, Satan and Lucifer appear, there suddenly arose a very high wind which made the house shake. And presently, the back door flying open, there came five spirits ... in the likeness of ragged boys, some bigger than others, and ran about the house where she had drawn the staff, and the witch threw upon the ground crumbs of bread which the spirits picked up, and leaped often over the pan of coals in the midst of the circle, and a dog and a cat of the witch's danced with them.

Anne Bodenham's undoing came through her association with the Goddard family. The deranged wife of Richard Goddard, fearing that her own daughters were trying to poison her, sent her young maid Ann Styles to Bodenham to obtain some arsenic to use against her offspring. When news of the plot leaked out, Styles helped herself to some of the Goddard family silver and fled; subsequently apprehended, she attempted to save herself by attributing all blame for the affair to Bodenham. According to Styles, she had been seduced into the Devil's service after Bodenham turned herself into a black cat and then persuaded her to sign a PACT WITH THE DEVIL in her own BLOOD, pricking the maid's finger to wet her pen. As a reward for selling her soul to the Devil, Ann had been given a silver coin by an imp.

The trial of Anne Bodenham depended largely upon Ann Styles's evidence. Particularly damning was the discovery of a mark on the maid's finger, said to correspond with the wound that Bodenham had inflicted in signing the pact, and the dramatic seizures that Styles suffered when describing the 'black man without a head' who threatened to take her soul. Whenever Anne Bodenham herself was brought into the courtroom Styles appeared to go into a deep trance, from which she only emerged after the defendant had gone. As confirmation of guilt, examination of Bodenham's body revealed two WITCH'S MARKS, one on her shoulder and another in her genitals. The trial caused a sensation and, as the antiquary John Aubrey reported, 'the crowd of spectators made such a noise that the judge could not hear the prisoner, nor the prisoner the judge; but the words were handed from one to another by Mr R. Chandler, and sometimes not truly recorded'.

Protesting her innocence to the last and refusing to forgive either her accusers or her gaolers, Anne Bodenham was hanged at Salisbury in 1653. Her plea that she be given some beer so that she would be drunk when the time for execution came was denied.

Dodington, George Bubb *see* HELL-FIRE CLUB.

dog Tradition has it that the DEVIL often appeared on Earth in the form of a black dog, in which guise he might preside at SABBATS or stalk his victims. In former times many people expressed nervousness if they found they were being followed by a black dog and viewed this as an omen of death. The chances were that the dog was either the Devil himself or a witch's FAMILIAR (as evidenced by the investigations conducted by Matthew HOPKINS, whose victims described familiars in the shape of greyhounds and legless spaniels, and the canine familiars claimed by the PENDLE WITCHES).

The tradition of the dog being associated with the forces of evil might, it is speculated, be traced back to the 'Old Religion', in which the HORNED GOD was often depicted in company with his faithful hunting dog. This was not, of course, the only canine to be equated by primitive man with the gods: in Egypt the god Anubis, the hunter, was conventionally depicted with a jackal's head.

A number of witches confessed that the Devil had seduced them at sabbats in the form of a large black dog and others maintained that the Devil habitually manifested as a dog when the time came for the 'obscene kiss', in which all present were required to kiss their overlord on the buttocks. In 1640s England rumours abounded that Boye, the dog that Prince Rupert draped over his saddle during his Civil War campaigns, was really the Devil (the dog was killed at the Battle of Marston Moor in 1644). Necromancers of more recent times, meanwhile, have allegedly confined themselves to a diet of dog flesh and black unleavened and unsalted bread in preparation for the ritual raising of the dead.

doll *see* IMAGE MAGIC.

Dornheim, Gottfried von *see* BAMBERG WITCHES.

drawing blood *see* SCORING ABOVE THE BREATH.

Driver, Ellen *see* FAMILIAR.

Drownestown, Eva de *see* KYTELER, ALICE.

Drummer of Tedworth   Poltergeist haunting of a house in Tedworth (now Tidworth) in Wiltshire, which was widely blamed on the activities of DEMONS. At a time when authorities often failed to differentiate between such supernatural phenomena as ghosts and the nefarious deeds of demons and witches, the events at the home of the magistrate John Mompesson in 1662–3 gave rise to much speculation that the lawyer was being victimised by devils.

The affair began when Mompesson confiscated a drum belonging to a vagrant named William Drury, a former regimental drummer turned trick dancer at country fairs. Subsequently the sound of drumming was heard throughout the magistrate's home, although the source of the thumping and tapping could not be located. When the vagrant's drum was destroyed, these noises grew louder still. Drury was arrested again early in 1663 on a charge of stealing pigs and was sentenced to transportation. After escaping from the convict ship he acquired a new drum. Mompesson had the vagrant seized once more and the drummer found himself charged with witchcraft and pig-stealing. Drury was alleged to have admitted to a visitor while he was in prison that he was responsible for the disturbance, but the witchcraft charge could not be proved. He was transported to Virginia, however, for the other offence.

Those who claimed to have heard the noise explained that the unseen drummer seemed to tap out responses to their questions. Contemporary demonologists regarded various other phenomena reported at the house as significant and clearly indicative of the demonic origins of the trouble – they drew obvious conclusions, for instance, from the smell of sulphur that was said to pervade the house. Other reports spoke of strange lights, children being lifted into the air, furniture being moved by unseen hands, Bibles being covered in ashes, chamberpots being emptied on to beds, drops of blood being found and bedclothes being disturbed. On occasion the cacophony was loud enough to wake up the whole village.

The extraordinary phenomena attributed to the 'Drummer of Tedworth' continued for two years, then ceased without anyone tracing the root cause. Charles II became interested in the case and sent a committee to investigate, but its members failed to witness anything unusual. Joseph GLANVILL, who also investigated the case, announced himself convinced that the phenomena were genuine and underlined the impressive qualifications of John Mompesson, who witnessed many of the incidents, calling him 'a discreet, sagacious and manly person'. So many people reported inexplicable happenings at the house with such honesty, Glanvill stressed, that there was no option but to consider the haunting real, particularly as the Mompessons themselves had nothing to gain from the affair.

ducking *see* SWIMMING.

Duke, Alice *see* SOMERSET WITCHES.

Dummy The nickname of an otherwise unidentified man who was subjected to the ordeal of SWIMMING as a suspected witch at Sible Hedingham, Essex, at the late date of 1863. Dummy was an eccentric eighty-year-old, thought to be of French origins, who was unable to speak because his tongue had been cut out (for unknown reasons) many years before. Living alone but for the company of his three dogs in a modest hut, he cut an odd figure about the village, customarily wearing several hats and coats at once. He was well known in the area as a fortune-teller and some said he was also skilled as a WHITE WITCH.

The tolerance shown to Dummy by his neighbours changed dramatically one night when the old man, drinking at the Swan Inn, was accused of casting the EVIL EYE over a woman named Emma Smith. According to Smith, Dummy had caused her to suffer a prolonged illness in punishment for once refusing him a room at her house. When Dummy declined to go home with Smith to lift the spell he was accused of casting, his accuser became hysterical, attacking him with a stick and loudly repeating her allegations for all to hear. The hysteria quickly spread through the crowd present at the inn and it was decided that the old man must be tested as a witch there and then by the ancient (and only dimly remembered) procedure of swimming.

The luckless Dummy was carried out of the inn and taken down to a brook in nearby Watermill Lane. Several times the old man was thrown into the water, although it seems that the mob (perhaps ignorant of the original theory of swimming) were less interested in testing his guilt by observing whether he sank or floated than in punishing a known witch and breaking his power. As tempers gradually cooled, common sense finally prevailed and the mob dispersed. Two kindly women saw the terrified and soaking-wet old man home, but the experience proved too much for him and shortly afterwards he died in the Halstead Workhouse from the effects of his ordeal.

Emma Smith and the ringleader of the mob, a young man named Samuel Stammers, were charged with unlawful assault at Castle Hedingham Petty Sessions and were tried in Chelmsford. A ten-year-old child named Henrietta Garrod, it transpired, had witnessed the whole affair and, largely on the strength of her testimony, both adults were sentenced to six months' hard labour. The official report of the court into what it called a 'disgraceful transaction' sternly condemned the readiness of the villagers to accept the accusation of witchcraft that had been made against the old man, particularly as the majority of those involved had not been illiterate agricultural labourers, as might be expected, but men 'of the small tradesmen class' who, in the opinion of the court, ought to have known better.

Duncan, Gilly *see* NORTH BERWICK WITCHES.

Dunlop, Bessie *see* SCOTLAND.

Duny, Amy *see* BURY ST EDMUNDS WITCHES.

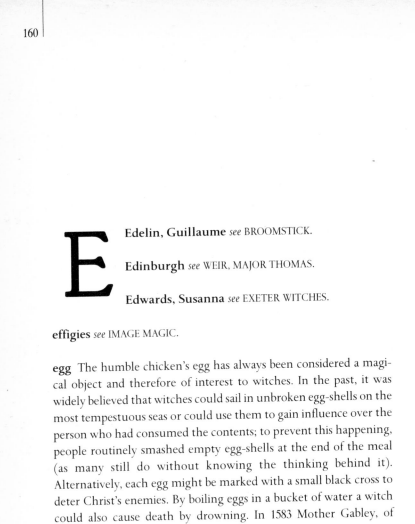

E Edelin, Guillaume *see* BROOMSTICK.

Edinburgh *see* WEIR, MAJOR THOMAS.

Edwards, Susanna *see* EXETER WITCHES.

effigies *see* IMAGE MAGIC.

egg The humble chicken's egg has always been considered a magical object and therefore of interest to witches. In the past, it was widely believed that witches could sail in unbroken egg-shells on the most tempestuous seas or could use them to gain influence over the person who had consumed the contents; to prevent this happening, people routinely smashed empty egg-shells at the end of the meal (as many still do without knowing the thinking behind it). Alternatively, each egg might be marked with a small black cross to deter Christ's enemies. By boiling eggs in a bucket of water a witch could also cause death by drowning. In 1583 Mother Gabley, of King's Lynn in Norfolk, was condemned to death for performing magic of this kind and causing the deaths of fourteen sailors in a storm.

In some parts of the world eggs could also be used to bestow protection against the power of the EVIL EYE. In Albania, for instance, an egg might be smashed and thrown across the face of a newborn baby to keep it safe from the attentions of evil spirits. In Greece, meanwhile, an egg would be passed before a baby's face while the mother intoned: 'Mayest thou live, my little one. Mayest thou grow old, with hoary hair and eyebrows, with a hoary beard and moustache.'

Eichstätt Witch German witchcraft trial staged at Eichstätt near Ingolstadt, Bavaria, in 1637, which was typical of many thousands of similar trials but is known about in more detail than most because the record made by the official scribe of the proceedings still survives. Written as events unfolded both in the courtroom and in the torture chamber, it throws much light upon the appalling inevitability of the process by which an accused witch was 'proved' to be guilty.

The unnamed defendant, a peasant woman aged forty, was pressed repeatedly to admit to such offences as attending SABBATS, exhuming corpses and passing through locked doors by magic. Initially she denied all these and other preposterous charges with some spirit. According to the record of her testimony, the accused woman naively declared that 'she will suffer anything, but cannot admit she is a witch'. When the first charges were read to her she 'laughs heartily and declares she prefers death'. The scribe then made the chilling note: 'Inasmuch as the accused does not respond to merciful treatment, she is brought to the torture chamber.'

Following discovery of the DEVIL'S MARK on the right side of her back, the accused woman was subjected to torture over a period of some two weeks. To begin with she was stretched repeatedly on the LADDER, but later she was subjected to more severe agonies through such means as the BOOTS and STRAPPADO and was obliged to start making up the sort of extravagant confession which she clearly believed her interrogators wished to hear. At times the pain became too much and all that the scribe was able to record were her piteous words as she called on God and Christ to save her.

First the woman admitted to an affair with the hangman, and then to being seduced by the DEVIL in the guise of the hangman. From the Devil she had received a mysterious green powder with which to work evil against man and beast (which officials then produced in court). On the Devil's orders she had also secured the deaths of three of her own children. When she showed signs of wanting to recant her confession she was flogged and encouraged to admit further wrongdoing, such as continuing to have intercourse with the Devil (which she found painful) in her prison cell. She also kept an INCUBUS called Gokhelhaan. However, once the torture ended she withdrew her confession in full, claiming that 'in all her life she never saw the devil nor had intercourse with him'. As a result she was returned to the torture chamber by the judges, who condemned her for her 'stubborn devilish heart'.

By the time the torturers had finished with her the accused was in such a state that she appeared to believe genuinely in the reality of the accusations against her and offered no further resistance. The denunciations of fifteen other witnesses had, in any case, made any protestations of innocence on her part futile. In court, where she was routinely denied any defence, the judges seemed interested primarily in obtaining from her the names of other accomplices. In deference to their wishes the defendant gave copious details of the sabbats she had attended, listing the names of many of the other witches allegedly present and those of their attendant demons. Among other misdeeds she had, she admitted, used magic to raise storms and to enter locked cellars and had also exhumed the corpses of children and desecrated the sacred host.

By now the accused had furnished the court with more than enough evidence to pass a guilty verdict and also to proceed with charges against numerous other suspects. A final perfunctory note in the scribe's record, for Friday, 17 December 1637, reads: 'She dies penitent.'

Many other similar trials were staged in Eichstätt both before and after this case. It has been estimated that between one and two thousand accused witches were burned in the town during the period of the witch hysteria.

See also BAVARIA; GERMANY.

elder Judas was said to have hanged himself from an elder tree and Christ's cross was also reputed to have been made of elder wood, hence its evil reputation. Superstition had it that elder plants were often inhabited by spirits, and furthermore that if elder was burned on the domestic hearth the DEVIL himself would come down the chimney. Because of such ominous associations, witches favoured elder for their WANDS – although the pungent smell of cut elder was reputed to deter witches, and a household could be protected from their spells if a bough of elder picked on the last day of April was hung over the doorway (or if the inhabitants took to wearing AMULETS made of the wood). Elder was never to be taken indoors, however, as it would bring death in with it, and children beaten with elder sticks would fail to grow properly. Decorating a cradle with elder was especially dangerous, for FAIRIES would steal the baby lying in it.

More usefully, however, if anyone who suspected witchcraft was at play dabbed a little elder juice on their eyes they would be able to perceive what witches in the neighbourhood were doing. One tradition further had it that cutting a stem of dwarf elder would cause injury to any witch in the vicinity.

Elder was frequently included in the ingredients of witchlore recipes. This might have been because the stems of dwarf elder become reddish in the autumn, suggesting to the uneducated eye that BLOOD ran within the plant (the plant was said to prosper only where human blood had been spilt). Among the medicinal applications of elder was the old belief that if a person wore a piece of elder against the skin they would be cured of rheumatism.

elements The four basic elements of fire, air, earth and water, of which the whole of creation was once believed to be composed. This ancient notion, long predating Christianity, survived into the philosophy of medieval scholars and was one of the laws governing the pseudoscience of alchemy. Man himself was thought to be ruled by the four elements, fire (or yellow bile) representing irascibility, air (or blood) representing confidence, earth (or black bile) representing melancholia, and water (or phlegm) representing calmness. These elements had to be in balance for an individual to prosper, and medical treatment often depended on adjusting the ratio between the four parts. In broader terms, fire and air were considered the active, creative and masculine elements, while earth and water were thought to embody the passive, negative and feminine values.

The theory of the four elements played a significant part in witchcraft ritual. In modern practice their influence is especially obvious in the conventional initiation ceremony. In the course of this the initiate lies on the floor within a MAGIC CIRCLE with the limbs stretched towards the four quarters, or elements, while the head corresponds to a fifth point (as in a PENTAGRAM) to represent the occult force that rules the four 'humours'.

elf-shot In rural communities of former times, any unexplained decline in the health of a person or animal was often blamed on the malevolent interference of witches or FAIRIES, and the hapless victim was widely considered to be 'elf-shot'. According to tradition, malign beings might cause injury and illness in both human and animal victims by firing 'magic' arrows at them. These were sometimes found in the vicinity of the ailing victim as proof of ill doing (carefully preserved arrows have since been identified as prehistoric flint arrowheads).

The Scottish witch Isobel GOWDIE described, in the course of her lengthy voluntary confession, how she had been taught to fire such arrows made by the Devil himself. According to her testimony: 'The Devil sharps them with his own hand, and delivers them to Elf-boys, who whittles and dights them with a sharp thing like a packing needle.' When it came to firing the arrows, Gowdie explained, witches did not use a bow but 'span them from the nails of our thumbs'. The Devil took Gowdie and her friends hunting and between them they shot and killed a ploughman, while Gowdie herself boasted of killing a woman in this way.

Ellis, Dorothy *see* FAMILIAR.

Elphen, Queen of The queen of the elves, who featured in a number of witches' confessions from the sixteenth and seventeenth centuries. The Queen of Elphen was a mysterious figure who sometimes presided over SABBATS in company with the DEVIL himself.

Clearly a variation upon the ancient figure of the GREAT GODDESS, she often demanded the same obeisance from COVEN members that the Devil himself did, insisting that they KISS her buttocks and then taking her choice of the male witches present. According to confessions extracted from the ABERDEEN WITCHES in the 1590s, for instance, she is 'very pleasant, and she can seem old or young when she pleases, and she makes whoever she likes king, and lies with whoever she likes'. She may have been synonymous with the 'Queen of the Faeries' that Isobel GOWDIE described, 'bravely clothed in white linen, and in white and brown clothes'.

Endor, Witch of The 'witch' through whom Saul communicated with the dead, as related in I Samuel, chapter 28, of the Old Testament. The passage concerning the Witch of Endor, who acted as a medium for Saul when he sought advice in the face of a Philistine assault, was often quoted by those seeking to justify the systematic persecution of witches. At Saul's request, the witch conjured up the spirit of Samuel (or a demon impersonating him, according to some critics) and Saul was able to hear Samuel's voice through her.

In reality, the identification of the woman as a witch owes more to niceties of translation than to the Bible, for in the original Hebrew she is described rather as a 'pythoness' (a woman telling fortunes through the inspiration of a python or a spirit). In the English Authorised Version of 1611, however, the translators are quite clear about the nature of the incident, subtitling the chapter with the legend 'Saul consulteth a witch' and describing her as possessing a FAMILIAR (although the concept of every witch possessing such an imp was a relatively new idea, restricted largely to the English witchcraft tradition). This obfuscation had the advantage of appearing to give divine approval to such measures as the Witchcraft Act passed under JAMES I in 1604. As early as 1584 Reginald SCOT questioned the validity of citing the story of the Witch of Endor as justification for the witchcraft persecution, stating that, on the evidence of the original Hebrew, if Saul saw anything at all it was 'an illusion or cozenage'.

England The witchcraft hysteria came relatively late to England, although for many centuries up to 1500 proven evil-doing by any means, including sorcery, had been deemed to deserve severe punishment. In the Middle Ages witchcraft was interpreted as a crime against man, rather than against God, and was dealt with in much the same manner as other offences: cases depended largely upon hard evidence of actual criminality, such as damage to crops or proven threat to life through poisons or spells. Witches were thus judged by their deeds, and proof of MALEFICIA was necessary to obtain a conviction. Records exist of several suspected witches in medieval times being released by the courts or suffering only the mildest of punishments because no one could provide proof of any harm they had done. As late as 1560, indeed, eight men who had actually confessed to conjuration and sorcery were released after a brief stay in the pillory and after promising not to practise witchcraft in the future.

In common with other suspected criminals in medieval times, witches could elect to undergo trial by ordeal. The very first person to be charged with sorcery in England was Agnes, wife of Odo, who was arraigned in 1209 but acquitted after successfully undergoing the ordeal of grasping a red-hot iron. The ecclesiastical courts investigated alleged cases of sorcery and witchcraft until the fourteenth century, handing condemned persons over to the secular authorities for punishment. The first witchcraft trial to be heard in the secular courts took place in 1324, when twenty-seven people were charged in Coventry with consulting necromancers in a plot to kill the King.

English society was fortunate in that the INQUISITION never enjoyed much success on that side of the Channel, largely because it was denied the use of torture to obtain confessions and because the civil courts by tradition would not accept unsupported confessions as evidence and demanded fairly substantial proof of *maleficia*. Cases in which noblemen were implicated were taken rather more seriously by the civil courts, because they involved a risk of treason against the Crown, and defendants might be brought before the Privy Council or arraigned before a court of bishops (*see* COBHAM, ELEANOR, DUCHESS OF GLOUCESTER; WOODVILLE, ELIZABETH).

The first statute to deal specifically with witchcraft was passed in 1542, during the reign of Henry VIII. It made no reference to PACTS WITH THE DEVIL, but was otherwise stern in dictating harsh penalties against alchemists and witches who aimed to perform *maleficia* through black magic, including the use of waxen images. Witchcraft itself, however, was still no grounds for a case – and, as things turned out, only one suspect (later pardoned) was arrested under the Act before it was repealed by Edward VI in 1547. A new Act was prepared in 1559 but failed to become law, and for a few years there was no statute prohibiting witchcraft in English law.

The climate changed significantly in 1563 when new legislation designed to control witches was issued under Elizabeth I. The Queen herself had been the target of various witchcraft plots, and she evidently appreciated that allegations by fortune-telling sorcerers that the monarch had little time to live could easily provoke a rebellion led by those looking to the succession. Several of Elizabeth's Protestant bishops had been influenced by witch burnings that they had witnessed in other countries, and pressed repeatedly for sterner measures to be taken at home. Bishop John Jewel, preaching before the Queen at Oxford around 1560, broke from his prepared text to deliver an alarmist warning about the activities of witches throughout the realm, claiming that because of witches 'Your Grace's subjects pine away even unto death, their colour fadeth, their flesh rotteth, their speech is benumbed, their senses are bereft.'

The Act of 1563 introduced the death penalty for those found guilty of committing murder by sorcery, and terms of imprisonment as well as appearances in the pillory for witches guilty of less serious crimes. Although the new legislation was less severe than laws passed elsewhere in Europe, it was from the date of this Act that the witch mania really took hold in England.

Among the first important witchcraft trials to be based on the 1563 Act were those of the CHELMSFORD WITCHES in 1566 and the ST OSYTH WITCHES in 1582, both in the county of Essex, and that of the WARBOYS WITCHES in Huntingdon in 1593. Essex, a centre of Protestant dissent in the first half of the fifteenth century, came to be considered a hotbed of witchcraft activity and the majority of cases based on Elizabeth's Act came from the south-eastern counties, although subsequent decades saw concentrations of cases in Lancashire and Somerset among other areas. Another Act, in 1581, tightened up the prohibition against fortune-tellers and witches in general, and in all 535 indictments on charges of witchcraft were issued during the Queen's reign. Eighty-two of the witches tried were put to death, the first being sixty-three-year-old Agnes Waterhouse, hanged in Chelmsford in 1566. This was not to say, however, that the courts ignored some of the more dubious evidence: several celebrated cases resulted in the exposure of hoaxes (as, for instance, in the matters of the BURTON BOY in 1597 and the BILSON BOY in 1622, after Elizabeth's reign).

A much more stringent Act altogether replaced earlier measures when it was introduced under JAMES I in 1604. Death by hanging now became mandatory even for first offences if *maleficia* were proved, and it did not matter whether the victim had actually died or not – it was more than sufficient if he or she had, by magic, been 'killed, destroyed, wasted, consumed, pined or lamed in his or her body, or any part thereof'. Making a pact with the Devil also became a felony, as did keeping or consorting with 'any evil and wicked spirit', digging up corpses to use in spells, preparing LOVE POTIONS and divining the whereabouts of hidden treasure. The 1604 Act remained on the statute book until 1736, and it was under this Act that many of the most important English witch trials were prosecuted, including those of the PENDLE WITCHES in 1612, when nine were hanged, and the later generation of Chelmsford Witches in 1645, which resulted in the biggest mass execution during the whole of the English hysteria. In America the act was cited as the basis for the prosecution of the SALEM WITCHES.

The worst years of all were the 1640s, when English society was in any case in considerable turmoil as a result of the Civil War. Most notorious of the English witch-hunters who emerged at this time was Matthew HOPKINS, the self-styled Witchfinder-General who instigated a reign of terror in the Puritan counties of the east in the years 1645–6. Because of the law's reluctance to accept unsupported confessions and to demand proof of guilt, much emphasis was placed by Hopkins and his confederates on the business of PRICKING and searching for the DEVIL'S MARK, which they successfully argued was substantial and undeniable physical proof of a person having made a covenant with the Devil. Also prominent in the confessions that Hopkins and others extracted were detailed descriptions of witches' FAMILIARS. These attendant demons, usually taking the form of domestic animals such as CATS and DOGS, were a peculiarity of the English witchcraft tradition – few Continental witches ever mentioned such creatures.

Unless found guilty of treason, condemned witches were usually hanged rather than burned alive at the stake as they were in Scotland and on the Continent of Europe. Neither were they subject to excessive torture to obtain confessions, although witchfinders such as Matthew Hopkins became adept at extracting testimony by such means as sleep deprivation (a process known as WATCHING AND WAKING, enforced walking (*see* WALKING A WITCH) and restricting suspects to a diet of bread and water. Another favourite witch test was SWIMMING, until it was banned by a Parliamentary Commission in 1645.

Typical victims – although there were exceptions – were confused old peasant women, resented by their neighbours and feared because of their solitary and sometimes antisocial ways. All too often the cases against them depended upon hearsay or on highly unreliable testimony obtained from young children, encouraged in their denunciations by witch-hating fanatics, ill-intentioned relatives or gullible priests and judges.

The witchcraft mania gradually died down, as elsewhere in Europe, in the latter half of the seventeenth century, not least through the enlightened attitude taken by such judges as Sir John HOLT, the Chief Justice who acquitted every witch brought before him. The 1604 statute under which most of the trials had been conducted was finally repealed in 1736, during the reign of George II, and the last hanging on a charge of witchcraft took place in Exeter in 1684, when Alice MOLLAND was executed. The last person to be convicted on charges of witchcraft was Jane WENHAM, tried in Hertford in 1712 and later pardoned. The last serious attempt to have someone tried on charges of witchcraft was made at Leicester in 1717, when Jane Clarke and her son and daughter, all from Great Wigston, were accused – after undergoing the ordeals of swimming and SCORING ABOVE THE BREATH – of various offences by no fewer than twenty-five of their neighbours. They were allowed to go free after the jury threw out the indictments against them.

It is impossible to state for certain how many people were put to death in England for witchcraft during the years 1542–1736, but most authorities agree that there were at least a thousand victims.

After this time, although witchcraft was no longer illegal, people throughout the land continued to fear the activities of witches for many years. In 1751 Ruth OSBORNE, suspected by locals of being a witch, was beaten to death by an angry mob whose ringleader was later hanged for murder. Belief in the reality of witchcraft was widespread until the middle of the nineteenth century, and as late as 1879 a man named William Bulwer, of Etling Green in Norfolk, was brought to trial for assaulting and insulting an eighteen-year-old neighbour called Christiana Martins and her mother, both of whom he had accused of being witches. When the magistrates tried to get to the bottom of the quarrel Bulwer made no bones about his doubts concerning the Martins:

> Mrs Martins is an old witch, gentlemen, that's what she is, and she charmed me, and I got no sleep for her for three nights, and one night at half-past eleven o'clock, I got up because I could not sleep, and went out and found a walking-toad under a clod that had been dug with a three-pronged fork. This is why I could not rest; she is a bad old woman, and her daughter is just as bad, gentlemen. She would bewitch anyone; she charmed me and I got no rest day and night for her, till I found this walking-toad under the turf.

Isolated cases of witchcraft belief have continued to surface into modern times, with the occasional apparently ritual killing or the discovery of disturbed graves and so forth. The twentieth century saw a revival in interest in witchcraft as an occult science speculatively descended (though the link is highly tenuous) from pre-Christian cults. The last references to witchcraft were finally removed from the statute book by the British Parliament in 1951.

See also BATEMAN, MARY; BURY ST EDMUNDS WITCHES; CROWLEY, ALEISTER; DARRELL, JOHN; DEE, DR JOHN; DR LAMB'S DARLING; DRUMMER OF TEDWORTH; DUMMY; EXETER WITCHES; FAIRFAX, EDWARD; FAVERSHAM WITCHES; FLOWER, JOAN; GARDNER, GERALD; GLANVILL, JOSEPH; GOLDEN DAWN, HERMETIC ORDER OF THE; GUNTER, ANNE; HALE, SIR MATTHEW; HARSNETT, SAMUEL; LEICESTER BOY; MAIDSTONE WITCHES; NORTHAMPTON WITCHES; ST ALBANS WITCHES; SOMERSET WITCHES; WALTON, CHARLES; WAPPING WITCH; WICCA.

esbat The monthly gathering of a modern witches' COVEN. Ideally, esbats are timed to coincide with nights when there is a full moon, and may be held either in the open air or indoors. Traditionally, every coven holds thirteen esbats in a year, in accordance with the lunar calendar. Modern witches believe that only three magical rites (to provide assistance to someone when they are ill or in trouble, for instance) may be attempted at a single esbat, as more would exhaust their potency. At the close of a modern esbat participants may partake of crescent-shaped cakes and wine as an expression of thanksgiving.

See also SABBAT.

Essex, Countess of *see* OVERBURY, SIR THOMAS.

Essex Witches *see* CANEWDON WITCHES; CHELMSFORD WITCHES; ST OSYTH WITCHES.

evil eye The bewitching of a person or an animal by 'overlooking' them. In the past, the power of the evil eye was much feared and suspected witches were frequently accused of causing injury and even death by such 'fascination', which usually consisted of a baleful stare. Among the more notable trials in which allegations of fascination were voiced in court were those of Janet Wishart, one of the ABERDEEN WITCHES, Elizabeth Device, one of the PENDLE WITCHES, and Bridget Bishop, one of the SALEM WITCHES.

References to the evil eye are to be found in the BIBLE and in the writings of Virgil, among others of the ancient world. The English demonologist William PERKINS, writing in the late sixteenth century, was clearly conscious that the tradition was of ancient origins:

> It is an old received opinion, that in malicious and ill-disposed persons, there proceed out of the eye with the beams noisome and malignant spirits, which infect the air, and do poison or kill not only them with whom they are daily conversant, but others also whose company they frequent, of what age, strength, or complexion so ever they be.

Anyone with a squint, uneven or deep-set eyes, eyes of different colours, cross-eyes or any other abnormality of a similar kind might be accused of overlooking victims, particularly if they were caught staring at them or shooting them a severe glance. People with piercing blue or green eyes were considered particularly likely to possess such power.

Superstitious people once took elaborate measures to protect themselves from the influence of the evil eye (see WITCH BALL). Children and livestock, especially pigs, were said to be particularly vulnerable to such magic and were consequently made to wear AMULETS or inscribed rings reputed to deter such threats. One counter measure was the carrying of a knotted cord, the KNOTS in which had been ritually tied while chanting certain NAMES OF POWER (a procedure still practised by witches and occultists today). Other amulets that might be worn included pieces of coral, red ribbons, and necklaces of betony leaves, bittersweet, woody nightshade or blue beads.

If, despite these precautions, such magic was still thought to be at work, various incantations might be uttered in an attempt to avert disaster. In extremis, one remedy was to spit in the guilty party's eye, while another involved burning the carcass of any animal killed through the influence of the evil eye in order to inflict excruciating pain upon the person responsible. Sticking pins in an effigy of the person suspected of using the power of the evil eye was also reputed to break the spell. Alternatively, making the sign of the cross, the 'fig sign' or the 'Devil's horns' (holding down the middle two fingers of the hand with the thumb) in the direction of the suspect might have the desired effect.

If all else failed, recourse might be made to a WHITE WITCH, who would typically recite a counter-spell of his or her own. An example from medieval England ran thus:

Three biters hast thou bitten
The hart, ill eye, ill tongue.
Three biters shall be thy Boote,
Father, Sonne, and Holy Ghost or God's name.
In worship of the five wounds of our Lorde.

A strikingly similar counter-spell was recorded in Spain well into the twentieth century:

Three have done evil to you.
Three have to be taken away.
Who are the three persons of the Holy Trinity?
Father, Son, and Holy Ghost.
Shepherd who came to the fountain,
Take away the Evil Eye
From whom you put it on.

Rather different was the procedure outlined by Scottish witches to solve the same problem: 'Go to a ford, where the dead and the living cross, draw water from it, pour it into a coggie [drinking vessel] with three girds [rings] over a crosset [medieval coin], and then sprinkle the water over the victim of the ill eye.'

Belief in the power of the evil eye has survived into modern times, with gypsies and fortune-tellers often being suspected of such skill. In the 1930s no less a personage than the exiled king of Spain, Alfonso XIII, was widely rumoured to be able to harm the fortunes of his enemies simply by 'overlooking' them.

See also EGG.

executions Condemned witches were executed by a wide variety of means throughout the witch mania of the sixteenth and seventeenth centuries. In England and colonial America they were usually hanged, being burned alive only if found guilty of treason (which could include 'petty treason' against one's husband). In Scotland and most of Continental Europe, however, witches were generally put to death in the manner previously reserved for heretics, usually by burning at the stake.

It was the INQUISITION which established burning as an appropriate method of execution, although the Inquisitors handed condemned witches over to the secular authorities for sentences to be carried out; numerous authorities subsequently confirmed this as the best method, reflecting the seriousness of the crimes involved. In Italy and Spain condemned persons were traditionally burned alive, although the German, Scottish and French courts generally permitted them to be garrotted at the stake or hanged before their bodies were burned to ashes (as they had to be in order to destroy the magical powers of the accused completely). They were burned alive, however, if they withdrew their confessions before execution.

In 1608 the Earl of Mar complained to the Privy Council about one appalling incident in which the accused were still alive when the fires were lit, writing that 'some of them died in despair, renouncing and blaspheming; and others, half burned, broke out of the fire and were cast alive in it again until they were burned to the death'. In cases where the court was disinclined to show a particularly stubborn witch mercy the fire would be built of green logs so that it burned much more slowly and prolonged the death agony.

Many children were among those executed by the witch courts. Although some judges chose to take account of extreme youth in convicted witches and sentenced them to terms of imprisonment or flogging rather than death, children as young as eleven are recorded to have died at the stake. Nicolas REMY, for instance, expressed regret that as a judge he had contented himself in the main to sentencing children to flogging as they saw their parents burned.

Executions were big public occasions, often conducted with some ceremony. Spectators were alerted to the imminence of an execution by the blaring of trumpets or the tolling of bells, which might be wrapped in wet cloth to make the sound more chilling.

The crowds were frequently swollen by large numbers of children, who were given a holiday in order to see executions take place. Condemned prisoners were led out in procession and made to listen to a recitation of their crimes, after which they were required to confirm their guilt. If they refused to do so they might be returned to the torturer. Attendant priests might deliver lengthy sermons on the evils of witchcraft, and very occasionally the condemned person was allowed to say a few words. Hymns might be sung as the prisoner was put to death. In some parts of the Continent it was quite common, once the execution had been duly carried out, for the mayor and other officials to sit down to a lavish meal paid for out of the estate of the dead witch.

It is impossible to know how many witches were executed throughout Europe and America in the years 1450–1750, with different authorities suggesting anything from fourteen thousand to two hundred thousand (perhaps thirty thousand at the hands of the Inquisition). Half of these were put to death in the German states (in contrast to the thousand or so who died in England and the 4400 or more killed in Scotland).

See also BURNING OF WITCHES.

Exeter Witches The case of Susanna Edwards, Temperance Lloyd and Mary Trembles, three destitutes who were tried for witchcraft in Exeter in 1682. One of the last major witchcraft trials staged in England, that of the Exeter Witches centred on the Devon port of Bideford, where the three were suspected of being members of a COVEN. Temperance Lloyd, queen of the alleged coven, had twice been tried for witchcraft already, while Susanna Edwards had been recruited by the DEVIL himself (whom she met in the guise of a black-dressed gentleman crossing Parsonage Close) and Mary Trembles had been invited to join by Edwards.

On being arrested, Susanna Edwards grave her gaoler a long glare: when he was immediately seized by a fit, accusations that she had the power of the EVIL EYE were inevitably voiced. Edwards's account of her meeting with the Devil on Parsonage Close caused a sensation and the three women's voluntary confessions, imaginative and shocking, left little room for doubt concerning their culpability in the eyes of the public. None the less, some of the evidence brought against the Bideford women was tenuous in the extreme. One 'witness' gave as the sum total of his testimony the fact that he had seen a CAT jump in at the window of one of the accused. According to Roger North, who wrote an account of the trial, 'This informant saith he saw a cat leap in at her window, when it was twilight; and this informant further saith, that he verily believeth the said cat to be the devil, and more saith not.'

The judge, described as a 'mild, passive man', was inclined to take pity on the three impoverished and clearly confused and frightened old women before him, but the whole of Exeter seemed to be of a different opinion. As North reported:

> The women were very old, decrepit and impotent, and were brought to the assizes with as much noise and fury of the rabble against them as could be shewed on any occasion. The stories of their acts were in everyone's mouth ... all which the country believed, and accordingly persecuted the wretched old creatures.

It became evident that there would be a riot if the three women were acquitted, and in the end the judge capitulated. Susanna Edwards, Temperance Lloyd and Mary Trembles were sentenced to death and all three were hanged on 25 August 1682. It was reported that Susanna Edwards and Mary Trembles both wept on their way to the gallows, while Temperance Lloyd chewed nonchalantly on a piece of bread.

See also MOLLAND, ALICE.

exhumation *see* GRAVE-ROBBING.

exorcism The expulsion of DEMONS or other evil spirits reputed to have taken POSSESSION of a person, place or object. In its simplest form, an exorcism required no more than a dousing of holy water accompanied with orders or threats directed at the demon concerned. Records of one seventeenth-century exorcism describe how a demon quitted its victim in horror after the exorcist who was called in condemned it as a 'ninny, a drunkard and a sow'. Other evil spirits took more dislodging, requiring lengthy rituals, prolonged argument between exorcist and demon and thrashing of the victim's body with sticks.

The Christian service of exorcism is regarded with a doubtful eye by many modern priests, but requests for the ceremony continue to be made (now mostly in connection with hauntings) and some – mostly Catholic – priests, with special authorisation from their bishop, specialise in such rituals. WHITE WITCHES too will perform services of exorcism, similarly invoking the assistance of God, Christ and the twelve Apostles (and perhaps other friendly spirits) to drive out unwanted demons. The latter type of exorcist draws a MAGIC CIRCLE in which to work and may advise carrying out a symbolic sacrifice or perhaps a ritual involving sex magic.

The ceremony of exorcism was mentioned in the New Testament and candidates for baptism were routinely exorcised of the demons that were presumed to have infested them before they turned to Christ. In subsequent centuries exorcists were often called in to deliver the possessed from the demons that tormented them, causing them fits and terrible pain or leading them into mischief. Originally it was believed that only certain gifted individuals could perform such services, but later any priest was deemed capable of undertaking the procedure, which was known in many different variations.

Fetching the exorcist was often the first line of defence adopted by the authorities in the much-publicised cases involving young girls incarcerated in French convents in the seventeenth century (*see* AIX-EN-PROVENCE NUNS; AUXONNE NUNS; BAVENT, MADELEINE; LOUDUN NUNS) and similar action was taken in many other cases. Often the attentions of the exorcist (or the satisfaction to be had at attracting great public interest) was sufficient to bring the symptoms to an end.

The ritual of a full exorcism was complex, demanding considerable perseverance and patience on the part of priest or white witch. If an exorcism failed on the first attempt it might be repeated time after time until a satisfactory result was obtained. The exorcist, ideally holding the service at midnight, sternly demanded that the demon depart from the body it inhabited; the modern service begins with the adjuration: 'I rebuke thee! I rebuke thee! I rebuke thee! I abjure thee and summon thee forth from this man/woman.' Further pressure was applied in the form of prayers and by the use of holy water. A variation of the 'bell, book and candle' procedure used in the process of excommunicating someone might also be carried out. In former times, the victims of possession were encouraged to breathe noxious fumes in the hope that this would smoke out the demon lurking within. Once this had been achieved (one account described how the demon was drawn out of a victim's nostrils) the nine openings of the body were sealed to prevent the exorcised spirit from regaining entrance. FLAGELLATION was also said by some to be of help. The exorcist attempted to identify the demon by name, and to establish how many devils were involved and whether they were prepared to leave of their own accord, before he set about expelling them by force.

The ritual of exorcism, with its alternation between prayer and threats, might sometimes have had a beneficial psychosomatic effect upon allegedly possessed people, but there have been instances when it has had the opposite effect. In 1975 a Yorkshireman exorcised by a priest of the demons he claimed were tormenting him went out and killed his wife shortly afterwards, ripping out her eyes and tongue so that she choked on her own blood.

Fairfax, Edward *c.*1580–1635. English scholar and gentleman of Fewston in Yorkshire, who in 1621 instigated a witchcraft trial involving six local women. The affair began when the distinguished scholar's two young daughters started to suffer fits and to complain of visions. The symptoms went on for months and doctors were unable to suggest any medical cause. The two girls laid the blame for their afflictions at the feet of Elizabeth Fletcher and five other women from the Forest of Knaresborough, who, they claimed, met at Timble Gill to share midnight feasts with the DEVIL and had sent their FAMIL-IARS to trouble their victims. When one of the Fairfax girls, Helen, was found wandering the moors on her own, she alleged that she had been carried there by one of the witches and had got a glimpse of the coven gathered around a blazing fire.

Edward Fairfax found no reason to doubt the testimony of his daughters and consequently took his suspicions to the courts. His allegations gained credence when a neighbour, John Jeffray, claimed that his daughter Maud had also been bewitched by the women. The six suspects were taken to the Assizes at York to be examined. When the girls were brought into their presence all three fell into a trance-like state and had to be taken out of the room to recover. The justices were cautious, however, and questioned the young victims closely, perhaps remembering the warnings from JAMES I against accepting unsupported accusations. Maud Jeffray quickly retracted her allegations and confessed that her father had put her up to it. Although the Fairfax girls refused to make any similar confessions, it was presumed that they had been influenced by the Jeffrays and the trial was soon halted. John Jeffray was thrown into prison and the six women were released.

Edward Fairfax's transcript of the trial, illustrated by the Reverend Miles Gale of Keighley, remains an interesting record of the affair.

fairies The mythical 'little people' who for centuries past have been claimed to haunt secluded rural locations, working magic and indulging in mischief against unsuspecting humans. There are many different types of fairy, some friendly, but others – such as the boggarts, brownies and goblins – decidedly hostile towards humans. Opinions have differed as to their nature: some have identified them as the spirits of the dead, while others have described them more in terms of minor deities of the countryside, perhaps relics of some diminutive Celtic race, or as fallen angels. They are said to inhabit a realm beneath the ground, accessible through certain caves or hillsides.

The lore of fairies sometimes overlaps that of witches and sorcerers, and belief in their existence was certainly strong throughout Europe when the witch hysteria was at its height. Indeed, in the seventeenth century many people believed it was risky even to utter the word 'fairy' and used such euphemisms as 'the good neighbour' instead. In Ireland, where the witch mania never really gripped the popular imagination as it did elsewhere, many people none the less greatly feared the active interference of fairies, usually in the guise of malevolent leprechauns, and persecuted as witches those who were said to consort with them (*see* CLEARY, BRIDGET).

Like witches, fairies were unpredictable and could prove both friendly and hostile, and their powers were to be feared.

Exercising their own brand of magic, the fairies – whose attributes included the power to make themselves invisible – were reputed to steal human babies and replace them with changelings, baleful creatures whom the parents were tricked into caring for. They were also alleged to shoot magic arrows at livestock and humans: many a farmer, on discovering one of his animals to be in a poor physical state, would conclude that it had been ELF-SHOT, either by a fairy or by a witch. Interestingly, the Scottish witch Isobel GOWDIE, who described how she was once taken to meet the King and Queen of the Fairies, claimed to have been taught how to shoot such magic arrows as part of her training in witchcraft. As further evidence of the popular link between witches and fairies, the interrogators of JOAN OF ARC in 1431 tried to make her confess that as a child she had danced round a Fairies' Tree and hung garlands upon it. Other witches, such as Agnes Hancock in 1438 and John Walsh in 1566, admitted to treating wounds made by fairy magic and to consulting the 'little people' for advice.

According to tradition it was particularly hazardous to venture near spots where fairies were said to roam on HALLOWE'EN, when the little people – like the witches – were said to be especially active. Many eyewitness accounts exist of people accidentally coming across fairy processions in progress from one fairy hill to another, but the witnesses were usually punished for their temerity in spying on such activities. Anyone daring to venture into the underground kingdom of the fairies was equally likely to come to grief. Penalties imposed on those who trespassed on the fairy realm might range from mild practical jokes to death. A typical punishment was blinding: in 1555, for instance, an alleged witch called Joan Tyrrye claimed that she had lost the sight of one eye after catching a glimpse of a fairy at Taunton market.

Some visitors were made welcome, however. An unnamed Yorkshireman, accused of witchcraft practices in 1653, confessed that a fairy who had taken pity on his penniless condition had admitted him to the fairy kingdom. There he had been shown how to administer a special fairy powder to treat the sick, and was thus enabled to make a living. The jury eventually acquitted the accused man, who was described as 'a very simple and illiterate person'.

See also FAIRY RING; HAGSTONE.

fairy ring Dark green ring on a lawn or in a meadow caused by the presence of fungi in the soil, but traditionally identified as a favourite haunt of the FAIRIES. Legend had it that the fairies danced round these rings at midnight and that any human foolish enough to fall asleep within one would fall into their power. These sites, claimed by some to mark the location of fairy villages, have long been reputed to be magical places where occult power is concentrated. They were therefore favourite locations for performing spells and ceremonies.

familiar A demon or imp, usually in the outward form of an animal, that was assigned to a witch or sorcerer to carry out magic on their command. The concept of the witch's familiar was largely an invention of the English and Scottish witchcraft tradition; there were relatively few cases from the Continent in which alleged witches were accused of keeping such supernatural beings, although the idea was probably descended from primitive animal worship of the kind once common throughout Europe. The notion crossed the Atlantic with English settlers and featured in several famous American cases, including that of the SALEM WITCHES.

Under the terms of the Witchcraft Act of 1604 it became a felony in England 'to consult, covenant with, entertain, employ, feed, or reward any evil and wicked spirit'. The idea of the witch's familiar really came into its own, however, in the 1640s, when the notorious Witchfinder-General Matthew HOPKINS extracted from various suspects details of their supernatural attendants. On his first investigation into witchcraft, conducted against Elisabeth Clarke of Manningtree, Essex, he even claimed to have laid eyes on her familiars himself. He was able to describe at some length the five assorted imps that came into the room where he was questioning Clarke, who by then had been kept awake for three days and nights on end (*see* WATCHING AND WAKING). Hopkins recalled the appearances of these five imps, before ten witnesses, in his *The Discovery of Witches*:

1. Holt, who came in like a white kitling.

2. Jarmara, who came in like a fat spaniel without any legs at all, she said she kept him fat, for she clapt her hand on her belly, and said he suckt good blood from her body.

3. Vinegar Tom, who was like a longlegg'd greyhound, with an head like an ox, with a long tail and broad eyes, who when this

discoverer spoke to, and bade him go to the place provided for him and his Angels, immediately transformed himself into the shape of a child of four years old without a head, and gave half a dozen turns about the house, and vanished at the door.

4. Sack and Sugar, like a black rabbit.

5. Newes, like a polecat. All these vanished away in a little time.

The familiar, usually identified as one of the minor deities of Hell, was a gift from the DEVIL at a witch's INITIATION, although in practice familiars were often passed from one witch to another or inherited. The idea of such low-ranking demons serving accused witches was convenient to those who supported the witchcraft persecution, because it bypassed the criticism implied by those who scoffed at the idea that the Devil himself would deign to be at the beck and call of often half-witted old crones.

In many cases the familiar took the form of a domestic animal, most commonly a CAT, TOAD, HARE, BLACKBIRD, CROW or DOG (exactly the sort of creature, in fact, that a lonely old woman would be most likely to keep as a companion). But there were also cases in which the accused person was alleged to have a familiar in the shape of a HEDGEHOG, WEASEL, ferret, mole, mouse, rat or insect, such as a bee or grasshopper, among other creatures. Larger animals, for instance HORSES and stags, were known as 'divining familiars' and, although they were not kept by any particular witch, could be consulted for information about the future.

Some witches described much more outlandish creatures that combined the attributes of more than one animal, although few independent witnesses ever claimed to have seen them. Bridget Bishop of Salem was one of those to have contact with such a being, describing 'a black Thing ... the Body was like that of a Monkey, the Feet like a Cock's, but the Face most like a man's ...'. Another witch startled her interrogators by claiming to have a familiar in the form of a cat that was brilliant blue in colour. Many familiars were also apparently able to transform themselves from one shape to another at will.

In some cases familiars took human form, and several witches talked of handsome young men in black who performed their every wish in exchange for the promise of their soul at a future date. Margaret Johnson, one of the PENDLE WITCHES, was attended by a well-dressed man who called himself Mamilion, while Anne Chattox, also from Pendle, spoke of her familiar being 'a thing like a Christian man'. Under questioning in 1645 Ellen Driver, of Framlingham in Suffolk, actually claimed she had married her familiar, who was human in every aspect but for a pair of cloven feet: they had two children (both changelings) before he died or otherwise 'disappeared'. Another accused witch described how her familiar manifested in the form of the prophet Daniel, and records exist of another familiar preferring the shape of a bishop who vomited streams of fire. Usually, however, these familiars in human shape were assumed to be the Devil himself rather than one of his minions (as in the case of Alice KYTELER and her 'Robin Artisson').

Some witches confessed to owning more than one familiar spirit. Ursula Kempe, one of the ST OSYTH WITCHES, admitted to keeping no fewer than four familiars – a grey cat called Tyttey, a black cat named Jack, a toad called Pygine and a lamb named Tyffin (defying the presumption that no demons could manifest in the form of lambs or doves because of their holy associations). Another of the St Osyth Witches, Cicely Celles, evidently had trouble keeping her familiar spirit in check. Her nine-year-old son described how a black imp not dissimilar in form to his sister had seized him by the toe, at which he had cried out to his father to rescue him: 'Whereat his father said to his mother, "Why, thou whore, cannot you keep your imps from my children?" Whereat she presently called it away from her son, saying "Come away, come away." At which speech it did depart.'

Even if a witch was not found to possess any animal that might be suspected of being her familiar, this was not necessarily an insurmountable obstacle to those seeking her conviction. Any animal that had been seen anywhere in her vicinity, from a passing dog to a cat leaping on to her windowsill, might be confidently identified as her attendant demon.

Familiars were baptised at a special ceremony, often being given bizarre un-Christian names such as Pyewackit, Gibbe, Peckin the Crown and Rutterkin. They were often well fed and were traditionally rewarded for their work by a few drops of their master's or mistress's blood. Some witches added a few drops of their blood to the food they gave their familiars, while Ursula Kempe claimed that she allowed her imps to suck blood from her thigh. Others boasted a supernumerary nipple at which they suckled their demonic attendants; discovery of such a nipple was taken as convincing proof of guilt (*see* WITCH'S MARK).

Typical outrages supposedly executed by familiars on behalf of their masters or mistresses ranged from souring milk and damaging livestock and property to committing murder. Some witches were also reported to fly on the backs of their familiar spirits rather than upon the conventional BROOMSTICK. One case involving murder was that of Dorothy Ellis of Cambridgeshire, who admitted in 1647 that her cat-familiar had killed some cattle belonging to Thomas Hitch, had lamed John Gotobed after he had thrown stones at her and had procured the death of the infant daughter of Thomas Salter, who had caused her some unrecorded offence. Other notable examples of trials that were much influenced by evidence of familiars included that of the CHELMSFORD WITCHES, several of whom confessed to owning in turn a murderous cat-familiar called Sathan, among other imps, that of the WARBOYS WITCHES, and that of the notorious Scottish witch Isobel GOWDIE. Gowdie alleged, apparently without coercion, that 'Each one of us has a spirit to wait upon us, when we please to call him.'

When the time came for a witch's trial it was usual for the alleged familiars to go missing, and there are no records of familiars reappearing to rescue their erstwhile owners once they had been confined in prison. If such demons in disguise could be located, they were immediately burned to death.

See also FLOWER, JOAN.

fascination *see* EVIL EYE.

Faust, Dr fl.1500–40. Semi-legendary German theologian and magician, whose dealings with the DEVIL were memorably dramatised by Christopher Marlowe and Johann Wolfgang von Goethe among others. According to the legend and to the many plays and books based on it, Faust was a brilliant scholar who made a pact with BEELZEBUB, selling his soul for a few years of pleasure and uninhibited knowledge-seeking on Earth. Among other excesses he was reputed to have committed, he once swallowed a rival magician whole and on another occasion attempted (unsuccessfully) to fly all the way to Venice. As the hour of his descent into Hell approached, however, he came to regret his decision – a salutary lesson to all those who might be considering a similar deal.

The relationship between the Faust of the theatre and the Faust of reality is uncertain. It seems there was indeed a magician of the name in sixteenth-century Germany, but attempts to identify him as Johann Fust, a printer born in 1400 who died of the plague in 1466, are now dismissed by most authorities. Another contender was Georgius Sabellicu Faustus Junior, a necromancer, astrologer, alchemist, soothsayer and clairvoyant recorded in Germany in the early sixteenth century. This luminary was sacked as a teacher after being suspected of indulging in indecent behaviour with his pupils, and some years later he was banished from Ingolstadt for soothsaying. One Johann Faust, meanwhile, gained a theology degree in Heidelberg in 1509. Maybe the Faust of fiction is an amalgam of several people. A book on demonology, attributed to Faust, was published in Germany in 1505.

Marlowe's play *Dr Faustus* depicts the pact made between the learned doctor and Mephistopheles (*see* PACT WITH THE DEVIL) and relates the wayward scholar's tragic end, carried off to Hell by the Devil himself. A celebrated theatrical legend describes how the famous English actor Edward Alleyn, playing Faustus, once succeeded in accidentally summoning up a real devil in the scene where the doctor invokes Mephistopheles. Alleyn's shock at finding a demon waiting for him in the wings was sufficient, the legend claims, to persuade him to give up the stage permanently and to devote himself to good works, which included the foundation of Dulwich College in London.

Faversham Witches An outbreak of witchcraft hysteria that seized the town of Faversham, Kent, in 1645. The case was typical of many others of the period, depending largely upon confessions extracted under duress and expanding to take in more suspects before it finally petered out.

Crucial to the development of the case was the confession of Joan Williford, who admitted a wide range of witchcraft practices. She had, it was claimed, become first acquainted with the DEVIL when he appeared to her in the form of a small DOG and invited her to give him her allegiance. She accordingly sold him her soul and signed the pact in her own blood (*see* PACT WITH THE DEVIL), in return for revenge against one Thomas Letherland and his wife Mary Woodruff, and was further rewarded by promises that she should never want for money. She was also granted a FAMILIAR called Bunnie, whose services to her over the ensuing twenty years included depositing an enemy, Thomas Gardler, in a cesspool.

Also named as witches in Williford's confession were Jane Holt, Joan Argoll and Elisabeth Harris. A specific charge against Harris was that she had put a curse on a boat belonging to one John Woodcott after her own son had drowned while sailing in it. As a result of the curse, it was alleged, the boat was lost. Argoll, meanwhile, had laid curses on a man called Major and another called John Mannington, both of whom had suffered in consequence.

Williford's confession, which ended with a claim that the Devil had twice visited her in prison in the form of a mouse in order to suck her blood, was more than enough to seal her fate. She and her accomplices were all executed at Faversham on 29 September 1645.

fern Plant that was once widely believed to boast a variety of magical powers. Sometimes ominously referred to as the 'Devil's brushes', ferns were often considered evil plants that would bring harm to anyone who cut or touched them. Others, though, claimed that they were lucky and would ward off evil spirits if used to decorate a horse's collar. If brought into the house they reputedly provided protection against lightning. Some people carried fern flowers as these were believed to ward off witches, although others were anxious that anyone who carried the leaf of a fern would attract adders.

Witchlore suggested that by tossing a fern flower in the air and noting where it fell a person might locate buried treasure. It was also said that fern seeds collected on Midsummer's Eve and carried on the person bestowed the power of INVISIBILITY and were an essential ingredient of FLYING OINTMENT. The seeds might also be consumed as a sure remedy for stomach ache (as long as they came from a plant growing on an oak tree). Potions made from the seeds were used for the treatment of minor wounds, coughs and inflamed eyes, among other conditions.

The male fern, sometimes popularly called Lucky Hands, was particularly prized for its efficacy against witchcraft. Anyone who picked a male fern on Midsummer's Eve, stripped it down to five unfurled fronds (which look rather like fingers) and then smoked it over a bonfire until hard could enjoy complete immunity from the threats of witches and evil spirits by carrying this 'lucky hand'.

Fery, Jeanne b.1559. French nun, whose alleged POSSESSION by no fewer than eight devils in the years 1573–85 attracted much interest. Fery suffered from violent hysterical fits, in which she was subjected to agonies inflicted by DEMONS identified by the curious names Hérésie, Traitre, Art Magique, Béléal, Vraye Liberté, Namon, Sanguinaire and Homicide. These demons first tormented Fery soon after she was allegedly seduced by the DEVIL when she was fourteen years old, and remained with her until she underwent a service of EXORCISM some eleven years later. The severity of the fits was reduced by bathing in holy water, upon which she would vomit copious amounts of 'filth' and 'hairy worms'. She also displayed a tendency to throw herself out of windows and into rivers. Of particular interest to her contemporaries were the visions of Hell that she said were vouchsafed to her during her possession. The demons also caused her internal pain and forced her to swear and blaspheme. At other times she was overcome with a sense of childish happiness.

The exorcism that took place on 24 May 1585 produced some odd effects. At first Fery went completely rigid, her eyes fixed on a statue of Mary Magdalene, then she giggled, trembled, beat her heart and lost the power of speech, before gradually returning to what was considered a more normal state.

The case of Jeanne Fery was re-examined three hundred years later when an account of it was republished by Dr Magloire Bourneville as an illustration of mental instability.

festivals *see* HALLOWE'EN; WALPURGIS NIGHT.

fetish A CHARM or AMULET that is supposed to have innate magical properties (rather than because it is possessed by some spirit or demon). African tribes have always treasured certain stone and wooden figures reputed to have magic potential, and modern witches and occultists are similarly convinced that certain objects carry with them a magic force that may be tapped in their cere-monies. Witchcraft fetishes range from bones and chalices to mystic symbols such as the HEXAGRAM.

Fian, John d.1591. Scottish schoolteacher from Saltpans (now Prestonpans), near Edinburgh, sometimes identified by the name John Cunningham, who found himself heavily implicated in the trial of the notorious NORTH BERWICK WITCHES which began in 1590. Fian was identified as the leader of the coven that was alleged to have plotted the death of James VI of Scotland (later JAMES I of England), and on 26 December that year he was arrested on charges of witch-craft and high treason. On behalf of the treacherous Earl of Bothwell he was reputed to have acted as secretary for the covens of southern Scotland, keeping records of all who attended meetings.

The details of Dr Fian's indictment were nothing if not fanciful. As well as plotting to have James drowned while sailing to Denmark to join his intended wife, he had also made a PACT WITH THE DEVIL in order to avenge himself on a workman with whom he had argued, had worshipped Satan in North Berwick church, had allowed him-self to be transported to various mountains while in a trance, had robbed graves for ingredients to be used in a variety of spells, had broken into houses by breathing on locks to open them, had flown through the air by magic, had raised storms, had cast horoscopes and had seduced a widow through the use of love charms. It was said that while in pursuit of his aims he had been spotted riding at night on a horse decked out with blazing magic candles. His magic was not, however, infallible: as a result of one spell that had gone awry, Fian had accidentally bewitched a cow into falling in love with him instead of directing the magic successfully at a certain young lady (see LOVE POTION).

The charges may have been laughable, but the treatment to which Fian was subjected most certainly was not. The first stage in his torture was a procedure known as 'thrawing', which involved the victim being jerked roughly about by means of a rope securely tied around his head. After an hour of this abuse had elicited no response from the accused the torturers switched to the infamous BOOTS, crushing Fian's legs three times in succession before the schoolteacher lost consciousness. This lapse into senselessness was blamed as a trick by the Devil to escape further pain, and Fian was searched for charms. Two pins were discovered stuck into his tongue (they had probably been placed there by the gaolers themselves). At this point, in the presence of King James himself, Fian made a complete confession, admitting whatever accusations his interrogators chose to make.

According to one account of the affair (probably fictitious), fortune smiled on the hapless schoolteacher the following night and he managed to escape from prison and to make his way back to Saltpans – though one can only speculate how he did this in view of the hideous injuries to his legs. Rumour had it that the Earl of Bothwell had bribed the gaoler and at Saltpans insisted that Fian recant his confession, which threatened to expose his own involvement; he also provided him with a drug to help him endure further torture. Whatever the truth of the matter, the King expressed alarm at the escape and it was not long before Fians was intercepted and brought back to gaol.

On a second appearance before the King Fian seemed to enjoy a new courage and withdrew his confession, claiming that it had been given only to avoid further pain. This recantation was understandably not well received. Determined to secure a conviction, the authorities, who suspected that the Devil was the source of the accused's renewed resolution, decided on an unusual torture generally associated with the INQUISITION and countries of the Middle East. Using a pair of pincers called a 'turkas', the schoolteacher's fingernails were broken and pulled off, after which the whole length of two needles was forced into the bloodied nailbeds up to and beyond the first joint, causing the most excruciating pain. Incredibly, Fian still refused to confess that he was a witch. Recourse was made once more to the boots, and Fians legs were crushed to the point where 'the blood and marrow spouted forth in great abundance, whereby they were made unserviceable for ever'. Still the schoolteacher refused to cooperate.

Although denied the convenience of a confession, the court, with the support of King James, decided to press ahead with the charges and had no hesitation in imposing the death penalty to make Fian an example for others. On one of the last Saturdays of January 1591 he was strangled on Edinburgh's Castle Hill and then burned as a witch. Dr John Fian's resilience in the face of the cruellest torture remains perhaps the most remarkable feature of a remarkable case.

fig sign *see* EVIL EYE.

Filastre, La *see* CHAMBRE ARDENTE AFFAIR.

Finland As in the other Scandinavian countries, the history of the witchcraft mania in Finland began in the mid-fifteenth century, when measures were taken against sorcerers who sought to divine the future through such means as casting lots and interpreting dreams. The subsequent history of witchcraft in Finland was much influenced by events in Sweden and Germany, which were reported by Scandinavian soldiers and other travellers, although the country was largely spared the excesses that traumatised society in those countries.

Finnish fortune-tellers and witches were excommunicated by the Church in 1573 and the secular authorities became increasingly active against such persons, although suspects were not accused of HERESY as elsewhere in Europe at the time. The first official witchcraft trial in Finland took place at Pernaja in 1595, when an unnamed woman was condemned to death on charges of using magic to harm other people and to induce illnesses, which she later purported to cure. Witch trials became more frequent in the late 1620s, notably in the regions of Pohjanmaa and Ahvenanmaa, where the population was mostly Swedish-speaking, and the clergy were instructed to preach more regularly and sternly on the subject. The panic reached a peak in the 1650s with the worst excesses being witnessed in the Pohjanmaa region, where some fifty cases were brought to trial.

Perhaps the blackest period in the witchcraft hysteria in Finland was the 1670s, when several witches were burned to death on charges that appeared to mirror those alleged in the infamous trial of the MORA WITCHES in Sweden during the previous decade. There was also a rash of cases in Ahvenanmaa between 1666 and 1678, apparently after local judges came under the influence of the works of German demonologists. These trials were unusual in the Finnish experience in that the authorities adopted inquisitorial methods, encouraging the accused to implicate other relations and acquaintances. One notable victim was Karin Persdotter, a beggar's wife, who was persuaded to name another thirteen witches, who were then brought to court.

Proven cases in which MALEFICIA were alleged laid the accused open to the death penalty, while lesser offences led to fines. Laws passed in 1683 directed death by hanging for male witches guilty of murder and burning for their female counterparts. Four years later the death penalty was also imposed on anyone found guilty of making a PACT WITH THE DEVIL, while witches convicted of lesser crimes faced imprisonment on a diet of bread and water, running the gauntlet or whipping. In contrast to proceedings in some other countries, torture was prohibited and accused persons were allowed to produce witnesses in their defence (most of those who died fell into the category of the poor and friendless). As a result there were relatively few instances of the death penalty being imposed: only fifty to sixty suspects were thus condemned, and not all of these were actually executed. There are no records of anyone being put to death as a witch after the death penalty was renewed by an Act of 1734, and the statute itself was abolished in 1779.

Firth, Violet Mary *see* FORTUNE, DION.

five-fold kiss *see* KISS.

Flade, Dietrich d.1589. German judge, who became perhaps the most distinguished person found guilty of being a witch during the witchcraft mania in Germany. Flade was rich, well connected and widely respected in the secular courts. He oversaw the suppression of Protestantism under the Prince-Archbishop of Trevès from 1559, and was rewarded for his service first with the Vice-Governorship of Trèves in 1580 and then by being made Rector of the University in 1586.

The reasons for Flade's downfall were primarily political. Although he approved in theory of the persecution of witches, he had grave doubts about how the laws were being interpreted in the courts and was inclined to leniency in such cases.

This attitude led to criticism from various highly placed witch-hunters, who began to talk of Flade as a 'witch-protector'. Matters came to a head under Johann von Schönenburg, who succeeded to the See of Trèves in 1581. Action against heretics of all kinds was stepped up, with first the Protestants, then the Jews and ultimately witches being singled out for persecution. The first witch to come to trial in Trèves, in 1582, suffered nothing worse than exile, but the Suffragan Bishop Peter BINSFELD and the new Governor, Johann Zandt, who was appointed in 1584, were impatient for examples to be made and felt that Flade was holding them back. A plot was hatched to get rid of the stubbornly lenient judge.

First, Zandt hinted to the Archbishop that he was at risk of being poisoned by Flade, offering as proof of his suspicions the testimony of a slow-witted boy who claimed he had witnessed a SABBAT at which the judge was present. He also reported to the Archbishop that a condemned witch called Maria had named Flade as a witch shortly before her own execution in Pfalzel in June 1587, and that similar accusations had been made in confessions by several other convicted witches. The Archbishop responded to these allegations by ordering Flade to be more severe when passing sentence in witch-craft cases. Then Zandt closed for the kill, presenting to the Archbishop a witch named Margarethe of Euren who claimed to have attended a sabbat at which Flade had called down a curse on the harvest. This was a particularly sensitive issue, as only two good harvests were gathered anywhere in the region in the years 1580–99, the rest having suffered damage from bad weather and from plagues of mice, snails and grasshoppers. Flade had allegedly ensured silence from those present at the sabbat by commanding them to eat a frit-ter made from a child's heart, which would keep their lips sealed under torture – but Margarethe had only nibbled a little of hers.

The seriousness of the charges led to the setting up in July 1588 of a commission to investigate the matter. By October the com-mission had collected so much evidence against Flade, including accusations by many known witches, that the judge attempted to escape from the city – only to be captured and placed under house arrest. The fact that Flade had tried to escape the charges was itself deemed indicative of his guilt.

The Archbishop of Trèves finally ordered the judge's arrest in March 1589, although the reluctance of the courts to arraign so senior a figure led to delays and he was not committed to prison until the end of April. Flade was now brought face to face with his accusers and a court was, with some difficulty, assembled for his prosecution. In order to obtain a confession he was subjected to the torture of STRAPPADO, which proved particularly painful in his case because of a hernia. It was not long before the learned man had con-fessed to attending sabbats, having intercourse with the Devil and indulging in such evil-doing as making slugs out of pellets of earth and then sending them to blight crops. He also named various accomplices, but still the torture continued until at last he admitted plotting the death of the Archbishop himself.

Flade was strangled and his body burned on 18 September 1589. Among the most distinguished of all victims of the witchcraft hysteria, he is remembered now as a man who defended common sense and humanity at a time when the trend was decidedly against them.

    See also TRÉVES WITCHES.

flagellation The use of whipping and beating to achieve a state of ecstasy, as allegedly practised by many witches even today. Extreme religious sects often indulged in self-flagellation in order to 'cleanse' the spirit and to show humility before gods and goddesses in order to win their favour. In ancient Rome, during the Festival of Lupercalia, it was traditional for men to strike with whips any women they met as this was said to please the gods and thus to promote the fertility of both parties. Early Christians similarly employed flagellation as a means to cleanse the mind, in particular to drive out thoughts of lust.

    Actual or symbolic flagellation was long a feature of the witch-craft tradition. Isobel GOWDIE, for instance, claimed that she provoked the DEVIL at her coven into beating her with cords, as this gave her both pain and pleasure. As far back as the thirteenth century flagellation was considered a stimulant to sexual desire and this would seem to be the prime reason why such activity continues to be practised by modern covens – although other authorities suggest that it is used purely to elevate the consciousness of the person involved, so that he or she may more easily commune with the world of demons and spirits. Gerald GARDNER enthusiastically rec-ommended the use of ceremonial flagellation to his followers, setting a pattern followed by many modern covens.

fleeting *see* SWIMMING.

Flower, Joan d.1618. English peasant woman who was tried at Lincoln in March 1618, in company with her daughters Margaret and Philippa Flower, on charges of causing death by witchcraft. Mother Flower was described as a 'monstrous malicious woman', who was widely considered a witch. Her daughter Margaret was in charge of the laundry at Belvoir Castle, the seat of Francis, Sixth Earl of Rutland, a friend of JAMES I, while Joan and Philippa often worked there too as cleaners. When Margaret was dismissed from her post on suspicion of stealing food and staying out at night, the girls allegedly turned to their mother for revenge through magic against the Earl and his family.

Accordingly, Joan Flower cursed the Earl in public and told the girls to obtain from the castle various personal possessions of his family. Among the items subsequently brought to her was the right glove of the Earl's eldest son, Henry, Lord Rosse. Joan Flower rubbed the glove on the back of her FAMILIAR (a cat-demon called Rutterkin) and placed it in boiling water. She then pricked the glove and buried it in order to bring misfortune to its erstwhile owner. Lord Rosse died shortly afterwards, and some four or five years later the Earl's two surviving sons were afflicted with illness, allegedly after similar spells were enacted against them. Feathers from the Countess's bed were also obtained, and these were rubbed against the cat's belly to render the Earl and his wife infertile.

Suspicion of witchcraft was aroused by the misfortunes visited upon the Earl and his family, and the curse that Joan Flower had uttered was now remembered. All three women, who clearly believed in the efficacy of their actions, were arrested and committed for trial, as were other alleged accomplices. During the proceedings that ensued the accused freely admitted plotting evil against the Earl's children and also gave details of various rituals that the coven observed on Blackberry Hill in the Vale of Belvoir. They also made confessions in which they admitted committing various misdeeds and keeping various familiars, in the form of an owl, a white dog, a white mouse and a kitten called Pusse.

When Joan Flower belatedly realised that they were condemning themselves by their own evidence she retracted her confession and, to support her innocence, made the melodramatic gesture of thrusting some dry bread into her mouth with the words: 'May this choke me if I am guilty.' Unfortunately, in front of a startled court, she did indeed choke to death. The judges, Sir Henry Hobart and Sir Edward Bromley, had little hesitation in finding the remaining five women – the two Flower girls, Anne Baker of Bottesford, Eileen Greene of Stathern and Joan Willimot of Goadby Marwood – guilty as charged, and they were hanged at Lincoln on 11 March 1619.

As a footnote to the sorry affair, the tomb of the Sixth Earl of Rutland, who died in 1632, was adorned with carvings representing his children and a note that they 'dyed in their infancy by wicked practice and sorcerye'.

flying *see* TRANSVECTION.

flying ointment   The mysterious ointment that witches were reputed to smear on themselves in order to enjoy the power of flight. Tradition had it that witches smeared both their own naked bodies and sometimes their BROOMSTICKS or other means of flight with the ointment, which was given out by the Devil or prepared according to his instructions, before setting off for their SABBATS. There was some disagreement, however, about how much of the body had to be coated: some authorities claimed that only the breasts, armpits and genitals or the forehead and wrists needed to be smeared, while others insisted that the entire body be covered (to the depth of two inches, by one report). According to Jean de Nynauld in 1615, the skin had to be rubbed with the ointment until it was red so that the mixture might penetrate more deeply.

Ingredients of the ointment, which was usually described as black or dark green, were variously identified as the boiled and reduced fat of babies, the blood of bats, soot and samples of aconite, poplar leaves, fern, hellebore, hemlock and belladonna. In 1608 Francis Bacon wrote that 'the ointment that witches use is reported to be made of the fat of children digged out of their graves; of the juices of smallage, wolfbane, and cinquefoil, mingled with the meal of fine wheat'. In view of the toxic nature of some of the ingredients, it may be that the ointment was itself enough to make the user delirious and to persuade them that they were actually flying.

Reginald SCOT, writing in 1584, discounted the idea that witches actually flew but none the less offered a detailed recipe for flying ointment given to him by an expert in such brews:

The fat of young children, and seethe it with water in a brazen vessel, reserving the thickest of that which remaineth boiled in the bottom, which they lay up and keep, until occasion serveth to use it. They put thereunto *eleoselinum, aconitum, frondes, populeas,* and soot. Another receipt to the same purpose ... *Sium, acarum vulgare, pentaphyllon,* the blood of flittermouse, *solanum somnferum et oleum.* They stamp all these together, and then they rub all parts of their bodies exceedingly till they look red and be very hot, so as the pores may be opened, and their flesh soluble and loose. They join herewithal either fat, or oil instead thereof, that the force of the ointment may the rather pierce inwardly, and so be more effectual. By this means (saith he) in a moonlight night they seem to be carried in the air, to feasting, singing, dancing, kissing, culling and other acts of venery (saith he), with such youths as they love and desire most: for the force of their imagination is so vehement that almost all that part of the brain, wherein the memory consisteth, is full of such conceits.

Under questioning by examiners, relatively few witches openly confessed to using flying ointment. In 1664 Elisabeth Style, one of the SOMERSET WITCHES, described how when the time for the sabbat approached she and her companions would 'anoint their Fore-heads and Hand-Wrists with an Oil the Spirit brings them, which smells raw', while her fellow coven-member Anne Bishop talked of flying after her forehead had been 'anointed with a Feather dipt in Oyl'. Similar confessions were extracted from a small number of accused witches elsewhere in Europe, including Belgium, Sweden and France – although confessions also exist of witches who claimed to enjoy the power of flight without using any flying ointment at all.

In his *De la Lycanthropie* of 1615, Jean de Nynauld gave a number of recipes for flying ointment and discussed their use at some length. Among the anecdotal evidence he quoted in support of his contention that flying ointment could and did work was a curious story he claimed to have been told by a Frankfurt physician in 1603. The physician suspected that his aunt was a witch and spied on her as she rubbed ointment on to her skin before making a night flight. When she had gone he tried some of the ointment on himself and found himself whisked through the night sky to the sabbat, mounted on a calf. As punishment for his temerity in attending the sabbat the calf deposited him in the Rhine on the way home, and he had to be rescued from drowning by a friendly miller.

See also TRANSVECTION.

Fontaine, Françoise fl.1575–1610. Young French girl whose detailed claims of demoniacal POSSESSION led to her trial as a witch in Louviers in 1591. The episode began, as in many similar cases, with the girl being subjected to hysterical fits and convulsions in which she claimed she was being tormented by DEMONS. According to surviving records of the trial she was also prone to fainting, trembling, leaping, paralysis and other easily recognised symptoms of the possessed. At a time when civil war was ravaging France the inhabitants of Louviers were not inclined to take allegations of supernatural activity lightly and, after Françoise claimed that an evil spirit was coming down her chimney to visit her and to provoke poltergeist phenomena, she was put in prison as a precaution.

When the gaolers reported that strange things had begun to happen shortly after Fontaine's arrival it was decided to put her on trial on charges of witchcraft. EXORCISM was attempted, and the girl was then taken to a church where, in front of a large audience, she was stripped and shaved of all hair so that she could be searched for incriminating marks (see WITCH'S MARKS) and subjected to PRICKING.

The evidence presented by Françoise at her own trial was remarkable and caused a considerable stir, not least because of its frank sexual nature. She confessed to signing a PACT WITH THE DEVIL and to having intercourse on a nightly basis with her demon lover, who visited her in her room in the form of a bearded man in black with flashing eyes. The court revelled in the description she gave of his '*membre viril*', which she said was so large and so stiff ('as hard as flint') that she experienced considerable pain on penetration; on one occasion the two partners had become locked together in intercourse and had been unable to separate themselves for some time. Sometimes he had sex with her without even troubling her to remove her clothes. His semen she described as 'very cold'. As proof of these exchanges the girl bared her breasts in court in order to show the love bites he had given her.

A highlight of the court proceedings was the accused girl's sudden seizure by convulsions. Those present were startled to see Fontaine assume the stance of someone being crucified, her arms stretched out to either side where she lay on the ground in the shape of the cross. All attempts to free her arms from their locked positions failed, and observers were alarmed to see her throat swell up and her eyes protrude from her head as sweat broke out on her brow. When someone thought to check if she was still breathing no sign of life could be detected, although her pulse and temperature remained normal.

Curiously, considering the severe attitude taken by other courts in similar cases around the same time, no attempt was made by the authorities to track down the guilty party who was presumed to have bewitched Fontaine. Neither was the girl subjected to torture beyond pricking, nor was any attempt made to secure the death penalty against her on the basis of her freely given confession. Perhaps, it may be speculated, her mental instability was so obvious that even in that age of witchcraft hysteria no one felt inclined to take her allegations very seriously. Whatever the case, the affair was gradually forgotten and, instead of being burned as a witch as she would undoubtedly have been elsewhere, Françoise Fontaine actually seems to have recovered her senses in time, got married and led a relatively normal life.

Forman, Simon *see* OVERBURY, SIR THOMAS.

Förner, Friedrich *see* BAMBERG WITCHES.

Forster, Anne fl. seventeenth century. English countrywoman who was prominent among a group of suspects tried for witchcraft in Morpeth, Northumberland, in 1673. The Morpeth case is interesting for the wealth of detail surrounding the allegations, and also because it implies, in the eyes of some authorities, the existence of a loosely organised system of COVENS throughout Northumberland during the seventeenth century.

At the heart of the case against Anne Forster was the evidence of Anne Armstrong, a maidservant from Stocksfield-on-Tyne, who claimed that she had been bewitched by Forster into carrying her to a sabbat one night just before Christmas. According to Armstrong, she had first met Forster when sent to buy some eggs from her. Following the encounter she had been much troubled by fainting fits, and had been warned by a beggar whom she met that the other woman was a witch and that she would try to ride her spirit like a horse.

With Christmas approaching, Armstrong met Forster once more and this time the alleged witch forced a bridle over Armstrong's head, upon which the maid lost all power to resist her will. Armstrong was subsequently obliged to carry Forster cross-legged to join her companions at Riding Mill Bridge, where the witches held their sabbats. In so doing she got a good look at Forster's confederates, who included several people she knew (and named in court). Most striking of these was a 'long black man riding on a bay galloway, as she thought, which they called their protector'. The members of the coven ordered her to sing for them while they danced and amused themselves changing from one shape to another. Anne Baites, a witch from Morpeth, in quick succession changed into a CAT, a HARE, a greyhound and a bee in an effort to please the Devil (rather than actually changing form, it is likely that she acted out the roles of different animals while pursued by the master of the coven as part of a ritual mating dance). At the end of the proceedings the luckless Armstrong was obliged to carry Forster back home again.

According to Armstrong's testimony, Anne Forster met with her friends on numerous occasions; sometimes it was Forster who used Armstrong as her mount, although other witches demanded similar service of her too. Armstrong was garrulous in describing the details of the ceremonies that she witnessed, recalling in particular a lavish banquet at which no fewer than five covens of thirteen witches each were present. A rope hung down over the gathering from the ceiling, and the witches pulled on it to obtain any food they desired, which was magically produced. The maidservant also described how she had seen the witches bow down in obeisance before a certain large stone, reciting the LORD'S PRAYER backwards in the course of their veneration.

Armstrong went on to make further serious allegations that Forster and the other witches had used their magic to harm enemies and their livestock, saying that she had learned of their misdeeds when they boasted of them to the Devil. Mary Hunter and Dorothy Green had cast a spell over John March's mare, resulting in the animal's death – an accusation that tallied with the story of John March himself, who described how his horse had been pestered by a swallow one evening and had then become ill and died four days later. Elizabeth Pickering of Wittingstall, meanwhile, claimed that Foster had procured the death of a neighbour's child through magic, although other alleged offences were more trivial in nature.

Anne Forster and the other accused witches all denied Armstrong's accusations and it seems from the inconclusive trial records that they were all acquitted (although two of the group were briefly imprisoned). Anne Armstrong herself may have been for a time a willing member of the coven, which may well have existed in some form or other, but many of the events she claimed to witness probably owed more to her imagination than to reality.

Fortune, Dion 1891–1946. English occultist, born Violet Mary Firth, who became one of the best-known magicians of contemporary times. Firth, a Londoner, was much influenced by the writings of the Christian Scientist Mary Baker Eddy as a young woman but subsequently joined the Hermetic Order of the GOLDEN DAWN and became an associate of Aleister CROWLEY. Interested in developing her own psychic powers, she split from the Order after fighting a 'psychic battle' with its leader, Moina BERGSON, who allegedly sent a horde of black cats against her. Having founded her own Fraternity of Inner Light, Firth began to explore the 'Old Religion' from which some authorities claimed modern witchcraft was descended. She expanded her ideas in various books published under the name Dion Fortune. These volumes, in which the author claimed that she had gained knowledge through contact with what she termed 'elemental forces', are still widely read by students of the occult. Central to her system of belief was the notion that all people have magical power, but most lack the knowledge of how to turn it to their use.

fortune-telling *see* DIVINATION.

foxglove Woodland plant with purple or white flowers that has long been associated with witchcraft. Originally called Folk's Glove or Witches' Glove, the foxglove was a frequent ingredient in a range of potions concocted by witches and herbalists over the centuries. Many witches' remedies and plant extracts were harmless and cannot have had more than psychosomatic benefits for those who consulted the local 'Wise Woman' for treatment of physical or mental ailments. In the case of the foxglove, however, witchcraft had stumbled upon a plant with powerful healing potential – an accident that was to have a profound impact on Western medicine.

In 1741 a Shropshire doctor and botanist called William Withering heard of a witch who was having remarkable success with patients suffering from dropsy, which she treated with a herbal tea. Having obtained the recipe from her, he found that the main ingredient was foxglove. From the soft leaves of the plant he subsequently managed to extract the hitherto unrecognised drug digitalis. This breakthrough was to make Withering famous, for digitalis proved highly effective as a treatment for heart complaints, improving weak hearts and assisting patients to pass excess water and salt. As a result of Withering's findings based on the unnamed Shropshire witch's potion, a whole new family of medicines was made available to science.

France The history of the witch mania in France began early and claimed thousands of victims before the panic eventually subsided towards the end of the seventeenth century. The influence of the INQUISITION had a profound effect upon attitudes to witchcraft in the fourteenth and fifteenth centuries and did much to promote the witch-hunts pursued by the civil authorities in later times. Ultimately witchcraft came to be detected in the most unlikely places, notably in convents throughout France and in the French royal court.

In the Middle Ages, southern France was the scene of several ruthless campaigns against those suspected by the Inquisition of HERESY, and the decision that witchcraft was also a heresy signalled a new wave of persecutions in the early fourteenth century. Sorcerers had been subject to severe punishment by law since the passing of the Salic Act around AD 500, but cases depended chiefly upon evidence of actual poisoning or magic, rather than merely on the accused's belief in witchcraft. The crucial link between heresy and witchcraft was forged gradually over several centuries, through discussions between prominent theologians. Once the reality of PACTS WITH THE DEVIL and other related matters had been accepted, the business of sorcery made the transition from mere magic to an activity with religious overtones and was recognised as dangerous to the established Catholic Church. Witchcraft consequently qualified as a heresy and thus came within the gambit of the Inquisition, which was then running short of victims, having already stamped out with great efficiency such heretical sects as the Albigensians and the Waldensians and driven out of existence the Order of the KNIGHTS TEMPLAR.

The pattern for the first witchcraft trials in France had already been established to a great extent by the proceedings against heretics, in which similar evidence – including pacts with the Devil and consorting with DEMONS – had often been presented to the courts. Back in 1275, indeed, a woman named Angèle de la Barthe had been accused of eating babies and having intercourse with the Devil. She was subsequently burned by the Inquisition in Toulouse, making her arguably the first person to be executed for witchcraft. A few decades later, in 1335, Anne-Marie de Georgel and Catherine Delort, also from Toulouse, confirmed by now conventional notions about the activities of French witches. They admitted being seduced by the Devil, travelling by magic to regular SABBATS presided over by a GOAT, using magic to work evil against their enemies and indulging in orgies of sex and feasting on the corpses of babies.

Reports of witchcraft being practised among the highest in the land for political purposes did much to accelerate the speed with which the hysteria spread throughout society. Bishop Peter of Bayeux and his nephew were tried in 1278 for using sorcery against Philip III; Bishop Guichard of Troyes was charged in 1308 with using magic against Philip le Bel and other aristocrats; Alips de Mons and various associates were accused in 1314 of using IMAGE MAGIC against Louis X; Count Robert d'Artois was banished in 1331 for fashioning a wax figure to use against the King's son; and in 1398 various suspects were beheaded for causing the madness of the French monarch (see also JOAN OF ARC; RAIS, GILLES DE). By 1500 belief in the reality of witchcraft was much in evidence at all levels of French society, and large numbers of witchcraft trials were held virtually every year for the next 170 years or so.

The secular authorities joined the Inquisition in the campaign against witches around 1390, when the first such cases were brought before the civil courts (see PARIS WITCH TRIAL), and in time most cases ended up before the secular courts. In the early years witchcraft investigations were carried out in much the same way as examinations of other heresies, with suspects being asked leading questions and then tortured until they gave the desired answers. Accused witches were routinely required to name their associates, turning single cases into the starting-point for a series of mass trials. Later the secular courts attempted to observe some of the more important legal doctrines in trials involving witchcraft, but all too often the most unlikely evidence was accepted virtually without question.

The death penalty was imposed with increasing regularity from the mid-fifteenth century. Between 1428 and 1450 no fewer than 110 women and 57 men were burned alive as witches in Briançon, Dauphiné, for instance. Several more died at Arras in 1459 (see ARRAS WITCHES) and there were notorious mass trials at Béarn in 1508, at Luxeuil in 1529 (see LUXEUIL WITCH), at Toulouse in 1557 (when forty were put to death) and at Poitiers in 1568 (when four died). When the magician Trois-Echelles was put on trial (and subsequently executed) in Paris in 1571, he claimed that there were a hundred thousand witches in France. Others told of sabbats at which as many as ten thousand witches were present.

The Inquisition, meanwhile, was particularly occupied in investigating alleged cases of demonic POSSESSION involving nuns. Alarm at the numbers of nuns apparently under the influence of the Devil's minions confirmed the Catholic Church's fears that Christianity itself was under concerted attack, and that all witches were agents recruited by the Devil in an attempt to win control of the Earth. This paranoia quickly communicated itself to judges and other civil authorities, who were consequently even more merciless in passing sentence on the condemned. Witchcraft was blamed for any national ill, from failed harvests to the poor health of the King.

The hysteria reached a peak in France between 1575 and 1625. In 1579 the death penalty was extended to 'every charlatan and diviner, and others who practise necromancy, pyromancy, chiromancy, hydromancy', and possession of a GRIMOIRE was prohibited by the Church in 1581. Among the worst individual outbreaks during this period was the trial and execution of eighteen witches at Avignon in 1582, under the direction of the Inquisition. Central France, including Paris, escaped the worst excesses, but thousands more were put to death in Alsace, Lorraine, Normandy and Burgundy. As an illustration of the strength of popular belief in witchcraft, when King Henri III stepped in to secure the discharge of fourteen witches at Tours in 1589 he was himself promptly accused of being a witch-protector.

The panic died down gradually after 1625, although atrocities against alleged witches still took place from time to time (*see* GORDEL, DOMINIC). In 1670 Louis XIV had cause to deliver a stern rebuke to the Parlement of Normandy after 525 people were indicted on charges of witchcraft in Rouen: on orders from the King the sentences of the accused, who had their property restored to them, were reduced to banishment from the province, despite fierce protests from the local authorities. When his own court was threatened by a serious witchcraft scandal in 1682 (*see* CHAMBRE ARDENTE AFFAIR), Louis determined to end the hysteria once and for all. That year he formalised his opposition to the persecutions in a celebrated edict which effectively brought to an end orchestrated witch-hunts in France. The reality of witchcraft was officially denied (although those who stubbornly persisted in it were still liable to the death penalty).

Isolated cases continued to occur for some years, but after 1682 only on an irregular basis. When a man was burned for making a

LIGATURE in 1718 it proved to be the last execution for witchcraft in Bordeaux. Father Bertrand Guillaudot (and subsequently five accomplices) was burned alive at Dijon in 1742 for using magic to divine the whereabouts of treasure, but the last victim of all was Father Louis Debaraz, who was burned alive at Lyons in 1745 for performing sacrilegious masses in an attempt to find treasure. This did not mean, of course, that belief in the reality of witchcraft was stamped out everywhere: as late as 1885, in Sologne, a woman enlisted the aid of her husband to burn her own mother, whom the couple suspected of being a witch.

See also AIX-EN-PROVENCE NUNS; ALLIER, ELISABETH; AUXONNE NUNS; BASQUE WITCHES; BODIN, JEAN; BOGUET, HENRI; CADIERE, MARIE-CATHERINE; CIDEVILLE WITCH; FERY, JEANNE; FONTAINE, FRANÇOISE; LANCRE, PIERRE DE; LATEAU, LOUISE; LILLE NOVICES; LOOTEN, THOMAS; LOUDUN NUNS; LOUVIERS NUNS; MEDICI, CATHERINE DE'; REMY, NICOLAS.

Francis, Elizabeth *see* CHELMSFORD WITCHES.

Freeman, Alice *see* DARRELL, JOHN.

Fressingfield Witch A certain Mrs Corbyn of Fressingfield, Suffolk, who was the focus of allegations of witchcraft in 1890. This very late outbreak of the witchcraft mania was made public at the inquest into the sudden death of a baby in the village. Medical examination of the child's body revealed that it had died of shock as the result of the application of an unidentified irritant. The infant's parents were quick to state that they believed witchcraft was involved and named as the culprit the child's step-grandmother, Mrs Corbyn, who had died on the same day. On her deathbed the old woman had warned that the baby would not long outlive her, words that were remembered when the child died a few hours later. George Corbyn, husband of the dead woman, admitted that he had always suspected his wife of being a witch and had consequently taken care never to anger her for fear of the consequences.

G

Gabley, Mother *see* EGG.

Galrussyn, John, Ellen and Syssok *see* KYTELER, ALICE.

Gardner, Gerald 1884–1964. British occultist, who styled himself 'King of the Witches' and did much to promote the revival of the 'Old Religion' in the twentieth century. Claiming descent from one Grizell Gairdner, who was burned at Newburgh in Scotland as a witch in 1640, Gardner became interested in the occult in the course of the many years he spent in the Far East working in the tea and rubber trades and as a civil servant. He retired in 1937 and settled at Christchurch, near Bournemouth, where he initiated contact with a local Rosicrucian group. Subsequently he made the acquaintance of the notorious Aleister CROWLEY, who in due course admitted Gardner into the mystical Order of the Temple of the Orient, which claimed to have rediscovered the secret magic of the KNIGHTS TEMPLAR.

When Gardner heard about the existence of a coven of witches in the New Forest, near his home, he immediately set about joining it, and in 1949 he published a book in which he detailed some of the secrets that had been revealed to him. Another book, entitled *Witchcraft Today*, followed in 1954; it generated considerable interest in the subject and many people contacted him in order to learn more. Subsequently Gardner settled in the Isle of Man, where he managed a museum of magic and witchcraft and continued to spread knowledge about primitive magic and occult practices.

Later books included *The Meaning of Witchcraft* and *The Book of Shadows*, a text detailing secret rites that had to be copied by hand by initiates to the coven.

According to Gardner, who was influenced in this regard by the writings of the anthropologist Margaret Murray, modern witchcraft could be traced directly back to the Stone Age (although most authorities dispute this theory). The ancient fertility spirits known as the HORNED GOD and the GREAT GODDESS – variously addressed as Aradia and by inner initiates by a secret name – were thus the focus of veneration.

Participants in Gardner's covens celebrated their magic in the open air once a month. Ceremonies were always performed with the participants in the nude and included such practices as FLAGELLATION and giving the 'five-fold KISS'. Sex – to the scandalised delight of the popular press – played a prominent role in many of the ceremonies designed to honour the deities, with the High Priest and High Priestess having intercourse in front of other members of the coven at the culmination of what Gardner termed the 'Great Rite'. Tools used by Gardnerian witches included the PENTACLE, the WAND, the ATHAME, a SWORD and a horn with which to summon spirits.

Numerous covens on the Gardner model were set up throughout the UK, Europe and the USA. Although by now an old man, the 'King of the Witches' himself ran a coven on the Isle of Man until his sudden death on a passenger ship off the coast of Africa. Following Gardner's demise, there was an unseemly conflict between his disciples over who would succeed him as the pre-eminent witch for the next generation; the contest was eventually won by Alex Sanders.

Gardner's reputation suffered somewhat after his death when it emerged that he had probably fabricated his academic qualifications. In addition, some people claimed that, contrary to his own declarations, he had invented rather than rediscovered the mystic and ancient religion that came to be called WICCA.

garlic Herb that was widely believed to be a powerful witch and vampire deterrent. Legend had it that garlic sprang up where SATAN placed his left foot after departing from Paradise (while onions grew where he trod with his right foot). Garlic gathered in May was thought to be particularly effective against evil, although precautions (such as chewing garlic) had to be taken when collecting it, as demons might lurk nearby. To fend off vampires, garlic was placed near windows and worn as a necklace. In Italian folklore it was also used to adorn a baby's cradle to keep demons away in the vulnerable time between birth and baptism. WHITE WITCHES revered garlic for its efficacy against such complaints as worms, dropsy, sunstroke, smallpox, plague, leprosy, toothache, whooping cough, hysterics, snakebite, earache and bedwetting.

Gaufridi, Father Louis *see* AIX-EN-PROVENCE NUNS.

Gaulter, Catherine *see* POSSESSION.

Georgel, Anne-Marie de *see* SABBAT.

Germany The German states, then under the rule of the Holy Roman Empire, witnessed the worst of the witch hysteria that traumatised European society in the sixteenth and seventeenth centuries. For every witch who was put to death in England during that period a hundred or so were executed in Germany. In all, some hundred thousand people died after being found guilty in the German courts on charges of witchcraft, although the hysteria only got into full swing in Germany at the relatively late date of around 1570, when the Jesuits stepped up the campaign against non-Catholics of all descriptions. Under the terms of the Holy Roman Empire's CAROLINA CODE, drawn up in 1532, all witches had to be condemned to torture and the death penalty. Torture was officially sanctioned by the authorities in most states (though interpretation of the Code varied from one area to another) and accused persons routinely suffered the most excruciating torment before going to the stake.

Such was the slaughter throughout Germany in these years that many towns and villages boasted a small forest of stakes at which the condemned were put to death. In the Silesian town of Neisse, the executioner went to the trouble of constructing a huge oven in which, over a period of nine years, he roasted more than a thousand condemned witches, some as young as two years old: in 1651 alone, forty-two women and girls were put to death in it. In the town of Quedlinburg, in Saxony, 133 witches were publicly burned in just one day in 1589 (the executioner took it on himself to spare four of the most beautiful girls condemned to death). Records for the region presided over by the Abbey of St Maximin near Trèves indicate that between 1587 and 1594 two villages were entirely wiped out after all the inhabitants were executed for witchcraft, and in two others only two women were reported to be left alive in 1586. Many places boasted special 'witch houses', gaols where those suspected of witchcraft were incarcerated and tortured.

Mere suspicion of witchcraft was sufficient to get a person arrested and thrown into a witch house, there to await the attentions of the torturer. Suspicions were often voiced by personal enemies out for revenge or by people motivated by the rewards that were frequently offered for such information. Secular and ecclesiastical authorities were particularly keen to have proceedings instituted against the richest citizens, as – in accordance with the example set by the INQUISITION – they were then able to sequestrate the victim's possessions. Many witches were arraigned simply on the strength of unsupported accusations made by suspects under torture or by young children who clearly had little conception of the possible outcome of their fantasies.

Yet more fell victim to the malevolent activities of professional WITCHFINDERS, who made fortunes through their denunciations of witchcraft. No one was immune from the danger, and victims ranged from the stereotypical poverty-stricken hag of popular legend to members of the richest families in German society. The Prince-Bishop of Würzburg, Philipp Adolf von Ehrenberg, had his own son and heir burned as a witch on the advice of the Jesuits; later he regretted this, and brought a halt to all witchcraft trials in the bishopric around 1630. Once one member of a family had been accused, suspicion automatically fell upon other family members and close associates, and the accused person would be pressed to confirm that they too were involved in devil worship.

A letter to Count Werner von Salm, written in the early seventeenth century by a priest in Bonn, vividly depicts the extent to which everyone was subject to the threat of being exposed as a witch. As well as reporting the arrest and execution of priests, monks and prominent political figures, he finds that children too are being suspected:

> Half the city must be implicated; for already professors, law students, pastors, canons, vicars and monks have been arrested and burned ... The Chancellor and his wife and the Private Secretary's wife have already been apprehended and executed. On the Eve of Our Lady's Day there was executed here a girl of nineteen who had the reputation of being the loveliest and most virtuous in all the city, and who from her childhood had been brought up by the Prince-Bishop himself ... Children of three or four years have devils for their paramours. Students and boys of noble birth, of nine, ten, eleven, twelve, thirteen and fourteen years of age, have here been burned. To sum up, things are in such a pitiful state, that one does not know with what people one may talk and associate.

Torture was vicious and could be repeated many times. One woman is recorded to have been handed over to the torturers on no fewer than fifty-six occasions. The ingenuity of the torturers, bent on obtaining confessions and the names of other witches, knew no bounds. The accused – who had little chance of being acquitted once allegations had been made – were subjected to such diabolical torments as the BOOTS, STRAPPADO and the THUMBSCREWS.

Attempts to withdraw in court confessions earlier obtained by torture were rarely successful, in part because, in line with the model established by the Inquisition, the accused were denied witnesses in their own defence and were generally presumed to be guilty until proved otherwise. Anyone who did retract their confession was liable to find themselves once more in the hands of the torturers. Accusations against alleged witches were fairly formulaic, usually involving allegations that they had made PACTS WITH THE DEVIL, had bewitched their enemies, had attended SABBATS and had indulged in intercourse with DEMONS. Securing a confession to the charges, even under torture, was usually enough to justify the death penalty.

The conventional punishment was death by burning. Many condemned witches were burned alive, although others were strangled first or run through with a sword as a gesture of mercy from the courts. Towards the end of the period, when the death penalty became less automatic, many guilty persons were sent into exile instead (often hopelessly crippled as a result of the torture they had suffered).

The witch terror in Germany, which spanned both Catholic and Protestant society, reached a climax during the Counter-Reformation around 1570 and again during the Thirty Years' War (1618–48), with some of the worst excesses taking place in connection with the mass trials staged in Würzburg and Bamberg in the 1620s and early 1630s (see BAMBERG WITCHES; WÜRZBURG WITCHES). Also excessive even by the standards of the day was the ruthless campaign conducted by the Lutheran Benedict CARPZOV in Saxony, which is reputed to have cost the lives of some twenty thousand suspects.

Those who opposed the systematic persecution of Germany's alleged witches did so at their own peril, it should be noted. Persons suspected of being 'witch lovers' were likely to find themselves subjected to the same treatment as the victims with whom they sympathised – or else disposed of in a more subtle manner (see SPEE, FRIEDRICH VON).

The terror finally began to calm down towards the end of the seventeenth century, first in the Protestant states, although isolated outbreaks continued to occur for many years. The last witch trial in Prussia, for instance, took place in 1728, while the last execution for witchcraft in the whole of Germany did not occur until 1775, when Anna Maria SCHWÄGEL was put to death in Kempten on the order of the Prince-Abbot Honorius.

See also AUSTRIA; BAVARIA; BLANCKENSTEIN, CHATRINA; BÖFFGEN, CHRISTINE; BUIRMANN, FRANZ; COLOGNE WITCHES; EICHSTÄTT WITCH; FLADE, DIETRICH; GWINNER, ELSE; JUNIUS, JOHANNES; LEMP, REBECCA; MOUSE-MAKER; RENATA, SISTER MARIA; SCHÜLER, JOHANN; TRÉVES WITCHES; WÜRZBURG WITCHES.

ghirlanda delle streghe *see* LIGATURE.

ghost Modern popular thinking maintains a gulf between the subject of ghosts and hauntings and the world of witches and demons, but in former times the boundary between the two phenomena was often blurred. This was particularly true in the case of poltergeists, the invisible psychic entities bent on causing mayhem within a household through various kinds of mischief. As far back as the fifteenth century, authorities on witchcraft were writing that a favourite sport of devils was the execution of such pranks as tossing ornaments through the air, throwing stones, pulling at bedclothes, starting fires or overturning dinner tables. These devils had in all probability been ordered to inflict such miseries upon their victim by a witch, who might then be charged with causing the trouble.

Many noted authorities on the occult in the sixteenth and seventeenth century insisted, indeed, that there was no such thing as a ghost and that any apparition or poltergeist that manifested itself was in reality a demon in disguise. This attitude is reflected in the attention that was given to such celebrated cases as the DRUMMER OF TEDWORTH, which to modern eyes looks more like a straightforward poltergeist haunting. Many cases of alleged demonic POSSESSION, meanwhile, incorporated psychic disturbances such as rappings, tappings, hallucinations of spirits and the manifestation of small objects apparently out of thin air. As an illustration of the confusion, an account of a seance conducted by a Parson Rudall in Cornwall in 1665 includes the cleric commanding the spirit summoned to the MAGIC CIRCLE to confirm it is a 'true spirit and not a false fiend'.

At about the same time that witchcraft's grip on the popular imagination began to loosen, in the early part of the eighteenth century, interest in the spirit world and in the associated business of NECROMANCY intensified, developing over the years into the quite distinct discipline of spiritualism. By the nineteenth century the study of ghosts and poltergeists was a science in its own right.

Several of the measures that may be taken to protect oneself against the threat of witchcraft were also said to be effective against ghosts. These included guarding the doors and windows of a house with GARLIC and carrying a stick of ROWAN wood. Convention had it, though, that the devils who caused poltergeist phenomena often proved impervious to rituals of EXORCISM (in contrast to the devils that might be expelled in cases of demonic possession).

See also BARGARRAN IMPOSTOR; CIDEVILLE WITCH; GLENLUCE DEVIL; MAGEE ISLAND WITCHES.

Gifford, George d.1620. English cleric and writer, author of two of the earliest and most influential English books on witchcraft. A Nonconformist preacher from Maldon, Essex, Gifford presented his critical view of witchcraft in *A Discourse of the Subtle Practices of Devils by Witches and Sorcerers* of 1587 and *A Dialogue Concerning Witches and Witchcrafts* of 1593. Although Gifford agreed that some truly thought themselves witches, and that these deserved the death penalty as blasphemers, he cautioned judges in examining their evidence, claiming that their testimony could not be relied upon. If any supernatural force was at work, Gifford contended, the real culprit in such cases was the DEVIL himself, who was clever enough to work his evil without enlisting the aid of old women. Even so, the influence of Satan should not, Gifford stressed, be overstated – for this only encouraged the gullible to turn for protection to WHITE WITCHES when they should really turn to their Christian faith.

Gifford dismissed the idea that witches kept FAMILIARS with supernatural powers and denied that any old woman, whether she believed herself to be a witch or not, was capable of causing harm to man or beast by magic. Lamenting that 'much innocent blood is shed' because juries were inclined to accept unsupported allegations of witchcraft without question, Gifford singled out the 'Cunning Men' of rural communities who made it their business to identify witches and to offer magical protection by live sacrifices and so forth (practices that Gifford suggested were pagan in origin).

Gifford was admired by later generations for his determination to challenge the gullibility of the superstitious at a time when the majority were fairly convinced of the reality of the witchcraft threat.

Gilles de Rais *see* RAIS, GILLES DE.

Girard, Jean-Baptiste *see* CADIÉRE, MARIE-CATHERINE.

Glanvill, Joseph 1636–80. English cleric, philosopher and writer on the occult who did much to strengthen belief in the reality of witchcraft in English society in the seventeenth century. Chaplain to Charles II and a Fellow of the Royal Society Glanvill was the author of *Saducismus Triumphatus* (1681), which investigated twenty-six notable cases in which suggestions of supernatural activity or witchcraft were involved.

Glanvill was firm in his belief of the Satanic origins of evil and applauded those who aimed to seek out and suppress witchcraft wherever it was suspected. Despite professing an interest in scientific exploration of the subject he was inclined to accept much far-fetched testimony as true, and countered those who dismissed witchcraft as a delusion by warning that denial of the existence of ghosts and witches was but a step on the road to atheism. He did, however, question whether many witches had the powers which they claimed, remarking that it was 'very improbable that the devil who is a wise and mighty spirit would be at the beck of a poor hag, and have so little to do as to attend to the errands and impotent lusts of a silly old woman'.

In an attempt to furnish more evidence for the reality of the supernatural, Glanvill – who is often described as the 'Father of Psychical Research' – often met with the scientist Robert Boyle and others at Ragley Castle, where the group conducted seances with the assistance of leading mediums. Among the most celebrated cases that Glanvill examined were those of the DRUMMER OF TEDWORTH and the SOMERSET WITCHES.

Glendower, Owen *c.*1350–*c.*1416. Welsh rebel, who was called 'King of the Witches' by his devoted followers. Claiming descent from Prince Llewelyn ap Gruffud, he launched a guerrilla war against the English lords of the Marches in 1401 and proclaimed himself Prince of Wales. In the space of five years he ran the English out of much of Wales, but the military skill of the future Henry V eventually turned the tide against

Glendower and his men and he gradually lost virtually all the ground he had previously taken. Details of his death are obscure.

Despite the efforts of Christian missionaries over the centuries Glendower's people were in the main worshippers of the GREAT GODDESS and his claim to power rested largely on his status – through matrilineal descent – as her consort on Earth. Among other rituals, it is thought that Glendower may have been required to make human sacrifices to this goddess of witches, and may also have had ceremonial sexual intercourse with her.

In the twentieth century, Alex Sanders claimed direct descent from Glendower and assumed his title 'King of the Witches' (as had Gerald GARDNER before).

Glenluce Devil The apparent poltergeist haunting in 1654–6 of a family in Glenluce, near Newton Stewart in Galloway, Scotland, which was attributed by many local people to witchcraft. The disturbances troubling the family of Gilbert Campbell, a weaver, began after his son Thomas was fetched home from grammar school in Glasgow. Tom evidently feared that his schooling would be cut short and he would have to go into his father's trade, which he disliked. The demon that then manifested itself in the house clearly sympathised, demanding that Tom be allowed to continue his education and threatening revenge on the boy's parents.

Blind to the obvious source of the happenings, which came and went as Tom did and included stone-throwing, eerie whistling noises, acts of petty vandalism and arson, the weaver and his wife, supported by the local minister and subsequently a specially convened Synod of Presbyters, decided it must be witchcraft. It was recalled that a beggar called Andrew Agnew had called at the house and, when denied alms, had muttered various threats. It was consequently assumed that he must be the cause of the trouble (although the 'spirit' in the house had laid the blame not on Agnew but on local witches). The luckless Agnew was accordingly hunted down and hanged in Dumfries for blasphemy, and the supernatural manifestations ceased. As late as 1685 the incident was being included in collections of allegedly genuine episodes of witchcraft.

Gloucester, Duchess of *see* COBHAM, ELEANOR, DUCHESS OF GLOUCESTER.

Glover, Goody *see* GOODWIN CHILDREN.

goat The goat was the favourite disguise of the DEVIL, and the animal is consequently widely associated with rank virility and the forces of darkness. The classical deity Pan was conventionally depicted in half-man, half-goat form, and – though a direct link between Greek mythology and witchcraft remains to be proved – the Devil of European witchcraft similarly retained a human torso and arms in combination with a goat's head and horns, legs, tail and cloven hoofs (and, occasionally, a pair of wings). Also influential may have been the goat-demons of ancient Jewish lore, which lusted after human women, and the ancient Egyptian tradition of venerating male goats, which were reportedly allowed to copulate with female devotees. Whatever the origins of the idea, the goat became indelibly linked by peoples throughout Europe with the demonic. Superstition, for instance, claimed that all goats absented themselves once every twenty-four hours in order to have their beards combed by the Devil as a token of their allegiance to him.

As early as 1335 the French witches Anne-Marie de Georgel and Catherine Delort described how they had had intercourse with the Devil in the form of a goat, and many subsequent confessions included claims that the Devil had appeared at COVENS in such a shape (though, oddly enough, never in England or Scotland). Some witches claimed to ride to their SABBATS on goat-shaped demons and also confessed to kissing the hindquarters of a goat (*see* KISS) in the belief that the creature was SATAN himself. The goat that manifested at such covens was usually described as black in colour, but sometimes sported a red beard.

High Priests and Priestesses of modern covens often wear goat masks while performing their ceremonies, sometimes with a candle fixed between the horns.

Golden Dawn, Hermetic Order of the British secret society, founded in 1887, which devoted itself to the study and practice of occult magic. The Order was established by three Rosicrucians, of whom Samuel Liddell MATHERS emerged as the group's first leader. Mathers assumed control apparently at the command of the 'Secret Chiefs', some superior beings who communicated with Mathers one night in the Bois de Boulogne in Paris and dictated to him what was to be the constitution of the society. Other members attracted to the Order included the Irish poet W. B. Yeats, who devised some of the rituals to be practised, Algernon Blackwood and the young Aleister CROWLEY. Branches were subsequently opened in Edinburgh, Paris, Bradford and Weston-super-Mare.

Among other activities the Golden Dawn members learned about the use of magic, being taught how to consecrate talismans and how to draw MAGIC CIRCLES and so on, though without recourse to drugs or sex. They also explored the complexities of the CABALA.

The Order of the Golden Dawn gradually lost direction in the early years of the twentieth century, with Mathers and Crowley falling out and Yeats questioning whether it could continue. Crowley eventually left to found his own Order and the Golden Dawn effectively ceased its activities.

Good, Sarah *see* SALEM WITCHES.

Gooderidge, Alice *see* BURTON BOY.

Goodwin Children Witchcraft case based on the testimony of some Boston children that led to a notorious American trial in 1688. The affair centred on four of the six children of stonemason John Goodwin and was in many ways a precursor to the infamous trial of the SALEM WITCHES in the same city a few years later.

The four Goodwin children, aged between five and thirteen years old, began to suffer fits after one of the girls fell out with the laundress, Goody Glover, over some missing linen. The aged Goody Glover had, most unwisely as it turned out, spoken very harshly to one of the girls. She and three of her siblings consequently experienced a series of epileptic fits and periodical loss of hearing, sight and the power of speech. To the horror of their parents and others, the children would seem to suffer temporary dislocation of their jaws and limbs and to lose control of their tongues, which protruded 'to a prodigious length' or were drawn down their throats. At other times the children cried out in pain as their bodies were contorted, or else found themselves paralysed and unable to move at all.

Medical examination failed to reveal the origins of the problem and witchcraft was the next cause suspected by the family, in which all the children were being conscientiously raised on strict religious lines. Demons, it was presumed, lay behind the physical torments of the children and were also responsible for the contrary and stubborn behaviour to which the four were prone – violent arguments would break out over such minor issues as getting dressed or washing their hands. With no improvement in the condition of the children seeming likely, the distraught John Goodwin took his case to the magistrates. He alleged that the only conclusion he could draw was that his children had been bewitched by Goody Glover, although he could offer no proof whatsoever to support his allegations. Glover's house was searched and a number of small figures were found: the old woman soon confessed that she used these to influence the children, stroking them with a wet finger to cause their agonies. When required to recite the LORD'S PRAYER, the crone failed to do so without making an error. She was unable to furnish the authorities with details of her dealings with the Devil, but there was enough 'evidence' for the court to find her guilty and to condemn her to death as a witch. One of those judges who passed sentence was Judge Stoughton, who was later to preside over the Salem trial.

The children's fits gradually ceased after a second suspect was put to death as an accomplice in the case. Among those deeply impressed by the whole affair was Cotton MATHER, a witch-hunting minister who wrote his own full account of the happenings surrounding the Goodwin children and concluded: 'I am resolved after this never to use but just one grain of patience with any man that shall go to impose upon me a denial of devils or of witches.'

Gordel, Dominic fl.1631. French priest whose examination on charges of witchcraft in the Lorraine region of France in 1631 bears witness to the suffering inflicted on accused people by witch-fearing courts in the seventeenth century. Like many another defendant, Gordel, the parish priest of Vomécourt, was implicated in witchcraft through accusations made by local children and after his name was mentioned in the confessions of suspected witches already under examination. He clearly believed himself to be innocent of the charges laid against him. However, this was hardly enough to ensure his acquittal in an age when the testimony of children as young as two was admissible in cases involving sorcery and witchcraft and the usual rules of evidence were suspended in the interests of fighting the threat posed by the powers of darkness. Straightforward denials of guilt, for instance, were stubbornly interpreted as attempts by the Devil to deflect attention.

Father Gordel's case is notable chiefly for the detailed records, signed by the Bishop of Side in his role as Vicar-General for the region, that have survived and detail the horrific tortures to which he was subjected as a suspected witch. His involvement in witchcraft had been suggested by two condemned witches, Claude Cathelinotte and Hanry Gaubart of Béthencourt, as well as by four local children, all of whom claimed to have seen Gordel at SABBATS and in the course of these committing a variety of evil acts. Gordel denied the charges and the court gave permission for torture to be applied.

The proceedings got under way, in the presence of various court representatives, in a tower of the episcopal palace of Toul on 25 April 1631. A surgeon and a doctor were also present to guard against 'unreasonable violence' being used against the accused. The hangman first applied the THUMBSCREWS to the priest's fingers and then to his toes, but no confession was forthcoming. Next the torturers resorted to the LADDER, stretching the luckless Gordel three times while repeatedly demanding from him the truth about the sabbats he had attended. The pain was severe and Gordel called time and again on Jesus and the saints to release him from his agony, while consistently denying he had ever been to a sabbat or even knew what a sabbat was. Now, with Gordel still upon the ladder, the torturers applied the BOOTS, upon which the priest shrieked that he was dying but still denied that he was a sorcerer or that he had attended any sabbat.

The verbatim record of the court officials, written up on the same day as the events described, coolly relates how the bewildered priest was exposed to increasing agony in an attempt to obtain the desired confession:

> After this, we ordered the vice applied to his left arm, thigh and left leg; to all this he said that he had never been at a sabbat and 'I am dying! I am broken! Jesus, Maria! I renounce the Devil!' With this we ordered him to be crushed more severely, whereupon he cried that he told the truth and that he had never been at a sabbat, always saying, 'Jesus! Maria! Mother of God have pity on me! Never have I had any compact with the Devil, secret or otherwise. I have never consented to his temptings!' Pressed more tightly, he shrieked, 'Jesus! Maria! Father everlasting, help me! I am broken! I never saw a sabbat. I was never at a sabbat. I renounce the Devil and confess the Holy Trinity. I deliver myself into the hands of the good angels. Mercy, I beg God for mercy!'

The record of Father Gordel's sufferings, a rare glimpse of the horror of the torture chamber, is incomplete. It seems unlikely that he was allowed to survive the accusations, and that, like many others, he met his death either at the stake or at the hands of his torturers.

Gordon, Sir Robert 1647–1704. Aristocrat who became one of the most notorious witches in Scottish history. Many local legends tell of Sir Robert Gordon's dealings with the DEVIL. According to these, Sir Robert gave his shadow (widely believed to be a manifestation of the soul) to the Devil in 1678 in order to escape death. Fearing that the Devil would demand further sacrifices of him in the future, Sir Robert subsequently constructed a fortress called the 'Round Square' at Gordonstoun in Moray, in the hope that, with the assistance of a minister, he would be able to keep the Devil out. The minister whom Sir Robert consulted, however, insisted that he would be safer in a church and in 1704 he persuaded the aristocrat to accompany him to Birnie church near Elgin. Unfortunately the Devil caught up with them on the road and snatched Sir Robert from his escort, galloping away with him to Hell as a demon hound buried its fangs in the luckless man's neck. His home is now the site of the famous Gordonstoun public school.

Gowdie, Isobel d.1662. Scottish witch whose detailed confessions to the authorities at Auldearn in Morayshire, given without torture in 1662, ensured that hers became the most celebrated name in the annals of witchcraft north of the border. Gowdie, the childless wife of an ill-educated farmer named John Gilbert, was young, red-haired and attractive but apparently also deranged, believing that she possessed all manner of supernatural powers which she voluntarily described to her astonished and appalled interrogators. The revelation that she was a witch was a shock to all who knew her, since apparently even her husband had been ignorant of the fact until she spoke to the authorities (she explained that she had bewitched him by leaving a BROOMSTICK in the bed when she departed for the COVEN).

According to her own confession, Gowdie was initiated as a witch at Auldearn kirk in Nairnshire in 1647, shortly after encountering the DEVIL – 'a man in grey' – for the first time while out on the downs one day. At the Devil's instructions she refuted her baptism as a Christian and, placing one palm on her head and the other under her feet, promised to him everything between her hands. She was then baptised with the name Janet by the Devil, who made his mark by nipping her shoulder and sucking blood from the wound to sprinkle over her head. The ritual closed with the Devil reading from the pulpit.

The covens which Gowdie attended comprised thirteen members, who learned to transform themselves into various animals, to perform obscure rites using the corpses of unchristened children, to shoot 'elf arrows' (*see* ELF-SHOT), to take crops for the Devil, to steal cows' milk, to destroy enemies by making clay models of them, to raise storms and various other feats of magic. Gowdie also explained how she had been taught to fly to SABBATS on a straw or a beanstalk by uttering the words: 'Horse and hattock in the Devil's name!' Each witch in the coven had her own FAMILIAR, Isobel's being a black-dressed spirit called the Read Reiver. She further claimed that she had enjoyed frequent sexual intercourse with other coven members and with the Devil, finding that his huge genitals gave her more pleasure than those of ordinary mortals even though his semen was icy cold.

Despite displaying no confusion when she made her surprisingly coherent confession, Gowdie did express some remorse for her conduct and seemed fully aware of the likely outcome of her unparalleled statements, lamenting at her trial that she deserved the harshest of tortures. Although the records for the trials of the AULDEARN WITCHES are incomplete, it seems probable that Gowdie was duly hanged and her body burned to ashes in the usual manner.

Authorities on witchcraft have since seen in Isobel Gowdie the archetypal witch of the seventeenth century, claiming as she did the full range of powers attributed in other cases. Quite why she made the extraordinary confession that almost certainly led directly to her death and that of other members of her coven has been much debated. Some authorities have speculated that she was mad or emotionally unbalanced and, bored by her lonely life, desired the attention that her confession would bring her, regardless of, or simply uncomprehending, the cost. Others have suggested, but without any corroborating evidence, that she may have been chosen as a sacrificial victim by her coven or that she was obsessed by the urge to avenge herself on her confederates after some quarrel.

Grandier, Urbain *see* LOUDUN NUNS.

grave-robbing The plundering of graves by witches to obtain ingredients for use in spells has long been alleged by their enemies, and it would seem that such acts of desecration have indeed taken place. Many of the most powerful spells that witches were claimed to perform appropriately enough required the use of ingredients that were virtually impossible to find. A number of spells, including some deadly potions, would only work if samples of human remains were available to the witch concerned – hence the traditions of witches bribing executioners for the bodies of victims hanging on the gallows and practising 'corpse-lifting' in the dead of night.

Most prized of all were the corpses of those who died violent premature deaths, because these bodies were presumed to have some trace of unused vitality still in them. According to Paulus GRILLANDUS, a judge in sixteenth-century Italy, 'some take a small piece of buried corpse, especially the corpse of anyone who has been hanged or otherwise suffered a shameful death ... the nails or teeth ... the hair, ears or eyes ... sinews, bones or flesh'. Alice KYTELER, Ireland's most famous witch, was said to employ the SKULL of a thief in her magic, and also made use of hair taken from a corpse.

Also sought after were the corpses of babies, ideally those of children who died before baptism. Isobel GOWDIE, the celebrated Scottish witch who made a voluntary confession in the seventeenth century, described in some detail how she and other members of her coven had exhumed the bodies of newly buried infants to use in their spells. These corpses were then split up and the pieces shared with other covens in the area. Gowdie and her fellow witches buried their own portion of the spoils in a farmer's field in order to 'steal' his crops by magic.

Even in recent years there have been much-publicised cases of grave-robbing, apparently by members of Satanic sects. In 1968 coffins were broken into at Tottenham Park Cemetery, Edmonton, in north London, and a year later the bones of a girl buried in the cemetery of a derelict church at Clophill in Bedfordshire some two hundred years before were found laid out inside the church after apparently being used in some obscure ceremony (*see* CLOPHILL WITCHES).

Measures taken to deter witches from robbing graves have ranged over the years from scrawling runic symbols on gravestones to carving on them elaborate curses threatening the well-being of anyone disturbing the remains below.

See also HAND OF GLORY; NECROMANCY.

Great Beast The Anti-Christ, a terrifying demon that, on biblical authority, ranks high in the hierarchy of Hell. Following the expulsion of SATAN from Heaven, the Great Beast, with ten horns and seven heads, rose up from the sea and, with power granted by Satan, waged war with the saints. After he had ruled the Earth for three and a half years the forces of good and evil did battle and the Great Beast was cast into a lake of fire and brimstone, there to remain for eternity. The identity of the Beast is not revealed, but it is given a number, 666, perhaps because Christ was crucified on the sixth day of the Jewish week. It is conjectured by various authorities that the Great Beast, with its seven heads, represented Rome with its seven hills, and that the number 666 can be translated as a numerical code for the name of the hated Emperor Nero.

Many latter-day witches and sorcerers have claimed to have raised up the Great Beast during rituals conducted within MAGIC CIRCLES. Aleister CROWLEY included the Great Beast in his personal occult philosophy, adopting the number 666 as his own and calling himself 'The Great Beast'.

Great Goddess Pagan deity, who, under a variety of names, became one of the principal figures allegedly venerated by witches through the centuries. The female equivalent of the HORNED GOD, the Great Goddess represented to early man the virtues of procreation and fertility, and indeed life and nature itself. Depictions of this deity, usually with a distended belly, have been found in prehistoric cave paintings and she subsequently reappeared in various guises in pre-Christian cultures throughout Europe. To the Babylonians she was Ishtar; to the Egyptians she was Aset; to the Phoenicians she was Astarte; to the Greeks she was Hera and Isis; to the Canaanites she was ASHTAROTH; to the Romans she was the Good Goddess, Juno and DIANA. Jewish lore identified her as LILITH, the first consort of Adam, but Christians had little use for her and her followers were much persecuted by the early Church.

Many people clung to the 'Old Religion', however. In England, the Saxons venerated the Great Goddess as Goda or Frig, while later names included the Queen of Heaven, Marian and, in Wales, Rhiannon and Arianrhod. Among the more distinguished of her devotees in post-medieval times was Catherine de' MEDICI, who acted the part of Venus in rites dedicated to the Great Goddess, offering herself naked as an altar, and Madame de MONTESPAN, mistress of Louis XIV of France. The Great Goddess was also venerated in the sex rituals of the English HELL-FIRE CLUB and many covens were reported to celebrate the union of the Great Goddess, impersonated by the senior female witch, with the Horned God, who was played by the master of the coven.

Worship of the Great Goddess was revived in the twentieth century. Many modern witches perform ceremonies in her honour, identifying her by such names as Diana or Aradia.

Great Rite *see* GARDNER, GERALD; WICCA.

Greensmith, Rebecca *see* CONNECTICUT WITCHES.

Grierson, Isobel d.1607. Scottish peasant woman whose trial as a witch before the Supreme Criminal Tribunal in Edinburgh on 10 March 1607 caused a sensation. The wife of a labourer named John Bull, of Prestonpans, East Lothian, Grierson was a vindictive woman who had many enemies among her neighbours, all of whom were terrified of her and only too willing to testify against her. The opportunity to do so finally came when Grierson was accused of employing witchcraft against a man called Adam Clark, with the intention of causing him harm over an eighteen-month period leading up to the trial.

Evidence was obtained to the effect that Grierson had disguised herself as a CAT to gain entrance into Clark's house during the hours of darkness in the company of other cats in order to frighten the inhabitants; that she had recruited the DEVIL in the form of a naked infant to procure the death of one William Burnet in 1605; that in 1598 she had inflicted sickness upon one Robert Peddan until the latter had paid her money that he owed her; that in 1604 she had caused the ale being brewed by the same Robert Peddan to turn foul by the simple expedient of stroking his cat; that she had cursed Peddan's wife Margaret Donaldson with sickness on no fewer than three occasions since 1600; and that she had peddled various charms and potions and cast spells as a sorceress and witch.

The readiness of witnesses to come forward and the fact that the accused was denied any defence sealed Grierson's fate. The friendless woman was found guilty and shortly afterwards strangled at the stake and then burned on Edinburgh's Castle Hill.

Grillandus, Paulus fl. sixteenth century. Italian papal judge who presided over many witch trials in the Rome district and recorded his experiences in the influential *Tractatus de Hereticis et Sortilegiis* (*Treatise on Heretics and Witches*). Grillandus's book was one of the most influential publications on the subject produced during the sixteenth century, furnishing many details of witchcraft practice and warning of the dangers threatened by unchecked witchcraft activity.

Accepting the reality of the often extraordinary confessions that he heard, Grillandus related various 'proofs' of such phenomena as TRANSVECTION, LIGATURE, the making of PACTS WITH THE DEVIL, demonic POSSESSION and metamorphosis of witches from one form to another. Among other details he repeated, without questioning their validity, claims by witches that they were transported to SABBATS on DEMONS in the form of GOATS, that they enjoyed sexual intercourse with the Devil 'with the greatest voluptuousness' and that they exhumed corpses to use in their SPELLS.

One anecdote retold by Grillandus concerned a man who persuaded his wife to take him to her sabbat, which she agreed to do provided he did not cause offence by mentioning God or Christ. Unfortunately, when the witches sat down to eat the man demanded SALT (which demons detest), and when it arrived called out: 'God be praised, here comes the salt!' At this point the sabbat vanished and he found himself a hundred miles from home. On his return he denounced his wife as a witch and she was burned to death by the INQUISITION.

grimoire A book of SPELLS. So-called 'black books', containing spells often attributed to Solomon himself, were reputedly in widespread use during the Middle Ages, the earliest of them being written in Constantinople before its capture by the Turks in 1453. Many of these hand-written volumes drew on Jewish lore, the best known of them being the *Key of Solomon*, which purported to pass on some of the magic of the biblical king of that name (a copy is now preserved in the British Museum). Legend has it that Pope Honorius III was in possession of such a book, and after his death Pope Innocent VI held a ceremonial public burning in which a copy of it was destroyed. The first printed edition of a grimoire purporting to be by Honorius was produced in Rome in 1629 and was subsequently translated into several languages.

In more recent times Gerald GARDNER insisted that his protégés laboriously copy out by hand his own *Book of Shadows*, detailing the procedure to be followed in certain rituals. Many modern witches are required to create their own grimoires in a similar fashion in the course of their apprenticeship.

Typical contents of such volumes describe the ceremonial robes and tools to be used in magic ceremonies, together with advice on how to choose the right time and place for the performing of a particular ritual, how to draw a MAGIC CIRCLE and what NAMES OF POWER to use to summon spirits, find hidden treasure, open locks and so forth. Spells described in these volumes range from those designed to obtain magical influence over someone to the procuring of murder by magic.

Guaita, Stanislas de fl.1900. French aristocrat who led a famous Rosicrucian lodge in Paris in the late nineteenth century. The Marquis de Guaita gathered around him a COVEN of magicians and witches with similar views, of whom the writer Oswald Wirth made a permanent record in *The Book of Thoth* (1889), in which he detailed their beliefs and also discussed the interpretation of tarot cards. Trouble loomed, however, when Guaita's attention was drawn to the activities of a rival coven led by Joseph-Antoine BOULLAN in Lyon. Having ascertained the sexual abandon with which Boullan's followers pursued their magic, the Marquis wrote to Boullan and informed him that he had been condemned to death. A campaign of psychic warfare developed between the two covens, each despatching DEMONS to attack their opponents. The battle ended when

Boullan suddenly died. Accusations followed that his death had been caused by the Paris lodge, as a result of which duels were fought between prominent members of the two groups – fortunately no one was seriously hurt. The Marquis's coven gradually disintegrated in the ensuing years and Stanislas de Guiata himself died prematurely of a drug overdose, aged just twenty-seven.

Guazzo, Francesco-Maria fl.1600–30. Italian friar who wrote one of the standard demonologies of the seventeenth century. *The Compendium Maleficarum (Handbook of Witches)* was written in 1626 at the request of the Bishop of Milan to publicise the evil-working of witches everywhere. Having served as an assessor in numerous witchcraft trials, Guazzo was well placed to explore his subject and clearly believed in the reality of the supernatural powers popularly attributed to witches. Among other items he listed the many symptoms of demonic POSSESSION (including contortions and vomiting) and repeated the rumour that the Protestant reformer Martin Luther was the offspring of a nun and the Devil.

One remarkable story included by Guazzo in his highly influential book concerned a party of French soldiers who fired into a black cloud over Calais after they heard voices emanating from it. Out of the sky fell a fat, drunk, naked old woman wounded in the thigh.

Guernsey *see* CHANNEL ISLANDS.

Guibourg, Abbé *see* CHAMBRE ARDENTE AFFAIR.

Gunter, Anne b. 1590. English girl, the daughter of a respected gentleman of North Moreton, Berkshire, who was at the centre of a notorious witchcraft trial held at Abingdon in 1605. Gunter was prone to fits and hysteria and at the age of fourteen began to suffer such symptoms as foaming at the mouth and temporary blindness and deafness, along with a tendency to produce pins from various parts of her body. These ailments she blamed upon the sorcery of three local women, Elizabeth Gregory, Agnes Pepwell and Mary Pepwell.

The allegations caused a considerable stir and the three women were sent for trial. The case was, however, thrown out and Gunter herself came under suspicion of fraud. She was personally questioned by JAMES I on three occasions, at Oxford, Windsor and Whitehall, and he committed her to the care of experts who quickly confirmed the King's doubts about her honesty. The King assured the girl that she would not be punished if she told the truth; she subsequently admitted that the entire story had been a fabrication and that she had exaggerated her symptoms at the order of her father, who wished to have revenge upon a neighbour. Both Anne Gunter and her father were charged with conspiracy.

The case of Anne Gunter was significant in that it was the first important trial investigated by the King in which fraud was seen to be manifestly at work, and the outcome doubtless had a considerable impact upon James's subsequent attitude to the assessment of evidence in witchcraft trials (and consequently that of his judges). Historians have noted various similarities between the Gunter case and that of the widely reported WARBOYS WITCHES and it seems probable that the girl got her inspiration largely from pamphlets about the earlier trial.

Gwinner, Else d.1601. German baker's wife, who resisted the most hideous tortures after being charged with witchcraft in Offenburg in Baden in 1601. The trial of Else Gwinner was typical of many others prosecuted in Catholic towns and cities throughout GERMANY during the period, and it remains a good example of the determination that the authorities – who stood to benefit financially through convictions – often displayed in getting what was to them the 'right' result.

Else Gwinner (born Else Laubbach) came under suspicion of being a witch as a result of the political machinations of Rupprecht Silberrad, who plotted the downfall of a rival councillor, Georg Laubbach (Else's father). Else's mother had been burned as a witch in 1597 and this provided Silberrad with a golden opportunity to frame other members of the family with the same crime. Accordingly, in 1601 Silberrad publicly denounced Georg Laubbach's daughters

Adelheid and Helene for bringing about the death of his own son by means of magic. Else was added to the list of the accused after two vagrants also suspected of witchcraft named her, among other women of the town, while under torture on charges arising from the theft of some grapes.

Such accusations were taken very seriously in Offenburg, which was dominated by the Jesuits, and Else Gwinner was quickly arrested and put to torture to obtain a confession. She endured the terrible agony of STRAPPADO without admitting anything, and her young daughter Agathe was taken into custody in order to get incriminating evidence from her. This ploy failed, however, and in their frustration the authorities subjected Else to another, more severe, testing by strappado. Still she said nothing. After flogging, however, Agathe broke down and confessed all that was suggested to her about her mother. The use of the THUMBSCREWS forced out of Else an admission that she had enjoyed intercourse with DEMONS and that she flew to SABBATS. Subsequently she was thrown into an icy dungeon and subjected to further tortures that wrested from the exhausted and wretched woman the names of two accomplices.

The court's satisfaction was short-lived, however, for Else quickly withdrew her confession once she had partially recovered and nothing that the authorities could do seemed to weaken her resolve to remain silent. Even the threat of worse torture did not have any effect upon her. In the face of such stubbornness, the judges abandoned their campaign to get a confession and sentenced her to death by burning. Else Gwinner duly died at the stake on 21 December 1601.

Agathe, meanwhile, was too young for burning and after pleas from her father she was banished (to the intense irritation of Silberrad and his confederates). Charges were also dropped against Adelheid and Helene Laubbach. The tables were briefly turned when Silberrad, the instigator of the whole tragic affair, was himself placed under house arrest, but it was not long before he managed to secure his release (together with substantial compensation) through his friends in the Church.

Haecke, Father Louis van 1828–1912. Belgian Catholic priest who led notorious devil-worshipping sects in Bruges and Paris. Father Haecke had a great weakness for women and as a young man manipulated his position of influence over those who came to him for confession, in order to seduce them. He perfected a technique of psychic suggestion in which he encouraged the women to think of him in terms of a lover, until they were obsessed by him and the ensuing seduction became easy.

Admired by the faithful at Bruges, Father Haecke gathered around him a circle of occultists and set about developing his own variation of the Catholic mass, introducing various pagan elements and making the idea of sex central to each celebration. The extraordinary proceedings were watched over by a statue of a naked god, complete with devilish leer and erect penis. Typical rites culminated in the desecration of the sacred host and a wild and indiscriminate orgy, in which all tastes were catered for. Haecke himself directed the ritual wearing a skull-cap with horns.

Eventually, Father Haecke's involvement in black magic was revealed by the writer Joris-Karl HUYSMANS, who had persuaded a woman named Berthe Courrière to join the Bruges coven and report to him what she saw. Huysmans wrote up Courrière's experiences of the coven in a novel and the Bishop of Bruges launched his own inquiry into the wayward priest's activities. In the end, however, the matter was allowed to drop.

See also BOULLAN, JOSEPH-ANTOINE; GUAITA, STANISLAS DE.

hagstone Small holed pebble, otherwise known as a 'witch-stone' or 'fairystone', which was reputed to ward off witchcraft and other varieties of evil. In former times, owners of livestock habitually hung up such holed stones in their stables or in the cow-byres, or round the animals' necks, in order to fend off any threat from evil spirits. Some people also carried stones of this kind about their person, both to protect themselves against witchcraft and to safeguard their luck. At night the stones would be hung on the bedstead to keep away the demons that caused nightmares.

Some authorities insisted that hagstones were only effective if properly consecrated in a special ceremony, which comprised a curious mixture of Christian and pagan elements and included reciting the following incantation:

> I conjure thee, by all Hosts of Heaven,
> By the Living God, the True God,
> By the Blessed and Omnipotent God ...

The ceremony ended with the presiding magician crying out: 'May it protect you against all evil forces and curses, Amen.'

See also AMULET; CHARM; PROTECTION AGAINST WITCHCRAFT.

Hahn, Dr Georg *see* BAMBERG WITCHES; JUNIUS, JOHANNES.

hair Because the hair, like other body parts, is reputed to retain a mystic link with the body even after it has been cut off, it has always been much valued by practitioners of witchcraft (particularly as the head is the seat of a person's psychic power). Many witches arraigned before church and civil authorities in former times admitted to using the hair of both living and dead people to achieve their nefarious ends.

Possession of just a few strands of a person's hair was alleged to be enough to enable the practised witch to obtain magical influence over the person concerned. A witch could, for instance, summon anyone they desired to their presence by the simple expedient of boiling a single one of their discarded hairs. Burning a strand of hair, meanwhile, was supposed by many witches to cause the erstwhile owner unbearable pain. A few strands of a person's hair could also be incorporated into a wax figure made in their likeness, providing the magical link through which the witch could work some IMAGE MAGIC.

Defences against such powerful spells were few, and those fearful of becoming the victims of witchcraft took the greatest care in disposing of their cut hair (as did Aleister CROWLEY, for instance). Ideally, cut hair was buried rather than burned, because the owner would need it again when resurrected in body on the Day of Judgement. It was most unwise, superstition claimed, for a doting parent to save a lock of their child's hair (or, indeed, their own), as this could all too easily fall into the hands of a witch. By extension, lovers traditionally exchanged locks of each other's hair as a sign of their complete trust in one another, a token of faith that the other would not use it for the purposes of witchcraft.

If the worst was suspected and image magic was thought to be at work, cutting off a lock of one's hair (or perhaps part of a finger) as a sacrifice might, it was believed, be sufficient to prevent further bodily damage. Another possibility was to use a little of one's own hair in the preparation of a WITCH BOTTLE.

Hair could be used for less malevolent magic, however, and was often listed as a desirable ingredient in recipes to improve the health or to obtain the love of another. In the past, WHITE WITCHES consulted for the treatment of children suffering from whooping cough sometimes recommended feeding a dog with a sandwich containing a strand of the patient's hair: the illness would be transferred to the dog and the child would allegedly recover.

Witches were once shorn of all their body hair in preparation for inspection of their bodies for WITCH'S MARKS, or otherwise just before execution. This measure not only made searching their bodies easier, but was also reputed to deprive the suspect of his or her supernatural powers, forestalling the chance of the condemned prisoner making a last-minute escape. Demons hiding in the witch's hair could use their magic to help the accused person withstand the pain of torture, or else whisper misleading information into the prisoner's ear so as to deceive any interrogators.

Haizmann, Christoph d.1700. Bavarian artist who in 1677 wrote a startling autobiography in which he claimed to have sold his soul to the DEVIL and to have indulged in various witchcraft practices. Lavishly illustrated with pictures of the demons he had encountered, the book was based on a confession that Haizmann made to the police at Pottenbrunn in 1677 after suffering a fit. Haizmann had always experienced visions of various kinds, but now he claimed that nine years earlier he had actually sold his soul to the Devil on two occasions and requested protection because the day was approaching when he was supposed to meet his part of the bargain. He had signed the pact in his own blood under the words: 'I sell myself to this Satan, to be his own bodily son, and belong to him both body and soul in the ninth year.'

Extraordinary though his story was, Haizmann was believed by the authorities and, showing suitable signs of contrition, was sent to the shrine at Zell, where he underwent a ritual EXORCISM that lasted three days and nights. In a vision, Haizmann saw the Virgin Mary snatching his pact from the Devil and he declared himself free of Satan's influence, but soon afterwards he returned to the shrine, fearing he had been mistaken. In a further vision, he saw the Virgin snatch the second pact he had signed and tear it to pieces.

Haizmann recorded his impressions of the Devil and his minions in his unique autobiography. The Devil he depicted as a weird creature combining a human abdomen with female breasts, horns and the legs and claws of a bird.

In gratitude for his deliverance from the Devil, Haizmann spent the rest of his days as a monk at Neustadt, Bavaria. His writings subsequently furnished material for a case history by Freud, who read into them evidence of an Oedipus complex and castration anxieties.

Haldane, Isobel fl.1623. Scots woman who was tried for witchcraft at Perth in May 1623. The trial of Isobel Haldane is unusual in that fairly detailed records survive of her interrogation before the Session of Perth, allowing a glimpse of how Scottish witchcraft trials were pursued at the height of the witchcraft hysteria in those parts.

Haldane appeared before the court charged with being a witch largely on the strength of various reports that she had used magic to effect the cures of certain sick people – a skill that she could only have acquired, it was assumed, by selling her soul to the Devil (*see* PACT WITH THE DEVIL) – although she protested that she had in fact learned her craft from the FAIRIES. She had also prophesied the death of various local citizens, which had then come about exactly as she had foretold.

When questioned about her dealings with the supernatural, Haldane confessed to a strange adventure, according to the official record: 'Ten years since, lying in her bed, she was taken forth, whether by God or the Devil she knows not, and was carried to a hillside. The hill opened and she entered in there. She stayed three days, viz., from Thursday to Sunday at twelve o'clock. She met a man with a gray beard, who brought her forth again.' From the 'man with the gray beard' the accused had learned the identities of those fated to die in the near future.

Various witnesses admitted going to Isobel Haldane to seek her assistance. Patrick Ruthven, a skinner from Perth, had consulted her in order to be freed of a spell cast by a woman named Margaret Hornscleugh, while others had asked her to wash their sick children, thus transferring the disease to the soiled water and restoring them to good health. Others she had treated with herbal remedies. On one occasion, it was alleged, she had visited a sick child and, deciding that it was a changeling and not the real child, had fed it a lethal potion that quickly brought about its death.

The records of the case of Isobel Haldane do not include the outcome of the trial, but the likelihood is that she was found guilty of witchcraft, strangled and burned.

Hale, Sir Matthew 1600–76. English judge, whose reputation as one of the most learned and acute legal authorities of his day was permanently marred by his evident belief in witchcraft and by his conduct in several notorious witchcraft trials.

Brought up in the Puritan tradition, called to the bar in 1637 and raised to the post of Chief Justice of the King's Bench in 1671, Hale demonstrated his strong prejudice against accused witches on several occasions and undoubtedly played a leading part in securing guilty verdicts. When the evidence inclined towards acquittal, his usual practice was to make no reference at all to matters of evidence in his summing-up and rather to arouse the superstitious leanings of the jurors.

The most shameful trial with which Hale was connected was that of Rose Cullender and Amy Duny at Bury St Edmunds in 1662 (*see* BURY ST EDMUNDS WITCHES). Many of those present in the courtroom detected fatal flaws in the evidence being presented against the two women, depending as it did upon the statements of hysterical children around the age of ten, but Hale displayed unmistakable satisfaction in the guilty verdict that eventually came in after he had worked on the jurors' susceptibilities. The fact that ostensibly disinterested witnesses were revealed to have personal connections with the 'victims' of the accused was conveniently disregarded, and allegations that the children were being tormented by malevolent spectral forces were readily accepted despite the fact that no one else could see them. Cullender and Duny were duly hanged.

Hale's culpability in the case of the Bury St Edmunds Witches did not end there, for his ruling in the trial was used as a model to similar effect by the judges in the trial of the SALEM WITCHES a few years later. Such was the cloud that the case cast over Hale's name that as early as 1682 his biographer, Bishop Gilbert Burnet, carefully avoided any mention of the Bury St Edmunds case.

Hale's involvement with witchcraft cases is often contrasted with that of his successor as Chief Justice, Sir John HOLT, who is revered for his steadfast refusal to be influenced by the witchcraft mania of the times and in this way did much to bring it to an end.

Hallowe'en In the Church calendar, the eve of the Feast of All Hallows or All Souls' Day, which is traditionally the night of the year most closely associated with witchcraft and the forces of darkness. Hallowe'en, celebrated on 31 October, marks the end of the Celtic year and is the point in the sun's cycle when it reaches the lowest part of its course. Legend has it that the sun actually enters the underworld for a time, and when the gates open to admit it hordes of ghosts and demons escape to visit Earth. It is, as a result, the best time to attempt to tap occult powers, which are then at their strongest.

This is the night when witches throughout Europe are reputed to take to the air on their BROOMSTICKS or in sieves or egg-shells (*see* EGG), travelling to SABBATS to work their spells and consort with demons. The ABERDEEN WITCHES put on trial in 1596 admitted to DANCING round the market cross at midnight on Hallowe'en and then cavorting to the music of the Devil himself at the foot of the hill at Craigleuch. Modern witches still meet on this date to draw MAGIC CIRCLES and to perform various ceremonies.

In pre-Christian culture, Hallowe'en was the date of the pagan festival of fire and the dead. In the folklore of the Celts it was the festival of Samhain, marking the beginning of winter and the time when cattle were brought in from the pastures and moved to their winter quarters. Attempts by the Church to displace this with a Christian festival in honour of the saints and martyrs, first introduced in the seventh century AD, have proved only partly successful.

The bonfires that were once a central feature of the pagan festival have, in England at least, been transferred to 5 November, the anniversary of the failed Gunpowder Plot of Guy Fawkes and his associates in 1605 – although Hallowe'en was still celebrated by dancing round large fires in parts of England until the end of the nineteenth century. Bonfires still occasionally burn in Scotland at Hallowe'en, and in the last century it was customary for boys in the Aberdeenshire and Buchan areas to ask neighbours for 'a peat to burn the witches' on this date. As the fire burned the children shouted, 'Fire! Fire! Burn the witches', and when the last embers went out they screamed, 'The devil take the hindmost!' and then ran helter-skelter for home in the belief that demons would snatch the slowest of them. An effigy of a witch was sometimes burned on these fires, much as Guy Fawkes is in towns and villages throughout England.

The terror that the festival inspired in pagan worshippers is evoked now by the grotesque PUMPKIN heads that are carved out as decorations for the night in question, and in the fancy dress parties, horror movies and so forth that are a highlight of Hallowe'en festivities on both sides of the Atlantic. The pumpkin heads, incidentally, are intended not so much to scare humans as to frighten away any ghosts or demons walking abroad on the night.

The business of children going from house to house to play 'trick or treat', a custom that originated in the USA, is derived from the old tradition of putting out offerings of food and drink to appease any of the dead revisiting their old homes. The children, disguised as ghosts, witches, goblins or the like, now demand these (or some substitute such as sweets) on pain of the householder suffering from some prank or other – rather in the manner of the witches who are reputed to work their evil on their enemies at this time.

hand of glory The severed hand of a hanged man, which was supposedly prized by witches for its special magical properties. The tradition of the hand of glory is common to the witchcraft beliefs of several European countries, including England and Ireland. One of the most complete accounts of the preparation of such a hand is to be found in *Marvellous Secrets of the Natural and Cabalistic Magic of Little Albert*, published in Cologne in 1722, although similar recipes are given in many other handbooks on the black arts.

Taken from the corpse while it was still on the gibbet, the hand (which was kept wrapped in a piece of shroud) was squeezed dry of fluid and pickled in an earthenware jar with salt, nitre, long peppers and a mysterious powder identified as 'zimit' (possibly zimar-verdigris). After two weeks the hand was removed from the jar and dried thoroughly in the sun in the so-called 'dog-days' of the month (or else by heating in an oven with fern and vervain). The pulp extracted from the hand was mixed with nitre, salt and other ingredients, reduced to a powder and left to dry thoroughly before being stuffed back into the hand.

A candle was then made with fat from the corpse combined with virgin wax, sesame and another ingredient called 'ponie' (tentatively identified as horse dung). This candle was fixed in position between the fingers and lit. It was alleged that anyone sleeping in the vicinity of the candle would be robbed of all power of speech and movement until the hand was removed. Alternatively, the hand was simply dried and pickled and the fingers themselves were lit. If the thumb refused to ignite, this was interpreted as a warning that someone nearby was awake and thus not subject to the hand's power to prevent them waking from a stupefying sleep.

Many witches were accused during their trials of possessing a hand of glory, and such grisly candleholders became an essential witch's accessory in the popular imagination. According to six- teenth-century demonologists, witches would light a hand of glory while preparing poisons to ensure that their brew acquired the desired lethal qualities. Thieves were also reputed to use hands of glory to keep themselves safe from discovery during house burglary (possession of such a hand also meant that locks opened magically to the touch). Tradition has it that they would sometimes intone the following to enhance the power of its influence:

> Let those who rest, more deeply sleep;
> Let those awake their vigils keep.
> Oh, hand of glory, shed thy light
> And guide us to our spoil tonight.

One celebrated story from the sixteenth century relates how a thief, arriving at a house in the guise of a beggar, used a hand of glory to keep his hosts from waking while he ransacked the contents. A servant girl, however, found the hand and, after failing to rouse the sleepers, finally succeeded in extinguishing the burning fingers by dowsing them with milk (water and beer having had no effect): the thief was captured and in due course hanged. Variants of this tale have been recorded elsewhere, including Huy in the Low Countries. The antiquarian John Aubrey referred to a similar story in the seventeenth century, while as late as 1831 thieves left behind a hand of glory when they were disturbed during a burglary at Loughcrew, County Meath, Ireland. Countermeasures to the baleful influence of the hand of glory were said to include smearing the threshold of the main door and other entrances to the house with a special ointment made from the gall of a black cat, the fat of a white hen and the blood of a screech-owl.

An example of a hand of glory is preserved in Whitby Museum, North Yorkshire.

hare Reputedly, a favourite disguise of witches when going about their nefarious business. Considered sacred by some pre-Christian societies, the hare, with its eerie cry and ability to stand upright like a human, has long been widely regarded with mistrust. In the past, the mere appearance of a hare near livestock was considered a calamity: the creature was undoubtedly a witch in disguise, threatening harm to both the animals and their owners.

It was claimed that witches often disguised themselves as hares in order to milk cattle without being detected. Many stories survive of farmers failing to kill hares with ordinary bullets and finding that only a SILVER one would do the job (the traditional method of shooting a witch). Marksmen who succeeded in wounding hares left behind many tales of how some old crone in the locality subsequently appeared with a bandage on the equivalent limb, 'proof' that she had been wounded while in the guise of the animal in question.

A typical case in which it was alleged that a witch had turned herself into a hare involved a woman named Mrs Julian COX, who was tried at Taunton in Devon in 1663. Among the witnesses against Cox was a huntsman who had happened upon a hare not far from where the woman lived. Having trapped the hare in a bush, and wishing to save it from being torn apart by his hounds, he went round the other side of the bush and leaped on it – upon which it turned into human shape. Recognising Mrs Cox, he retreated in terror, as did his dogs. The luckless woman was found guilty of witchcraft and executed.

Isobel GOWDIE, the celebrated self-confessed Scottish witch of the seventeenth century, recounted that while transformed into a hare she had had to run through her own house and out into another in order to escape a pack of dogs. It has been speculated that this 'hare and hound' story may have developed out of a ritual dance recorded in the confessions of several witches from different regions, in which the master of a COVEN played a hound and chased the female witches playing hares, copulating with them when he caught them.

The connection between hares and occult magic is remembered today in the 'lucky' hare's feet that are commonly sold as keyfobs or in the form of some other lucky charm.

See also RABBIT.

Hargreaves, Jennet *see* PENDLE WITCHES.

Harris, Elizabeth *see* FAVERSHAM WITCHES.

Harsnett, Samuel *see* DARRELL, JOHN.

Hartford Witches *see* CONNECTICUT WITCHES.

Hartlay, Edmund d.1597. English conjuror and herbalist whose involvement in a notorious case of demoniacal POSSESSION at Cleworth Hall, Leigh, Lancashire, led ultimately to his trial for witchcraft. The trouble at Cleworth began in 1594, when the children of one Nicholas Starkie, John and Anne, were afflicted by violent fits and bouts of nervous shouting. Edmund Hartlay, described by contemporaries as an itinerant conjuror and faith healer, was asked to help and for some months his assistance, based on the use of herbs and CHARMS, seemed to improve their condition. When Hartlay announced that his work was over, however, the two children (who were evidently very fond of the conjuror) were seized by fits and hysteria once more, and it was consequently arranged for him to remain permanently at the Hall.

When Hartlay was paid less than he had asked for, however, he threatened a deterioration in the situation. Sure enough, three girls living at Cleworth and two women servants then came down with symptoms of demoniacal possession. Hartlay, who found himself the target of assault by the evil spirits involved, now employed a MAGIC CIRCLE (despite the fact that these were forbidden by law) in order to quell the DEMONS threatening the household, but the fits carried on as before and Starkie, in desperation, sought advice from the celebrated Dr DEE.

Dee criticised Hartlay but otherwise declined to help, even when approached by the children themselves. Hartlay, who probably genuinely thought he could help the children, was incensed by Starkie's lack of faith in his abilities and the problems in the house were redoubled. Questions began to be asked about Hartlay's integrity, and soon allegations were being made that he was a witch and was himself the source of the trouble. A servant named Margaret Byrom revealed that the DEVIL had twice manifested himself in her bedroom in Hartlay's form, and both she and the children appeared to lose the power of speech when Hartlay was brought before them.

After Hartlay was unable to recite the LORD'S PRAYER without breaking down he was arraigned before the local magistrates and then sent to the court in Lancaster. The story of the magic circle he had drawn up in order to vanquish the demons proved damning evidence of his guilt, and he was sentenced to death as a witch and hanged in March 1597.

After Hartlay's death the case was put in the hands of the celebrated exorcist John DARRELL. He spent three days subjecting the seven possessed people in the house to a regime of fasting, prayer and preaching, and then declared six of them free of their tormenting devils. The seventh victim, Jane Ashton, was a Roman Catholic and it took another day's effort before she too was cured.

Harvey, William *see* PENDLE WITCHES.

hat The tall black steeple-crowned hat of the witch is a stereotype of time-honoured standing, reinforced in the twentieth century by countless illustrated children's stories and Disney films. However, the earliest extant descriptions of witches make no mention of them sporting any distinctive headwear, and it was conventionally believed that witches went to their COVENS entirely naked. The tall black hat of the stereotypical witch is, however, an interesting historical record of the witch hysteria: such hats were commonly worn by Puritan women in England and the English colonies in the first half of the seventeenth century – and it was Puritan England of the 1640s that witnessed the worst of the witchcraft panic at its peak in northern Europe.

Hatfield Peverel Witches *see* CHELMSFORD WITCHES.

Hathaway, Richard *see* HOLT, SIR JOHN.

hawthorn Like other thorn trees, the hawthorn has a somewhat dubious reputation and is often mentioned in connection with witchcraft. Tradition suggested that the crown of thorns placed on Christ's brow came from the hawthorn, and the tree was thus cursed. Its spikes were allegedly used by witches to inflict pain in IMAGE MAGIC or in other black magic rituals, being driven into the hearts of such animals as sheep and bats. The unwitting were particularly warned not to sit under a hawthorn on HALLOWE'EN, as they were reputed to attract fairies and other malevolent spirits. By contrast the hawthorn was, however, sometimes recommended as a witch deterrent, the theory being that witches entering a house would get tangled up in the spikes if the rooms were decorated with hawthorn blossom (although many people observed a taboo against bringing hawthorn blossom into the house, which was thought to be unlucky). In much the same way, parents of young babies in former times sometimes used to decorate their infants' cribs with hawthorn as a means of protection against evil spirits.

Haynokes, Susannah *see* WEIGHING AGAINST THE BIBLE.

hazel The hazel was much prized by the superstitious for its varied magical qualities, not least of which was its apparent ability to ward off fire and witchcraft. Considered sacred in Norse mythology and by the Celts, hazel was widely valued for its medicinal properties and was also one of the preferred woods of diviners and dowsers. Carefully cut on MIDSUMMER'S EVE by approaching the tree backwards and cutting the stem using both hands between the legs, a forked hazel twig could be used, it was claimed, to divine for hidden treasure. Twigs of witch hazel would often be tied over doors to keep witches from entering, and would protect the house from lightning and other threats. Sailors took bits of hazel to sea with them to keep themselves safe from shipwreck, while in Wales sprigs of hazel were worn in the cap to protect a person's luck.

Because of its magical potential, hazel was traditionally favoured by witches and sorcerers as the best wood from which to make a magic WAND. It was also used by WHITE WITCHES in the treatment of rheumatism and lumbago, among other complaints. The nuts themselves could be used for DIVINATION at HALLOWE'EN. The procedure was to place two nuts in the fire: if they jumped in the air, a lover was deemed to be unfaithful.

heart According to superstition, the heart was the seat of the soul and therefore a focus of occult power. In a variety of sympathetic magic, practitioners of witchcraft cut out felt hearts and pierced them with pins and thorns in order to cause great pain to an enemy. To procure someone's death, one method was to cut out the heart of a HARE and to stick it with pins before burying it in the ground: as the heart deteriorated, so the health of the victim went into decline. Conversely, farmers suspecting that their livestock had been bewitched to death were known on occasion to cut the heart out of the dead animal and to drive pins and thorns into it in the belief that this would cause unbearable pain to the witch responsible for the deed, thus revealing their identity.

hedgehog A traditional disguise of witches and a form in which they were reputed to rob cows of their milk and to obtain entry to homes and farm buildings. The association between hedgehogs and witchcraft was so strong that in the past many people killed hedgehogs on sight, especially if they were discovered in or near the home. It was considered most unwise to discuss one's personal business if a hedgehog was nearby, as it was probably a witch eavesdropping.

Records also exist in the English witchcraft tradition of FAMILIARS occasionally taking the form of hedgehogs. One notable instance concerned Christian Green, one of the SOMERSET WITCHES tried in 1665, who claimed that the Devil was in the habit of coming to her at five o'clock in the morning in the guise of a hedgehog and sucking milk from her left breast. According to her testimony, it was a less than pleasant experience: 'She says that it is painful to her, and that she is usually in a trance when she is sucked.'

Hell-Fire Club Notorious society which was devoted to the enjoyment of a hedonistic variety of SATANISM. The original Hell-Fire Clubs were groups of aristocrats who met in London at the beginning of the eighteenth century and dedicated themselves to the pursuit of blasphemy and various vulgar diversions, but better known than any of these was the more refined society founded by Sir Francis Dashwood (later Baron Le Despencer) in 1750.

Dashwood's Hell-Fire Club met at Medmenham Abbey, Buckinghamshire, altered by him to reflect the current vogue for ivy-clad ruins in the Italian style. It comprised a 'Superior Order' of twelve members, all rakes drawn from the English aristocracy, and an 'Inferior Order' of another twelve, composed of guests at Medmenham and selected neighbours (although these were excluded from the rites themselves). The 'Monks of Medmenham' included the politician John Wilkes, the satirist Paul Whitehead (who was the club's secretary and steward), Thomas Potter (whose father was the Archbishop of Canterbury), the eccentric George Selwyn (who attended executions in the guise of an old woman), Charles Churchill, Sir Henry Vansittart, Robert Lloyd, the Prince of Wales, the Marquis of Bute, the Marquis of Queensberry, the Earl of Sandwich and the relatively lowly born but very wealthy George Bubb Dodington (later Lord Melcombe).

The fraternity gathered for two weeks every June to celebrate various orgiastic rites parodying Christian ceremonies in the chapel at Medmenham, which was appropriately decorated with lewd wall-paintings. Typical highlights of these outrageous gatherings included veneration of the GREAT GODDESS (represented by a naked girl laid on the altar with her legs spread), FLAGELLATION, bondage and other sexual perversities. This was usually followed by feasting, drinking and whoring with prostitutes specially brought from London for the purpose. The motto of the club, borrowed from the writings of Rabelais, was: '*Fay ce que voudras*' ('Do what you will').

It is unclear how serious the members of the Hell-Fire Club were in their pursuit of Satanism (details of the rituals were destroyed by Whitehead shortly before his death). On one occasion the group seemed to have succeeded in raising the Devil when a hideous black figure leaped up and grabbed a screaming Earl of Sandwich; the demon turned out, however, to be a monkey wearing false horns and a long cloak, a practical joke perpetrated by Wilkes.

Dashwood's Hell-Fire Club ceased its activities at Medmenham in 1762 after Wilkes and his confederate Charles Churchill made public the Club's activities in an attempt to score political points against Bute (now Prime Minister), Dashwood (Chancellor of the Exchequer) and Dodington (a member of the Cabinet). Possibly fearing further disclosures, Dashwood, the Earl of Sandwich and the Marquis of Queensberry had Wilkes hounded out of Parliament and forced into exile in France. Dashwood subsequently attempted to reform the fraternity using chalk caves excavated at his estate at West Wycombe (now open to the public) and hosting small parties in a hollow golden ball added to the tower of the nearby church of St Lawrence, where he amused himself delivering parodies of the Psalms at the top of his voice.

Dashwood's Club inspired other similar groups throughout Britain and Ireland. Among the most notorious of these was the Dublin Hell-Fire Club, which included among its ranks such distinguished personages as the Colonels Clements, Ponsonby and St George, and Henry Barry, Fourth Lord Santry. These roués caused considerable scandal with their high-spirited japes, which ranged from wagering huge sums of money on the most eccentric wagers to setting fire to cats and burning down churches. They were also rumoured to celebrate BLACK MASSES on a regular basis and were presumed to be in cahoots with the DEVIL. Memory of their deeds is kept alive at such sites as the Dower House at Killakee, where they are said to have taunted and suffocated a deformed youth simply 'for sport'; in 1968, the skeleton of a small youth with an oversize skull was unearthed in the garden there during building work.

hemlock Poisonous plant which was consequently widely associated with the DEVIL and with the business of witchcraft. Hemlock featured in a host of brews and potions supposedly concocted by witches over the centuries. As well as being useful as a poison it was prized for its apparent ability to summon DEMONS, to cause dissension between lovers, to bring about madness and to render animals infertile. Hemlock was often listed as one of the prime ingredients in the mysterious FLYING OINTMENT with which witches are alleged to smear themselves before taking to the air on their broomsticks.

henbane Poisonous plant said to be a favourite ingredient in witches' spells. According to the folklore of witchcraft procedures, henbane was burned in order to release fumes which were said to induce the appearance of DEMONS. If eaten, it was reputed to cause a person to go mad (consumption of henbane could actually lead to convulsions and death). On a more positive note, the plant was supposed to assist in clairvoyance and to have aphrodisiac qualities, making it useful in the preparation of LOVE POTIONS; it was also used to ease injuries caused by witchcraft. The time-honoured practice of smoking henbane in the belief that it would reduce the pain of toothache was risky in the extreme, as it could easily prove fatal.

Henri III 1551–89. King of France (1574–89) who was widely suspected of witchcraft practices. The son of Catherine de' MEDICI, Henri distinguished himself as a military commander against the Huguenots and succeeded to the French throne on the death of his brother. Legend has it that he was brought up by his mother in the tradition of the 'Old Religion', even though he was outwardly a Catholic. Supported by the Catholic League headed by Henri, Duc de Guise, who was destined to become an enemy, Henri was king of a country divided throughout his reign by civil war. In his private life also he encountered controversy, not least through his barely disguised homosexuality.

Surrounding himself with a circle of personable young men, he was alleged to have worshipped the old gods at his own private altar, at the side of which stood the silver-gilt figures of two satyrs, complete with horned heads and erections. These were positioned with their backs to a relic purported to be a sliver of wood from Christ's cross, presumably as a gesture of contempt for Christianity.

Little is known of the nature of the ceremonies conducted by the King and his followers at this altar, but after his death an ominous indication of their tenor was discovered at his palace in the shape of the cured skin of a child. Henri is also said to have kept a talisman that belonged to his mother, which bore on one side a depiction of Catherine de' Medici in the role of the GREAT GODDESS.

Rumour had it that witchcraft was also employed by Henri III's enemies. Followers of the Duc de Guise were known to have cursed the King through the use of an effigy (*see* IMAGE MAGIC) and when he began to show signs of premature ageing, losing his hair and teeth while still comparatively young, this was blamed by many on spells cast by his political opponents. In the end Henri put paid to such plots, if they existed, by the simple expedient of having the Duc de Guise murdered by his own escort. In his turn Henri himself fell victim to a murderer: he was stabbed to death by a Dominican friar, Jacques Clement, who resented the King's opposition to the Catholic League.

Whatever the truth of the allegations that the King of France was a practising witch, or at least a sympathizer with pagan beliefs, it is undoubtedly true that during his reign many thousands of his people were executed on charges of witchcraft at the instigation of the Catholic Church.

Henry V *see* JOAN OF NAVARRE.

Henry VI *see* COBHAM, ELEANOR, DUCHESS OF GLOUCESTER.

Herd, Annis *see* ST OSYTH WITCHES.

Hereford, Bishop of *see* LAUDUN , SIR WALTER.

heresy An opinion or doctrine that is contrary to the teachings of the Church. The word comes from the Greek for 'free choice', a concept that was anathema to the Establishment throughout medieval Christian society. The Roman Catholic Church considered heresy a heinous sin deserving of death, and the INQUISITION was created specifically to deal with cases in which heresy was suspected, including (in its later history at least) those in which witchcraft was alleged. Because heresy was rather more than a crime ordinarily punishable under civil law, the usual rules of evidence were often ignored and persons found guilty of it were routinely excommunicated.

Heresy was categorised by the Roman Catholic hierarchy into several types. Those most relevant to witchcraft were the Albigensian and Waldensian forms. The Albigensian heresy, a variation of the Catharist movement, maintained the reality of SATAN as a god of evil on Earth and its adherents were regularly accused of sexual perversity. In the early thirteenth century they were persecuted throughout southern France, where the sect was strongest (they were named after the town of Albi). The Waldensians, meanwhile, emerged in the late twelfth century and claimed the Bible as the ultimate authority in a bid to combat immorality among clergymen. Again strongest in southern France, where they were also known as the Vaudois, the Waldensians were much persecuted on papal command in the fifteenth century.

A decision by the Lateran Council in 1215 made the death penalty for all cases of heresy a rule of Canon Law and thus, when witchcraft itself came to be classed as a heresy under pressure from the Inquisitors, it too carried the death penalty. Besides the death penalty, heresy bequeathed to witchcraft the notions that the Devil's adherents signed away their souls by means of pacts in BLOOD (*see* PACT WITH THE DEVIL), that they could fly through the air, that they showed their obeisance to the Devil by kissing his hindquarters (*see* KISS) and that they celebrated the BLACK MASS (accusations that formed the basis for countless witchcraft trials).

Hermetic Order of the Golden Dawn *see* GOLDEN DAWN, HERMETIC ORDER OF THE.

Herne the Hunter Legendary English witch whose ghost is said to haunt Windsor Great Park to this day. Tradition has it that Herne the Hunter was a keeper of the Park in the reign of Henry VIII and that he was hanged from an oak tree (identified thereafter as Herne's Oak) after being found guilty of dabbling in the occult. Many tales were subsequently told of his ghost, clad in deerskin with forehead surmounted by a magnificent set of stag's antlers, thundering through the park on a fire-breathing horse with a company of spectral hounds. Anyone who saw the ghost was fated to misfortune, although this did not prevent Henry VIII, for one, claiming to have seen the apparition.

An alternative version of the legend suggested that as a keeper Herne the Hunter saved the life of Richard II by killing an injured stag that was attacking the King. In the process Herne was badly wounded himself, but a mysterious stranger appeared and, by binding the stag's antlers to Herne's head, brought him back to health. The King promised to make Herne head keeper but this offended the other keepers, who threatened to kill the stranger unless he did something to prevent Herne taking the office. The stranger agreed, after extracting the keepers' consent to accepting Herne's curse. Soon afterwards, Herne found that all his knowledge of hunting had deserted him and the King reluctantly dismissed him, upon which the luckless keeper hanged himself. His ghost subsequently hounded each of the other keepers to their death.

Authorities on the occult have since made the obvious connection between Herne the Hunter and Cerne or Cernunnos, the HORNED GOD of the 'Old Religion' (and the prototype DEVIL of the witchcraft tradition).

Herodias *see* DIANA.

Hewit, Katherine *see* PENDLE WITCHES.

hex CURSE or malevolent spell, the aim of which is to bring harm to a person or to his or her livestock or property. Aggrieved persons once sought out witches in order to get a hex placed on their enemies; victims, meanwhile, had the option of seeking out a 'hex doctor', a witch specialising in the business of removing curses and lifting the power of the EVIL EYE. Conventional safeguards against such ill-intentioned magic include the wearing of AMULETS bearing certain mystic symbols, and protecting entrances to the house with similar designs and patterns.

See also MALEFICIA.

hexagram Occult symbol, otherwise known as the Star of David. Comprising two triangles superimposed, one pointing upwards and the other downwards, the symbol was traditionally used in a variety of ritual magic ceremonies. The triangles represented the contrasting qualities of male and female, 'above' and 'below', and fire and water. When sacrifices were demanded in the course of black magic ceremonies, they were usually enacted at the centre of a hexagram. The 'Seal of Solomon', in which the hexagram design was enclosed in a MAGIC CIRCLE, was reputed to grant the magician great influence over the spirit world, as well as offering a degree of protection against the DEMONS that he or she might raise. Such designs were sometimes used to decorate ceremonial robes, usually with the name of an occult demon added (the so-called 'double hexagram').

See also PENTACLE.

Hinchcliffe, Joseph and Susan *see* CHILD ACCUSERS.

Holda-Perchta *see* DIANA.

Holt, Sir John 1642–1710. English judge, who retains respect for his consistent determination not to be influenced by the contemporary hysteria in cases concerning alleged witches. Born in Thame, Oxfordshire, and called to the bar in 1663, he succeeded the witch-fearing Sir Matthew HALE as Lord Chief Justice of the King's Bench in 1689. Unlike his predecessor, he showed a positive will to defend suspected witches from their accusers by directing juries to ignore superstition and to act on the principles of judicial fairness and common humanity.

Holt presided over eleven notable witchcraft cases. In 1691 he saw to it that two witches accused of casting a spell over a woman named Mary Hill of Frome, Somerset, were acquitted (a third suspect had already died in prison): Hill quickly returned to her normal self. In 1694, in Bury St Edmunds, Suffolk, he obtained the acquittal of Mother Munnings, who had been accused of keeping imps and of killing her landlord by witchcraft: the chief witness in the case had been on his way home from the alehouse at the relevant time and no clear link could be made between the accused and the death of her landlord. That same year, at Ipswich in the same county, Holt secured a not guilty verdict concerning one Margaret Elnore, who had been accused of having the DEVIL'S MARK and also with causing infestations of lice. A year later, at Launceston in Cornwall, he was able to set free one Mary Guy, who was alleged to have caused a local girl to be possessed. In 1696, at Exeter, he obtained the acquittal of Elizabeth Horner on charges of causing the POSSESSION of three children (one of whom was allegedly given to walking up the wall to the height of nine feet).

In 1701, at Guildford, Holt cleared Sarah Murdock of casting a spell over an apprentice blacksmith called Richard Hathaway, who was given to fits. This decision led to angry protests, with outraged crowds threatening to 'duck' the unfortunate woman, and also to an apparent worsening in the condition of the young blacksmith, who suffered more frequent fits, could not eat or drink, was struck blind and dumb and was given to vomiting copious amounts of pins. But Holt was unrepentant: Hathaway was put under observation and, when it was discovered that his physical condition was faked and that the pins (strangely dry) were emanating from his pocket and not his mouth, he was charged with fraud. As a warning to others who might be considering levelling witchcraft charges in the future, Hathaway was fined, imprisoned for a year and also sentenced to three sessions in the pillory.

The most curious (and very possibly apocryphal) case in which Holt was involved was of particular personal interest to him. When a woman was brought before him accused of being a witch, the evidence consisted of a piece of parchment on which was written a charm for curing fevers. This was not, however, the first time that Holt had seen the piece of paper. As a young man at Oxford University he had lived a dissolute life and on one occasion, finding himself unable to settle a tavern bill, had paid his debt by scribbling a charm to cure the landlady's daughter of ague: this was the charm now presented to him by his erstwhile landlady. Needless to say, the case was thrown out.

Holt's example in repeatedly directing acquittals of suspected witches, regardless of any contemporary prejudice against them, was inevitably imitated by judges in lesser courts, thereby doing much to bring the witchcraft hysteria of seventeenth-century England to an end.

holy water   Water blessed in the course of religious services was once considered a powerful witch deterrent. It was also believed to be highly effective in curing WARTS. Such was the scale of belief in these notions that it was once necessary for fonts to be covered with locked lids to prevent all the water being used by parishioners anxious to rid themselves of witches and other evil spirits or to wash away warts and other incriminating imperfections on the skin.

Water used in services at Easter was most valued for its power to ward off witches and demons. Water saved from Palm Sunday, meanwhile, was reputed to prevent storms. Superstition detailed how holy water could also be used to detect witches who were suspected of having transformed themselves into CATS. The procedure was to place the cat in question in a bowl that had been used to carry holy water: if the creature attempted to escape, it was undoubtedly a witch in disguise.

See also WATER.

Holyday, Magdalen b.1654. English servant girl who in 1672 demonstrated startling signs of demonic POSSESSION. A maidservant at the parsonage of Saxmundham, Suffolk, she was suddenly taken ill after experiencing a sharp pricking sensation in her leg. Over the ensuing three weeks she vomited up a huge variety of extraordinary objects, ranging from egg-shells, bits of brass and bones to pins, bodkins and other objects. Finally, having brought up a length of blue cloth into which were stuck a whole row of pins, she seemed to be freed from her indisposition, which was inevitably blamed by everyone on witchcraft. Magdalen herself could think of no one who might have wished to do her harm, although she did recall refusing an old crone a pin when she had asked for one. Whatever the origins of the case, the symptoms never returned and Magdalen settled down to become in time the wife of Sir John Hevingham's steward.

Hopkins, Matthew c. 1621–47. English witchfinder, who was responsible for the ruthless persecution of scores of alleged witches during the witchcraft mania that swept parts of England under the Puritans. The son of a minister, Hopkins was raised in Essex, a staunchly Parliamentarian county with a long tradition of witchcraft. He studied law and may have worked as a clerk in marine insurance in Amsterdam and as a lawyer in Ipswich but failed to prosper until he hit upon the idea of establishing his reputation as a self-appointed witchfinder back in the Essex parish of Manningtree and Mistley in the mid-1640s. This was an ideal time to launch a career as a witch-hunter, for the Civil War was ravaging England and tension throughout Puritan society was high. Anyone who suggested a scapegoat for the nation's ills was more than likely to get a hearing.

Hopkins, then aged twenty-four, levelled his first charge of witchcraft against a one-legged crone called Elizabeth Clarke, claiming that she was a member of a COVEN in the Manningtree area. Clarke was duly arrested and questioned in Chelmsford in March 1645. As a result of her 'confessions' many more women were quickly brought before the Assizes (see CHELMSFORD WITCHES), of whom no fewer than nineteen were hanged.

After adopting the self-styled title of Witchfinder-General Hopkins acquired two assistants, John Stearne and Mary Phillips, whose job it was to search for the DEVIL'S MARK, and began a tour of the eastern counties of England, apparently obsessed by his mission to obtain confessions of witchcraft. To those who questioned his qualifications for such work, pointing out that he had never studied the subject, he replied simply that his expertise issued 'from experience, which though it be meanly esteemed of, yet the surest and safest way to judge by'. Such was the demand for his services that he made a handsome profit from his work (he charged 40 shillings for each investigation that he was asked to make, and his total bill amounted to as much as £23 when proceedings in a single town were complete).

In the space of little more than a year Hopkins brought over a hundred women, typically old, impoverished and physically unattractive, to the gallows in Essex alone, extracting the desired confessions by such relatively subtle means as PRICKING, SWIMMING and WATCHING AND WAKING. The fact that the women whom he charged with witchcraft fitted so closely the conventional idea of a witch doubtlessly did much to advance his chances of getting a conviction.

Particularly notorious was the involvement of Hopkins and his confederates in the trial of nearly two hundred suspects in the BURY ST EDMUNDS WITCHES case, which culminated in the execution of many of the accused. Victims included an eighty-year-old Royalist clergyman, John Lowes, who had made the mistake of antagonising his parishioners at Brandeston in Suffolk. Lowes consequently found himself on the gallows after being accused by the Witchfinder-General of sinking a ship by magic (even though his motives for doing so were never revealed and no one ascertained that a ship had in fact been lost on the day concerned). Other unfortunates were hanged at the instigation of Hopkins and his assistants in the adjacent counties of Cambridgeshire, Northamptonshire, Huntingdonshire and Bedfordshire.

Hopkins's motivation remains obscure: he was not a government or church agent but acted possibly out of religious zeal – although he may have been equally attracted by the prospect of becoming one of the most feared men in the country and also by the fortune waiting to be made out of such exposures. Whatever his motives, he declared himself quite convinced of the existence of witches. On one occasion he voiced genuine, perhaps paranoid, fears that a coven had dispatched a bear with orders to kill him. Much of his activity was directed towards identifying the guilty parties on what he claimed was his 'Devil's List', a document that was reputed to name every witch in Britain.

The Witchfinder-General's nightmarish career was mercifully brief. Doubts about his methods led to the setting up of a parliamentary commission to watch over each trial and to restrict the use of torture by the investigators. Hopkins was forced to give up the swimming torture but he continued to torment victims with sleep deprivation, starvation and other abuses. A more serious setback followed in April 1646 when the Reverend John Gaule of Great Staughton in Huntingdonshire objected to the presence of Hopkins and his assistants in his county and delivered a powerful tirade against their investigations. Gaule condemned the duress applied by Hopkins and pointed out that 'every old woman with a wrinkled face, a furrowed brow, a hairy lip, a gobber tooth, a squint eye, a squeaking voice or a scolding tongue' was likely to be pronounced a witch under such circumstances. Magistrates began to resist pressure from the Witchfinder-General and convictions fell off.

Hopkins suspended his activities, either because of the mounting opposition to his campaign or because of ill health, in May 1646. In 1647 he felt obliged to lay down an account of his methods in a pamphlet, *The Discovery of Witches*, in order to counter criticism by those who had misgivings about his activities and who questioned his integrity. To those who accused the witchfinder of operating solely for financial gain, and of concocting allegations against the innocent regardless of the evidence, he answered thus:

You do him a great deal of wrong in every of these particulars. For, first,

1. He never went to any town or place, but they rode, writ or sent often for him, and were (for ought he knew) glad of him.

2. He is a man that doth disclaime that ever he detected a witch, or said, Thou art a witch; only after her tryall by search, and their owne confessions, he as others may judge.

3. Lastly, judge how he fleeceth the Country, and inriches himself, by considering the vast sum he takes of every town, he demands

but 20 shillings a town, and doth sometimes ride 20 miles for that, and hath no more for all his charges thither and back again (and it may be stays a week there) and find there three or four witches, or if it be but one, cheap enough, and this is the great sum he takes to maintain his company with three horses.

Eventually, Hopkins became the victim of the hysteria he had helped to whip up. Legend has it that when he arrived in a new town and set about his usual business of charging local women with witchcraft, the townsfolk took exception and instead accused Hopkins himself of being a witch. Bound thumbs to toes, he was subsequently tried by his own methods and subjected to the ordeal of swimming. When he failed to sink, as an innocent man would, he was hauled out of the water and run out of town. One time-honoured version of this almost certainly apocryphal tale has it that he was actually hanged. In reality, Hopkins's demise was probably much less spectacular, although it may have resulted indirectly from the rigours of his ceaseless travelling in search of more victims – his health, it seems, had never been good and John Stearne reported him dying 'of a consumption' at his home in Manningtree in August 1647.

The location of Hopkins's grave is unknown and, although his burial is recorded in the Manningtree parish register, there has been diverting speculation that he went into hiding with the support of well-placed sympathisers. One remarkable theory has it that he emigrated to New England – where some playfully suggest that as an old man he may even had had a hand in the notorious trial of the SALEM WITCHES.

It is thought that in all Hopkins and his associates were responsible, over a period of just fourteen months, for at least two hundred deaths.

Horned God   Pagan deity who was venerated by many pre-Christian societies and later became identified with the DEVIL reputed to hold court at witches' SABBATS. In contrast to the GREAT GODDESS, who represented summer and the good things associated with it, the Horned God represented winter. Thus his appearance evoked the hunt and the business of killing for food, and he was usually depicted with stag-like antlers, animal skin and cloven hoofs.

In Stone Age society, when average life expectancy was as low as fourteen years and few reached sexual maturity, those who were the best hunters were revered by the rest of their tribe and were depicted in cave paintings throughout Europe wearing animal skins and horns. Emphasis was often given in these paintings to their sexual organs – the probable beginnings of the Horned God tradition. When farming developed, the Horned God retained his importance, becoming a symbol of fertility and ensuring through his ritual union with the Great Goddess that the crops grew and that both humans and livestock multiplied. In time, horns became a sign of divine power (Moses adorned his altar in honour of Yahweh with brass-covered horns, and centuries later Michelangelo carved a statue of Moses complete with a set of horns to denote his divine status).

The Celts brought their version of the Horned God with them to Britain a thousand or so years before Christ, and the curious figure with erect penis cut into the chalk hillside near Cerne Abbas in Wiltshire is generally agreed to be a representation of Cerne, or Cernunnos, the Horned God. Evidence of early veneration of the Horned God has been found far and wide: when, for instance, the altar at Nôtre Dame in Paris was repaired towards the end of the eighteenth century a much older altar was found within it, bearing a carving of this pagan deity beside the name Cernunnos. The Horned God, however, had no place in Christian doctrine and so he was transformed from a powerful fertility-promoting benefactor to a figure of evil whose followers merited the death penalty.

The degree to which early religious beliefs influenced the development of witchcraft is debatable – most authorities argue that there is no connection at all, and that the link suggested by followers of modern-day WICCA is a fiction. The Horned God did, however, endure longer than the Great Goddess as a cult figure, and it seems possible that the SATAN figure described by many witches owed at least his physical appearance, complete with cloven hoofs and horns, to this model (although the Horned God was probably not the only influence).

See also HERNE THE HUNTER.

horse-charming The bewitching of horses by the use of certain spells and charms, as blamed on many a suspected witch over the centuries. The economic value of the horse meant that in former times any illness or other problem suffered by the animal could often present a serious threat to the owner's livelihood. Horse-owners were therefore particularly sensitive about any suggestion of black magic being directed against their animals. It was once considered sensible throughout Europe to protect stables with reliable charms, such as horseshoes and boughs of ROWAN, which were reputed to ward off witchcraft. Similarly, the animals themselves wore HAGSTONES or shiny horsebrasses (the glare of the metal would supposedly dazzle any evil spirit that approached) and their tails were carefully plaited with ribbons, so that any demons in the vicinity would be transfixed by the intricacy of the KNOTS.

In some parts of Europe it was claimed that witches assumed the form of horses to fly through the air to their covens. Elsewhere, they 'borrowed' other people's horses to get to their meetings: in the morning the unlucky owners would find their animals in a sweaty and exhausted state and realise that they had been 'hagridden'. Witches were also reputed to have the power to halt whole teams of horses in their tracks and to keep them rooted to the spot for as long as they desired – though this magic would not work if the driver of the team carried a rowan whip.

Records remain of numerous cases in which the accused were charged with directing the EVIL EYE at the horses of their neighbours. In 1578, for instance, Margery Stanton of Wimbish, Essex, was alleged to have used magic to destroy a white gelding and a cow, while in 1610 Katherine Lawrett of Colne Wake, also in Essex, was similarly charged with causing the death of a horse through the employment of 'certain evil and devilish arts'. Such beliefs die hard. In the middle of the nineteenth century Priss Morris, of Cleobury North, Shropshire, incensed local farmers and others by allegedly causing their horses to remain stock-still until she was persuaded, after much difficulty, to utter the words: 'God bless you and your horses' – upon which the creatures immediately recovered their power of movement. Even later, Anne Blackmore, a resident of Withypool in Somerset at the end of the nineteenth century, was said to have the power to make horses rear and plunge uncontrollably under their riders should they cause her offence.

Howard, Frances *see* OVERBURY, SIR THOMAS.

Howgate, Christopher *see* PENDLE WITCHES.

Hunt, Alice *see* ST OSYTH WITCHES; SOMERSET WITCHES.

Huntingdonshire Witches *see* HOPKINS, MATTHEW; WARBOYS WITCHES.

Hutchinson, Francis 1660–1739. English cleric, Bishop of Down and Connor, whose *Historical Essay Concerning Witchcraft* of 1718 helped to bring popular belief in witchcraft in England to an end. When vicar of Bury St Edmunds in Suffolk, which had suffered considerably as a result of the witchcraft mania earlier in the seventeenth century, Hutchinson heard many stories dating back to the infamous trials held in the area. These inspired him to interview those with memories of the trials and to publish his book in an attempt to underline once and for all the manifest absurdities of the witchcraft delusion. In particular, he condemned the acceptance of evidence from children and the cruelty and partiality of the legal process.

Such was the effectiveness of Hutchinson's work that it was later claimed that 'few men of intelligence dared after that avow any belief in the reality of witchcraft; it is probable that very few men even secretly cherished such a belief'.

Huysmans, Joris-Karl 1848–1907. French novelist of Dutch origin who wrote up his experience of devil-worship in the sensational novel *Là-Bas* (1891). Born in Paris, Huysmans established his reputation as a novelist of the ultra-realist school, mixing with writers such as Émile Zola and Gustave Flaubert, but subsequently he became interested in the occult and formed links with the Rosicrucian group of the Marquis Stanislas de GUAITA in Paris, with the Church of Carmel run by Joseph-Antoine BOULLAN in Lyons and with the coven headed by Father Louis van HAECKE in Belgium.

When Huysmans exposed the activities of such groups in 1891 he differentiated between the relatively mild and beneficent sex magic of Boullan and the more hedonistic and uncontrolled rites practised by van Haecke, whom he depicted, thinly disguised as the villain of his plot, as a fully fledged devil-worshipper. The Marquis de Guaita was also offended by the book and directed several death-wishing spells at the author, as a result of which (so Huysmans claimed) he was often woken at night by a flurry of blows from an invisible assailant.

Boullan taught Huysmans how to defend himself against psychic attack, but he died not long afterwards and the author subsequently turned to the Roman Catholic Church for the stability he craved. Huysmans did, however, keep close contact with Boullan's followers, making his mistress and 'Apostolic Woman' Julie Thibault his housekeeper for a time. Retreat to a Trappist monastery failed to relieve him from supernatural interference, however, and he complained of being much troubled by a SUCCUBUS, which came to his cell and seduced him in his sleep.

Huysmans's last novels reflected his decision to devote himself to a chaste Christian life, and in 1905 his writings were acknowledged by the French state when he was raised to the rank of Officier of the Légion d'Honneur.

I **image magic** The use of an image fashioned in the likeness of a living person in order to obtain magical influence over that person, usually to their detriment. The employment of such 'sympathetic' magic, in which it was presumed that whatever happened to the image would be duplicated in real life, was long associated with the activities of witches all over the world. Many witches confessed in court to taking effigies of their enemies to sabbats to have them inspected and baptised by the DEVIL.

The image or poppet was traditionally shaped out of wax or clay, although often carved from wood or taking the form of a rag doll. Some witches insisted that, in order to work, a figure had to incorporate certain magically potent ingredients such as soil from a fresh grave, human bones reduced to ashes, black spiders and the pith of ELDER. The usual stipulation was that the image must also incorporate some trace of the real person if it was to work as intended. Such images would therefore include a few strands of the person's HAIR, their fingernail clippings, threads from their clothes, their handkerchief, their saliva, blood, sweat, tears or sexual fluids – or something else that had been produced by, or had been in close contact with, their body. Even soil taken from the centre of a person's footprint might be enough to establish the magical connection. In the past, to counter such malevolent magic people were very careful about the disposal of their personal belongings: they meticulously burned trimmed fingernails, locks of hair and so forth to prevent them falling into the wrong hands. Even water used for washing the body had to be carefully disposed of because it carried traces of a person's soul.

Once made, such images would be stuck with pins, nails or thorns (or alternatively melted, placed in water or buried) in order to bring pain and even death to the victim. Penetrating the figure's head with a nail would make the person it represented go mad, while driving one into the heart inflicted death either instantaneously or within a short time (perhaps nine days). Burying the figure in the ground meant that the victim would slowly and painfully waste away as the likeness itself rotted. A refinement of the practice observed by voodoo sorcerers was to send the actual figure to the person concerned, thus heightening their fear and laying them open to further magical interference. Others claimed that making a figure was not necessary, as a portrait or photograph – or even a wheatsheaf twisted into the shape of a man and named after the victim – would serve just as well. Records also exist of witches torturing and killing live animals as substitutes for their enemies.

The only defence against image magic was for the victim to find the image and to burn it, or else to rely upon the witch concerned relenting and not causing further harm. Time was when mere possession of a waxen image, or something that resembled one, was enough to confirm a suspect's guilt and to condemn them to the gallows or the stake.

Typical targets of image magic over the centuries included rivals in love, opponents in business affairs and those in positions of power and prestige (and therefore largely immune from assault from the aggrieved individual by more conventional means). Several notable cases hinging on the use of malevolent image magic concerned members of royal families or the nobility. Elizabeth I seems to have suffered in this way more than most. The discovery of three waxen images in the royal stables in 1578 caused a considerable stir, especially when one of them was found to bear the name Elizabeth (although it was suggested by Reginald SCOT that these were in fact love charms fashioned by a young man in pursuit of three ladies of his acquaintance). Two years later Nicholas Johnson, from Woodham Mortimer, was charged in court at Colchester in Essex with making a wax image of the Queen. Among other notable cases in which the highest in the land were allegedly involved were those of Eleanor COBHAM, the NORTH BERWICK WITCHES (who plotted the death of JAMES I), the AULDEARN WITCHES and Elizabeth WOODVILLE. Among Continental figures of importance who allegedly found themselves the target of image magic were Philip VI of France, who levelled charges at Count Robert of Artois, and Pope Urban VIII who had one of his cardinals' nephews executed for sticking pins into a wax figure.

As a tool of the sorcerer, the use of waxen images can be traced back all the way to ancient Egypt. Predating the development of witchcraft as such was a case recorded in AD 963, when a widow and her son from Ailesworth, Northamptonshire, were accused of making an effigy of Aelsi, father of Wulfstan, and driving nails into it; the son escaped justice and became an outlaw, but his mother was drowned at London Bridge. Some six centuries later belief in the effectiveness of image magic was just as strong. In 1594 a waxen image was found concealed in the bedroom of the ailing Ferdinand Stanley, Earl of Derby. The image was immediately destroyed in order to break the spell causing the Earl's condition, but this time action must have been taken too late for the Earl's health was not restored and he died six days later (despite the efforts of his doctors and of a WHITE WITCH recruited to combat the suspected evil). It appears, in fact, that the Earl had been poisoned and that the image may have been introduced as a means of concealing the true cause of his decline.

One of the most detailed descriptions of the use of waxen images in image magic was left by Mother Demdike, one of the PENDLE WITCHES, in 1612:

> The speediest way to take a man's life away by witchcraft is to make a picture of clay, like unto the shape of the person whom they mean to kill, and dry it thoroughly. And when you would have them to be ill in any one place more than another, then take a thorn or pin and prick it in that part of the picture you would so have to be ill. And when you would have any part of the body to consume away, then take that part of the picture and burn it. And so thereupon by that means the body shall die.

In 1960 an eighteenth-century doll was found in the cellar of council offices in Hereford; attached to the skirt was a piece of paper with the name Mary Ann Wand and the legend: 'I act this spell upon you from my whole heart, wishing you to never rest nor eat nor sleep the restern part of your life. I hope your flesh will waste away and I hope you will never spend another penny I ought to have.'

Reports of clay figures being used in witches' spells continued with some frequency even into the nineteenth century, especially in Scotland, and isolated instances have also occurred in modern times. In 1900 a critic of President McKinley burned his pin-studded effigy on the steps of the American Embassy in London, while during the Second World War an effigy dressed in the uniform of an officer in the Woman's Auxiliary Air Force was found in Gloucestershire with a pin driven into one of the eyes.

Image magic of this kind was not, however, always directed against someone's well-being. White witches used such images in casting spells designed to benefit a person's financial prospects, their health or their love life. Images were also used to promote fertility and, in a variation of the conventional service of EXORCISM, priests sometimes used to fashion wax images representing the demons they were called upon to drive out, plunging these into a fire while chanting appropriate verses from the Bible.

An unusual physical illustration of image magic may be inspected at the so-called 'Image House' near Bunbury in Cheshire, a modest cottage with a number of small stone figures set into its outer walls and in the garden. Legend has it that the house was built by a local poacher, who returned to Bunbury after serving an eight-year term of transportation as punishment for killing a gamekeeper in a fight. He cursed the stone figures in the names of the judge, the sheriff's officers, the witnesses and others involved in his prosecution, and set them in place around his house as he waited for the magic to have the desired effect. History does not record what fate befell his intended victims.

See also CANDLE MAGIC.

imp *see* FAMILIAR.

impotence *see* LIGATURE.

incantation *see* SPELL.

incubus Demon or goblin that engages in sexual intercourse with women. The original definition of an incubus – from the Latin *incubo*, I lie upon – was that it was a fallen angel, subverted by an unnatural lust for women (though the incubus may have descended ultimately from the satyrs and fauns of classical mythology). Such demons ravished women as they slept, causing them erotic dreams. As early as the fifth century AD such beings were acknowledged by St Augustine in his *De Civitate Dei* as a very real threat: 'It is a widespread belief that sylvans and fauns, commonly called incubi, have frequently molested women, sought and obtained coitus from them.'

The idea that such a being could have actual physical relations with mortals posed a problem, for the conventional view of the early Church was that demons had no corporeal existence. One way round this dilemma was to postulate the theory that a demon wishing to have intercourse with a human might take over a corpse or another human's body, or else fashion a body of sorts by magic. By the thirteenth century it was generally agreed that demons could freely adopt physical form by such means and aimed by their actions to bring degradation down upon hated Christianity. Other accepted traditions included the idea that incubi were particularly attracted to women with beautiful hair and the curious notion that they boasted two sexual organs with which to desport themselves.

Such demons were said to serve witches as FAMILIARS, and they might also be identified as the supernatural creatures with whom witches were alleged to enjoy intercourse at their SABBATS. In the latter case, they often took the form of a male goat (although they were reputed to be able to take several other shapes, including those of sexually desirable young men). These sexual encounters were reported to be especially satisfying, as it was in the interest of the incubus to ensure that the women thus seduced had fulsome orgasms. Married women, it was claimed, could keep such illicit liaisons secret from their husbands by always having intercourse with their incubi on the left side of the bed, which ensured that their human partners would not wake up. In the case of less willing partners, incubi might deceive women by assuming the outward appearance of their husbands or lovers.

Authorities on the subject claimed that it was possible for a woman to become pregnant through intercourse with an incubus, but also that a demon could produce no semen itself. The necessary seed had, therefore, to have been previously stolen from some other man, possibly after he had been bewitched into intercourse with a SUCCUBUS, the female version of an incubus. According to some accounts, succubi had the power to change sex, transforming themselves into incubi and thus passing on the 'stolen' semen. Favourite targets for such attentions included strong and very masculine men in their prime, whose semen was presumed to be particularly potent and likely to be produced in generous quantities. Alternatively an incubus might steal semen from corpses.

Any child produced in this way was likely to be born a monster, half human and half animal. Legend had it that Plato, Merlin and Martin Luther were among those born as a result of such exchanges between the Devil and mortal women. In 1275 Angela de Labarthe, of Toulouse, reportedly gave birth to a monster with a wolf's head and a serpent's tail – she subsequently became the first person known to have been executed for intercourse with a demon.

No doubt the idea of the incubus proved convenient on many an occasion when an errant wife was suspected of dalliance with a lover or was found to be pregnant when her husband had been absent at the time of conception. One celebrated instance, related by Reginald SCOT in his *Discovery of Witchcraft* in 1584, concerned a Bishop Sylvanus, who was alleged to have seduced a nun – the bishop insisted that an incubus had taken his form in order to deceive the nun and that he was in no way to blame. The authorities, a little gullibly perhaps, accepted his contention without a murmur. Nuns were, inevitably, considered a favourite target of incubi, and many records exist of sisters complaining of lustful dreams and of demons seducing them in their cells. If the nuns proved too virtuous to be seduced, as several saints were reputed to have been, the incubi allegedly tormented them, singing lewd songs and trying every trick to lure them into indecent acts.

Attempting to disguise immoral behaviour by blaming the attentions of incubi was, however, a risky business, for sex with an incubus was classed as bestiality and therefore considered more serious even than the sin of fornication. Any woman found guilty of entertaining incubi had furnished her husband with grounds for divorce and could be sentenced to death by burning. Much depended upon the degree of willingness that a woman betrayed in her dealings with such supernatural beings: if she showed any sign that she had given her consent to such exchanges, she was probably a witch.

Getting rid of incubi was no easy matter, for services of EXORCISM and the use of various holy relics often failed to remove the nuisance. Indeed, incubi affronted by such measures might exact revenge through poltergeist phenomena such as those reported in the case of the DRUMMER OF TEDWORTH.

See also NIGHTMARE.

initiation The acceptance of new witches into a COVEN was always (and still is) accompanied by various arcane rituals. The precise details of the ceremony varied considerably over the years and also from one country to another, but certain features were common to most versions.

On a given night (usually a Friday) the new recruit was presented by an existing member of the coven – often an older relative – to the DEVIL or to his representative, who might be disguised as an animal of some kind. An oath of allegiance might be sworn, which included a promise that the secrets of the coven would never be divulged. The apprentice witch, who in former times could be just seven years old or even younger, might also be required to promise to recruit further members to the coven and to perform various misdeeds in honour of his or her demonic master. At this point the Devil would mark the aspiring witch as one of his own, tainting the skin with a blemish or by branding, or perhaps drawing BLOOD from the person's ear (*see* DEVIL'S MARK). The blood might be used to sign a pact, under the terms of which the new recruit promised his or her soul to the Devil in exchange for enjoying riches and other pleasures on Earth, sometimes for a stated number of years (*see* PACT WITH THE DEVIL). The initiate, anointed in imitation of the Christian baptism, might also be given a new name and then be ordered to bestow the obscene KISS, pressing his or her lips to the Devil's buttocks as a gesture of obeisance. According to many confessions, the Devil might then insist on ratifying the pact by having sexual intercourse (often painful) with the initiate.

The coven usually went on to devote itself to the customary business of performing parodies of Christian ritual, working spells, feasting, dancing and enjoying orgiastic sex. The apprentice witch might also be presented with certain tools of the trade at this first gathering, among them FLYING OINTMENT and possibly a BROOM-STICK and a FAMILIAR to act as a loyal servant.

Innocent VIII, Pope 1432–92. Genoese-born Pope (1484–92), born Giovanni Battista Cibo, who instigated the witch-hunting mania that was to traumatise European society for some three hundred years. Innocent VIII was one of the less reputable popes, whose personal vices included keeping a mistress by whom he sired two children, causing the death of three boys whose blood was used for transfusions to improve his health and, at the end of his life, taking sustenance by sucking milk from a woman's breasts. Another weakness which he displayed shortly after gaining the highest office in the Roman Catholic Church was a passionate hatred of witches, whose activities he was inclined to interpret as a direct challenge to the authority of Christianity. He was particularly incensed by the leniency showed by many of his underlings towards suspected witches, and wrote numerous letters stressing the need to adopt a firmer line.

In December 1484, shortly after his election as pope, he issued the papal bull entitled *Summis desiderantes affectibus*, which aimed to promote the prestige of the INQUISITION and to intensify the campaign against those accused of such crimes. The invention of printing meant that the bull, which gave the ultimate authority to aspiring WITCHFINDERS and encouraged them to seek out witches at all levels of society, was widely read and had a much more profound influence than earlier papal missives. It took as real the rumoured wickedness of Europe's witches: the faithful were reminded that among other outrages witches conjured up INCUBI and SUCCUBI, murdered children and destroyed livestock through magic, blasted crops, inflicted pain and disease on their enemies, hindered lawful sexual relations between husbands and wives and blasphemed against the Church:

> It has recently come to our attention, not without bitter sorrow, that in some parts of northern Germany, as well as in the provinces, townships, territories, districts and dioceses of Mainz, Cologne, Trèves, Salzburg and Bremen, many persons of both sexes, unmindful of their own salvation and deviating from the Catholic Faith, have abused themselves with devils, incubi and succubi, and by their incantations, spells, conjurations and other accursed superstitions and horrid charms, enormities and offences, destroy the offspring of women and the young of cattle, blast and eradicate the fruits of the earth, the grapes of the vine and the fruits of trees; nay, men and women, beasts of burden, herd beasts, as well as animals of other kinds; also vineyards, orchards, meadows, pastures, corn, wheat and other cereals of the earth. Furthermore, these wretches afflict and torment men and women, beasts of burden, herd beasts, as well as cattle of all other kinds, with pain and disease, both internal and external; they hinder men from generating and women from conceiving; whence neither husbands with their wives nor wives with their husbands can perform the sexual act. Above and beyond this, they blasphemously renounce the Faith which they received by the Sacrament of Baptism, and at the instigation of the Enemy of the human race they do not shrink from committing and perpetrating the foulest abominations and excesses to the peril of their souls, whereby they offend the Divine Majesty and are a cause of scandal and dangerous example to very many.

The bull was specifically addressed to Catholics in Germany, where the Pope's inquisitors Heinrich Kramer and Jakob Sprenger had recently experienced considerable opposition in their efforts to secure convictions on charges of witchcraft. Those who continued to block trials were hereby warned that 'upon him will fall the wrath of God Almighty'. Kramer and Sprenger became two of the most powerful and feared men in Europe, being granted wide powers to investigate charges of witchcraft 'against such persons of whatsoever rank and high estate they may be, and to correct, punish, imprison, and mulct, as their crimes merit, those whom they have found guilty'. Anyone who opposed the inquisitors or molested them in any way risked 'excommunication, suspension, interdict, and yet more terrible penalties, censures and punishments'.

The bull of 1484 was subsequently quoted many times in defence of the witch-hunts that were mounted by witchfinders throughout Catholic Europe, and later observers have seen it as a landmark signalling the beginning of the witchcraft hysteria.

Inquisition Roman Catholic tribunal, which was founded in the twelfth century to suppress HERESY throughout the Christian world and subsequently acquired a legendary reputation for brutality in the Church's campaign against witchcraft. As early as AD 430 the leaders of the Christian Church had declared heresy punishable by death, although it was not until the advent of the Inquisition, which made heresy the basis of all cases that it examined, that such severe penalties were sought on a regular basis from the secular courts. In the thirteenth century a common punishment for those found guilty of heresy was to have to wear two large yellow crosses on their clothing, as a sign to the world of their culpability. The situation slowly changed after the institution of the Inquisition (in Toulouse in 1233 and in Aragon in 1238) to root out heresy in all its forms. As early as 1258 the Inquisition petitioned Pope Alexander IV to allow it to extend its frame of reference to encompass divination and sorcery – although the Pope on this occasion decided against such a change, it was not long before offences of this kind were being regularly investigated by the organisation. One of the early targets of the Inquisition were the KNIGHTS TEMPLAR, who were accused of all manner of occult crime and were persecuted without mercy by the Pope's representatives until the Order was effectively destroyed.

The idea that witchcraft was a heresy was debated for a considerable time. Gradually it was accepted that the Inquisition had a legitimate interest in investigating cases of witchcraft and sorcery as well as other varieties of heresy, and by the fourteenth century it was left to the Inquisitor himself to decide if a case involved heresy. The hierarchy of the Inquisition were keen to be allowed to investigate cases of sorcery and witchcraft because by the late fourteenth century, as a result of their own murderous zeal, they were running short of heretics to accuse on existing grounds.

Some of the earliest concerted campaigns by the Inquisition against witches were staged in southern FRANCE in the 1320s and 1330s, following the decision by Pope John XXII that devil-worshippers were a rightful target of persecution by the organisation. By 1350 some one thousand people had been prosecuted by the Inquisition at Toulouse and Carcassonne on charges of sorcery, and six hundred of them had been burned. Mass burnings of suspected witches continued throughout southern France under the direction of the Inquisition in the late fourteenth and early fifteenth centuries. Subsequently its influence spread to parts of Switzerland, northern ITALY and GERMANY among other countries.

The activities of the Inquisition against witchcraft were stepped up after Pope INNOCENT VIII issued his papal bull of 1484, sanctioning witch-hunts and granting greater powers to his two inquisitors in Germany, the Dominicans Heinrich Kramer and Jakob Sprenger. These two became the authors of the notorious and influential *Malleus Maleficarum*, otherwise known as the *Hammer of Witches*, which justified the persecution. One country where the Inquisition failed to make inroads, however, was England, where the common law forbade the use of TORTURE except where sanctioned by an act of the Royal Prerogative. Without torture the confessions deemed necessary for a successful prosecution could not be secured.

The conventional view held by the inquisitors was that Europe was under threat from the powers of darkness, which were waging war on mankind through demonic POSSESSION in various forms and were recruiting an army of agents, sorcerers and witches to undermine their enemies. To defend society against this threat, the normal rules of evidence observed by secular and church courts were set aside and much harsher measures adopted.

The Inquisition, whose officers were chosen from the Dominican Order, was answerable only to the Pope himself, who despatched individual inquisitors to areas that he feared were particularly susceptible to the enemies of the Church. The proceedings instituted by these inquisitors set the pattern for the persecution of witches in both church and secular courts, formalising indictments and establishing torture as an accepted method to obtain confessions upon which whole cases could be decided (usually, of course, against the accused). The sequestration of property by the Inquisition was also an example that other courts were quick to emulate.

Accused persons were presumed guilty until proven otherwise, in imitation of the attitude taken by legal authorities under the Roman Empire. The normal rules of evidence were set aside in view of the serious nature of the crimes alleged, and unsupported hearsay was deemed sufficient to justify the arrest of a suspect. All crimes considered to fall within the remit of the Inquisition were tried as heresy, which carried the death penalty. The identity of witnesses was kept secret, making defence of accused persons well nigh impossible. Testimony by persons whose evidence would not be admitted in other courts was acceptable when trying cases of heresy, with accusations being gathered from young children, other heretics and convicted perjurers. Retraction of evidence by a witness laid the person concerned open to a charge of perjury, and the original testimony was left before the court or dropped at the judge's discretion. Until a certain relaxation of the rules in the mid-seventeenth century, the accused were allowed no witnesses in their favour and the court disregarded pleas for clemency on the grounds of previous good character. The judges themselves sometimes took part in the inquisitorial process, and were permitted to use whatever deceit they thought necessary to trick suspects into confessing.

The use of torture was approved by a papal bull in 1257. In 1623 its use was restricted, senior figures in the Vatican acknowledging that it had sometimes been employed to excess in the past, but it was not forbidden officially until 1816. Although technically torture was not to be repeated, it could be 'continued' after a break and most suspects were subjected to three sessions, in which they were exposed to the most exquisite and sometimes life-threatening agonies until a confession was obtained.

Confessions had to be repeated by the accused once their torture had ended so that the inquisitors could claim that their statements had been made while free from such pressure. These confessions had to include the names of accomplices. Once found guilty, condemned prisoners had no right of appeal and their property was confiscated by the Inquisition. Many inquisitors became rich this way, although a large share of the wealth obtained was supposed to be sent back to Rome or shared with the civil authorities. A condemned person's only hope of escaping the death sentence was to arrange to buy off the inquisitors, perhaps with a guaranteed yearly payment.

Death sentences were not usually carried out under the auspices of the Inquisition itself. Condemned prisoners were instead handed over to the secular authorities with hypocritical requests for their lives to be spared (although judges who did so were likely to be charged with heresy themselves for showing leniency to proved heretics).

Interestingly, with the exception of Spain (where the Inquisition acted on its own authority and trials of witches continued to be pursued with vigour through the sixteenth century), the countries where the Inquisition held sway were among the first to see a calming of the witchcraft hysteria. Here the Inquisition instituted relatively few trials after 1500, although the mania was then at its height elsewhere. Those cases that did come to light were generally left in the hands of the secular authorities, with both Catholic and Protestant courts adopting similar procedures. Members of the Inquisition did, however, maintain their status as authorities on the business of hunting down and trying witches. They also published a steady stream of books on the subject throughout the seventeenth century, fanning the dying embers of the mania even while not actively involved in the trials themselves.

It is estimated that the Inquisition was responsible for the burning of some thirty thousand alleged witches in the years 1450–1600.

See also SALAZAR Y FRIAS, ALONZO DE.

invisibility   Many witches claimed that they had the power of making themselves invisible, usually a gift from their FAMILIAR or from the DEVIL himself. There were various other ways in which invisibility might be achieved. One method recommended by English witches was to mix the spittle of a TOAD with the sap of a sow-thistle and then apply this special lotion to the body in the shape of a cross. Alternatively, carrying agate or the right eye of a BAT about the person was reputed to have the same effect, as did exchanging shirts with a dead body.

Ipswich Witchcraft Case   Witchcraft scandal that erupted in Salem, Massachusetts, in 1878 and threatened to cause serious embarrassment to Mary Baker Eddy and the other founders of the Christian Science movement. The affair began when two of those drawn to the sect fell out and one of them, Lucretia Brown of Ipswich, alleged that the other, Daniel Spofford, was a mesmerist who had used his occult powers to cause her physical harm.

With encouragement from others, Lucretia Brown took the matter to the courts, charging Spofford with inflicting on her various ailments such as spinal pain and neuralgia. Somewhat reluctantly, Mary Baker Eddy allowed herself to be recruited to Lucretia Brown's cause, while another Christian Scientist, Edward Arens, took on the job of presenting the case in court. Perhaps predictably, the case failed to prosper, as the court considered it no business of theirs to attempt to control Spofford's mental processes. The press, delighting in the link to be made with the now infamous trial of the SALEM WITCHES 186 years before, took the opportunity to deride Baker and her followers. Not long after the farcical trial Mary Baker Eddy's husband was arrested for the attempted murder of

Arens (this case too was eventually thrown out) and within two years Mrs Eddy herself was doing what she could to distance herself from the whole sorry affair, blaming Arens for instigating the charges in the first place.

Ireland Irish culture, although famous for its rich and detailed folklore, remained relatively immune to the witchcraft mania that swept Europe between the fifteenth and seventeenth centuries. Reasons advanced for Ireland's deliverance from such troubles have included geographical remoteness from the hotbeds of the witchcraft hysteria, the difficulty thus entailed in getting hold of books on witchcraft, and the degree to which the Protestant ruling class kept itself apart from the Roman Catholic populace.

The first notable trial took place in 1324, when Dame Alice KYTELER of Kilkenny and several of her servants and acquaintances were charged with a long list of heretical practices and occult activities (which seem to suggest that they were merely observing some vestige of pre-Christian religious observance). This first trial was instigated largely at the insistence of the Bishop of Ossory, an Englishman trained in France, who may have seen the opportunity to profit by introducing to Ireland the witchcraft trials of mainland Europe. As a result of the investigations carried out in Kilkenny by the Bishop, Kyteler's maid Petronilla de Midia (or Meath) became the first recorded victim of the witchcraft hysteria on Irish soil, being burned at the stake on 3 November 1324 after the extraction of a confession under torture. Other accomplices may have followed her to the stake, although records of the case are incomplete. Kyteler herself escaped similar retribution by exiling herself to England.

The sensational events surrounding the Kilkenny case did not, however, inspire further trials elsewhere and outbreaks of the witchcraft mania remained relatively infrequent over the next three centuries or more; Alice Kyteler herself retained her reputation as Ireland's most celebrated witch. In 1447 the Irish Parliament declared that it believed it impossible for any man to ruin or destroy another through sorcery or necromancy.

Kilkenny became the scene of another witchcraft scare in 1578, when three witches – one of them black-skinned – were executed 'by natural law', after no statutory offence could be proved against them. There is, incidentally, no other record of a black-skinned person being executed for witchcraft either in Ireland or in mainland Britain.

The passing of a Witchcraft Act by the Irish Parliament in 1586 was invoked in the prosecution of individual cases over succeeding years, but none of these triggered the mass flare-ups that traumatised English society at much the same time. Records exist of only half a dozen trials between the first, in 1324, and the last, in 1711. In every case but the first, the defendants were Protestants tried by Protestants. Charges in two of the cases related to divining the future by calling up spirits; another, in 1609, concerned a young girl who was possessed by demons until magically restored by a holy girdle from Holy Cross Abbey, near Thurles. Rather more serious were the trials of Florence NEWTON, the 'Witch of Youghal', who was charged with bewitching a servant girl in 1661, and that of an unnamed beggar woman who was condemned to death and burned as a witch around 1699 for causing fits in a nineteen-year-old girl who had given her alms. The Witchcraft Act was finally repealed in 1821.

See also CLEARY, BRIDGET; HELL-FIRE CLUB; MAGEE ISLAND WITCHES.

iron Of all metals, iron (which is forged in fire) is considered the most magical and in the past was widely used as a witch deterrent. In ancient Egypt iron objects were often placed in the tombs of the dead in order to keep away evil spirits, while similar associations were shared by the early Chinese, who claimed that iron frightened off dragons, and throughout Europe, where many peoples believed that it also fended off lightning.

Because iron deterred witches, knives and scissors were often concealed under doormats at the threshold of the home so that no witch could enter. An iron horseshoe positioned over a doorway was thought to have a similar effect, and an old scythe hung above the bed was said to keep witches out of the bedroom. Touching something made of iron was once believed to ward off the EVIL EYE and magicians seeking to raise spirits might sometimes place a chain of magnetised iron around their MAGIC CIRCLE to reinforce its protective qualities. Iron nails, meanwhile, are among the more commonly mentioned ingredients used in ritual magic.

Italy The history of witchcraft in Italy reached an early climax under the INQUISITION. However, relatively few records of the witchcraft hysteria survive from the Reformation period, perhaps because the Church exercised more complete control over state affairs in Italy than it did elsewhere.

Sorcery was a crime punishable by death under the laws of ancient Rome, and many practitioners were crucified or thrown to the lions for such offences as bewitching enemies through the use of waxen images or preparing poisons. With the advent of Christianity, all sorcerers – with the exception of those responsible for public augury – continued to be persecuted, being periodically driven out of Rome and, in later centuries, sold into slavery. Memories of '*La Vecchia*' (the 'Old Religion') lingered, however, and it is probable that in remote areas some communities clung to their pagan beliefs, venerating such gods as Bacchus, DIANA Herodias and Venus. Legend has it that bands of witches swarmed across the night skies behind their leader, the goddess Diana Herodias, and these gatherings may have inspired the SABBATS that subsequent generations of European witches were rumoured to attend.

The 'Wise Women' of isolated Italian villages became the target of the Inquisition in the early years of the fifteenth century. Despite the fact that many of these victims did little more than concoct potions from wild herbs or tell fortunes, the inquisitors persecuted them with great ruthlessness. Also targeted were the fortune-tellers who made a living probing the future for well-heeled clients in the towns and cities (although astrologers were generally tolerated and even consulted by the ruling classes). The authorities were particularly concerned to prosecute anyone who was suspected of preparing poisons, and the concoction of any potion whatsoever was outlawed as early as the twelfth century.

The papal bull passed by Pope INNOCENT VIII in 1484 opened the floodgates, effectively signalling the start of the witch mania throughout Europe. The belief grew that Christian society was under threat from a huge army of witches dedicated to serving the forces of darkness. In the panic that ensued, the determination to stamp out heresy right across Italian society led to mass burnings on the flimsiest of evidence. Within months of the bull being published, in Como alone forty-one alleged witches were put to death on the orders of the Inquisition.

As elsewhere, the typical witch was an elderly crone living on her own and long suspected by the locals. The most savage TORTURE was routinely employed and confessions thus obtained were carefully recorded and studied, until a consensus of opinion was reached about what a sabbat was and how witches worked their evil and might be recognised. Outrages allegedly committed by Italian witches included child murder, cannibalism, sex with demons, desecration of the sacred host, the procurement of abortions and bewitching to death. A curiosity limited to Italian witchcraft was '*La Volta*', a fast and furious dance incorporating hops and leaps that witches danced at their sabbats and which was said to have been invented by the Devil himself (*see* DANCING).

Notable mass trials took place in 1510, when 140 witches were burned at Brescia; in 1514, when another three hundred were executed at Como; and at Valcanonica, where seventy died and another five thousand were suspected.

Around 1520 the Venetian Council of Ten attempted to restrict the mass executions that the Inquisition were undertaking in northern Italy, fearing the threat of depopulation, but Pope Leo X responded by confirming that the Inquisition had the ultimate authority in such cases. The only duty of the secular courts was to confirm the sentences that the Inquisition chose to impose. In 1633 one of Leo's successors, Urban VIII, was revealed to have been the intended victim of a witchcraft plot, the aim of which was to have him replaced by Cardinal d'Ascoli.

Typical of the later Italian witchcraft trials was that of an aged woman called La Mercuria in Castelnuovo in 1646. Subjected to torture, she named various accomplices and gave details of the sabbats she had attended in order to worship Satan and work evil against various enemies; as a result of her testimony eight people were beheaded and then burned. Among the most celebrated victims was Count CAGLIOSTRO (Giuseppe Balsamo), who was sentenced to death in 1789 for offering the services of sorcerers to various high-born guests at his villa in the Piazza Farnese in Rome. Thanks probably to his distinguished connections he was allowed to live, but was kept in prison for the rest of his days.

The witch hysteria in Italy died down gradually from the mid-fifteenth century, but sporadic outbreaks continued for some two centuries. Even today, the people of remote parts of southern Italy retain their reputation for adhering to ancient pagan beliefs.

Izzard, Anne fl.1808. English countrywoman who was the central figure in a late upsurge of witchcraft hysteria that swept the village of Great Paxton, Huntingdonshire, in 1808. Izzard had long had the reputation of being a witch, and locals were only too ready to believe the allegations of two village girls who claimed that they had been 'overlooked' by her (see EVIL EYE). As a result of Anne Izzard's influence, the girls explained, they had both suffered a marked decline in their health. A mob of incensed locals broke into the woman's house and scratched her face (see SCORING ABOVE THE BREATH) in an attempt to break the spell. A threat to subject her to the ordeal of SWIMMING came to nothing, but the mob attacked her a second time a few days later.

The authorities heard of the affair and several of the mob's ringleaders were thrown into gaol. When two more women scratched Anne Izzard's face with a pin, they too were imprisoned. Although the courts refused to countenance such unlawful action against the suspected witch, and pointed out that the illness of the two girls dated back to a day when they had got wet trying to cross the frozen River Ouse, the villagers – true to the beliefs of rural Englishmen and women two centuries before – remained steadfast in their stubborn opinion that Anne Izzard was to blame. In the end, the threat of further assaults obliged the unhappy woman to leave the village and she spent the rest of her life in St Neots.

J **Jacquier, Nicholas** b.1402. French Dominican inquisitor who confirmed witchcraft as a HERESY, justifying the persecution of witches throughout the Roman Catholic world by the representatives of the INQUISITION. In his role of inquisitor Jacquier conducted savage campaigns against heretics of all kinds in Tournai (1465), Bohemia (1466) and Lille (1468–72).

In 1452 he discussed the theory of heresy and witchcraft in the influential *Flagellum Haereticorum Fascinariorum* (*A Flail Against the Heresy of Witchcraft*) and concluded that of all heresies witchcraft was the most culpable, since its adherents knowingly and deliberately denied Christ's Church.

Among other things, he argued in particular against allowing anyone accused of attending a SABBAT to claim that the Devil had impersonated them – if this was their defence, they must prove that God had given permission to the Devil to impersonate them (clearly an impossibility). Jacquier's unforgiving views were subsequently developed and refined by later demonologists.

James I 1566–1625. King of Scotland (as James VI) from 1567 and of England (as James I) from 1603 who, despite his reputation for learning and open-mindedness, is remembered as one of the prime movers behind the instigation of the witch-hunting hysteria that swept England and Scotland in the seventeenth century. In 1597, indeed, he published a classic tract stressing the need for vigilance against witchcraft, and this work was considered by many to bestow the royal seal of approval on those who believed in the systematic persecution of witches in their midst.

James became convinced of the reality of witchcraft as a young man, probably while wintering with his bride-to-be in Denmark. Here he came into contact with many notable European intellectuals, who happened at that time to be much distracted by the perceived threat of witchcraft and were actively developing the theory that the whole of the civilised world was being invaded by Satan's hordes. Shortly after his return home, the King's anxiety about this threat seemed to him to be confirmed when, at Holyrood Palace in 1591, he personally interviewed Agnes Sampson and other suspects in the infamous case of the NORTH BERWICK WITCHES. Under torture, which was witnessed by the King in person, Sampson confessed her guilt and also (perhaps conveniently for James) implicated the King's ambitious cousin, Francis, Earl of Bothwell, as the leader of a COVEN who had plotted against the throne.

James let it be known that he was especially alarmed by Sampson's claims that she and her accomplices had plotted to murder him when he sailed off to visit his intended wife, Anne of Denmark. According to Sampson's confession, the witches had taken to the waters of the Forth in magic sieves when the King set sail for Scandinavia and had thrown a CAT, tied up with parts of a dead corpse, into the sea to raise a storm. The fleet had indeed encountered bad weather and one ship had gone down, although it was not the vessel on which the King was travelling. When this plot had failed, the witches had fashioned a waxen image of James, identifying it as the King as they passed it from one to another prior to roasting it over a fire.

James listened carefully to the testimony of Sampson and the others and expressed doubts about the truth of much of it. Ultimately he lost patience with them and called them all 'extreme liars', but he changed his tune very quickly when Sampson reportedly whispered in his ear the exact words that James and his new bride had exchanged in private on their wedding night. The startled James, who admitted that 'all the devils in hell could not have discovered the same', had no option now but to accept Sampson's culpability and to support the guilty verdict that was brought against her (she was subsequently executed at Haddington). When another of the accused, Barbara Napier, was acquitted because she was pregnant, James – in what was called the 'Tolbooth Speech' – accused the judges of 'an assize of error':

> For witchcraft, which is a thing grown very common amongst us, I know it to be a most abominable sin, and I have been occupied these three quarters of this year for the sifting out of them that are guilty herein. We are taught by the laws both of God and men that this sin is most odious. And by God's law punishable by death. By man's law it is called *maleficium* or *veneficium*, an ill deed or a poisonable deed, and punishable likewise by death.
>
> The thing that moved [the judges] to find as they did, was because they had no testimony but of witches; which they thought not sufficient. By the civil law I know that such infamous persons are not received for witnesses, but in matters of heresy and *lesae majestatis*. For in other matters it is not thought meet, yet in these matters of witchcraft good reason that such be admitted. First none honest can know these matters. Second, because they will not accuse themselves. Thirdly, because no act which is done by them can be seen.
>
> Further, I call them witches which do renounce God and yield themselves wholly to the Devil; but when they have done, then I account them not as witches, and so their testimony sufficient.

The judges were obliged to apologise for their leniency (although Napier seems to have survived). Bothwell was obliged to go into exile and ceased to be a serious challenge to the throne.

Politically motivated though it might have been, James's interest in the trial of Sampson and other members of her coven prompted him to record his thoughts on the subject in his *Daemonologie*, which was published in the form of a lengthy dialogue in 1597, the same year as the mass trial of the ABERDEEN WITCHES. This tract was written partly in response to Reginald SCOT's sceptical *Discoverie of Witchcraft* of 1584 and supported, on the whole, the idea that witchcraft was a real threat. James did, however, question the validity of some theories about the powers and practices of practitioners of the black arts and warned against accepting accusations without corroborating evidence, as well as discounting the existence of WEREWOLVES. On the other hand, he supported the practice of SWIMMING and the searching out of the DEVIL'S MARK to confirm guilt. The book, republished south of the border in 1604, found a ready audience throughout the kingdom. All copies of Scot's book, meanwhile, were destroyed in 1603 by royal command.

In the first year of James's reign in England he pushed through a new Witchcraft Act which was much sterner in character than the previous Act of 1563, increasing penalties and consequently intensifying the witch-hunting mania. In line with Continental practice, courts now looked for suggestions that the accused had made a PACT WITH THE DEVIL, rather than concentrating upon evidence of actual MALEFICIA. In James's defence, his reservations about the quality of the evidence in many cases became well known and undoubtedly curbed some of the judicial excesses that might otherwise have occurred. On several occasions, indeed, he went out of his way to make public criticisms of judges who failed to question adequately wild accusations that relied upon hearsay alone.

In 1616 James demonstrated his cautious approach to evidence in specific cases when he interviewed a thirteen-year-old boy, John Smith, who was at the centre of a trial at the Leicestershire Assizes (*see* LEICESTER BOY). Nine witches had already been hanged for causing the lad to suffer fits, and another six were awaiting examination on the same charges. James questioned the boy and decided he was faking his evidence: the Archbishop of Canterbury agreed, and finally the boy confessed. James delivered a stiff rebuke to the judges – Sir Randolph Crew and Sir Humphrey Winch – who had sent nine innocent women to their deaths, and demanded that in the future judges assess evidence much more stringently. The case of the BILSON BOY in 1620, which resulted in the acquittal of the accused after the boy concerned similarly admitted he had made up the allegations, strengthened James in his scepticism.

It is unlikely that James ceased to believe entirely in the principle of witchcraft, but certainly towards the end of his life he retreated from many of the conclusions he had drawn in his famous book. In the last nine years of his reign only five people are recorded as having been executed for witchcraft. None the less, passages from James's *Daemonologie* continued to be widely quoted in courts as justification for the prosecution of accused witches, and the 1604 Act that he sponsored remained on the statute books until 1736.

The circumstances of James I's early death are shrouded in mystery and some contemporaries detected a further link between the monarch and witchcraft, alleging that Dr LAMB, associate of the Duke of Buckingham, had used magic to poison the King. Lamb himself was subsequently hunted down by the London mob and stoned to death in Cheapside amid accusations that he was a wizard. His assistant, Anne Bodenham, stood trial as a witch, accused of supplying poisons, and was hanged (*see* DR LAMB'S DARLING).

See also GUNTER, ANNE.

Jeanne des Anges *see* LOUDUN NUNS.

Jeffray, John and Maud *see* FAIRFAX, EDWARD.

Jenks, Roland *see* CANDLE MAGIC.

Jersey *see* CHANNEL ISLANDS.

Jewel, John, Bishop of Salisbury *see* ENGLAND.

Joan of Arc *c.*1412–31. French patriot and martyr, born Jehanette/ Jehanne Darc and also known as La Pucelle, who inspired French resistance against the English occupiers of the country during the Hundred Years' War, but was ultimately burned at the stake for HERESY and was popularly regarded by many of her enemies as a witch. Born into a peasant family in Domrémy on the borders of Lorraine and Champagne, Joan had a keen intelligence though little education. In 1428, at the age of sixteen, she announced that she had heard the voices of St Michael, St Catherine and St Margaret ordering her to drive the English out of the Paris region (the saints had first appeared to her three years earlier). When Joan related her story to the local military commander, Robert de Baudricourt, he sent her home, but she came back six months later to repeat her claims. De Baudricourt had her exorcised but gradually became convinced of the authenticity of her claims and decided to present her to the Dauphin, the disputed heir to the French throne, at Chinon in the Loire valley.

A first test of Joan's supernatural abilities, in which the girl was ordered to pick out the disguised Dauphin from among his courtiers, proved no problem to her and her contention that he was indeed the true heir to the throne of France went down very well. To the Dauphin's evident surprise, she was also able to recite accurately the words of his personal daily prayer. After subsequently impressing her interrogators when she was brought before an ecclesiastical court in Poitiers she was sent, with the approval of the Dauphin's court, to join the French army at Orleans, which was then under siege by the English. Clad in white armour and carrying her own personal banner, she proved an inspiration to the dispirited soldiers and she entered the city with them on 29 April 1429; the siege itself was lifted on 8 May. Over the following months the English were forced to withdraw from the Loire and Joan made a great show of escorting the Dauphin triumphantly through English-occupied territory to be crowned at Rheims.

The Dauphin, now crowned as Charles VII, showed some reluctance to rely further on the young girl's apparently divine gifts of leadership, however, and he resisted her plans for other military excursions which included the relief of Paris. In 1430 Joan determined to raise the siege of Compiègne, then being attacked by the Burgundians under Jean de Ligny of Luxembourg, but the expedition proved a military disaster and she was captured during a skirmish. An attempt to escape from imprisonment in Beaurevoir Castle by jumping from a high tower resulted only in her sustaining minor injuries. Three days after her capture, with the ungrateful Charles VII doing nothing to ransom the woman to whom she owed his throne, Jean de Ligny handed her over to the pro-English Pierre Cauchon, Bishop of Beauvais, for a price of ten thousand crowns.

Chained by the neck, hands and feet, Joan was then locked in a cramped iron cage and taken to the castle of Rouen to await trial for heresy and sorcery before Bishop Cauchon and Friar Martin Billorin, Inquisitor-General of France.

The outcome of the trial was a foregone conclusion, but Joan impressed everyone with her courageous demeanour. Physical examination confirmed that she was a virgin (evidence which proved to many that she was not a witch) and investigation into her early life at Donrémy failed to uncover any incriminating stories about her. The judges tried to extract from her admissions that could be interpreted as confessions of occult practice, asking her whether her angels had appeared to her naked and whether she had danced round a tree locally reputed to belong to fairies, but none of these was forthcoming.

None the less the trial continued, with much of the proceedings taking place in the prisoner's cell. When Joan refused to withdraw her claims that she had heard the voices of angels, it was suggested to her that what she had really heard were the voices of devils – but she skilfully evaded the dangers implicit in this and other questions. Neither would she confirm that she possessed some magic rings which ensured her victory on the battlefield. In the end, lacking corroborating evidence, the court was obliged to strike out all the charges which implied that the accused was a sorceress or witch, and of the original seventy counts on which she was indicted only twelve were left standing. They included the offences of wearing men's clothes and wilfully disobeying the authority of the Church. These twelve charges were declared proved, and Joan was formally condemned to death as a heretic.

Attempts were made by the authorities to persuade Joan to recant, but these failed. Torture was considered, but rejected on the grounds that the court had no wish to appear to have forced a confession from her. On 24 May 1431 Joan was taken to the churchyard of St Ouen in Rouen for execution, but the terror of the occasion proved too much for her and she unexpectedly admitted her errors, promising to obey the Church and to deny her visions. She signed a confession, and was thrown into gaol to begin a life sentence. Here the English gaolers gave her only men's clothes to wear and, when she finally out of necessity consented to wear them, she was immediately accused of lapsing once again into heresy.

Joan now withdrew her confession entirely and, refusing all attempts to make her change her mind, she resigned herself to her fate. On 30 May 1431 she was excommunicated and then, at the age of nineteen, burned alive as a heretic on a pyre in the Old Market Place in Rouen. To guard against the possibility that the dead woman had indeed been a witch, the executioner is reported to have cut out her heart and entrails and to have burned them before throwing the ashes into the Seine.

In 1456, to validate the legitimacy of Charles VII's coronation, the trial was declared irregular. Ultimately, Joan of Arc, the 'Maid of Orléans', was canonised by the Roman Catholic Church in 1920. From time to time various authorities on the life of Joan of Arc have attempted to put the case that she really was a witch and a follower of the 'Old Religion', but the theory has still to be convincingly proved.

See also RAIS, GILLES DE.

Joan of Navarre 1370–1437. French princess who married Henry IV of England in 1403 but subsequently fell from grace after she was accused of witchcraft by her stepson, Henry V. The daughter of Charles the Bad, King of Navarre, Joan married the Duke of Brittany at the age of sixteen but was courted by Henry IV after her first husband died in 1399. The match was desirable chiefly for political reasons, and in due course the two were married and Joan became the new Queen of England. She was reportedly an attractive woman, but the marriage was not very happy. Henry died ten years later and his eldest son by his first marriage was crowned Henry V.

For six years relations between Joan and her stepson were warm and harmonious, but this all came to an abrupt end when Henry suddenly accused her of plotting his death by witchcraft. The allegation was based on the testimony of Joan's confessor, a Franciscan friar named John Randolf, who had confessed to plotting with the King's stepmother to secure Henry's death 'in the most horrible manner that could be devised'. Henry was alarmed enough at this confession to request the Archbishop to say prayers for his protection and he immediately set about foiling the alleged conspiracy. Both plotters were thrown into prison, Joan being confined in Pevensey Castle in Sussex. Henry hesitated, however, before taking the matter further in view of the political repercussions that such action would entail.

Three years later, aged thirty-four, Henry died and Joan was released from her prison after promising to live quietly and never to come to court. She spent the remaining fifteen years of her life at Havering-atte-Bowe in Essex, without attracting any further controversy, and was eventually buried at her husband's side in Canterbury. According to one authority Randolf died in prison when his brains were dashed out by his gaolers, while another version of his end describes how he was murdered by a mad priest who attacked him first with a stone and then with an axe and subsequently buried his body beneath a dunghill.

John XXII, Pope *c.*1245–1344. French pope at Avignon (1316–34), born Jacques Duèse, who was the first pontiff to promote the theory of witchcraft and who also sanctioned an intensification of the campaign by the INQUISITION against all heretics, sorcerers and witches. John XXII was deeply superstitious and was obsessed with the idea that his life was constantly under threat from demonic forces sent against him by his enemies. A year after his election he ordered the torture of three suspects accused of using such magic, and had the satisfaction of hearing their confessions to the charges. In 1318 he considerably widened the scope of legal action against alleged heretics, passing a bull that permitted accusations against dead suspects to be heard in court.

In 1320 the Pope instructed the Inquisition in FRANCE to move against anyone alleged to have made sacrifices to devils or otherwise to have dabbled in the black arts by making waxen images and so forth, or to have blasphemed against the Church, and to confiscate their property. Witch-hunts were subsequently pursued throughout southern France on the Pope's direct orders in 1323, 1326, 1327 and 1331.

A further bull of 1326 emphasised the reality of the threat posed by witchcraft, accepting as proved the contentions that witches denied Christ, made sacrifices to devils, used waxen images, rings, mirrors and so on to harm their enemies, divined the future by questioning demons and employed the said demons to pursue their own evil ends.

John XXII, for all his anxieties, seems to have remained immune from the witches whom he feared and loathed with such ferocity. He was deposed by Louis of Bavaria in 1334, but enjoyed his last years in Avignon surrounded by the great wealth he had amassed as supreme pontiff.

Johnson, Margaret *see* ROBINSON, EDMUND.

Johnson, Mary *see* CONNECTICUT WITCHES.

Jørgensdatter, Siri b.1717. Norwegian peasant girl who in 1730 was examined by local magistrates after she had made various accusations of witchcraft against her own grandmother.

The case of thirteen-year-old Siri Jørgensdatter began when she publicly alleged that her late grandmother had been a witch and that she had tried to initiate her into a coven of devil worshippers. The girl claimed that she had seen her grandmother smear FLYING OINTMENT on a pig and that she had then been taken for a ride through the air to a place called the Blocula, where she had been introduced to the Devil himself and had shared a meal with him. At the end of the meal a blue flame had entered through a trap door and out of it had come a horde of little demons. On a second visit in company with her grandmother the DEVIL had stuck a knife into the girl's finger and had then bitten her right ear – on examination it was found that Siri had no feeling at either of the two sites she described. On other occasions, she had seen her grandmother magically milk cows by sticking a knife into the wall and tying to it three straps, which she then milked as she would a real animal.

Siri alleged that when the old woman lay dying she had given her granddaughter a wooden cup containing some flying ointment, and also named Anne Holstenstad and Goro Braenden as her accomplices. Unfortunately, Siri's aunt had then found the ointment and Siri's broomstick and had burned them. When questioned further by her aunt, Siri confessed everything (although warned not to do so by various demons and her grandmother's fellow witches) and she was brought before the local dean and parson for examination.

Despite the fact that the dean and parson were deeply impressed by Siri's evidence and passed the case on to the Bishop and the local governor, Siri's tale failed to make much further headway. The similarities between her story and the widely reported Swedish case of the MORA WITCHES in 1669 was considered suspicious, and it was quickly decided that the girl had made up her allegations on the strength of what she had read about the earlier affair. The case was dismissed, and little more was heard of Siri Jørgensdatter and her dealings with the Devil – a vivid illustration of how allegations that a bare sixty-one years previously could lead to the deaths of eighty-five suspects could now be totally disregarded, failing to satisfy the simplest legal tests in a less credulous age.

Jourdemain, Margery *see* COBHAM, ELEANOR, DUCHESS OF GLOUCESTER.

Junius, Johannes d.1628. German burgomaster (mayor), who became one of the more distinguished victims of persecution during the infamous campaign against the BAMBERG WITCHES. The case of fifty-five-year-old Junius is remembered for two reasons: first, he was the burgomaster of the town, and second, shortly before his execution he smuggled out of prison a letter – a document that not only sheds light on the process by which such prosecutions were brought to a conclusion but which also evokes the reality of the agonies and suffering to which the innocent victims of the witch-hunters were exposed.

Junius had the misfortune to be burgomaster in Bamberg at a time when the witch hysteria in Germany was at its height. In the years 1623–33 some six hundred of the town's residents, including many of its most respected citizens, were put to death on charges of witchcraft, often on the flimsiest of evidence. Junius had been appointed to his post in 1608 and appears to have lived a blameless life until 1628, when he was arraigned as a suspected witch on the strength of a confession, extracted under severe torture, by Georg Hahn, the Vice-Chancellor of Bamberg. Junius's wife had already been executed on a similar charge, and this fact alone was enough to confirm his guilt in the minds of the judges.

Throughout his trial before the representatives of the witch-hunting Prince-Bishop Gottfried Johann George II Fuchs von Dornheim, Junius denied any knowledge of witchcraft and was vehement in claiming that he had never renounced God or attended a SABBAT. Testimony to the effect that he had been seen at sabbats by various other witnesses (all of whom had been tortured into making these accusations) was then presented, but still Junius continued to resist the urgings of the court that he make his own confession. Inevitably, he was handed over to the torturers. According to the surviving records of the case, the THUMBSCREWS and the BOOTS had little effect, but after repeated subjection to STRAPPADO he finally broke down and requested time to consider his position. Discovery of the DEVIL'S MARK in the form of a blemish on his right side, which appeared impervious to pain, was but another piece of 'evidence' that made his case quite hopeless.

Alone in his cell, the wretched burgomaster managed to write a last letter to his daughter Veronica, although he had some difficulty holding a pen because of the torture he had suffered:

> Many hundred thousand good-nights, dearly beloved daughter Veronica. Innocent had I come into prison, innocent I have been tortured, innocent must I die. For whoever comes into the witch prison must become a witch or be tortured until he invents something out of his head and – God pity him – bethinks him of something.

In this moving last message, dated 24 July 1628, Junius apprised his daughter of his situation and urged her to flee Bamberg until the panic had died down. He described how Georg Hahn and his other accusers, before going to their own deaths, had apologised to him for implicating him in the affair, explaining that the torture had been too much for them to bear. Of his own torture in the thumb-screws, he recalled how 'the blood spurted from the nails and everywhere, so that for four weeks I could not use my hands, as you can see from my writing'. Of the experience of strappado he could only say, 'I thought heaven and earth were at an end. Eight times did they draw me up and let me fall again, so that I suffered terrible agony.' In private, he wrote, the executioner had urged him to con-fess the truth or else to make something up in order to escape further agonies: 'Now, my dearest child, see in what hazard I stood and still stand. I must say that I am a witch, though I am not – must now renounce God, though I have never done it before.'

He tells his daughter that he will compose a confession, even though in his heart he will know it to be untrue. The letter goes on to describe how the interrogators have insisted upon him naming accomplices, taking him on a tour of the town and picking out the witches he recognised street by street. The heart-rending text of the letter ends with the simplest of farewells: 'I have taken several days to write this – my hands are both crippled. I am in a sad plight ... Good night, for your father Johannes Junius will never see you more.'

Junius subsequently made a lengthy statement to the court describing his various crimes. Among other offences, he admitted to renouncing God after the Devil had seduced him in the form of a young woman, to keeping and having intercourse with a SUC-CUBUS·named Vixen, to desecrating the sacred host and to riding through the air to sabbats on a BLACK DOG. He had, however, refused to obey Vixen's demands that he murder his children using a grey powder, and had administered the powder to his horse instead. In response to the court's demands he also made allega-tions against various accomplices. The court accepted the confession and Johannes Junius, a representative of hundreds of others thus maltreated, was sentenced to death. On 6 August 1608 he was burned at the stake.

Kelly, Edward 1555–95. English necromancer, alchemist and scientist, born Edward Talbot, who in 1582 became assistant to the celebrated Elizabethan scholar Dr John DEE. Generally considered a charlatan, Kelly none the less shared Dee's intellectual fascination with the occult.

Born in Worcester, where he worked for a time as a chemist's apprentice, Kelly was reputed to have made a first attempt to raise the dead in a graveyard at Walton-in-le-dale in Lancashire, in collaboration with a man named Paul Waring. The two men dug up a freshly buried corpse and by means of various incantations reportedly persuaded it to speak. The scene later became the subject of a famous seventeenth-century print, in which the two men stand in a protective MAGIC CIRCLE while questioning a skeletal form in a shroud.

Kelly took it on himself to make the acquaintance of Dee at his home in Mortlake, London (although he later hinted that he had been sent there in order to obtain evidence that Dee dealt with the DEVIL, thus facilitating his trial). Dee quickly appreciated Kelly's skill in the business of SCRYING and the two became partners in the quest for knowledge of the mystic arts. Kelly related to Dee details of the spirit world gleaned from his crystal-gazing, reporting conversations with angels on an almost daily basis.

One of the pair's communicants was St Michael, who dismayed Kelly by insisting that he take a wife, which he soon did – though, he claimed, only with the greatest reluctance. The newlyweds moved into the Dee household, causing some friction, but the work went on and the two men and their wives also made lengthy visits to the courts of Europe, where they were generally honoured as scholars and mystics. While abroad, Kelly is said to have perfected the science of alchemy, producing real gold from his experiments. This and other achievements led to his being granted a knighthood by Emperor Rudolf II while in Prague.

The most bizarre episode in Kelly's relationship with Dee occurred in 1587 and was eventually to bring the famed collaboration to an end. When Kelly reported that a spectral communicant called Madini had requested that the two partners and their wives should enter into an agreement by which they would share matrimonial rights, there was some consternation in the household. Eventually, however, all four signed the pact (which just happened to bring Kelly access to Dee's young and beautiful wife Jane). The domestic strain entailed in such an arrangement led to a parting of the ways some two years later.

After breaking with Dee in 1589 Kelly returned to Prague, but was flung into prison for several months after being charged with plotting against the Emperor. After his release following intervention by Elizabeth I he wandered north to Germany, but was again arrested as a sorcerer. In 1593, while attempting to escape pursuers, he jumped a wall and sustained internal injuries that led to his death two years later.

Kempe, Ursula *see* ST OSYTH WITCHES.

Key of Solomon *see* GRIMOIRE.

Kilkenny Witches *see* IRELAND; KYTELER, ALICE.

Killakee *see* HELL-FIRE CLUB.

killing ointment Poisonous ointment that witches were formerly reputed to smear on their victims in order to secure their murder by means of magic. Witches were once accused of such crimes on a fairly regular basis. The NORTH BERWICK WITCHES, for instance, confessed to attempting to obtain a garment belonging to JAMES I so that they might smear an ointment of this kind on it to cause his death. Those implicated in the CHAMBRE ARDENTE AFFAIR in Paris were similarly accused of practising such arts, making ointments incorporating arsenic, sulphur, vitriol, the blood of bats and toads, poisonous plants, semen and menstrual blood.

There were many recipes for killing ointments. Among the other ingredients allegedly used were leaves and other parts of such plants as HEMLOCK and NIGHTSHADE, venomous reptiles, animals and fish, consecrated wine and sacred hosts, bones, hair, metals, stones and, most notoriously of all, the fat of roasted human babies. Many tales were told of witches breaking open new graves, especially those of children and of executed felons, to procure raw materials.

Popular superstition had it that a killing ointment correctly made with such ingredients could cause wholesale disease and death. In 1545, for instance, Calvinist Geneva was hit by a mystery illness that claimed many lives. The use of killing ointments was suspected, and an alleged witch was tortured into confessing that he had smeared the foot of a hanged man with such an ointment and had then rubbed the foot against the doorbolts of many houses in the city so that the infection spread. Those found guilty of the crime were sentenced to have their flesh torn off with pincers and then to be burned, or, if they failed to confess, to be walled up and left to die. In 1630, many suspected witches were similarly tortured and put to death in Milan after an outbreak of plague in the city was blamed on sorcerers smearing a killing ointment on the city walls. In this last case it seems that the persecutions began after the Commissioner of Health himself was spied wiping his ink-stained hands on a wall: he was among the first to be tortured into a confession and burned.

kiss A kiss signifies many things, from simple affection to humility, obeisance, respect and lust. In witchcraft, the 'obscene kiss' (or *osculum infame*) that required apprentice witches to kiss the DEVIL 'beneath his tail' was an important feature of INITIATION ceremonies and was repeated at all SABBATS where the Devil was present as a renewal of allegiance to him. The first mention of such rituals can be found in writings as far back as the thirteenth century and they were also associated with the Waldensians, the KNIGHTS TEMPLAR and other heretical sects (*see* HERESY).

Most records suggest that the Devil conventionally manifested in the form of some animal when the obscene kiss was to be given, making the ritual doubly repellent to Christian thinking. According to the testimony of various confessions, witches might kiss their demonic master in the shape of a duck, a boar, a goose or a TOAD, but more frequently the Devil materialised in his familiar GOAT-headed form. Agnes Sampson, one of the NORTH BERWICK WITCHES, and others who admitted kissing the Devil's hindquarters at their sabbats, reported that his skin was icy cold to the touch and that on completing the ritual all memory of their previous Catholic devotions deserted them. The French witch-hunter Pierre de LANCRE claimed that one witch from south-western France revealed that the Devil had a second, black-skinned face beneath his tail, which devotees had to kiss. Other witches admitted kissing the footprints of the demon BEELZEBUB.

The fivefold kiss of modern ceremonial witchcraft is a form of obeisance demanded of male members of covens in the course of a ritual known as the 'Dance of the Wheel', which celebrates the solstice in late December. At a given point in the ceremony the male witches pair up with the females and honour them with five kisses, on the feet, knees, loins, breasts and lips. The females then bow in acknowledgement and the solstice festival continues. On other occasions it may be the female witches who perform the ceremony upon their male counterparts.

Knap, Elizabeth *see* CONNECTICUT WITCHES.

knife *see* ATHAME; IRON.

Knights Templar Order of knighthood, properly entitled the Poor Knights of Christ and of the Temple of Solomon, which was ultimately destroyed by the INQUISITION after various enemies accused its members of HERESY, occult worship and immorality. Founded by a group of nine French knights in Jerusalem in 1118, the Order celebrated the concepts of idealism, chivalry and religious piety. In the beginning, the Order prided itself on its poverty and its self-denying ways, the knights owning only their clothes and their weapons, cutting their hair and accepting the rule of chastity (even to the extent of refraining from kissing their own mothers). Their great seal showed two knights on one horse, a typical state of affairs in the early history of the Order when knights could not afford a horse each.

Such devotion inspired many admirers, who lavished gifts and lands on the Order until it grew to be one of the wealthiest enterprises in the whole of Europe. Together with the rival Hospitallers, the Knights Templar became one of the most important military orders involved in the Crusades – but the power that the organisation wielded had brought it many political enemies. In the end Philip IV of France (who had cast a greedy eye over the Templars' wealth) charged the Order with various offences, and in 1312 the Templars were suppressed with great ruthlessness by the Inquisition on command of Pope Clement V.

Charges on which the 231 knights were arraigned ranged from blasphemy and devil worship to sodomy and other unnatural vices. The secrecy surrounding their meetings and the wild rumours that were spread concerning bizarre initiation rituals and the like did much to promote public suspicion of the Order, and its destruction under the aegis of the Inquisition was total. Under torture, members of the Order admitted to renouncing Christ, to spitting or urinating on the cross, to indulging in all varieties of sexual perversity with demons and to venerating BAPHOMET and other evil spirits.

Those who confessed were generally allowed to live, but the Grand Master, who protested that the Order had never been guilty of such offences, was burned alive on 18 March 1314. As he died, he called on the Pope and Philip IV to meet him before God within the space of a year. Both men died within twelve months of the execution.

The destruction of the Knights Templar was significant in the early development of the witchcraft persecution in that it anticipated the methods and justification that were to be adopted by the Inquisition when it launched its campaign against witches. There was a marked similarity between the crimes of the Knights and those of the sorcerers and witches who were to follow, and in so successfully blaming the Order for the ills of society the inquisitors learned the value of the scapegoat – a role for which alleged witches were ideally suited.

knots The tying of knots to achieve certain magical ends was long considered one of the skills of the accomplished witch. The intricacy of a well-tied knot was reputed to have the power to entrance demons; hence the practice of tying knots in a handkerchief in order to remember something important – the knots would divert the Devil or any other evil spirit bent on making the person concerned forget what they were trying to remember.

WHITE WITCHES were known to treat WARTS and other sites of disease by touching them with knots and then burning or burying the string they had used. In the days of sailing ships, such 'Wise Women' sold cords with three knots tied in them to sailors anxious for good winds. When the first knot was untied, the sailor could expect a good following wind; when the second was loosed, a gale would spring up; but when the third was untied, his ship would be lashed by hurricane-force winds. Records exist of such 'wind sales' being made in many coastal areas, including the Isle of Man, Wales, Scotland and the Orkney and Shetland Islands. As late as 1814, the famed Scottish novelist Sir Walter Scott related in his diary how he had just 'bought' a wind in Stromness from a woman named Bessie Millie.

Such magic could also be employed for nefarious purposes, however. A witch could blight a marriage by tying a ritual knot in a length of cord, rendering the male partner impotent until, if the witch so chose, he paid for the knot to be untied. To deprive newly-weds of the pleasures of their marriage bed, a witch could recite curses upon them while tying knots (though a bridegroom could protect himself from such interference by leaving one shoelace untied as he walked up the aisle at his wedding). Surreptitiously tying knots in an expectant mother's bedding or nightclothes was reputed to prevent her from having an easy birth, while knots tied in a dying person's clothing were said to prolong the death struggle. *See also* LIGATURE.

Kramer, Heinrich *see* MALLEUS MALEFICARUM.

Kyteler, Alice fl. fourteenth century. Irish aristocrat who was the subject of the earliest known witchcraft trial in Ireland and who remains the best known of all Irish witches. Dame (or Lady) Alice (or Agnes) Kyteler, of Kilkenny in south-east Ireland, was rich and well connected, claiming descent from a respected Anglo-Norman family. She came under suspicion of witchcraft in 1324 when her fourth husband, Sir John le Poer (who was suffering from a wasting disease), became convinced that she was the source of his ill health. Sir John's suspicions were first aroused by a suggestion made by a maidservant in his household, and they were intensified when he discovered among his wife's belongings a wafer of sacramental bread stamped with the name of the DEVIL and various magical powders together with a phial of what was identified as FLYING OINTMENT.

Sir John reported his findings to Richard de Landrede, the Franciscan Bishop of Ossory, who had little hesitation in agreeing that witchcraft must lie at the root of the knight's troubles and ordered a full inquiry. It is speculated that the English-born Bishop may have been persuaded of the reality of witchcraft after hearing about trials on such charges during his training in France. The fact that he would be able to confiscate the wealthy suspect's fortune if she was found guilty may also have been an incentive.

Further allegations were gathered to the effect that the accused had denied God, had made sacrifices to the Devil, had consorted with a demon named Robin Artisson (who sometimes took the form of a CAT or a BLACK DOG), had probed the future with the aid of devils, had held sacrilegious services and had used magic to harm both human enemies and their livestock. Several of these accusations were furnished by the other children of Lady Alice's first three husbands, who were understandably resentful at finding themselves dispossessed in favour of her eldest son, William Outlawe.

Kyteler and ten other local devil-worshippers, it was alleged, met in secret at certain CROSSROADS in order to sacrifice cocks and other living animals to their demon masters, tearing the creatures limb from limb and using parts of their corpses in their spells. Potions of various kinds were brewed up in the SKULL of a beheaded robber placed over a fire of OAK logs. Other ingredients used by the coven included herbs, spiders, black worms, the flesh of serpents, hair and nails from corpses, and the brains and wrappings of an unbaptised child.

On one occasion, Lady Alice had been spotted sweeping the dirt in the streets of Kilkenny towards the front door of her eldest son while intoning:

> To the house of William, my son,
> Hie all the wealth of Kilkenny town.

She had also, it transpired, murdered her first three husbands with the assistance of Robin Artisson (described as one of the 'poorer folk of hell') in order to inherit their fortunes.

Whatever the truth behind the accusations, Alice Kyteler rallied considerable local support in opposing the allegations against her, drawn up as they were by an English bishop with few local sympathisers. After summoning William Outlawe to his court to answer a charge of HERESY, the Bishop found himself thrown into gaol for a period of seventeen days on the orders of Kyteler's highly placed friends and relations. Undeterred, he fought back by placing the whole diocese under an interdict, but this measure had to be lifted after Kyteler recruited the support of the Lord Justice. The Bishop subsequently had singularly little success in getting the secular courts, dominated by Lady Alice's family, to cooperate.

In the end, the Bishop succeeded in extracting qualified support from the senior Church authorities in Dublin. The pressure on Kyteler became too great and she fled to England, leaving the court in Kilkenny to find her guilty of witchcraft in her absence. Although excommunicated by the Bishop for her alleged misdeeds and deprived of her property in Ireland by the Church, it appears that Alice Kyteler never served any sentence for her crimes and she is thought to have lived out the rest of her life in peace in England.

Some of Lady Alice's 'accomplices' were less fortunate. Her middle-aged lady's maid Petronilla de Midia (or Meath) and others met far worse fates. Petronilla was flogged until unconscious six times in succession until she admitted that every charge laid against the accused was true, adding for good measure that she had learned her skills in the black arts from Kyteler herself. The doomed woman was then excommunicated before being burned alive, mouthing abuse at the Bishop to the last, in Kilkenny marketplace on 3 November 1324. Thus it was that Petronilla de Midia became the first person in Irish history to be executed as a witch. The others, identified as John, Ellen and Syssok Galrussyn, Robert of Bristol, William Payn de Boly, Alice Faber, Annota Lange and Eva de Drownestown, were sentenced to a variety of punishments, ranging from flogging and banishment to burning at the stake like Petronilla.

Encouraged by his success, Bishop de Landrede decided to try once again to get William Outlawe to answer for his offences. At length he managed to persuade the Justiciary of Ireland, the Chancellor, the Treasurer of Ireland and the King's Council to travel to Kilkenny to try the accused, who was obliged to cooperate. Outlawe obediently confessed that he had been in error and was ordered to make amends by going to mass three times a day for a year, by feeding the poor of the town and by paying for a new roof for the cathedral. Kyteler's son calmly agreed to all this and promptly forgot all about it once out of the court.

Next, de Landrede pursued Sir Arnold le Poer, Seneschal (magistrate) of Kilkenny and allegedly the HORNED GOD of Lady Alice's coven, who had earlier sought to frustrate the Bishop's campaign against the family, describing him as 'that good-for-nothing rustic runaway from England'. When the Bishop twice presented himself at Sir Arnold's court, wearing his full regalia and carrying the holy sacrament in a chalice, he was turned away on both occasions with only a minimum of decorum. Sir Arnold was forced to make a public (and none too convincing) gesture of reconciliation with the Bishop, but this was not enough for the latter who had the Seneschal committed to Dublin Castle. Here – to the fury of the

Bishop – he was treated as an honoured guest by the Chancellor, Roger Outlawe (another relation).

The Bishop now made the unwise move of accusing the Chancellor himself of heresy. Sir Arnold meanwhile died of natural causes in Dublin Castle and Chancellor Roger Outlawe got himself cleared of any hint of heretical practice by a sympathetic committee of clergymen (who were treated to a banquet at the Chancellor's expense). The Chancellor then spoke to the Bishop's superiors and de Landrede was summoned to see the Pope in order to explain his activities and, ironically, to answer a charge of heresy on his own account. While he was away, Alice Kyteler, through her influence at the English court, exacted further revenge by having the Bishop's lands and property confiscated by the Crown. These were eventually restored, but then seized once more after a second charge of heresy. The Bishop finally cleared himself of the charges in 1360.

L

La Voisin *see* CHAMBRE ARDENTE AFFAIR.

Labourd Witches *see* BASQUE WITCHES.

ladder Torture instrument that was extensively employed against suspected witches throughout Europe (chiefly in FRANCE and GERMANY) in order to obtain CONFESSIONS. The procedure was to lay the near-naked prisoner horizontally on the ladder (alternatively on a rack or slung by ropes fastened to two fixed hooks) and to bind his or her legs and arms with ropes, which were then joined in the form of a tourniquet knot. The knot could then be steadily twisted so as to draw tight the ropes binding the prisoner's arms and legs and thus stretch the victim to the point where muscles tore and bones broke. In an exquisite refinement of the torture, the hangman might be instructed to tie the prisoner to the ladder with many relatively thin cords, which were wound round the suspect's limbs and the uprights of the ladder itself. Sticks could then be inserted between these cords and twisted as in a tourniquet to apply the severest pressure to virtually any selected part of the body. Knots in the cords would be cruelly forced by the pressure into the victim's flesh, causing additional agony.

Horrific though the ladder was, it was considered one of the milder forms of torture and was employed in the early stages of questioning, after which it was followed by the much more savage procedures of STRAPPADO and SQUASSATION.

Laing, Beatrix *see* PITTENWEEM WITCHES.

Lamb, Dr John d.1628. English physician and occultist who became notorious for dabbling in black magic. Dr Lamb was personal physician to the Duke of BUCKINGHAM and was widely known not just as a doctor of medicine but also as an alchemist and magician, around whom many extraordinary stories circulated.

As a young man Dr Lamb courted disaster through his reputation as a wizard and was twice convicted at the Worcester Assizes, the first time on the serious charge of causing the death of Thomas, Lord Windsor, through witchcraft and the second time for raising evil spirits. On both occasions he was lucky to receive sentences of imprisonment rather than the death penalty. While in prison he continued his studies into the occult, and legend has it that his power was such that he could bewitch passing women into hoisting their skirts as they went by his barred cell window.

In 1624 he was released from prison on obtaining a pardon for his crimes and settled in London under the patronage of the powerful Duke of Buckingham, gaining the sobriquet 'The Duke's Devil'. When an action for impeachment of the Duke was considered in the House of Commons in 1626 and a violent storm broke out over the capital it was inevitable that Lamb was identified as the probable cause of the tempest through his STORM-RAISING magic. Other rumours connected to his name included the suggestion that he had provided the arsenic that gossips claimed had ended the life of JAMES I.

After years of speculation and rumour connected with his varied activities, Dr Lamb finally met his end in 1628 at the hands of a mob who beat him to death as a wizard at St Paul's Cross in London shortly after leaving the Fortune Theatre in Golden Lane. Charles I, hearing of the riot, went out into the streets to quell the disturbance, but arrived too late to save the unfortunate doctor. When the authorities failed to condemn the ringleaders of the mob the King, in a fit of fury, fined them the substantial sum of £600.

See also DR LAMB'S DARLING.

Lamia Alternative name for a witch or demon, as used since classical times. The original Lamia was a legendary queen of Libya whose beauty attracted the god Zeus, who became her lover. The goddess Hera, jealous of Lamia, robbed her of her beauty and turned her into a hideous hag, killing all the children she had borne her divine lover. Lamia in her turn vented her bitterness upon the children of others, but was also said by Roman mythology to resume her former beauty in order to seduce men and feed on their blood.

Subsequent generations of demonologists variously listed Lamia as a 'night monster' or vampire, who drank the blood of children and men and brought them nightmares. As early as the ninth century the name was being treated by some writers as synonymous with 'witch'.

Lammas Day *see* SABBAT.

Lancashire Witches *see* PENDLE WITCHES; ROBINSON, EDMUND.

Lancre, Pierre de 1553–1631. French lawyer who is thought to have sentenced some six hundred suspected witches to death during a four-month witch-hunt that he instigated in the Basque region north of the Pyrenees in 1609. Sent to the Pays de Labourd locality by Henri IV of France with orders to stamp out the witchcraft epidemic that was thought to be raging in the area, de Lancre struck terror into the populace as he identified scores of men, women and children for trial. Scornful of the Basque language and culture, de Lancre used his extensive knowledge of witchcraft theory and legal procedure to secure convictions on the flimsiest evidence, often basing charges on the unsupported accusations of children.

De Lancre, who was born into a wealthy Bordeaux family, saw himself as a crusader, making good the damage done through the leniency of previous judges and considering every witch he burned a moral victory. He had first become obsessed by the dangers of witchcraft when, passing through Rome in 1599 on his way to the Holy Land, he claimed to have seen a girl changed by the Devil into a boy. As a magistrate he took every opportunity to single out witches for persecution, a zeal that won him Henri IV's commission in 1609.

The results of his investigation in the Basque region convinced de Lancre that he had uncovered a vast and highly organised witchcraft conspiracy dedicated to the overthrow of the Christian world. Under the direction of the Devil himself an army of witches was being assembled, complete with ranks, rituals, a recognised pantheon of diabolic saints and a complex system of covens acting together to achieve their aims. To counter any accusations of paranoia de Lancre pointed to the similarities to be observed between the alleged crimes of witches across the length and breadth of Europe, and read into this a shared anti-Christian purpose. As proof of this intent, he emphasised the blasphemous nature of many of the rites that suspects were supposed to perform, the Devil being deliberately raised up in the place of Christ. According to de Lancre, he had heard confessions in which witches admitted to going down on their knees before the Devil, renouncing Christ and honouring their master with such greetings as 'Great Lord, whom I adore'.

Particularly shocking to de Lancre were the priests who were unveiled as witches, together with the women thus arraigned. He professed himself to be filled with amazement and revulsion when some of the women brought before him claimed to look forward to their SABBATS, with their feasting, DANCING and orgiastic sex. Indeed, he reported that they 'found the time too short because of the pleasure and happiness they enjoyed, so that they left with infinite regret and longed for the time when they could go again'.

The prevalence of witches in the Pays de Labourd, where the whole population, he concluded, was tainted by witchcraft, could, he argued, be explained by the geographical remoteness of the area. Once the 'pestilence' had been introduced to the region from Bearn in the late fifteenth century it had festered for many years undetected by anyone in the outside world.

De Lancre distinguished between two types of witchcraft. In his eyes, witches who specialised in poisons belonged to their own distinct group. It should be said, though, that few other authorities on the subject supported this categorisation. His involvement in cases of alleged SHAPE-SHIFTING, meanwhile, convinced him of the reality of LYCANTHROPY as another manifestation of evil in the Basque country.

De Lancre left detailed records of his witch-hunting activities in several books, which were widely read and much consulted by other witch judges. He described his own witch-hunting methods and the trials in which he was involved in his six hundred-page *Tableau de l'Inconstance des Mauvais Anges* (*Description of the Inconstancy of Evil Angels*) in 1612; other volumes by his hand included *L'Incredulité et Mescréance du Sortilège* (*Incredulity and Misbelief of Enchantment*), which was published in 1622, and *Du Sortilege* (*Witchcraft*), which appeared in 1627. Other observers, notably the Abbé Laurent Bordelon, sought to pour ridicule upon de Lancre's writings by publishing famous parodies of his *Tableau de l'Inconstance*, but many more took what he said to be gospel and adopted his theories to justify their own witch-hunts.

See also BASQUE WITCHES.

Lange, Annota *see* KYTELER, ALICE.

Langton, Walter fl. early fourteenth century. English prelate, Bishop of Coventry and Treasurer of England, who was charged with witchcraft, among other offences, in 1301. The extraordinary and long-running case against Langton had its roots in accusations made by Sir John Lovetot, who alleged that the Bishop had committed adultery with Lovetot's stepmother, that he had arranged the murder of Lovetot's father and that he was a sorcerer who had made a PACT WITH THE DEVIL, whom he had honoured with the posterior KISS.

The sensational nature of the charges against one of the most powerful men in England caused a furore and, although the Bishop denied them, debate over his guilt raged for some two years (to the intense irritation of Edward I, who stood resolutely by his Treasurer). Not until Langton had been summoned to see the Pope in Rome and a special royal commission had looked into the affair was Langton finally acquitted in 1303.

Historians agree that the case probably arose out of political reasons, coloured by hostility between the main parties. But it is interesting to note that as early as 1301, before the witchcraft mania had got a real hold on the European imagination, accusations of witchcraft could bring no less a personage than the Treasurer of England to the dock, where he was destined to experience the utmost difficulty in clearing his name.

Laudun, Sir Walter fl. twelfth century. English knight who brought to light an intriguing early case of witchcraft-connected vampirism. Hailing from one of the Welsh border towns, Sir Walter Laudun told Gilbert Foliot, Bishop of Hereford, an unusual tale which was later recorded in Walter Map's *De Nugis Curialum*. Apparently a Welsh sorcerer had recently died, but Laudun's home town was now being traumatised by his reappearance in the flesh every night.

According to Laudun, each night the dead man called the names of certain citizens of the town who immediately fell ill and died, to the consternation of their friends and relatives.

On the Bishop's advice, Laudun dug up the body of the sorcerer and had it beheaded and reinterred in the grave, which was then soaked in HOLY WATER. Unfortunately this countermeasure failed to work and one night Sir Walter's own name was called. In fear of his own life, Sir Walter followed the dead man back to his grave and then cut off his head with one blow from his sword before he could reach shelter. Happily, the sorcerer did not reappear.

Lawson, Mrs Nicholas *see* PITTENWEEM WITCHES.

lead Because lead was formerly used in the manufacture of coffins, it was widely regarded as a magically potent metal that had connections with death and witchcraft. Bullets made of lead would not kill a witch, it was claimed, and – according to the Scottish – might even rebound and kill the person who had pulled the trigger. Lead could, however, be used in certain circumstances to establish whether witchcraft was at work. One procedure was to drop a little molten lead into water and to observe whether it resolved into a discernible shape or not. If it did, evil was clearly present and the victim of the spell would be advised to wear the piece of lead over their heart as protection from further attack.

Caskets made of lead, which could not be penetrated by evil spirits, were much favoured both for burial and in the preservation of precious religious relics.

Leek, Sybil *see* WICCA.

left hand Since Christ is traditionally supposed to sit at God's right hand, the left-hand side became identified with the forces opposed to goodness, and therefore with demons and witches. In the conventions of witchcraft many operations, such as stirring the contents of a cauldron, had to be performed in a left-hand, anticlockwise or WIDDERSHINS direction, contrary to the passage of the sun through the heavens. In preparing potions and spells it was also believed that witches customarily used their left hand more than their right, because this hand was naturally more suited to the pursuit of evil. When the Devil made his pact of blood with a witch (*see* PACT WITH THE DEVIL) it was allegedly the initiate's left hand that he scratched to seal the agreement.

Inevitably, in past centuries, left-handed people were regarded with some mistrust in many communities, as this might be interpreted as a sign that the person was a witch. Modern-day witches, meanwhile, talk of the 'left-hand path' when discussing the pursuit of black magic and still favour the left hand when casting spells.

Leicester Boy The case of John Smith, a thirteen-year-old boy from Husbands Bosworth near Leicester, whose accusations of witchcraft directly or indirectly caused the deaths of ten innocent women in 1616. John Smith suffered from such violent fits that it took several strong men to hold him down. He publicly ascribed his affliction to various women of the town, providing full details of their FAMILIARS – as described in a contemporary letter:

> Six of the witches had six several spirits, one in the likeness of a
> horse, another like a dog, another a cat, another a foulmart,
> another a fish, another a toad, with whom every one of them tor-
> mented him. He would make some sign according to the spirit, as,
> when the horse tormented him he would whinny; when the cat
> tormented him, he would cry like a cat ...

Nine of the women were in due course tried as witches at the
Leicestershire Summer Assizes, found guilty and hanged. Another
six were thrown into prison to await similar examination.

At this point news of the trials reached the ears of JAMES I, who
was then passing through Leicester. On the King's orders, Smith was
brought into the royal presence and closely questioned. In the face
of such stern examination the boy broke down and confessed that
he had fabricated his evidence in order to enjoy the celebrity it
brought him. The Archbishop of Canterbury, to whom the boy was
despatched for further questioning, agreed with the King that there
was no reason for suspecting witchcraft and the King turned his
wrath on the judges, Sir Humphrey Winch and Sir Randolph Crew,
who had presided over the original trials. Five of the six women in
prison (the sixth had died) were released and the judges were
roundly condemned by James for their gullibility. He also permitted
the playwright Ben Jonson to ridicule the judges for their foolish-
ness in his play *The Devil Is an Ass*.

As a result of this very public rebuke English judges became
more circumspect in accepting uncorroborated accusations in
witchcraft cases, especially if they came from the mouths of
children.

Lemp, Rebecca d.1590. German witch-hunt victim, whose moving
letters to and from her family have survived as a testament to the
suffering that was inflicted upon many well-connected and innocent people during the hysteria that seized German society in the
late sixteenth century.

Rebecca Lemp was married to a respected accountant of
Nördlingen in Swabia and had six young children at the time of her

arrest for witchcraft in 1590. The first letter incorporated in the official court record of the case was written shortly after the arrest and was addressed to the unfortunate Rebecca from her children, who appeared to be unaware of the true reason for their mother's absence from home. They spoke of expecting her home soon, and in the meantime assured her that they were all well and 'not to be worried about the house-keeping till thou comest back to us'.

The second letter, from Rebecca to her husband, was similarly written in a relatively untroubled frame of mind. Although distressed at her situation, Rebecca emphasised her innocence of the charges brought against her and vowed not to confess anything. She clearly believed that she would come to no harm, writing: 'Therefore do not be alarmed; before my conscience and before my soul I am innocent. Will I be tortured? I don't believe it, since I am not guilty of anything.'

The tone of the third letter, written by Rebecca to her husband some months later, was very different. She had now undergone five sessions in the torture chamber and had had a confession dragged from her. Lamenting for her children, she could only beg her husband to obtain for her a means to escape further agonies: 'O thou, dearly beloved Husband, my heart is nearly broken! Alas, alas! My poor dear children orphans! Husband, send me something that I may die, or I must expire under the torture; if thou canst not today, do it tomorrow.' This third letter, it seems, was intercepted by the gaolers and read out in court as compounding evidence of her guilt, for suicide was a sin.

The last of the four letters was written to the court by Peter Lemp, Rebecca's husband, pleading for her life and stressing his belief in her innocence. He praised her as a wife and mother and promised that many well-respected people were prepared to vouch for her as 'a pious, chaste, honest housewife, foe to any evil'. He ended with a heart-felt plea for Rebecca's release 'in my name and in the name of my dear little children'.

The petition had no effect upon the court. After further torture, Rebecca Lemp was condemned to death and burned as a witch on 9 September 1590.

She was not the only victim of witchcraft paranoia in Nördlingen that year: in all some thirty-two people, all well placed in the local community, perished on similar charges. The hysteria that hit Nördlingen in the early 1590s only subsided in 1594, following the horrific torture of one Maria Hollin, who survived no fewer than fifty-six visits to the torture chamber without confessing. Public outrage at her suffering obliged the lawyers to desist from further trials.

Levi, Eliphas 1810–75. French occultist, born Alphonse Louis Constant, who became famous for his investigations into magical practices. Levi tried out many spells himself and reportedly collapsed in terror at the results he achieved. His research into the topic fascinated many distinguished people and he numbered the popular English novelist Edward Bulwer-Lytton among his friends and admirers. He brought together his thoughts on a wide range of occult subjects in the vast *History of Magic*, which became required reading for later generations of occultists. His illustration of a demon which he called the Sabbatic Goat, or Baphomet of Mendes, is often reproduced, attempting as it does to combine in one figure the goat-headed Devil of witches' sabbats, the god of the Templars and the Devil of tarot cards. In Levi's view this demon represented the supreme power in the universe, encapsulating both good and evil influences.

Leviathan One of the prime DEMONS of Hell, according to the demonologists of the sixteenth and seventeenth centuries. Linked by the demonologist Peter BINSFELD with the sin of sloth, Leviathan was often depicted as a dragon, echoing a long Christian tradition of equating dragons with the Devil. Popular superstition had it that the Devil sometimes chose the form of a dragon when he copulated with his witches.

levitation *see* TRANSVECTION.

ligature The use of sorcery to make a person impotent. The effect was usually achieved by two means, the first being through the magic of KNOTS and the second through potions. Such magic was much feared in classical times and its manifestation as one of the MALEFICIA of European witches in the sixteenth and seventeenth centuries was but a continuation of a very old tradition. Among the authorities who lent their weight to belief in the power of ligature was no less a figure than Thomas AQUINAS, who readily admitted the notion that by witchcraft a person might 'prevent carnal copulation'. Later authorities agreed that this was correct and that the Devil was responsible for such calamities, but added the codicil that God himself allowed him to exercise such power and that the only cure was to resort to abstinence and prayer.

According to Francesco-Maria GUAZZO, writing in 1608, there were seven ways in which a person's love life might be disrupted by the magic of ligature. Firstly, a couple could be made to hate each other. Secondly, they could be kept physically apart by some hindrance or other. Thirdly, the emission of semen at ejaculation could be prevented. Fourthly, the semen could be rendered infertile. Fifthly, a man could be deprived of the ability to sustain an erection. Sixthly, a woman could be dosed with potions to prevent her conceiving and, lastly, the genitalia of either sex could be made to retract or close up.

If the magic of knots (*aiguillette* in French, or *ghirlanda delle streghe* in Italian) was to be employed, the witch concerned had only to tie knots in a length of cord or leather and to keep this hidden from the victim. The spell could not be broken unless the knots were found and untied. According to an investigation into such magic that was reported by Jean BODIN in 1567, there were over fifty ways in which the knots might be tied, each having a particular effect upon a person's sexual potency.

Symptoms that suggested a person was subject to the magic of ligature included swellings on the body – one for each potential baby that was thus deprived of life. Any radical changes in the genitalia were also deemed significant (in one extraordinary Scottish case heard in 1590 two witches were accused of causing the sexual organs of certain men to be swapped with those of others).

Reginald SCOT, who sought to point out the absurdities of the witchcraft myth, related an anecdote to illustrate the ludicrous nature of such magic. After intercourse a young man discovered that his genitalia had been entirely removed, presumably as the result of a malevolent spell. In desperation he consulted a WHITE WITCH, who advised him that he would be able to replace what was missing from a selection lying in a nest at the top of a certain tree:

> She brought him to a tree, where she showed him a nest, and bade him climb up and take it. And being in the top of the tree, he took out a mighty great one, and showed the same to her, asking her if he might not have the same. Nay, quoth she, that is our parish priest's tool, but take any other which thou wilt. And it is there affirmed, that some have found 20, and some 30 of them in one nest, being there preserved with provender, as it were at a manger ... These are no jests, for they be written by them that were and are judges upon the lives and deaths of those persons.

Accusations that a person had caused harm through the use of ligature were not uncommon in historical witchcraft trials, but the demonologist Domenic de Soto for one doubted if such magic was often employed in reality – if only because the DEVIL delighted in fornication and was unlikely to consent to such restriction upon its practice. 'Proved' cases of ligature provided grounds for the annulment of marriages, and it seems highly probable that many dissatisfied husbands and wives extricated themselves from unhappy marriages by blaming such supernatural interference for their personal problems.

See also LOVE POTIONS.

Light, Thomas fl. early nineteenth century. English occultist who was famed throughout his native Shropshire and beyond for his skills in dealing with the supernatural. Light lived at Walton, near High Ercall, and was consulted for advice and assistance by both neighbours and people from all over Cheshire and Wales. Among other feats he was reputed to cure the sick, to help to make love affairs run more smoothly, to tell fortunes, to charm fighting cocks and to place spells on thieves, obliging them to return stolen property. According to his clients, his usual procedure was to retire to a private room and there to do battle with the supernatural until he had enlisted a spirit's aid.

One of the most famous wizards of his generation, Light credited much of his success to his treasured copy of *The Theomagia of John Heyden, Gentleman*, which was first published in 1662 and pretended to explain all manner of occult practice. Local legend has it that Light's own death came about as a result of the malevolent spells of a rival wizard, Jack of the Weald Moors.

Lilith The chief of all demonesses, who murdered young children and had intercourse with men as they slept. Probably descended from the Assyrian *lilitu*, a hideous monster with wings and long hair, Lilith was, according to Christian mythology, the first wife of Adam. She deserted him, however, in order to indulge herself with DEMONS, producing a hundred demon offspring every day. By way of consolation for Adam's loss, God then created Eve to be his new companion. Lilith, however, continued to terrorise men, often being attracted to couples having intercourse in the hope of stealing a few drops of semen with which to create more evil spirits. Those fearing attacks by Lilith were advised in former times to scrawl a MAGIC CIRCLE on the bedroom wall, completing it with the words 'Adam and Eve, barring Lilith'.

See also SUCCUBUS.

Lille Novices Case of apparent demonic POSSESSION that caused considerable concern at a convent in Lille, northern France, in 1658. The affair of the Lille Novices revolved around Antoinette Bourignon, who founded a home for orphans in the town in about 1653 and subsequently accepted most of them as initiates into her own convent, established in 1658. Although she kept good order at the convent, Bourignon was very gullible and failed to appreciate that her charges would learn to turn this fault against her. In order to escape punishment for minor misdemeanours, the girls habitually blamed the Devil for prompting them to misbehave. A pastor, brought in to investigate the girls' tales, quickly concluded that all thirty-two inmates of the convent were possessed by devils. According to the testimony provided by the girls, they were subjected to sexual abuse by the Devil in various guises on a daily basis and had been persuaded to fly with him to SABBATS, where they indulged freely in dancing, drinking, feasting and sex.

The bewildered Antoinette Bourignon admitted her confusion at finding herself sharing a house 'with two and thirty creatures who declared that they had all given their souls to the devil'. She considered sending her charges home, but then changed her mind when she envisaged the mischief they might get up to at the Devil's urging. Remarkably, no one thought of accusing Bourignon herself of bewitching the children, as happened in many other parallel cases. Instead, news of the case spread far and wide and she became a recognised authority on similar cases of demonic possession, recording her thoughts on religion and mysticism in such books as *La Parole de Dieu* (*The Word of God*) and *La Vie Exterieure* (*Mysticism for the Layman*). She was also credited with the acquisition of knowledge through supernatural means.

lily The lily was associated with the Virgin Mary and therefore regarded as one of the plants that could be relied upon to deter witches and evil spirits. Lilies were once popular as church decorations, reinforcing their reputation for good, and they featured strongly in the spells that WHITE WITCHES cast to counter black magic. It was also said that if lilies were planted near a house they would prevent GHOSTS from entering.

If a parent was worried that a daughter might have strayed from the straight and narrow, witchlore advised that the proper course was to feed her some powdered yellow lily. If she was indeed still a virgin, she would immediately feel a need to urinate. The plant could also be used to treat boils, sores and various growths.

Lilies did have their uses, however, in certain mischief-making spells. One of these required lilies to be mixed with the sap of a BAY tree and left to rot in manure. Worms gathered from this manure could then be slipped into the pocket of an enemy to rob him or her of sleep.

Lincoln Witches *see* FLOWER, JOAN.

lizard Superstition maintained a strong link between lizards and witchcraft and most myths concerning the creature were negative in character, reflecting this association with the forces of darkness. The witches in Shakespeare's *Macbeth* included lizard in the ingredients of the potion they prepared on stage and certainly the lizard appears to have featured in a variety of fabled potions, including preparations for the treatment of syphilis, impotence, WARTS and skin diseases. In ancient times the lizard was also supposed to have aphrodisiac properties (*see* LOVE POTION). According to the confessions of some witches their FAMILIARS sometimes chose the form of lizards, while other authorities theorised that lizards were the result of couplings between witches and the Devil.

Lloyd, Temperance *see* EXETER WITCHES.

Logan stone A large boulder that is so positioned that it may actually be rocked backwards and forwards. Such stones, found throughout Europe, were traditionally identified as favourite meeting places for COVENS of witches. In Cornish legend, touching a Logan stone nine times at midnight would instantly transform a person into a witch.

Looten, Thomas 1599–1659. Frenchman whose trial on charges of witchcraft at Bailleul, between Dunkirk and Lille, is known in some detail from surviving court documents made at the time. Very few contemporary official records of witchcraft trials have survived, so this account drawn up by the prosecutor is useful in understanding the way in which such matters were pursued in the French courts of the seventeenth century.

The circumstances by which Looten, aged around sixty, came to trial were commonplace enough. In September 1659 it was alleged by some of his neighbours that he had brought about the death of a child by feeding it bewitched plums. Public outrage at the alleged crime led to the accused going to the court asking for a trial in order to clear his name. Proceedings began as soon as the relevant witnesses had been traced and Looten's house had been searched for potions and other incriminating evidence. After the bailiff reported that he had evidence to prove the charges Looten was advised to get himself a lawyer, but the prisoner, clearly convinced that his innocence was self-evident, declined the suggestion. Unfortunately for Looten, the court then learned that the official torturer in Dunkirk was passing through town, and he was accordingly invited to test Looten for the DEVIL'S MARK. Using a bodkin in the usual manner, the torturer, who claimed 'that he himself had examined and executed between five hundred and six hundred witches', found a spot where he could thrust in the pin up to the head without the prisoner feeling any pain or shedding any blood.

On this evidence, the court agreed to sanction the torture of the accused. Seated on a wooden chair, Looten was fitted with a 'garotte', an iron collar that could be tightened by screws, and was interrogated over some two days while subjected to increasing pain. When this proved inadequate to obtain a confession, the torturer was allowed to inflict more savage torture after the prisoner was first sprinkled with HOLY WATER. Eventually Looten's resistance predictably broke down and he confessed to signing a PACT WITH THE DEVIL, whom he identified by the name Harlakyn, to attending SABBATS at which he partook of feasts and had sex with beautiful women, to flying by means of certain green ointments given to him by the Devil (*see* FLYING OINTMENT) and to poisoning the child of one of his neighbours by means of plums upon which the Devil had spat. Looten also named several accomplices, whose fate is unknown. He had endured the torture so long, he explained, through the Devil offering to suffer the pain on his behalf.

The following day Thomas Looten was found dead in his cell, his neck broken. The court, assuming that the Devil had killed the prisoner in order to prevent him confessing more details of his evil activities, ordered his body to be burned and the remains to be hung on a gibbet for all to see.

The official records of the Looten case include an illuminating list of the accounts relating to the trial. Among other expenses, the deceased man's estate was expected to reimburse the court for the cost of the search of his house, for his transport to trial, for the paper used by court officials, for the travel costs incurred by those accompanying the corpse to the gibbet, and finally for the wood that was used during his torture.

Lord of the Flies *see* BEELZEBUB.

Lord's Prayer Requiring a suspect to recite the Lord's Prayer without making a mistake was a widely respected test for witchcraft. Popular superstition insisted that the Devil would intervene to prevent one of his disciples delivering the prayer without some telling flaw, be it in hesitating, stuttering or simply forgetting the words. The test had no legal relevance, but was none the less brought up fairly frequently in court as evidence supporting a prosecution. Unfortunately, the typical victim of witchcraft allegations in many parts of Europe – old, ill-educated, uncooperative and perhaps mentally backward – was unlikely to be able to get through the prayer without making some error or other.

Among the most famous instances in which the test was tried in court was the trial of Mrs Julian Cox, one of the SOMERSET WITCHES, in 1663. When ordered by the judge to recite the prayer, she managed to say it several times without any mistake until she came to the line 'And lead us not into temptation': through false confidence, lack of thought or arguably because she was used to saying it that way it came out, damagingly, as 'And lead us into temptation'.

Loudun Nuns Case of demonic POSSESSION that caused a sensation in Loudun, France, in 1634. The story of the Loudun Nuns revolved around a handsome and somewhat dissolute young priest called Urbain Grandier, who was ultimately identified as a witch whose spells had caused mayhem in the Ursuline convent in the town. Before the scandal at Loudun broke he had already got into trouble with the authorities over his less than celibate lifestyle and for making critical remarks about the all-powerful Cardinal Richelieu. In particular he had incurred the wrath of his superiors through his entanglements with a succession of young women, only narrowly keeping his post in 1630 after investigation by his Archbishop into allegations that he had fathered a child by one Philippa Trincant, the daughter of the public prosecutor in Loudun. The prosecutor had him tried for immorality, on which charge he was found guilty, but Archbishop Sourdis of Bordeaux was persuaded to have the priest freed and returned to his duties. In the course of these escapades Grandier had made many enemies, who were determined to have their revenge upon him.

The crucial figure in his ultimate downfall was the Mother Superior at Loudun, Sister Jeanne des Anges, who had been appointed head of the convent at the young age of twenty-five because she came from a wealthy family. Once in control of the convent, Sister Jeanne vented her frustrated sexuality on those around her, ordering other nuns (who resented her appointment) to whip her. Deranged and hysterical, she saw in the young Urbain Grandier the very essence of physical sin and readily agreed to play her part in a plot to secure his undoing.

In order to blacken the priest's name Sister Jeanne and some of the other nuns feigned demonic possession, throwing fits in which their bodies assumed strange and sometimes indecent postures. Gibbering in unknown tongues and pulling faces, they blamed Grandier for causing their distress and alleged that he had raised two DEMONS, Asmodeus and Zabulon, to assist him. The accusations incensed the populace of Loudun and Grandier was obliged to seek the protection of Archbishop Sourdis of Bordeaux once more. The Archbishop had the nuns examined by his own doctor, who declared their possession to be faked. On the orders of the Archbishop all attempts at EXORCISM were ended and the women were confined to their cells, which brought about a temporary lull in affairs.

Unfortunately for Urbain Grandier, Cardinal Richelieu (who, it chanced, was related to one of the nuns at the convent) now saw his opportunity to gain political capital by having the nuns exorcised in public, thus stirring up the hysteria once more. If he could engineer an explosion of public concern the way would be prepared for the revocation of the Edict of Nantes, a piece of legislation which guaranteed freedom of worship for all religions. The exorcisms raised new charges against Grandier and the hapless priest himself was ordered to conduct a service of exorcism at the convent so as to release the women from his influence. Predictably, the service was not a success and the nuns elaborated sensationally on their initial accusations, claiming that Grandier had used his power to seduce them in the most shameless manner. Sister Jeanne herself claimed that she had witnessed the casting of the spell that now tormented them, reporting how the young man had tossed a bouquet of roses over the wall of the convent.

On the Mother Superior's evidence Grandier was arrested, taken to the castle of Angers and there searched for the DEVIL'S MARK. Surviving records indicate that the prisoner was first stabbed with the point of the lancet and then very gently touched elsewhere with the blunt end of the instrument – so lightly that there was little chance that he would notice this second contact while still writhing in pain from the first. Four Devil's marks apparently insensitive to the touch were located on Grandier's body, and he was handed over to the torturers.

At his highly irregular trial, presided over by lackeys of Cardinal Richelieu, there was consternation when the actual pact that Grandier had agreed with Lucifer, signed with his own blood, was produced for perusal by the officials of the court (*see* PACT WITH THE DEVIL). The unlikely story was that this pact, countersigned by Satan, Beelzebub, Lucifer, Elimi, Leviathan and Astaroth and tellingly written from right to left, against the usual conventions, had been purloined from the Devil's own files by the demon Asmodeus.

Grandier's defence was ignored and potential witnesses on his behalf were warned that, if they appeared, they might be suspected of involvement in witchcraft themselves. Some of the nuns themselves attempted to get a hearing, perhaps realising for the first time the consequences that their statements might have upon the young man. However, the court refused to countenance any withdrawal of evidence, arguing that this was simply a ploy by the Devil to save his servant. The nuns were also promised a pension from the Cardinal if they would appear for the prosecution. Even the melodramatic appearance in the court of the Mother Superior with a noose round her neck, threatening to hang herself if she did not get a hearing, did not sway the court.

The sentence of death was inevitable and, to the satisfaction of his enemies, the hapless young priest was condemned to be burned at the stake in the public square of St Croix. Before he was executed Grandier was tortured with extreme savagery in a bid to obtain the names of his accomplices. According to eyewitnesses the torture was so severe that the marrow was seen to ooze from the prisoner's shattered bones. He named no one. In retaliation for this resistance the Capuchin friars presiding over the interrogation ensured that the rope with which Grandier was to be strangled before burning was tied in such a way that it could not be drawn tight, so that their victim was still alive when he was surrendered to the fire. When the prisoner attempted to make a last public denial of guilt at the stake the friars supervising the burning drenched him in holy water to prevent his words being heard.

The apparent demonic possession of the nuns did not, however, end with Grandier's death. The continued fits and contortions that the nuns exhibited attracted widespread comment, as well as fuelling criticisms of the Cardinal and the government. People came from miles around to see the sisters throw fits and demonstrate the symptoms of demonic possession, as recorded in a contemporary account:

> They threw themselves back till their heads touched their feet, and walked in this position with wonderful rapidity, and for a long time. They uttered cries so horrible and so loud that nothing like it was ever heard before. They made use of expressions so indecent as to shame the most debauched of men, while their acts, both in exposing themselves and inviting lewd behaviour from those present, would have astonished the inmates of the lowest brothel in the country.

Tellingly, these demonstrations became less frequent once Richelieu withdrew the pension that the nuns had been awarded after appearing for the prosecution at Grandier's trial. Only after repeated attempts at exorcism and a visit to the tomb of St Francis de Sales in Italy in 1638 did Sister Jeanne herself finally enjoy a respite from the demons that she claimed were in residence within her.

All authorities now agree that Grandier was an innocent victim whose death had a political dimension. Expert opinion is divided about the motives of the Mother Superior, however. According to some she was an epileptic, while others suggest that she was suffering from schizophrenia or was simply a plain fraud interested only in attracting publicity to herself. Certainly she attained the status of a celebrity after the affair died down, becoming well known for her prophetic abilities, her powers of healing and her displays of stigmata, which manifested in the forms of the names of Jesus, Mary, Joseph and Francis de Sales upon her left hand. She was even brought before Cardinal Richelieu himself to demonstrate this last gift, which was judged 'admirable'. She died at Loudon on 29 January 1665.

Louviers Nuns *see* BAVENT, MADELEINE.

love potion A magic potion to capture the heart of an intended partner, regardless of his or her real feelings. Countless witches were credited with the power to concoct potions that would influence the emotions in such a way, and allegations that such potions had been administered were central to many historical trials. Anne BOLEYN was just one prominent figure rumoured to have ensnared a king through such love magic (in her case, Henry VIII). Such was the credence placed on this kind of magic in England that, by the Witchcraft Statute of 1542, anyone who employed 'any invocation of spirites, witchcrafts, enchantments or sorcerers to ... provoke any person to unlawful love' was guilty of a serious felony. Similar clauses in the Witchcraft Acts of 1563 and 1604 confirmed the illegality of such activity.

In many cases the potion – usually provided in liquid form – was supposed to cause the person taking it to fall in love with the next person whom he or she saw, although other brews could be more specific. The most effective love potions incorporated some trace of the desired victim's 'being', perhaps a few strands of their HAIR or some nail parings. By saying incantations over these and mixing them with certain herbs or other ingredients a witch or the client of a witch was reputed to be able to summon any person to his or her presence and to influence them in any way they chose.

Procuring samples from a victim was not always easy. In one celebrated story concerning the tragic Scottish teacher Dr John FIAN, who was tortured and put to death as a witch in 1590, the sorcerer desired to obtain the love of the sister of one of his pupils. He cajoled the boy into agreeing to purloin 'three hairs of his sister's privities', but the boy failed to do this without waking his sister, who complained to their mother. Their mother, who happened herself to be a witch, understood at once what was afoot and gave her son three hairs from a young heifer to take to the teacher. Consequently, when the unsuspecting magician worked his magic upon the hairs he found himself being pursued through the town by the lovestruck cow, which 'made toward the schoolmaster, leaping and dancing upon him'.

Among the plants supposed to have the greatest aphrodisiac properties were many with distinctive shapes or tastes. Some, such as asparagus, leeks and parsnips, resembled human genitalia, while others created a sensation of heat, and thus passion. At the more exotic end some witches were said to prefer above all else the MANDRAKE plant, pounded into liquid form and mixed with SALT, which had itself long been considered capable of rousing the passions. Another, more radical, spell required the marrow and spleen of a young man murdered while spying on some lustful scene. Less unusual, but also apparently effective in love magic, were such plants as MARIGOLD, St John's wort and periwinkle (which had to be made into a powder with some earthworms and then eaten with meat). Other ingredients ranged from narcotic perfumes, ginger and cinnamon to animal testicles, TOAD'S venom, ox bile, donkey lungs, human hearts, URINE and semen.

Witches were also said to offer 'an-aphrodisiacs' that would calm undesired passions. These included the common poppy, which was widely believed to subdue the passions. In medieval times many women set great store by so-called 'rings of oblivion', which enabled them to forget old loves and to concentrate on new prospects. More extreme solutions to the same purpose included the consumption of lizards dipped in urine and the application of liniments of mouse droppings.

Lowes, John *see* HOPKINS, MATTHEW.

Lowestoft Witches *see* BURY ST EDMUNDS WITCHES.

Lucifer One of the personal names by which the DEVIL, or SATAN, was often known. Lucifer, meaning 'Light-Bearer', was the name given by the Romans to the morning star, and in Christian mythology he was an archangel who, renamed Satan, became king of all the DEMONS after attempting to rival God. This former role as light-bearer was evoked in the conventional depictions of the demonic Lucifer complete with one or more black candles between his horns. Acolytes would light their own candles from that of Lucifer when he was present at their SABBATS. As the most powerful of all demons, and therefore the most dangerous, Lucifer was called on by witches and sorcerers when their spells demanded strong magic beyond the capabilities of his minions.

Lucifer was not, it should be noted, always synonymous with Satan. The sixteenth-century demonologist Peter BINSFELD, for instance, ascribed to Lucifer the deadly sin of pride, while Satan represented anger.

Worship of Lucifer as the supreme god was not confined to conventional witches – in thirteenth-century Germany a small Satanic cult who called themselves 'Luciferans' were persecuted as heretics. According to the confessions that were extracted from them by torture they named Lucifer, brother of Christ, as the source of all good things in the world and expected him one day to overthrow the Christian God. Like witches, they behaved in a manner calculated to offend Christian sensibilities, scorning Christian rites and desecrating the sacred host. They also observed the ceremony of the 'obscene KISS', for which Lucifer might manifest as a cat or a toad, and celebrated his presence with feasting and orgies.

Luxeuil Witch Madame Desle la Mansenée, wife of one Jean de la Tour, who was tried for witchcraft at the instigation of the INQUISITION in Luxeuil, Franche-Comte, FRANCE, in 1529. The trial was notable in that it demonstrated the continued, if covert, influence of the Inquisition in witchcraft cases even at this relatively late date.

The case was based on hearsay and gossip gathered secretly by the Inquisitor-General of Besançon in the village of Anjeux, Franche-Comté, where the woman lived. The mere fact that she had a local reputation as a witch was sufficient to seal her fate. As soon as a number of allegations had been collected against her, regardless of the quality of the evidence offered, Madame Desle la Mansenée was selected for trial and was clearly presumed to be guilty by repute even before the proceedings began. Bearing in mind this presumption of guilt the use of torture was automatic, and there was little hope of the suspect disclaiming the charges made in view of the fact that she was not even permitted to know the identities of those by whom she was accused.

With the encouragement of the Inquisitor-General, neighbours alleged that the accused had caused a wide variety of misfortunes to befall those who had crossed her, including the bewitching of children so that they fell ill. A six-man commission under the Inquisitor-General himself interrogated the suspected witch and, though she denied everything, she was handed over to the torturer. Exposed to the agonies of SQUASSATION, Madame Desle la Mansenée had no option but to admit all the charges against her. She admitted to denying her Catholic faith, to flying through the air on a stick, to dancing at sabbats, to having sexual intercourse with the Devil and to poisoning livestock with a mysterious black powder. Further torture wrested from her the names of various accomplices.

Convicted of HERESY, of renouncing her Catholic faith and of murder, Madame Desle la Mansenée was hanged on 18 December 1529 and her body burned to ashes.

lycanthropy The mysterious process by which a witch or sorcerer was once thought to be able to change into the form of a WOLF. The mythology of the 'werewolf' is closely related to that of the witch in that such metamorphoses were an essential feature of European witchcraft (see SHAPE-SHIFTING). Witches changed into HARES in order to steal milk from cows, into birds and CATS in order to spy on unsuspecting humans and into wolves in order to prey on children.

The myth of lycanthropy may have had its origins in ancient pagan wolf-worship and was nurtured by the many folktales common to all cultures in which men changed their form at will or through the casting of spells. In medieval times the authorities were divided as to whether lycanthropy could or could not happen. The Church rejected the notion because it appeared to trespass on the powers of God, and blamed delusions created by DEMONS for the confessions of those who professed to possess such gifts. The CANON EPISCOPI of the tenth century consolidated this view, but the suggestion that a new sect of witches had evolved undermined this attitude and by the fourteenth century scholars were once again questioning whether lycanthropy was merely a delusion. Some, including Jean BODIN and Henri BOGUET, were convinced – as were most of the public – that witches really could change their forms, while others protested that men who thought they could turn into wolves and other creatures were deceived by Satan or were merely suffering from mental derangement. Gervase of Tilbury, in his *Otia Imperialia* written in the early thirteenth century, accepted as fact that 'In England we often see men changed into wolves at the changes of the moon, which kind of men the French call *gerulfos*, but the English *werewulf*'. Other authorities suggested that gullible people were fooled by the Devil into thinking themselves wolves, and thus into thinking they had committed crimes on livestock and humans that had really been perpetrated by the Devil and his minions.

A number of witches, some clearly insane, actually confessed to adopting wolf shape in order to inflict harm, especially on the Continent of Europe. As wolves, they savaged livestock and ate babies; these confessions were often more than enough to ensure that the person concerned was sent to the stake, or at the very least incarcerated in a lunatic asylum. Like other witches, those who adopted wolf form would sometimes describe how they would gather in large numbers at SABBATS presided over by the Devil. Tales were told the length and breadth of Europe of wolves that had been shot or otherwise wounded while attacking livestock or humans, and of the same wounds being found on humans suspected of having the power of lycanthropy. Signs which indicated that a person was really a werewolf included hair on the palms of the hands and eyebrows that joined in the middle.

As wolves disappeared from the landscape, so witches were accused less often of adopting wolf form and were alleged instead to go about as cats, dogs or other domestic animals. Whatever the form that was assumed, however, it was widely agreed that the only way to kill a witch transformed in this manner was to shoot the animal with a bullet made of SILVER, a notion that is now part and parcel of modern werewolf myth.

Maclean, Euphemia *see* NORTH BERWICK WITCHES.

Magee Island Witches The last witch trial to be staged in IRELAND. The case, which centred on Magee Island near Carrickfergus in Antrim, was heard at Carrickfergus in 1711 and differed from the usual scenario in that it linked witchcraft with poltergeist activity.

The events from which the trial stemmed began in 1710 when the household of James Haltridge, the son of a deceased Presbyterian minister, was much disrupted by a series of pranks perpetrated by an undetected hand. Typical occurrences included bedclothes being pulled off beds and stones being thrown at windows. In February 1711 Haltridge's widowed mother felt a pain in her back and died a few days later. At this point neighbours began to discuss the possibility of witchcraft being at work and eighteen-year-old Mary Dunbar, who had arrived at the house as a servant shortly after the old woman's death, began to exhibit signs of demonic POSSESSION. As if to confirm the suspicions already in the air, the girl claimed she was being tormented by the spirits of several women. Soon afterwards she named eight local women as the witches who were sending these torments to her, and to support her claims went into violent hysterics when one of them was brought into the same room.

Suitably impressed by Mary Dunbar's seizures, the authorities had seven of the women arrested and brought to trial on 31 March. The proceedings were over within one day, with the prosecution relying almost entirely upon the 'evidence' of the servant-girl's torment. A large variety of unlikely objects that had supposedly been vomited by Mary Dunbar during her fits were presented for the judges to inspect: they included feathers, cotton, yarn, pins and two large waistcoat buttons. The prisoners had no counsel on their behalf, but testimony that they were regular attenders at church and were otherwise of good character complicated the matter somewhat.

In the end the three judges agreed to differ, but the jury had no such qualms and decreed that the women were guilty as charged. Their punishment was relatively light, however: each served a year in prison and underwent four appearances in the pillory.

magic circle Carefully prepared circular area of ground from the safety of which a sorcerer or witch may raise DEMONS without endangering themselves. The circle may be drawn with charcoal or chalk or scratched on the ground using a sword, knife (*see* ATHAME) or WAND. The convention is that the circle must be drawn in a clockwise direction unless it is to be used in black magic, in which case it is drawn in an anticlockwise WIDDERSHINS direction.

Everything used in the ritual of preparing a magic circle must be new and unsoiled, lest it be tainted by some previous misfortune. Convention has it that the outer circle must be nine feet in diameter, while a second circle eight feet in diameter is drawn within it. Various objects and substances with magical properties are then placed between the two circles to strengthen the barrier against any evil force that is raised. These might include bowls of WATER, crosses and crucifixes, NAMES OF POWER and various herbs that have a reputation for keeping evil at bay. The names used vary, but one accepted version makes use of the four magically potent names of the creator of the universe: Tetragrammaton (written between the east and south), Eheyt (between south and west), Elijon (between west and north) and Eloha (between north and east).

The sorcerer or witch may then enter the circle, carefully 'closing' it behind them. No gap must be allowed in the circles, for this will allow a spirit access to the centre. If the magic circle is drawn correctly, no malevolent spirit will be able to enter it and threaten the sorcerer or witch standing within its confines. The centre of the circle is usually decorated with further patterns and names, generally being divided into the shape of a PENTACLE or a similar arrangement of triangles. Candles may also be lit, incense burned and recitations chanted in order to promote the chances of success.

Witchcraft tradition warns against the sorcerer or witch being tempted to leave the protection of the circle until the ritual they have embarked upon is complete and any evil spirits have returned whence they came. Failure to observe this rule may result in the instant death of the person concerned: a seventeenth-century Egyptian fortune-teller called Chiancungi apparently left the protection of his magic circle too quickly and was crushed to death by a demon that he had raised.

Maid of Kent *see* BARTON, ELIZABETH.

maleficia The evil deeds that were formerly attributed to witches everywhere and which often formed the basis of the charges laid against them by the authorities. Above the theological and legal objections that many people felt when it came to the subject of witchcraft was the all-consuming dread of the harm that a witch might actually be capable of inflicting through magic. Because the source of witches' power was demonic it followed that their magic was in most cases malevolent, and the great mass of the populace lived in real terror of incurring the wrath of the local 'Wise Woman' or rumoured witch. This terror lay at the root of the persecution that was actively encouraged on virtually all sides over two centuries and more.

Witches and their enemies identified an almost endless list of felonies and offences that might be committed through the use of black magic. These ranged from STORM-RAISING, causing death by poison and blighting married couples with impotence (*see* LIGATURE) to bringing about illness in livestock and generally ill-wishing or cursing a person, place or animal (*see* CURSE). Through their SPELLS or the power of the EVIL EYE witches could steal milk from cows or the dairy, cause people to go mad or to suffer headaches and fits, damage crops, start fires, cause arguments between friends, make horses rear and plunge uncontrollably, spoil beer and butter and perpetrate a thousand other undesirable acts, both petty and serious to the point of high treason.

As early as 1435, the theologian Johannes Nider categorised *maleficia* into seven groups. According to his thesis, witches might cause harm by inspiring love, stirring up hatred, causing impotence, introducing disease, taking life, inducing madness, or injuring property or animals. Later authorities argued that any physical or mental infirmity that could not be understood or easily treated by a physician was due to witchcraft, and added to the list such misdeeds as raising storms and poisoning the air. Indeed, in some regions any event that could not be readily explained by normal means was automatically assumed to be the work of witches.

Lawyers routinely looked for details of *maleficia* as prima facie evidence against the accused. It was rarely necessary to prove a link between the event and the suspect – or even that the event itself had taken place as described (hence the court's acceptance of the allegation that one of the victims of Matthew HOPKINS had by magic sunk a ship, without anyone checking to see if a ship had been lost at all). In most cases, it was enough for a witness to recall some dim threat (formally a *damnum minatum*) uttered by the accused either recently or in the long-distant past and for some otherwise inexplicable harm (or *malum secutum*) to have then occurred. If information about past threats was not forthcoming the obvious next step was to inspect the neighbours for the most likely suspect, perhaps someone already rumoured to be a witch or simply fitting the popular conception of one. Discovery of corroborating evidence, such as a figure that might have been used in IMAGE MAGIC, was helpful but often almost superfluous.

Witch-hunters essentially sought to punish witches for their apparent rejection of the thinking of conventional Christian society. However, in order to carry popular opinion with them it was necessary to illustrate how this 'wrong' thinking had led to real, appreciable harm – hence the importance of identifying *maleficia* in the course of a trial. It was often left unclear how the culprit had actually perpetrated the alleged crime: as long as the witch had expressed some evil intent and some harm had followed it mattered little whether he or she had employed ointments, herbs, potions, effigies or the magic of KNOTS, or had enlisted the aid of the Devil or FAMILIARS to accomplish the act.

In order to make arresting a witch less perilous it was widely agreed that a witch's power to commit *maleficia* conveniently deserted her the moment she was touched by an officer of the law. To be on the safe side, representatives of the authorities faced with such challenges were advised to carry about their person exorcised SALT and consecrated wax in order to ward off supernatural attack. In some places they were warned not to let a suspected witch's feet come into contact with the ground, lest he or she be able to work *maleficia* to save themselves.

Malking Tower *see* PENDLE WITCHES.

Malleus Maleficarum The single most important publication ever written on the topic of witchcraft, long considered the most reliable authority upon virtually every aspect of the subject. Otherwise known as the *Hammer of Witches*, the *Malleus Maleficarum*, which was printed in 1486, was the work of two feared Dominican inquisitors, Heinrich Kramer (or Institoris) (*c.*1430–1505) and Jakob Sprenger (1436–95). Kramer had considerable experience as a witch-hunter in the Tyrol, where his activities had caused great unrest among the local population before he was finally expelled by the Bishop of Brixen. Sprenger, meanwhile, as Dean of Cologne University, was an established scholar whose name commanded some respect. Both men were apparently convinced of the need to expose the witchcraft threat and to secure the execution of as many of its practitioners as possible.

The text of Kramer and Sprenger's book detailed methods of interrogation suitable for cases of witchcraft, including TORTURE, and offered advice on how to secure the conviction of suspected witches as well as countering every possible argument that might be voiced by those who refused to believe in the reality of the witch-craft threat. It was also informative on the crimes that might reasonably be blamed on witchcraft and suggested appropriate punishments. Witchcraft, the authors claimed, was a serious threat and anyone who expressed disbelief in it was guilty of HERESY.

Approved by Pope INNOCENT VIII in his bull of 1484, the *Malleus Maleficarum* became an essential handbook for witch judges, going into fourteen editions by 1520 and being brought out another sixteen times between 1574 and 1669. The publication of the book, which linked folkloric beliefs in black magic with practices that the Church considered heretical, greatly intensified the growing panic that was being whipped up and reassured judges in witchcraft trials that in most cases the death penalty was the only sensible course to take. Countless trials were modelled on the procedures detailed in the book, with evidence being accepted from all quarters and legal niceties being given little consideration in the overwhelming need to counter the 'invasion' that the authors stressed was being mounted against the Christian world. Because the offence of witchcraft amounted to treason against God it was excusable for courts to withhold the names of accusers from the suspected person, to employ the severest torture to obtain a confession and to hear the testimony of convicted criminals and perjurers.

The book retained its status as the leading authority on the subject throughout the two hundred-year history of the witchcraft hysteria in Europe. It was accepted even by Protestant courts, despite the Catholic background of its authors.

malum secutum *see* MALEFICIA.

mandrake Plant with a distinctive human-shaped root which was long thought to be a favourite ingredient in witches' brews. In former times mere possession of a mandrake plant could prove enough to have a suspect condemned to death as a witch. Highly valued in medieval medicine for its magical properties, the mandrake was included among the most potent of all plants used for occult purposes. Witches were reputed to prize it for its soporific, aphrodisiac and purgative powers, and the root has been proved by science to contain an alkaloid that can suppress pain and promote sleep; taken in excess it can cause madness.

In ancient Egypt the mandrake was strongly associated with sex magic, and for similar reasons it was known popularly in English tradition the 'love apple' (a nickname later transferred to the tomato). In certain spells, it could apparently be employed as a potent influence upon sexual drive and appetite, a notion that went all the way back to the Bible. Other spells involving the use of the mandrake promised to promote a person's wealth, to fix broken bones, to ease the pain of toothache or rheumatism, to act as an anaesthetic before an operation, to cure depression, to enable the dying to recover, to prevent fits and even to enable them to give up smoking.

An elaborate spell involving the mandrake plant required the root to be dug up, watered with human blood and embellished with berries for eyes and mouth. If this was done correctly, the plant would acquire the gift of speech and would communicate the whereabouts of hidden treasure as well as sharing information about the future and opening locks. Care had to be taken, though, in digging up the root. Anyone who attempted to do so with their own hands would be struck dead or made impotent on the spot. The best method was to get a dog to dig the root up. As the root left the soil, superstition had it that it would utter a terrible shriek, which was itself enough to drive any living thing within hearing quite mad.

As a grim footnote, it was believed throughout Europe that the mandrake only grew naturally under a gallows, springing up from the semen that fell from the decomposing bodies of executed felons.

Manningtree Witches *see* HOPKINS, MATTHEW.

mare *see* NIGHTMARE.

Mareschal, Robert le *see* NOTINGHAM, JOHN DE.

marigold Garden flower that, like other yellow-centred blooms, was once considered an effective witch deterrent. Called the marigold because the Virgin Mary was supposed to have worn the flower at her breast, the flower was variously credited by witchlore as an aphrodisiac (hence the alternative names husbandman's dial and summer's bride) and as a protective against evil. In folk medicine, the flower could also be rubbed on the skin to ease the pain of wasp and bee stings and could be powdered to treat the ague. Inhaling the scent of the marigold was reputed to cure headaches and depression.

Martin, Susanna *see* SALEM WITCHES.

Mass for the Dead *see* BLACK MASS.

Mass of St Sécaire *see* BLACK MASS.

Mass of the Holy Spirit *see* BLACK MASS.

Mather, Cotton 1662–1728. US Congregational minister who is remembered as colonial America's most committed witch-hunter. The son of the respected Puritan leader Increase Mather, who himself published a book of cautionary tales designed to emphasise the ever-present danger posed by witchcraft, Cotton Mather played a key role in the tragedy of the SALEM WITCHES, the most famous witchcraft trial in American history.

Following education at Harvard, the youthful Cotton Mather was made head of the prestigious North Church in Boston and rapidly emerged as a prominent Congregationalist leader in New England. He developed the reservations that his father had harboured about the subject of witchcraft and became convinced that there was no forgiving such criminals, declaring: 'Witchcraft is the most nefarious high treason against the Majesty on high. A witch is not to be endured in heaven or on earth.' To disseminate his ideas on the subject, in 1689 he published *Memorable Providences Relating to Witchcrafts and Possessions*, in which he made clear his belief in a real, actively functioning Devil and stressed the reality of witchcraft.

Mather involved himself in numerous cases in which witchcraft was alleged, always pressing for strenuous action to be taken against the accused. When he was approached for advice concerning the events at Salem he had no hesitation in supporting those who felt that the suspects should be thoroughly investigated and exposed to the full vigour of the law: '... we cannot but humbly recommend unto the Government, the speedy and vigorous prosecution of such as have rendered themselves obnoxious, according to the directions given in the laws of God and the wholesome statutes of the English nation for the detection of witchcrafts'. When the judges appeared to be considering the reprieve of one of the accused, the Reverend George Burroughs, Mather is reported to have intervened personally to ensure that the execution was carried out as originally planned.

Subsequently, in 1693, when he felt called upon to justify the trials, Mather published *Wonders of the Invisible World*, which by all accounts only stirred up further anxieties about the presence of witches in the New England community. Mather admittedly expressed reservations about the acceptance of so-called SPECTRAL EVIDENCE (relating to apparitions) in witchcraft cases, but in all other respects he consistently supported the persecution of witches in the colonies.

In the wake of the Salem tragedy the tide of public opinion turned away from such stern responses and Mather became increasingly isolated, being passed over because of his views several times when he tried to win the presidency of Harvard. Embittered and ignored, he continued none the less to call for ruthless suppression of witchcraft until the end of his life.

See also GOODWIN CHILDREN; RULE, MARGARET; SHORT, MERCY.

Mathers, Samuel Liddell 1854–1918. British occultist who became head of the Hermetic Order of the GOLDEN DAWN. A Freemason and Rosicrucian, Mathers established his credentials as a leading occultist with his translation of an obscure manuscript on the CABALA and the art of tarot card reading that he picked up on a street bookstall. Having been invited to join the Golden Dawn movement, he quickly pushed out the original founders of the organisation and took over as its leader, claiming that he had met some supernatural beings called the Secret Chiefs in the Bois de

Boulogne in Paris and had been entrusted by them with a new constitution for the club.

Although the Order of the Golden Dawn had its headquarters in London, Mathers settled in Paris in 1892, decorating his house in the style of an ancient Egyptian temple and there performing bizarre 'Egyptian masses' in company with his wife and various guests. Among his associates was the Irish poet W. B. Yeats. He also worked on various books on magic, several of which were destined to have a profound influence upon contemporary occultists. His most significant publication was his translation into English of the *Key of Solomon*, which detailed the rites and procedures to be carried out in ritual magic.

Eventually, Mathers came into conflict with his erstwhile pupil Aleister CROWLEY, who sought to displace him as head of the Golden Dawn movement. Expelled from the movement, Mathers subsequently adapted the rituals so that he could perform them in public, presenting his *Rites of Isis* show at the Théâtre Bordinière in Paris. The relationship between Mathers and his rival Crowley rapidly deteriorated and they engaged in a lengthy psychic war in which they reputedly sent demons to attack each other. Crowley claimed to have raised up BEELZEBUB and forty-nine attendant demons, which he despatched to harm Mathers. Mathers's ultimate death (ostensibly caused by influenza) was blamed by some on Crowley's malevolent magic-making.

Mattsdotter, Magdalen *see* MORA WITCHES; SWEDEN.

Meath, Petronilla de *see* KYTELER, ALICE.

Medici, Catherine de' 1519–89. Regent of France (1560–3) during the minority of her second son, Charles IX, and effective ruler of the country until his death in 1574. Immensely powerful within France, and an upholder of royal authority, she was said by many enemies to be a witch. According to popular tradition, she often called on the forces of darkness for assistance and had BLACK MASSES said on her behalf.

As evidence of Catherine's involvement in the 'Old Religion' it was rumoured that she wore a gold talisman that bore various arcane symbols, including representations of the goddess Venus and the name of the demon ASMODEUS. The talisman was allegedly destroyed by Catherine's son Henri after her death, though a drawing of it survives.

As ruler of France Catherine sought to keep the peace between the Protestant Huguenots and the Catholics, but also devoted much energy to ensuring that her own children all became kings. When her son Charles, newly elected King of Poland at her instigation, fell seriously ill, Catherine had little doubt that witchcraft was to blame and singled out Cosmo Ruggieri, an astrologer then visiting Paris, as the source of the trouble. In a letter to the Procureur-General of Paris she complained that Ruggieri had made a wax image of Charles in order to bring harm to him. Ruggieri was arrested, but the young King's health failed to improve. In desperation Catherine, as recorded by Jean BODIN in his *Démonomanie des Sorciers* in 1580, ordered a BLACK MASS to be said on his behalf. On the Queen's orders a young boy was fed a white host and then murdered, his throat being cut to provide blood for the chalice to be used in the ceremony intended to restore Charles's fortunes. The ceremony was not, apparently, a success, for Charles died not long afterwards.

Mephistopheles One of the chief DEMONS of Hell, sometimes synonymous with the DEVIL himself. Mephistopheles, meaning 'he who loves not light' in Greek, originated in Mesopotamian religion and is conventionally depicted as half animal and half human. In Germany, he is addressed as 'the knight with the horse's hoof'. He is now best known for his role in the Faust myth, offering the central character a lifetime of pleasure and knowledge in exchange for his soul. His name features among those most often called upon for consultation by contemporary occultists.

metamorphosis *see* SHAPE-SHIFTING.

Midia, Petronilla de *see* KYTELER, ALICE.

Midsummer's Eve 23 June, the night before Midsummer's Day, is widely held to be one of the most magical times in the year and is thus a favoured date for the holding of witches' SABBATS. Marking the moment when the sun's power gradually starts to diminish and a time when the forces of darkness are reputed to be especially active, Midsummer's Eve was formerly considered an ideal time to probe into what the future might have in store. For this reason, witches throughout Europe once broke open hens' EGGS on this night in order to divine from the contents things to come, or would raise demons so as to question them about whatever might lie in wait.

Other witches might take advantage of the date to gather St John's wort, which was supposed to be of great benefit in the treatment of nervous disorders, in assisting barren women to become pregnant and in preventing the passage of malevolent spirits. The plant had to be gathered on Midsummer's Eve in order to be effective (some authorities stipulated that the person collecting it had to pick the plant while entirely naked) and care had to be taken not to step on the flower. If this happened, a fairy horse might rear up beneath the culprit and carry him or her off on a wild ride that might last all night and end up in some remote and desolate place.

Women who became pregnant on Midsummer's Eve were expected to bear children with the dubious gift of the EVIL EYE.

mirror The reflection, representing the soul itself, has always been considered magical in nature and mirrors therefore rank high among the tools of the conventional witch. In the past many sorcerers, including the celebrated Dr John DEE, were reputed to own magic mirrors by means of which they could see into the future (*see* SCRYING). Another tradition claimed that witches had a particular preference for mirrors framed on just three sides, which enabled them to see over immense distances.

Paradoxically, mirrors were also supposed to deter witches. Those fearful of witchcraft in former times purchased small WITCH BALLS of reflective glass, which were said to ward off the EVIL EYE, and during the seventeenth century there was a considerable fad for wearing small mirrors in the hat for the same purpose.

Molland, Alice d.1684. Englishwoman who was the last person to be executed for witchcraft in England. Hanged at Exeter, Alice Molland was not, of course, the last person to die in England as a result of being implicated in witchcraft, as several more victims lost their lives as a result of mob lynching or being subjected to such informal tests as SCORING ABOVE THE BREATH and SWIMMING. Her claim to be the last official victim is, however, generally agreed – although two probably fictitious pamphlets attempted to grant this 'honour' to two women hanged at Northampton in 1705 and to a woman and a child hanged in Huntingdon in 1716 (both cases otherwise unrecorded).

See also WENHAM, JANE.

Montespan, Madame de *see* CHAMBRE ARDENTE AFFAIR.

Mora Witches Outbreak of witchcraft hysteria that occurred at Mora in the Dalecarlia region of central SWEDEN and caused a major panic in Scandinavian society in the mid-seventeenth century. The case began in the summer of 1669 with a series of worrying reports which suggested many members of the community were practising witchcraft. In response to public alarm, the advisers of the young King Charles XI despatched a royal commission to investigate, although without the use of torture or imprisonment. Questioning of suspects only confirmed the initial anxiety, and, after attempts to redeem the accused through prayer only resulted in a further spreading of the hysteria, the commission levelled formal charges at some seventy adults. Subsequently twenty-three of the accused voluntarily confessed to their involvement in the occult, claiming that they met regularly with the DEVIL (calling himself Antecessoar) at a certain CROSSROADS. In exchange for their allegiance, the Devil enabled them to soar through the air mounted on GOATS, bewitched men or fenceposts to attend SABBATS at a large house in a meadow called the Blocula, where they denied their Christian faith, were baptised by the Devil, indulged in lavish feasts provided by their demonic master, engaged in DANCING and promiscuous sex and plotted various acts of MALEFICIA. They also, they claimed, attempted in vain to build a house in which all witches would find shelter at the Day of Judgement.

Particularly shocking to the astounded interrogators in the affair was the involvement of some three hundred young children in the case. While the adults sat and feasted with the Devil, these children, who were invited to attend by the adults, were allowed to watch proceedings from the doorway. The children, whose allegations had first brought the scandal to light, were all carefully questioned and their confessions were found to tally to a large degree with those of their elders. Some claimed that they looked forward to these outings, while others protested that they were dragged there against their will and forced to enrol in the Devil's ranks. The Devil himself had appeared to them as a red-bearded man, wearing a grey coat and a high-crowned hat wrapped with brightly coloured cloth. On his legs he wore red and blue stockings. After the feasting was over the company danced while the Devil played the harp before proceedings degenerated into a mass brawl and an orgy. As a result of these activities, several of the witches were alleged to have given birth to children by the Devil and to toads and snakes by each other.

Convinced of the seriousness of the situation at Mora, the royal commission passed the sentence of death upon eighty-five persons, including the twenty-three adults who had confessed to their crimes and fifteen of the children. The first of two mass executions took place on 25 August 1669, barely a fortnight after the commission had opened its proceedings. The condemned prisoners were first beheaded and then their bodies were burned to ashes. Another thirty-six youngsters, aged from nine to sixteen, were forced to run the gauntlet and were beaten with rods upon their hands once a week for a whole year. Twenty of the youngest children, all under the age of nine, were thrashed on their hands at the church door three Sundays in succession.

The hysteria that traumatised the population at Mora subsequently spread to other areas in Sweden and FINLAND, leading to further investigations in the Uppsala region and in Helsinki before reaching Stockholm in 1675. Here, following the execution of six more women, the delusion was finally laid to rest largely through the efforts of a young doctor called Urban Hjärne, who publicly declared the whole affair to be the product of overheated imaginations, madness or malice. The last straw came with the case of Magdalen Mattsdotter, who was accused of witchcraft by her own children and servant-girls (her daughter tried to persuade her to confess even as she was burned at the stake). Shortly after the luckless woman's execution it transpired that the whole affair had been dreamed up by the servant-girls out of jealousy, and they too were sentenced to death before reason prevailed and a stop was put to any more accusations. Scholars have since speculated that the Mora tragedy, which was first revealed by the local pastor, came about largely through the children being influenced by printed pamphlets describing witchcraft sensations elsewhere. In this respect, the episode bears comparison with the celebrated case of the SALEM WITCHES among other witchcraft trials that depended mainly on the evidence of children. Another factor in the case may have been the influence of the Swedish Lutheran Church, which was seeking to consolidate its power after a purge of liberal elements in the 1660s.

See also JØRGENSDATTER, SIRI.

Morgan, Nanny 1789–1857. Englishwoman of Westwood Common, near Much Wenlock in Shropshire, who was widely believed by her contemporaries to be a witch. Long after witchcraft had ceased to be a legal offence in England, belief in such supernatural activity remained strong in rural communities. Nanny Morgan was credited by many with the power of the EVIL EYE and neighbours feared her influence, quoting as evidence of her involvement in witchcraft the fact that she kept live TOADS in her cottage and her reputation as a fortune-teller, a skill that she was supposed to have learned from the gypsies with whom she had travelled for a time as a young girl after serving a term of imprisonment for theft. Few people dared to cross Nanny Morgan for fear of the possible consequences, but many others travelled miles to consult her on matters that seemed to demand her rather specialised knowledge.

The circumstances of Nanny Morgan's eventual death reflected the reputation she had as a witch. It transpired that her lodger, a man named William Davis, wished to leave her house, but was afraid that if he did so he would fall victim to the old woman's magic. On consulting other locals, Davis was advised of the ritual of SCORING ABOVE THE BREATH, which he was assured would free him of the witch's influence. Not long afterwards, Davis was seen leaving Nanny Morgan's house with bloodstains on his clothing. When the body of the old woman, who had died from multiple stab wounds, was subsequently found Davis was quickly traced and charged with her murder. Davis admitted the crime, explaining that he had not meant to kill the old woman but had merely attempted to draw blood so as to release himself from her power.

As a final indication of the seriousness with which such matters were taken in rural areas of England right up to the end of the nine-teenth century, it is illuminating to note that the authorities had the greatest difficulty finding anyone who was willing to lay the old woman's body out. In the end she was buried in the clothes she had been wearing at the hour of her murder.

Morton, Patrick *see* PITTENWEEM WITCHES.

Mother Goddess *see* GREAT GODDESS.

Mother Shipton *see* SHIPTON, MOTHER.

mountain ash *see* ROWAN.

Mouse-maker The case of Elsche Nebelings, a sixty-three-year-old German widow who was tried as a witch in an unidentified town in Saxony in 1694. This relatively late case illustrates how by the end of the seventeenth century a more rational approach to witchcraft was beginning to displace the more hysterical attitude commonly encountered in previous decades.

The allegations arose out of a conjuring trick Nebelings had taught a ten-year-old girl called Althe Ahlers. The trick, which the girl delighted in showing her schoolfriends, allowed her to produce a live mouse from an apparently empty handkerchief. The girl was promptly arrested on suspicion of witchcraft and, when the source of the trick was learned, Elsche Nebelings was also put on trial. Both the old woman and the girl denied being witches, but the case went ahead and the death penalty was demanded by the prosecution. Ultimately the judge consulted a university law faculty for advice, asking them whether they felt he should order the torture of the two suspects by means of thumbscrews and strappado and have them searched for the DEVIL'S MARK.

Fortunately for the two prisoners, the university scholars instructed the immediate release of the accused, who had already served a sufficient time behind bars. It was evident from this case that the tide was slowly turning, although it should be noted that in Germany parallel cases on equally ludicrous grounds all too often culminated in the torture and death of suspects until well into the eighteenth century.

mugwort Herb that was considered a powerful witch deterrent and was also believed to nullify the effects of poisons, spells and disease. Witchlore advised that mugwort was particularly effective in the treatment of women and could counter the ravages of consumption. Placed in the shoe, mugwort also prevented tiredness on long journeys. Any person who dug up mugwort on MIDSUMMER'S EVE would find a small coal beneath the plant: this could be carried on the person to provide protection against burns, the plague, carbuncles, fever and lightning.

Murdock, Sarah *see* HOLT, SIR JOHN.

Murray, Margaret Alice 1862–1963. British Egyptologist, archaeologist, anthropologist and authority on witchcraft who propounded the theory that witchcraft was but a continuation of a much older pagan religion (an idea promulgated by many witches in recent decades). In her book *The Witch-Cult in Western Europe*, published in 1921, Murray developed her thesis by making links between the details of witchcraft ceremonies described in witches' confessions and what could be surmised about the ceremonies of ancient religious cults. She claimed that witchcraft was an 'old' religion that had simply been driven underground by the Christians, and confidently identified the DEVIL as the successor of the HORNED GOD of the pre-Christian era. There was thus no deliberate heretical intent shared by witches, because their religion was much older than Christianity and belonged to a quite different tradition.

According to Murray's thesis, the old faith was kept alive through a complex and interlinked system of COVENS, which observed their own rules and rituals and usually comprised thirteen members – although this appears in reality to be a relatively recent invention. Participants in these covens ranged from the lowest peasant to members of royal families (she even ventured to suggest that Edward III instituted the Order of the Garter as a disguised coven). To support her notion of an organised pan-European secret cult, Murray emphasised the striking similarity between confessions recorded in different parts of Europe in different centuries. Unfortunately she failed to appreciate that the questions put to witches during torture often followed a standard pattern and were therefore more than likely to produce similar responses.

The theory nevertheless convinced a number of contemporary scholars and is still upheld by many modern witches, but the accepted view of scholars now is that the link cannot be justified by the evidence and does not hold up under close scrutiny. Most witches' confessions placed little emphasis upon the ritual ceremonies of alleged covens, suggesting that there was no real 'religious' intent behind their activities – assuming they took place at all. In cases where semi-religious rites were performed they were usually simple parodies of Christian worship or, at best, vague recreations of local rural dances or customs rather than expressions of a developed centuries-old faith.

Murrell, James 1780–1860. English herbalist and quack doctor from Hadleigh in Essex, who was widely known for his mastery of the occult arts and is remembered as perhaps the most famous of all

'Cunning Men'. Nicknamed 'Cunning Murrell', he was the seventh son of a seventh son and for this reason was credited with special prophetic and healing powers. According to Murrell, his powers were so great that he enjoyed dominion over the DEVIL himself and was personally immune from the threat of witchcraft. Trading in his native Essex as a herbalist, cattle-doctor and prophet, he was frequently asked in his capacity as a WHITE WITCH to exorcise ghosts, witches and demons, to employ the art of SCRYING in a looking-glass in order to locate lost property, and to make astrological predictions. He was especially famous for his skill in preparing WITCH BOTTLES to counter evil spells, and was also reputed to possess a copper AMULET that lost its lustre whenever anyone told a lie. As a final proof of his unique skills, he is said to have predicted with great accuracy the hour of his own death.

myrrh Gum resin, used as an ointment and perfume, which is usually associated with the Christmas story. One of the gifts brought to the infant Jesus by the three Magi, myrrh was highly prized in ancient times and continued to be revered in later centuries for its magical qualities. Like other strong-smelling perfumes, myrrh was linked with Saturn and was supposed by occultists to have considerable potential as a tool of the black magician. Thus it was listed as one of the ingredients used by Aleister CROWLEY in his 'Incense of Abramelin', which he used to conjure up demons.

N names of power The names of God and certain other divine beings that were supposed to have their own inherent magical properties, and which were allegedly recited by skilled witches or sorcerers in their SPELLS. Writing or reciting 'names of power' in preparing a MAGIC CIRCLE, for instance, was said to prevent any evil spirit penetrating the barrier that the witch or sorcerer thus constructed around him or herself.

The names themselves were derived from a range of historical sources, notably from ancient Hebrew and Greek tradition, although the origins of others cannot be traced. The theory was that, as the name was invoked, the magic associated with the spirit identified was channelled to the witch or sorcerer and could then be tapped in pursuance of the business in question. Among the most frequently used names of power were Adonai, Alpha, Asmodeus, Beroth, Craton, Delgaliel, Ehyeh, Eloa, Elohim, Emmanuel, Gabriel, Gomeh, Helim, Isis, Jehovah, Mach, Noth, Omega, Raphael, Sabaoth, Shaddai, Sibylla, Tetragrammaton, Uriel and Yod He Vau He.

Napier, Barbara *see* NORTH BERWICK WITCHES.

necromancy The practice of raising the dead in order to compel their spirits to provide answers to any questions that a witch or sorcerer might choose to put. Considered the most dangerous and dubious of all black magic pursuits, the possibility of raising the dead has fascinated scholars of the occult for centuries. Legend had it that many magicians attempted such feats in the ancient world, with varying degrees of success. The biblical story of the Witch of ENDOR, who raised dead souls through her magic, provided a model that inspired many subsequent explorers into the occult. Centuries later, such sorcerers as Dr John DEE and Edward KELLY were among the most famous practitioners of the art of necromancy, pursuing their experiments into the occult largely as an intellectual quest.

Others had more prosaic motives: in 1560, for instance, two priests were convicted of raising spirits through the use of three MAGIC CIRCLES in order to discover the whereabouts of a chest of gold. One of them was excommunicated for his trouble. Such cases were rare, however, and there was not a single trial on the basis of necromancy in England in the entire seventeenth century – either the rituals were too complicated for the average untutored witch or the dangers were too great. Those who attempted it were warned by some 'experts' on the subject that they did not raise real corpses but the Devil himself, who disguised himself thus in order to deceive them.

The risks involved in raising the dead meant that generally only the most experienced sorcerers dared to attempt such magic, carefully protecting their own lives from the demons they might invoke by preparing magic circles and taking other precautions. It was said that only those who had made a PACT WITH THE DEVIL had any chance of being successful. Other necessary measures included the burning of certain varieties of incense: the strong smell produced was said to ward off evil spirits. Careful observation of the positions of the planets and the moon was also required if a magician was to know the correct time and place to attempt the feat.

Dressed in used grave-clothes or in a special cloak bearing mystic symbols, the magician would recite NAMES OF POWER and then perform a long and elaborate ritual until the point came when he or she could summon a corpse to appear. At given points in these rites some magicians rang BELLS, which acquired the power to wake the dead after they had been laid in a grave for seven days. Some authorities decreed that the sorcerer must have abstained from sex for nine days before attempting to raise the dead and must have also kept to a rigid diet of dog's flesh, black unleavened and unsalted bread and unfermented grape juice. At the close of the ceremony the sorcerer laid the corpse to rest once more and drove a stake through its heart so that it might never again be used for necromantic purposes.

The art of necromancy still appears to have its practitioners. Every few years newspapers around Europe carry reports of disturbed graves and scattered bones, strongly suggesting that ceremonies designed to raise the dead have been staged. The so-called *culte des mortes*, closely related to voodoo, thrives to this day in Haiti. Its followers perform various rites in order to raise Baron Samedi, a grotesque spirit to whom questions about the future may be addressed.

Newbury Witch Unidentified woman who was summarily executed at Newbury in Berkshire in 1643 after she was suspected of witchcraft. The case arose when a group of Parliamentarian soldiers, passing through Newbury during the Civil War, happened to spy a woman apparently walking on the water of the River Kennet. When the woman reached the bank it was clear that she had crossed the river using a small board as a raft, but this plain piece of evidence was stubbornly ignored by the soldiers, who were convinced that they had caught a witch red-handed. When the women failed to answer their questions satisfactorily it was decided that she should be shot. One of the men then fired his weapon and the woman was hit in the chest, but the bullet rebounded and 'narrowly he missed it in his face that was the shooter'. The cherished legend reported in a contemporary tract to the effect that 'with a deriding and loud laughter at them, she caught their bullets in her hands and chewed them' may be discounted.

The wound was not fatal, and when another man similarly failed to dispatch the witch with a sword thrust it was remembered by someone present that a witch's power could only be broken by drawing blood 'above the breath' (*see* SCORING ABOVE THE BREATH). A pistol was discharged below the luckless woman's ear, 'at which she straight sunk down and died'.

Newton, Florence d.1661. Irish peasant woman, nicknamed the 'Witch of Youghal', who was tried as a witch at the Cork Assizes in 1661. The trial is known from the record made of it by Joseph GLANVILL, which was based on the recollections of the judge himself and thus allowed an insight into the way such proceedings were carried out in IRELAND in the seventeenth century.

Florence Newton was brought before the court of Sir William Ashton charged with causing the death by witchcraft of one David Jones and with bewitching Mary Longdon, a servant-girl. Mary Longdon had, it transpired, incurred the wrath of the accused witch by declining to give her a piece of pickled beef at Christmas, upon which the aggrieved woman had threatened that this meanness would be rewarded by some harm. A few days later, Florence Newton accosted Mary Longdon while she was carrying some laundry and 'violently kissed her'. From that point on, the girl was tormented by visions of Florence Newton and a 'little old man in silk clothes' and displayed such conventional symptoms of demonic POSSESSION as superhuman strength, loss of memory and the ability to vomit pins, wool, straw and other unlikely objects. Inexplicable showers of stones also fell wherever she went. When she managed to catch hold of one of these stones she noticed that it had a hole through it and tied it securely to her purse, believing that this would break the spell, but the stone vanished even though the knot by which it was secured remained tied.

The trial of Florence Newton was conducted with every effort to observe the requirements of the law and no undue pressure was put upon the accused – but fear of witchcraft still decided the matter. After an initial hearing the 'Witch of Youghal' was sent to prison, where an attempt was made to prove her guilt by PRICKING her with a lancet to see if she bled. At first no one could pierce her skin with the blade at all; when one of her hands was finally cut no blood came, to the satisfaction of those present (although it did after the other hand had been cut as well).

Glanvill's account of the affair ends prior to sentencing, but it seems certain that Florence Newton was convicted as charged and was probably executed by order of the court.

night flight *see* TRANSVECTION.

night spell A CHARM that may be recited on retiring for the night in order to be granted protection against NIGHTMARES, witchcraft and other evils during the hours of darkness. The medieval poet Geoffrey Chaucer cited an example of a night spell in 'The Miller's Tale', one of his *Canterbury Tales*:

> Jesu Christ and Saint Benedict,
> Bless this house from every wicked wight.

In 1619 the playwright John Fletcher quoted a similar charm in one of his plays, recommending sleepers to recite:

> St George, St George,
> He walks by day, he walks by night.

Francesco-Maria GUAZZO, in his authoritative *Compendium Maleficarum* of 1626, advised more elaborate precautions to the worried sleeper, suggesting psalms, prayers, making the sign of the cross, saying the Paternoster and other holy passages and, if possible, surrounding the bed with holy relics.

nightmare According to ancient superstition, nightmares were inflicted upon the sleeping by demons, who were in all probability acting on the orders of witches or the DEVIL himself. Evil spirits, usually identified as INCUBI or SUCCUBI, were formerly alleged to steal into bedrooms in the dead of night, often in the form of spectral horses (hence 'nightmare'), and to lie heavily upon sleepers, stifling their breath and restricting their power of movement. These unearthly intruders would delight in terrifying their victim with vivid and realistic visions of demons and so forth, or would seduce him or her with erotic dreams. Mare-demons (which also attacked ordinary horses) generally specialised in scary dreams, while incubi and succubi preyed on repressed sexual desires.

Such was the obsession with these demons that no fewer than sixteen major treatises were written on the subject between 1627 and

1740. Among other things, these stated that nightmares were more likely to strike those who slept on their backs, that sufferers always experienced a sensation of weight pressing down on their chest, and that other symptoms included palpitations, crying out and great anxiety on waking. In 1830, in *The Philosophy of Sleep*, Robert Macnish offered the following description of a nightmare demon: 'A monstrous hag squatting upon his breast – mute, motionless and malignant; an incarnation of the evil spirit – whose intolerable weight crushes the breath out of his body, and whose fixed, deadly, incessant stare petrifies him with horror and make his very existence insufferable.'

Remedies available to sleepers included pinning one's socks in the shape of a cross on the end of the bed, placing a knife or some other metal object nearby, placing one's shoes under the bed so that the toes pointed out, sleeping with the hands crossed and affixing straw crosses to the four corners of the bed. Spitting three times on getting up was recommended to dispel any lingering ill effects resulting from nightmares. Robert Burton, in his *Anatomy of Melancholy* of 1621, recommended marriage as a cure for bad dreams, indicating that he concurred with the school of thought which held that nightmares were attributable in large part to repressed sexuality (hence the many historical records of nuns and other celibates being afflicted with this problem).

See also NIGHT SPELL.

nightshade The poisonous nightshade was widely believed to be a favourite ingredient of witches and sorcerers. Witches were said to consume small amounts of deadly nightshade, the berries of which contain belladonna, in order to see into the future (too large a dose, however, could lead to madness and even death). Others were reputed to use it in preparing the FLYING OINTMENT that would enable them to fly through the air to their SABBATS.

Conversely, popular superstition had it that keeping a sprig of woody nightshade in the home or on the person would ward off evil spirits and that the plant could also be used to protect livestock from witchcraft and disease.

North Berwick Witches An alleged COVEN of Scottish witches who were brought to trial in 1590–2 accused of a host of crimes, including the attempted murder of James VI (later JAMES I of England). One of the most notorious of all Scottish witchcraft trials, it signalled the real start of the witchcraft hysteria in the British Isles, witnessing the most savage use of TORTURE and culminating in mass executions and the flight of Francis, Earl of Bothwell, cousin to the King and one of the most powerful men in the country.

The saga began ordinarily enough in 1590, with David Seaton, the deputy bailiff of Tranent, near Edinburgh, becoming suspicious of the nocturnal comings and goings of his servant-girl, Gilly Duncan. The girl had recently displayed skills as a healer and Seaton concluded that these new-found gifts could only be of Satanic origin. Accordingly, Seaton invoked his power as deputy bailiff to have the girl tortured in his own home by means of 'thrawing' (jerking her head violently by a rope), crushing her fingers in the 'pilliwinks' (thumbscrews) and inspecting her closely for the DEVIL'S MARK, which was found upon her throat. Subjected to these agonies and humiliations, Gilly Duncan confirmed her association with the Devil and she was brought before the authorities to give a formal confession.

Perhaps thinking that by cooperating fully with the court she might save her own life, Gilly Duncan provided a long list of 'accomplices' in the Edinburgh area. Of these, four were brought to trial: a respected schoolteacher from Saltpans, Dr John FIAN, who was identified as recorder for the coven, an elderly midwife called Agnes Sampson, and the aristocratically connected gentlewomen Euphemia (or Effie) Maclean and Barbara Napier. In view of the high social standing of some of the accused the case began to attract much attention in the city, and James I himself took on the role of interrogator of Agnes Sampson and some of the other defendants.

Agnes Sampson remained steadfast in her denial of any guilt, but the interrogators were not satisfied and, after ordering her to be completely shaved, inspected her closely for the Devil's mark, which was duly found in her genitals. Confident that they had a witch in their custody, the authorities had the woman fitted with a WITCH'S BRIDLE and ordered that she be deprived of sleep until she confessed.

After suffering the additional agony of being 'thrawed' with a rope as Gilly Duncan had been, the elderly woman could endure no more and admitted the fifty-three charges laid against her. Among other crimes, she confessed to employing CHARMS to cause disease, to administering various magic powders and to keeping a FAMILIAR in the form of a dog called Elva, which inhabited a well.

At the prompting of the interrogators, who demanded a full confession on pain of the torture being repeated, Sampson – described as 'grave and settled in her answers' – went on to describe how she had been present at a SABBAT of some ninety witches at HALLOWE'EN and how the company, after drinking their fill of wine, had sailed in sieves to North Berwick. There they had danced – always in a WIDDERSHINS direction – to the music that Gilly Duncan played on a Jew's harp. The song they sang as they danced was given as follows (the word 'cummer' meaning 'woman'):

Cummer, go ye before, cummer go ye.
If ye willna go before, cummer, let me.
Ring-a-ring a-widdershins
Linkin' lithely widdershins
Cummer carlin crone and queen
Roun' go we!
Cummer, go ye before, cummer, go ye.
If ye willna go before, cummer, let me.
Ring-a-ring a-widdershins
Loupin' lightly widdershins
Kilted coats and fleeing hair
Three times three.
Cummer, go ye before, cummer, go ye.
If ye willna go before, cummer, let me.
Ring-a-ring a-widdershins
Whirlin' skirlin' widdershins
And de'il take the hindmost
Who'er she be!

They had then offered their allegiance in North Berwick church, in the flickering light cast by black candles, to the Devil himself, kissing his buttocks as a sign of their devotion (*see* KISS). The Devil had manifested to them in the form of a man wearing a black gown and cap, and was reported to have hairy hands with claws. Subsequently they had plotted together how they might bring about the death of the King by raising a storm when he sailed for Denmark in order to fetch his bride-to-be.

James was duly impressed by this tale (he even had Gilly Duncan play him the tune she had allegedly played at the sabbat) but claimed he was still reluctant to accept that Agnes Sampson and her confederates were telling the truth. After further questioning he decided that the women were all lying, but at this point (according to James's own recollection of the affair) Agnes Sampson whispered to him the exact words he had exchanged with his bride on their wedding night – words that only the happy couple could possibly have known. Whether this really happened, or whether the King fabricated the story in order for the case to proceed and for the treason thus revealed to be suitably punished as a warning to others, James professed himself astounded and withdrew his former reservations.

Agnes Sampson's confession progressed from one startling revelation to another. The coven, she claimed, had tried once more to attack the monarch, preparing poison from the body of a black TOAD hanged by its feet for three days and attempting to obtain an item from the royal wardrobe so that the poison might be smeared upon it. Unfortunately for them, they had been unable to gain possession of any of the King's clothing. Next the witches had melted in a fire a wax figure verbally identified as James and had prepared a magic powder from a shroud and parts of a corpse. When it came to the possibility of drowning the King at sea by raising a storm, the witches had baptised a CAT, strapped the limbs of a dead man to its paws and then tossed the luckless creature into the sea. The first time they did this the animal got free and swam back to the shore, but the second time it drowned and a storm blew up (one ship went down and the King's ship narrowly escaped).

The tall stories told by Agnes Sampson and the other defendants stretched the credulity of the court to the limit, and at one point the jury decided to have the charges dismissed. The King, however, flew into a rage at the suggestion and the court was hastily reconvened in order to find the accused guilty. Those jurors who had argued for an acquittal were themselves tried for their error.

Barbara Napier, who was a relation of the Laird of Carschoggill, pleaded pregnancy and was allowed to go free, to the irritation of the King. Effie Maclean, however, was obliged to enlist the aid of six lawyers in an effort to prove her innocence. Unfortunately her links with the Earl of Bothwell, who as possible heir to the throne was rumoured to have instigated the plots against James in the first place, meant that the King was resolute in his determination that she should be executed, notwithstanding her social status as daughter of Lord Cliftonhall.

At the conclusion of the trial John Fian, Agnes Sampson and Effie Maclean were all put to death. Effie Maclean was denied the mercy of being strangled before being consigned to the flames and was burned alive. Another suspect, Margaret Thomson, died under torture.

The Earl of Bothwell, who was imprisoned for a time in Edinburgh Castle but escaped the death penalty after taking the precaution of packing Edinburgh with his armed supporters, eventually left Scotland after failing to dislodge James from power and spent the rest of his life in exile. To the end of his days he retained a reputation for being deeply interested in the occult.

Deeply affected by what he had heard during the confessions of the North Berwick Witches, James doubtless drew on his experience of the case for his highly influential treatise on witchcraft, entitled *Daemonologie*, which was first published some five years after the trial had ended.

Northumberland Witches *see* FORSTER, ANNE.

Norway As in the other Scandinavian countries (*see* SWEDEN and FINLAND), the history of the witchcraft hysteria in Norway (and Denmark, with which it was for several centuries united) was one of isolated outbreaks rather than sustained panic and suppression.

Belief in witchcraft was, however, of long standing and included similar features to belief elsewhere in Europe.

Norwegian witchlore emphasised the evil deeds that witches committed, rather than pacts with the Devil, and blamed witches for shipwrecks, murders and a host of lesser crimes. Witches were believed to gather in huge numbers at Christmas and Midsummer SABBATS at certain known sites, which included the summit of a mountain near Bergen and the volcano called Hekla in Iceland. They were widely rumoured to have the power of flight, and at their sabbats were reputed to indulge in feasting and drinking, dancing and sex.

The first recorded witchcraft trial in Norway was staged at Bergen in 1592 and culminated in the execution of Oluf Gurdal. Two more witches were burned in Bergen and another was exiled in 1594, but it was not until 1622 that the next case was heard. This time the accused, identified only as Synneve, strangled herself in gaol before the proceedings began.

The confession of Karen Thorsdatter in 1650 provided fuller details of the covert activities of Norway's witches. She confirmed that she flew to sabbats on bewitched animals and had plotted the deaths of local magistrates. Thorsdatter and an accomplice, Bodil Kvams, were burned at Kristiansand.

The year 1670 witnessed the trial of Ole and Lisbet NYPEN and also that of Karen Snedkers in Copenhagen. Snedkers was accused of using magic against Niels Pedersen, a councillor who suffered various ills after Snedkers allegedly sprinkled his clothes with salt, and also against the city clerk, Johan Worm, whose animals had fallen ill as a result of her spells. She confessed to her crimes and also admitted trying to sink a ship in which Pedersen had been sailing, being thwarted only by the prayer book he kept in his hand. Her confession implicated several people and the trial ended with Karen Snedkers and six others being burned to death.

The last recorded execution of a convicted witch in Norway took place after a trial in Sondmore in 1680, when a man named Ingebrigt was found guilty of poisoning cattle and attending sabbats. The last trial on charges of witchcraft was staged at Jaederen four years later, but the outcome is not known.

Notingham, John de d.1325. English sorcerer who was the central figure in a plot to kill Edward II, his favourite, Hugh le Despenser, and others by IMAGE MAGIC. John de Notingham lived in Coventry and, together with his lodger, Robert le Mareschal, had a strong reputation for his knowledge of the occult. In 1323 the pair were approached in secret by a group of twenty-seven burgesses of the city, who desired their help. In return for money and other rewards, the two magicians were asked to procure through magic the deaths of the King, Hugh Despenser, his father (the Earl of Winchester), and the prior of Coventry, at whose hands the burgesses had suffered various injustices. For good measure, they also desired the deaths of the seneschal and cellarer of the Coventry priory.

The deal was agreed and the two magicians retired to an isolated house on the outskirts of Coventry where they set about making wax figures of the intended victims. The six images were completed by April 1324, but it was decided that a trial should be run before the plot was carried out. Accordingly, the two men fashioned a seventh wax figure in the likeness of a neighbour called Richard de Sowe (with whom they had no particular quarrel). When all was ready, at midnight on 27 April, John de Notingham instructed Robert le Mareschal to thrust a shard of lead into the head of the figure. The following morning, Robert le Mareschal called at Richard de Sowe's house to find out if the spell had had any effect and to his satisfaction found that their neighbour had lost his reason overnight, failing to recognise anyone and repeatedly screaming the word 'Harrow!' There was no improvement in the man's condition over the weeks that followed, until finally the sorcerers removed the lead and thrust it into the heart of the wax figure. Richard de Sowe died several days later.

Convinced that their neighbour's death had been a direct consequence of their magic, John de Notingham and Robert le Mareschal prepared to repeat the operation upon the six remaining figures. At this juncture, however, Robert le Mareschal's nerve failed him and, rattled by enquiries into Richard de Sowe's mysterious death, he made a voluntary confession to the authorities in exchange for immunity from prosecution. Everyone implicated in the affair was flung into gaol and the case came to court in 1325. John de Notingham, however, died while in prison and the twenty-seven burgesses, for obscure reasons, were acquitted for their part in the plot. The fate of Robert le Mareschal is not known.

Nottingham Boy *see* DARRELL, JOHN.

Nouvelet, Father *see* AUXONNE NUNS.

Nutter, Alice *see* PENDLE WITCHES.

Nypen, Ole and Lisbet Norwegian couple whose trial for witchcraft at Leinstrand, Trondheim, in 1670 marked one of the few instances of witchcraft hysteria in the Scandinavian countries. Because the INQUISITION had never penetrated as far north as Norway there was no history of systematic persecution of witchcraft as such, although there were a few trials based on allegations of actual harm attributed to people locally reputed to have knowledge of the occult. There were no WITCHFINDERS, and local officials did not stand to make money out of successful witchcraft prosecutions as they did elsewhere in Europe.

The case of Ole and Lisbet Nypen began in 1667, when a man named Erik Kveneld denounced Ole Nypen as a witch while they were all present at a christening party. Kveneld blamed Nypen for the rheumatism in his hands and there was an unseemly brawl.

Three years later Ole Nypen started a case for slander against Kveneld, but attention was quickly diverted away from anything that the defendant had said and towards the Nypens and their alleged involvement in witchcraft. Under pressure, Lisbet Nypen admitted using CHARMS and SALT to cure disease, although she defended herself on the grounds that it was the prayers she had said while doing this that had done the healing. Erik Kveneld, meanwhile, contributed further allegations that the Nypens had caused his breasts to grow like a woman's. His wife, he alleged, had also suffered from their spells, her eyebrows growing so long that she could not see and her ears being made to extend until they dangled on her shoulders.

The Nypens were brought before the authorities on suspicion of witchcraft later in 1670, when numerous witnesses testified that the couple had a local reputation as witches (although little new evidence was offered). The accused couple consistently denied that they were witches, repeating that they had never made pacts with the Devil and had never harmed anyone.

A third hearing implicated Lisbet Nypen in the crippling of a young girl whom she had allegedly mistaken for one Kari Oxstad, whom she suspected of slandering her daughters.

At their subsequent trial the Nypens were indicted for taking the Lord's name in vain, for causing harm to their neighbours, for curing people by transferring the demons that tormented them to other enemies or to animals, and for having a generally evil reputation.

History does not record whether the couple were subjected to torture, but it does record that the pair were found guilty, despite their failure to admit their wrongdoing. Both were burned, Ole Nypen being first beheaded.

O **oak** The oak tree, according to time-honoured superstition, offered shelter from both evil spirits and witchcraft. Anyone standing under an oak, or keeping boughs of oak in the home, was deemed safe from magical interference. Some people wore oak leaves for the same purpose or kept a few acorns in the house to ward off lightning.

Cornish witchlore suggested that by hammering a nail into an oak tree a person could get relief from the pain of toothache, while Welsh witches advised that by rubbing sores on a piece of oak bark on Midsummer's Day the skin would quickly heal. Couples unable to have children or patients suffering from hernias were recommended to embrace the oak so as to benefit from its magic powers.

Oak trees planted at CROSSROADS were considered to be the most magically potent.

obscene kiss *see* KISS.

Ogg, Isobel and Margaret *see* ABERDEEN WITCHES.

ointment, flying *see* FLYING OINTMENT.

ointment, killing *see* KILLING OINTMENT.

orgies *see* SABBAT.

Osborne, John and Ruth Elderly English couple who were accused of witchcraft in Hertfordshire in 1751 and as a result lost their lives, some thirty-nine years after the last official conviction for witchcraft in England. The Osbornes, residents of the workhouse at Tring, first encountered trouble when they fell foul of a local farmer-turned-publican by the name of Butterfield. For reasons of his own Butterfield suspected the Osbornes of bewitching his calves, causing them to fall ill. According to him, the couple had inflicted this calamity in revenge for his refusal to give Ruth Osborne some buttermilk one day back in 1745. They had also caused him to suffer fits, and a WHITE WITCH from Northampton had confirmed that his difficulties were indeed attributable to witchcraft.

Butterfield's grievances got a sympathetic hearing from the neighbours who drank at his tavern in Gublecot, and it was agreed that the suspected couple should be swum as witches in order to prove their guilt. It appears that Butterfield believed that they had a legal right to swim suspected witches, provided the test was first announced in public. Accordingly, Butterfield and his friends had news of the planned SWIMMING proclaimed by the town criers in several local towns. No one came forward to oppose the test, although when the day came for the ordeal parish officials in Tring tried to shelter the Osbornes by removing them from the workhouse and hiding them in the church. The mob, determined to find the couple, ransacked the workhouse and threatened to kill its governor unless the Osbornes were produced. The parish officials gave in and the pair were handed over.

Led by Butterfield, the mob hauled the Osbornes, who were both in their seventies, two miles to the pond at Long Marston. The couple were stripped and their thumbs and big toes tied together crosswise, in the time-honoured fashion, before they were flung into the water. Ruth Osborne floated, but a chimney sweep by the name of Thomas Colley used a stout stick to push her under, repeating the act three times. The mob then dragged the old woman on to the bank, her face clogged with mud. When it was found that she was dead, the enraged mob beat and kicked her body. John Osborne was discovered to be still alive, but the injuries he had received led to his own demise some days later. When all was over Thomas Colley went round the crowd 'collecting money for the pains he had taken in showing them sport'.

The story of the brutal swimming at Long Marston quickly reached the ears of the authorities and thirty people were questioned. Three of them were subsequently tried for murder at the Hertford Assizes. Thomas Colley was sent to the gallows and his body was hung in chains as a warning to others who might be considering taking similar action against other suspected witches. On the day of Colley's execution a large crowd gathered, many of them voicing the opinion that it was unjust to hang a man for ridding the community of a known witch.

osculum infame *see* KISS.

Overbury, Sir Thomas 1581–1613. English courtier and poet whose sensational murder in the Tower of London was blamed by many upon witchcraft. The circumstances surrounding the death of Sir Thomas Overbury, a prominent member of the court of JAMES I, were the culmination of a life of scandal and intrigue and were finally exposed at a widely reported trial in 1616.

The train of events that led to Overbury's murder began when he attempted to prevent the marriage of the King's favourite, Robert Carr (later Earl of Somerset), to Frances Howard, the beautiful and precocious daughter of the Earl of Suffolk. By an arranged marriage in 1606, when she was thirteen, Frances Howard was already the wife of Robert Devereux, Earl of Essex, but it was not until 1609 that the Earl of Essex arrived at court to claim his bride, by which time the young girl had fallen in love with Carr. Faced with the urgent need to get rid of the Earl of Essex and the equally pressing desire to win the love of the King's favourite, Frances Howard turned to her friend Mrs Anne Turner and to Dr Simon Forman, both of whom were known for their skills in magic. From them she obtained a LOVE POTION to capture the heart of Robert Carr and another philtre to make the Earl of Essex impotent (some accounts suggest that a wax figure was used to this end). Allegedly as a result of this magic, Carr fell passionately in love with Frances Howard and the Earl of Essex failed to consummate his marriage, leaving his wife free to have the union annulled.

Free at last to marry her lover, Frances Howard then experienced a setback in the opposition of Sir Thomas Overbury, who, it is speculated, had a homosexual attachment to Carr and was blackmailing him into refusing her hand. Infuriated by this, Howard used her influence to have Overbury posted overseas, but he declined the position – upon which he was imprisoned in the Tower of London for disobedience to the King. At this point Howard allegedly turned once again to Mrs Turner and procured from her poisons which were then secretly administered through a servant to Overbury while in the Tower. The poisons made Overbury seriously ill but did not lead to his death, probably because his doctors were giving him regular purges and enemas. To finish him once and for all, Howard persuaded one of the doctors to mix poison into the prisoner's next enema. This ploy successfully brought about his death.

Overbury's demise in the Tower was unexpected, but murder was not at first suspected. However, when the doctor who had administered the fatal enema fell ill and, believing he was dying, made a full confession an investigation was started. Letters between Howard and Mrs Turner were found and, as proof of the employment of witchcraft, incriminating wax figures were discovered during searches of the Lambeth home of Dr Forman.

In 1616 Frances Howard, the Earl of Somerset (now her husband) and Mrs Turner, alongside others, were tried for Sir Thomas Overbury's murder. Sir Edmund Coke, Chief Justice of England, presided over the initial stages until James I himself decided to watch over events in person, in company with Sir Francis Bacon. All three accused were found guilty and condemned to death. Only Mrs Turner, Sir Thomas Overbury's servant and the Lieutenant of the Tower (who had taken no steps to prevent the murder) were actually hanged, however, as the King eventually decided to pardon his former favourite and his wife, leaving them to a quiet life together in obscurity on condition that they never ventured more than three miles from their home in Kent. Dr Simon Forman escaped punishment, having died of natural causes in 1611.

overlooking *see* EVIL EYE.

P

pact with the Devil The idea that witches made a pact with the Devil, promising him their soul in exchange for magical powers, was central to the mythology of witchcraft and was the basis upon which countless trials were prosecuted.

The concept of the pact with the Devil was promulgated enthusiastically in the early thirteenth century by the INQUISITION, which for its own reasons wished witchcraft to be classed a HERESY and thereby brought within its sphere of influence. By making out that witches acquired their powers through a deal with Satan, God's arch-enemy, such people were necessarily denying their Christian faith and were therefore heretics. Biblical authority for the pact was claimed through a passage in Isaiah (chapter 28, verse 15): 'We have entered into a league with death; we have made a covenant with hell.' Ancient stories of pacts with the Devil that were absorbed into the Western tradition from Byzantine sources around the ninth century were also quoted as examples of pacts that merited classification as heresy.

Regardless of the MALEFICIA that a witch committed having acquired magical powers from Satan, it was the pact itself that was the fundamental crime in the eyes of many Catholic and Protestant courts on the Continent of Europe. Maybe a witch did then cause harm through magic, maybe harming other men and livestock through magic was an impossibility, but if the witch had sealed such a pact with the Devil, or simply believed this to be so, this was usually enough to render his or her life forfeit. It did not matter, according to the sterner authorities, if the person concerned devoted themselves to 'white' witchcraft only (*see* WHITE WITCH): if they enjoyed demoniacal powers they must have made a bargain with the Devil and they were guilty.

Details of the circumstances in which a suspect had made a pact with the Devil were routinely demanded during interrogation and torture (although some courts were content to assume that such a pact had been made, regardless of any confirmation, if evidence of resulting magic powers was strong enough). Inevitably, to escape further torment, many hundreds of alleged witches furnished their captors with all the information they required, confirming in many people's minds the reality of such pacts.

Descriptions of how pacts were made varied considerably from region to region and from century to century. Early accounts of such dealings suggested that the ceremony was closely based on conventional Church ceremonies, but later descriptions added more outlandish elements, doubtless fuelled by the fevered imaginations of those giving confessions while undergoing torture. Johannes Nider described in his *Formicarius* (*c.*1435) how an initiate into the Devil's service was required to renounce his Christian faith, to pay homage to Satan and then to drink the blood of murdered children. Many subsequent accounts added to this relatively simple procedure the ritual KISS, in which the initiate displayed his loyalty to Satan by kissing him 'underneath the tail', the trampling of the cross underfoot, the denial of godparents, the writing of the initiate's name in the so-called 'Book of Death', the scratching of the initiate's head by the Devil so as to erase any trace of previous Christian baptism, and the renaming of initiates by the Devil. Initiates might also be required to surrender to the Devil a piece of their clothing to signify that they separated themselves from spiritual and terrestrial things, and, further, to promise that they would sacrifice young children to him at regular intervals. They might also have to swear not to honour the Christian sacrament or to use holy water or candles, to keep their dealings with the Devil secret and to persuade others to submit themselves to him. In most cases the Devil permanently marked the initiate by touching some part of his or her body (*see* DEVIL'S MARK) and might insist there and then upon ritual sexual intercourse to complete the deal.

In return for binding themselves to the Devil as his slaves, initiates were rewarded by the Devil agreeing to be available on command for the working of magic, whether it be in the pursuit of worldly pleasure, wealth, power or some other ambition. The apprentice witch might also be presented with a FAMILIAR spirit to act as their servant.

Sometimes the pact was made at a full SABBAT before the whole coven, sometimes it was made privately with the Devil (in which case it was more difficult to prove in court). On other occasions, it was claimed, the initiate made the pact indirectly through another witch. Often the pact was formalised through the signing of an actual piece of paper setting out the conditions of the bargain. Tradition insisted that this had to be written or signed in the initiate's own blood, taken from the apprentice witch's LEFT HAND. The Devil kept the pact, but there is at least one case on record of the actual agreement, written in Latin, being produced in court at the trial of a suspected witch. This was the pact presented to the judges in the case of Urbain Grandier in 1634 (*see* LOUDUN NUNS). The first part, inscribed in 'mirror-writing' and signed by Satan, Beelzebub, Lucifer, Elimi, Leviathan and Astaroth, ran as follows:

> We, the all-powerful Lucifer, seconded by Satan, Beelzebub, Leviathan, Elimi, Astaroth, and others, have today accepted the pact of alliance with Urbain Grandier, who is on our side. And we promise him the love of women, the flower of virgins, the chastity of nuns, worldly honours, pleasures, and riches. He will fornicate every three days; intoxication will be dear to him. He will offer to us once a year a tribute marked with his blood; he will trample under foot the sacraments of the church, and he will say his prayers to us. By virtue of this pact, he will live happily for twenty years on earth among men, and finally will come among us to curse God. Done in hell, in the council of the devils.

The second part of the pact, signed by Grandier himself, ran:

> My lord and master Lucifer, I acknowledge thee as my God and prince, and promise to serve and obey thee as long as I shall live. And I renounce the other God, as well as Jesus Christ, all the saints, the apostolic and Roman church, all the sacraments, and all the prayers and petitions by which the faithful might intercede for me. And I promise thee that I will do as much evil as I can, and that I will draw everyone else to evil. I renounce chrism, baptism, all the merits of Jesus Christ and his saints. And if I fail to serve and adore thee, and if I do not pay thee homage thrice every day, I give you my life as thine own. Made this year and day.

Once the pact was signed there was, it seemed, little chance that a witch could persuade the Devil to renounce the agreement voluntarily (as illustrated by the legend of Dr FAUST). There was always hope, however. A story related by the Puritan Increase Mather in seventeenth-century New England described how a young man who had signed a pact with the Devil in order to obtain money with which to pursue a dissolute lifestyle changed his mind and begged some Protestant ministers to pray for the return of the pact. Because the ministers were good men, whose prayers were heard by God, a cloud appeared above the group as they prayed and out of it dropped the very contract that the young man had signed. The reprieved youth quickly snatched up the pact and tore it to shreds.

Paisley Witches *see* BARGARRAN IMPOSTOR.

Pan Greek god, the spirit of woodlands and livestock, who was included among the pagan deities selected for worship by occultists in the late nineteenth century. The pipe-playing, horned and goat-footed Pan clearly bore more than a passing resemblance to the DEVIL of traditional witchcraft. Although it is impossible to draw a direct link between the Pan-worshipping cults of ancient Greece and latter-day witchcraft, there was a natural sympathy between the orgiastic revels and sacrifices of classical times and the SABBATS of more modern legend and it may just be that, in his common depiction as a goat, the witches' Devil, based on the Satan described by early Christians, was very distantly modelled upon the Greek original. Certainly, many magicians and sorcerers called upon Pan in their ceremonials; they included Aleister CROWLEY, who left instructions that his own 'Hymn to Pan' should be recited at his funeral in Brighton in 1947.

Paris Witch Trial The first secular trial for witchcraft to be staged in Europe, records of which have survived ever since 1390 when the proceedings took place. The trial was remarkable for the care that the Parlement of Paris took to apply the law soberly and correctly, with many lawyers being brought into the case and the prosecution being based for the most part on provable acts of MALEFICIA. The use of TORTURE was, however, sanctioned and thus rendered attempts to observe the spirit of the law futile.

The accused in the case was the thirty-four-year-old Jehenne de Brigue, known as 'La Cordiere'. She was alleged to have used sorcery to heal the seriously ill Jehan de Ruilly, who, according to Jehenne, was the victim of a spell cast by his lover Gilette. In reply to the charge Jehenne denied that she was a witch, but admitted using charms and also to neglecting to say her Paternoster on Sundays, among other offences.

Subsequently Jehenne admitted to being a witch, confessing that she consorted with the Devil, who called himself Haussibut. In exchange for Haussibut's assistance in the case of Jehan de Ruilly, she had rewarded him with some hemp seed and some cinders taken from her hearth. On the basis of this admission Jehenne de Brigue was sentenced to death by burning, but the sentence was postponed when she was discovered to be pregnant. It later transpired that she was not pregnant after all, but there was another delay while the case was heard on appeal to the Parlement of Paris.

At this point Jehenne was threatened with torture and strapped naked to the LADDER. The prisoner immediately agreed to confess more fully and explained that she had been approached by Ruilly's wife Macette in order to bewitch Ruilly so that Macette would be able to conduct an affair with a local curate. Together the two women had prepared a potion to procure Ruilly's death.

The Parlement had Macette arrested and tortured on the rack, upon which she confirmed the story that Jehenne had told. Both women retracted their confessions when released from torture, but the court decided that the accused must be burned (even though no murder had actually been committed). After further reviews of the case to check that it did fall within the court's jurisdiction and after the discovery of certain incriminating evidence – some hair, wax, a piece of sacred host and so forth – the sentence was confirmed. The two women were burned alive in the Pig Market on 19 August 1391.

Pearson, Margaret *see* PENDLE WITCHES.

Pendle Swindle *see* ROBINSON, EDMUND.

Pendle Witches COVEN of witches allegedly active in the Pendle Forest in Lancashire, whose mass trial in 1612 remains one of the most notorious of all outbreaks of the witch hysteria in England. Post-Reformation Lancashire was a scene of considerable religious conflict in the early seventeenth century, with a largely Roman Catholic population living under Protestant rule, and everywhere there was suspicion and counter-suspicion between neighbours. In this climate of mistrust accusations of witchcraft inevitably had a deep effect upon local communities, and the nascent hysteria finally erupted on a major scale when two old women long reputed to be rival witches were publicly accused.

The Pendle Forest, in east Lancashire, was the home of two rival peasant families, one headed by the eighty-year-old blind beggar Elizabeth Sowthern, a woman known as 'Old Demdike' and described as the 'rankest hag that ever troubled daylight', and the other by a 'withered, spent, and decrepit creature' dubbed 'Old Chattox', otherwise called Anne Whittle. With their wild, unattractive appearance and malevolent natures, both women fitted the popular image of a witch perfectly. Local legend had it that many mysterious deaths in the district could be attributed to the lethal potions that the two women concocted as heads of a coven based in the Forest. Certainly the two women appear to have capitalised on their reputations in order to exert influence over their neighbours and to promote their own trade in simple herbal potions and remedies.

The train of events that led to the eventual trial started around 1601, when the two hags, formerly close friends, fell out. This parting of the ways, which resulted in members of the two families embarking on a lengthy and ultimately bloody feud, resulted from the theft of some linen clothing and some meal from Alison Device, granddaughter of Old Demdike. The following Sunday, Alison Device claimed that she saw a missing band and coif being worn by Anne Redfearne, the married daughter of Old Chattox, and soon the two families were trading accusation and counter-accusation. In an attempt to prevent Old Chattox, apparently the more powerful of the two witches, using her supposed supernatural powers against his family, John Device, Alison's father, promised to pay her a yearly tribute of meal. This seems to have brought about a temporary truce that lasted until John Device's death a few years later.

Early in 1612 the revived feud between the two sides led to numerous complaints about both families reaching the ears of Roger Nowell, a local justice of the peace, and he determined to investigate the quarrel. He had little trouble persuading members of the two families to give evidence against each other, and accusation piled up on accusation until all involved were hopelessly compromised.

It emerged that Elizabeth Sowthern had become a witch many years before after meeting a 'spirit or devil in the shape of a boy' at a stonepit in the forest and agreeing to exchange her soul with him in return for anything she might want (*see* PACT WITH THE DEVIL). The Devil, who called himself Tibb, reappeared to her from time to time, variously assuming such guises as a brown dog or a black cat, in order to enquire if she had any new tasks she wished him to carry out on her behalf. Subsequently Elizabeth Sowthern had her son Christopher Howgate, her daughter Elizabeth Device and Elizabeth's children James and Alison also recruited as witches. Other converts included Anne Whittle, who sold her soul to a 'thing like a Christian man', and various neighbours and relatives.

After questioning Old Demdike, Old Chattox and Anne Redfearne, Roger Nowell decided that there was a case to answer and all three were confined in Lancaster Castle to await trial at the next Assizes. There they were joined by the eleven-year-old Alison Device on charges of bewitching an itinerant pedlar called John Law. It appeared that she and Law had had an altercation after he had refused to give her some pins. The exchange had culminated in Alison cursing the man, upon which he had collapsed, complaining of sharp pains in his side (modern medical opinion suggests that he suffered a stroke). Alison Device herself admitted that she had cursed the pedlar, and further claimed that she believed she was responsible for his illness and the permanent disabilities he had suffered as a result. Old Demdike, meanwhile, freely admitted to being a witch.

The trial of no fewer than eleven alleged witches, mostly members of the two families, was the largest mass witchcraft trial staged in England to that date and inevitably attracted much attention. (Another of the accused, Jennet Preston, was tried in her home town of York.) Huge crowds arrived at the court in Lancaster to witness the proceedings and to catch a glimpse of the accused, whose very appearance confirmed in many minds their guilt. Elizabeth Device in particular seemed the absolute epitome of a witch, with a deformed face and eyes that looked in different directions at the same time – a sure sign that she possessed the power of the EVIL EYE.

The trial itself lived up to expectations, and was in many respects typical of hundreds of other similar proceedings. Several of the charges laid against the accused involved murder by witchcraft. Old Demdike, it was claimed, had enlisted the aid of the demon whom she called Tibb to kill the child of one Richard Baldwyn after he had threatened to have her and her granddaughter Alison executed as witches. Old Chattox, allegedly aided and abetted by a FAMILIAR in the form of a 'spotted bitch', was accused of using sorcery to kill a local landowner called Robert Nutter (a charge that was also laid against Anne Redfearne). Perhaps belatedly realising the danger she was in, Old Chattox made some attempt to shift the blame by stressing that it was Old Demdike who had first introduced her to the Devil and that it was she who had arranged Nutter's death. Alison Device, meanwhile, wept bitterly when the pedlar she had accused of maiming was led into court, and begged his forgiveness.

Further charges related to a sensational report that ten days after the original arrests various members of the two families had plotted to blow up Lancaster Castle in order to rescue their imprisoned relatives. According to the court, the two families had temporarily shelved their differences and had met on Good Friday at Malking Tower, the Pendle home of Elizabeth Device, in order to plan a break-out. Over a substantial meal that included mutton stolen by James Device, the assembly hatched a plot to kill the gaoler at the Castle and to use gunpowder to release the prisoners. (Suggestions that the eating of a feast made this one of the very few occasions when English witches celebrated an actual SABBAT exaggerate the significance of what was probably an ordinary meal: no Devil was present and there was no performance of occult rites or dancing, sacrifices, orgies and so forth).

Of the eighteen women and two or three men who attended the meeting, sixteen were known by name – although only nine were located and brought to trial. Among these was a surprising name, that of the wealthy Alice Nutter of Rough Lee, mother of the deceased Robert Nutter, who was further charged with using witchcraft to murder a man named Henry Mitton. Her participation in the event was confirmed by several of the accused, but there was absolutely no concrete evidence against her (rumour had it that the charge was fabricated by those who stood to profit by her execution, and that Roger Nowell himself bore a grudge against her following a dispute over a boundary marker). In any event, to the very end she declined to admit any involvement in the affair.

The others indicted were Jennet Preston (who had come over from Gisborne-in-Craven to ask for aid in killing Thomas Lister of Westby), Elizabeth Device, James Device, Katherine Hewit (popularly known as Mould-heels), John and Jane Bulcock, Isabel Robey and Margaret Pearson. Katherine Hewit, it was alleged, had used witchcraft to kill Anne Foulds, identified as 'a child of Colne', while the Bulcocks had through their magic brought about the madness of a woman named Jennet Deane. Isabel Robey had used witchcraft to inflict physical pain upon parties identified as Jane Wilkinson and Peter Chaddock. In all, the accused witches were charged with responsibility for some sixteen deaths in the locality, as well as with causing harm to livestock and property and other lesser offences.

The case for the prosecution rested largely on the testimony of Elizabeth Device, her son James (a simple-minded labourer then in his twenties) and her nine-year-old daughter Jannet. Jannet's appearance in the witness box was unexpected and also illegal, as the testimony of children under fourteen was not admissible – a ruling that the court conveniently set aside. The young girl was placed on a table in the middle of the room and her subsequent confirmation of all that had been alleged prompted her mother to make a full confession (which she later retracted). According to James and Jannet, their mother was served by a familiar in the form of a brown dog called Ball and had caused at least three deaths through the use of IMAGE MAGIC and by other magical means. James informed the court that he had himself encountered 'a thing like a hare', which had begged from him some communion bread that he had been instructed to steal by his grandmother: the creature had disappeared when he made the sign of the cross. For his pains James too was accused of keeping a familiar, a dog by the name of Dandy, and of recruiting its powers to commit the murder of a Mistress Towneley, of the Carre.

At the close of proceedings the assembled crowd was not best pleased when Anne Redfearne was acquitted of the murder of Robert Nutter, but was somewhat mollified when she was found guilty of killing his father, Christopher Nutter, who on his deathbed had blamed witchcraft for his demise. On the strength of the confessions made by the accused and on the allegations they had traded between themselves, ten of the prisoners were sentenced to be hanged. Old Chattox made no attempt to deny her culpability but begged the court to spare her daughter; the others all protested vehemently that the charges against them were false. Old Demdike, meanwhile, had died in prison prior to the opening of the Assizes.

Old Chattox, Anne Redfearne, Elizabeth Device, James Device, Alison Device, Alice Nutter, John and Jane Bulcock, Katherine Hewit and Isabel Robey died on the gallows at Lancaster on 20 August 1612, by which date Jennet Preston had already been hanged in York as murderer of Thomas Lister (*see* BIER RIGHT). Margaret Pearson, who was found guilty of bewitching a mare to death, was sentenced to a year in gaol and made four appearances in the pillory, at the towns of Clitheroe, Padiham, Whalley and Lancaster.

The sensational details of the case were published the following year in a chapbook entitled *The Wonderful Discovery of Witches in the County of Lancaster*, written by Thomas Potts, clerk of the court, and approved as accurate by Sir Edward Bromley, the judge in the case. As a result people became familiar with the episode throughout the whole of northern England, and its influence was fated to be felt in many other trials.

The county of Lancashire was again traumatised by a mass trial of suspected witches from the Pendle Forest when, in 1634, a young boy brought charges against several women, including the now adult Jannet Device. This time, however, the boy eventually confessed to fabricating the charges, and those who had survived detention were released (*see* ROBINSON, EDMUND).

See also SALMESBURY WITCHES.

pentacle Five-pointed star pattern, also called a pentagram, that was traditionally reputed to have magical powers.

Considered to have a variety of supernatural properties by both the ancient Greeks and medieval astrologers, the pentacle became strongly identified with the business of magic and sorcery.

It was widely held that the pentacle was a highly effective defence against witchcraft and evil, and in former times such patterns were often scrawled or scratched on doors and doorways to deter witches. It was also adopted for use in the drawing up of MAGIC CIRCLES, because sorcerers believed it could act as a vehicle of transmission with the world of spirits.

The preparation of a pentacle for use in a magic circle was no simple task. Often inscribed on metal and decorated with certain symbolic and magical designs or words, the pentacle had to be specially consecrated before use in ritual magic. This was achieved through the magician either breathing on it or sprinkling over it HOLY WATER, oil, sexual secretions or BLOOD. The pentacle then had to be dried, using incense, chopped-up pubic hair or ash from human bones. Sealed in a darkened room for twenty-four hours, the pentacle was then 'charged' and ready for use.

pentagram *see* PENTACLE.

Perkins, William 1555 – 1602. English demonologist whose *Discourse of the Damned Art of Witchcraft* of 1608 ranked with the *Daemonologie* of JAMES I as one of the most authoritative texts on witchcraft to be published in England in the early seventeenth century. A Puritan preacher and an opponent of the Catholic Church, Perkins adopted an extreme evangelical position on witchcraft. Basing his arguments closely upon biblical authority, he condemned those who denied the reality of witchcraft, supported the death penalty for convicted witches and dismissed the miracles claimed by 'the popish church' as hoaxes. Like other demonologists of his era, he reserved special venom for those who sought to defend themselves on the grounds that they were WHITE WITCHES – in Perkins's eyes witchcraft of all kinds was to be suppressed with equal severity, and he even argued that white witches were the worst sort, because they attempted to conceal the diabolical origins of their magic.

The *Discourse* was published in Germany by 1610 and had a widespread influence upon contemporary thinking on the subject of witchcraft. Some ninety years later Cotton MATHER, the New England demonologist, was still recommending the book as an authority.

Perry, William *see* BILSON BOY.

Perth Witch *see* HALDANE, ISOBEL.

Peterson, Joan *see* WAPPING WITCH.

Petronilla de Midia *see* KYTELER, ALICE.

Philips, Mary *c.*1675–1705. English peasant woman who was executed after being tried for witchcraft at the Northampton Assizes. The story of Mary Philips is typical of hundreds of trials that culminated in the deaths of alleged witches in the British Isles, although hers was also one of the last executions before the witchcraft acts were finally repealed. The case against her was never more than circumstantial, and it was more by her reputation than by her deeds that she came to be hanged.

Mary Philips was born into poverty in the town of Oundle, Northamptonshire, and as a young woman eked a meagre living weaving stockings in the cottage she shared with her only close friend, Elinor Shaw. Both women had a reputation for immoral conduct and children were said to follow them in the street calling them whores. They were the outcasts of the local community and many inhabitants of the town, speculating that the pair were really witches, blamed them for the deaths of several people.

In 1705 the gossip crystallised in the form of complaints to the authorities, and the two women were taken to Northampton for trial. There they were persuaded to confess that they were witches and gave details of how they had been admitted to a local COVEN by a tall dark man, who pricked the tip of their third finger as a way of baptising them into worship of the Devil.

Whether or not Mary Philips really believed she was a witch is impossible to determine, but she certainly made the most of her short-lived notoriety, shocking listeners with her account of her life as a witch. When, as she was being taken by cart to Northampton gallows, she was asked by the attending priest to repent she merely laughed and invoked the name of the Devil. Before she could blaspheme any further, she and Elinor Shaw were hastily hanged.

Phillips, Mary *see* HOPKINS, MATTHEW.

Pickering, Elizabeth *see* FORSTER, ANNE.

Pierson, Allison *see* SCOTLAND.

pig *see* BOAR.

Pittenweem Witches A handful of men and women from the small Scottish fishing town of Pittenweem in Fife, several of whom suffered much ill treatment and even death in the early eighteenth century after being accused of witchcraft crimes. The case revolved around a sixteen-year-old blacksmith's apprentice named Patrick Morton, who in 1704 blamed a 'weakness in his limbs', fits and other physical ailments upon the malevolent magic of Beatrix Laing, wife of a former treasurer of Pittenweem. Morton had, he alleged, incurred the woman's wrath when he had refused to forge some nails for her because he was busy on other work. Beatrix Laing had vowed revenge on him and, assisted by her accomplice Mrs Nicholas Lawson and others, had tossed hot coals into water in order to cause him trouble. He was even able to show anyone who was interested the places on his arm where he claimed the witches had pinched him.

When Morton repeated his accusations to the local minister, Patrick Cowper, who had often warned his congregation about the dangers of witchcraft, he added for good measure that SATAN himself had appeared at his bedside in an attempt to persuade him to renounce Christ and join his own ranks. The Privy Council subsequently heard the case and ordered both the accused to be imprisoned. Beatrix Laing was searched for the DEVIL'S MARK and deprived of sleep for five days and nights (*see* WATCHING AND WAKING), following which she made a full confession in which she named as her fellow witches Mrs Lawson, Janet Cornfoot and Isobel Adam. Once recovered from her ill treatment, however, Laing withdrew her confession. She was placed in the stocks before being consigned to a dark dungeon, where she was allowed no light or human contact for some five months.

Eventually, the intervention of more enlightened authorities led to Beatrix Laing being released on payment of a small fine. But the reputation she had now acquired as a witch meant that she was no longer welcome at home, and she was doomed to wander forlornly from place to place, ultimately dying at St Andrews.

Beatrix Laing's accomplice Isobel Adam confessed that she had renounced her baptismal vows to 'a little black man with a hat and black clothes' who appeared to her at Laing's house and promised her 'riches as much as she could wish'. She had also plotted with other witches the death by strangling of a man called Alexander Macgregor. She was, however, permitted to buy her freedom through payment of a fine – a most irregular happening. By contrast, Thomas Brown – one of the others named by Adam – died in prison from starvation not long after his arrest. Another of the witches, Janet Cornfoot, was tortured into a confession, but she too withdrew her confession and had to be confined in a steeple so that her influence did not prompt others in gaol to recant in a similar fashion. She escaped, but was refused shelter by Cowper when she misguidedly sought his protection and had to lie low at the home of another suspected witch. On 30 January 1705 a mob seized Janet Cornfoot, beat her, and strung her up on a rope between the shore and a ship so that they could throw stones at her. After a further beating she was pressed to death, the mob resting a door on her and then piling heavy stones upon it until the life was crushed out of her. To ensure that the alleged witch was quite dead a horse and sledge was driven several times over her lifeless body. Cowper refused to give the corpse a Christian burial, and no legal action was taken against the ringleaders of the mob who had hounded Cornfoot to her death.

The eventual exposure of Patrick Morton as an impostor was a considerable embarrassment to the authorities and brought shame to the officials of Pittenweem. It seems likely that Morton concocted his evidence in imitation of the case of Christine Shaw some years earlier (*see* BARGARRAN IMPOSTOR), having heard Patrick Cowper read details of the case from pamphlets that were then widely available.

Thomas George Stevenson, writing in 1871, had little doubt where the real blame for the incident lay:

In places where the minister was inflamed with a holy zeal against the Devil and his emissaries (such as Pittenweem), the parish became a perfect hotbed for the rearing of witches; and so plentiful a crop did it produce, that it appeared nothing else could thrive. But in places where the minister had some portion of humanity, and a little common sense, the Devil very rarely set foot on his territories, and witchcraft was not to be found.

Pole, Arthur and Edmund *see* PRESTALL, JOHN.

poltergeist *see* GHOST.

poppet *see* IMAGE MAGIC.

possession Invasion of a person's body by a demon, spirit or other supernatural entity. The concept of possession, evidenced by all manner of abnormal behaviour, is very ancient and common to virtually all cultures and religions in one form or another. Christ himself cast out devils, according to the New Testament, and Church authorities (especially those in France, Spain, Italy and other Catholic countries) were only too ready to believe that such manifestations were real. The demonologists of post-medieval Europe generally admitted that the Devil could possess someone of his own will, but insisted that in most cases a person was taken over by DEMONS only at the behest of a witch.

Possession by the Devil or his minions was a subject much discussed in medieval Europe, and as the mythology of witchcraft developed demoniac possession emerged as one of the 'evidences' of the threat posed to the Christian world that WITCHFINDERS could claim. Evil spirits, it was agreed, gained access to the body through any unguarded orifice and once inside might resist all attempts at eviction for many years, even scorning those who tried to drive them out by EXORCISM and other means. One of the simplest ways for a witch to infect a person with demons was to hide her FAMILIAR spirits in some item of food, typically an apple, that was then offered to the intended victim.

The symptoms of possession were many and varied. Some victims were observed to alter facially or to suffer other physical changes, with internal pains, fits, convulsions, fainting, lapses into a catatonic state and copious vomiting of pins, straw, glass and other unlikely articles. Some would waste away, while others had distended bellies or suffered from paralysis, impotence or disturbance of their menstrual cycle. Other symptoms included changes to the voice, which might become unusually gruff, and the use of obscene and blasphemous language (which had a particular impact if the sufferer was a child or a member of a religious order). On rare occasions, the victim was discovered to be able to converse in several languages and to have access to apparently secret information. Many victims went into fits if religious artefacts were brought into the room or if someone recited prayers or read a passage from the Bible in Latin. (The fact that in some cases the possessed person also threw fits when non-religious passages by Latin authors were read led to the exposure of more than one hoax.)

Sometimes the sufferer was able to identify the witch who had caused the trouble and could give details of the names and nature of the devils inhabiting them. Records exist of some victims claiming that they were possessed by dozens, or even hundreds, of demons, ranking as high as BEELZEBUB himself. In 1583 a Viennese girl examined by the Jesuits was claimed to have been possessed by a total of 12,652 demons, which had previously been kept by the girl's grandmother in glass jars in the form of flies. The grandmother was tortured into a confession and burned alive.

In reality many instances of apparent possession were undoubtedly misdiagnosed cases of mental illness. Sometimes victims would be treated sympathetically and encouraged to reveal as much as possible about what they experienced. On other occasions they would be more sternly dealt with and accused of dealing with the Devil, because truly holy people were once deemed immune to such invasion of their being. Countless deranged or paranoid men and women were singled out for persecution as witches because of their claims that they were in touch with demons and spirits, or simply because the physicians could find no apparent medical reason for their behaviour.

By no means all victims of demonic possession were mad, however. A substantial number of individuals, often young children or inhabitants of celibate religious orders, were attracted to the possibility of drawing intense public interest to themselves by such behaviour and perpetrated hoax possessions to that end. Faking fits and babbling incoherently about demons and so forth was guaranteed to cause a stir in any community, and sensational accusations of witchcraft levelled at personal enemies or obvious scapegoats, such as persons already reputed to be witches, could make the accuser a national celebrity as well as providing an opportunity to settle old scores. Once one nun or child tried the ruse successfully it was inevitable that others close to them would follow suit, overwhelmed by the excitement or eager to share in the attention – hence the many records of epidemics of hysterical possession in various enclosed communities. The risks remained considerable, as the accuser could very easily be suspected of witchcraft on his or her own part – proven witches were often themselves described as 'being possessed by the Devil'. In some cases, however, accused witches successfully defended themselves on the basis that they were possessed and therefore not responsible for their own actions. Very often, as in the numerous cases of demonic possession in French convents, the motive was apparently less calculated and the symptoms were born out of what modern psychiatrists would recognise as hysteria rooted in sexual repression.

Some victims displayed originality, if not ingenuity, in their symptoms. The credulity of various observers was greatly tested by demonstrations of such feats as pin-vomiting or by the victim urinating blue fluid. In 1571 Catherine Gaulter of Louvain in Belgium, for instance, startled the authorities by throwing up:

> great flocks of hair, with filthy water, such as in ulcers, and sometimes like the dung of doves and geese, and in them pieces of wood, and those like new chips lately cut off an old tree, and abundance of skins like parchment shavings ... after this she vomited innumerable stones, some like walnuts, and like pieces broken out of old walls and with some of the lime on them.

Other sufferers contorted their bodies into impossible positions or gave displays of superhuman strength. Many hoaxes were exposed and the charges dropped as a result, but many more cases were accepted at face value and it was only after several people had been hanged or burned that the truth emerged (if at all).

Treatment was usually in the form of repeated exorcisms (prohibited in Protestant countries from around 1600) and prayer. Pilgrimages to holy sites were reputed to cure many people of their possession, though sometimes only after years of suffering. One curious trick tried by some courts was to place a wig on the head of the possessed person: when the next fit began, the wig was snatched off and thrust into a bottle in the hope that the demon had been plucked off with it.

The tradition of demonic possession died hard. As late as 1816 a Jesuit priest was ordered to desist from his activities after he had embarked on a campaign to free a young girl of Amiens in northern France from the three demons who she claimed had possessed her; it turned out that she had invented the story to conceal her pregnancy.

See also AIX-EN-PROVENCE NUNS; ALLIER, ELISABETH; AUXONNE NUNS; BAVENT, MADELEINE; BILSON BOY; BURTON BOY; BURY ST EDMUNDS WITCHES; CADIERE, MARIE-CATHERINE; CAMBRAI NUNS; COLOGNE WITCHES; CONNECTICUT WITCHES; DARRELL, JOHN; FERY, JEANNE; FONTAINE, FRANÇOISE; GOODWIN CHILDREN; GUNTER, ANNE; HAIZMANN, CHRISTOPH; JØRGENSDATTER, SIRI; LEICESTER BOY; LILLE NOVICES; LODDUN NUNS; MORA WITCHES; NEWTON, FLORENCE; PITTENWEEM WITCHES; RENATA, SISTER MARIA; ROBINSON, EDMUND; SALEM WITCHES; WARBOYS WITCHES; WENHAM, JANE.

potions *see* FLYING OINTMENT; KILLING OINTMENT; LOVE POTION; SPELL.

Potter, Thomas *see* HELL-FIRE CLUB.

Prelati, Francesco *see* RAIS, GILLES DE.

Prentice, Joan *see* CHELMSFORD WITCHES.

Prestall, John fl.1562–71. English conjuror and alchemist who was widely suspected of being involved in at least one plot to bring about the murder by witchcraft of Elizabeth I. John Prestall was among the most famous conjurors of his age and allegedly plotted with Arthur and Edmund Pole (relatives of his) and Anthony Fortescue to kill Elizabeth and have Mary Queen of Scots placed upon the English throne. His accomplice in the affair was another celebrated conjuror, Edward Cosyn, with whom Prestall was reputed to have raised DEMONS in order to hear their advice on the best way to set about killing the monarch.

The plot was exposed in 1562 and the conspirators were put on trial for treason (but not for witchcraft, because the previous Act prohibiting such activity had been rescinded in 1547 and another was not put in place until 1563). They defended themselves on the grounds that they had never initiated any campaign against Elizabeth since their supernatural informants believed she would die soon anyway, although they admitted their allegiance to Mary. Remarkably, Prestall and the others escaped the death sentence and were confined instead in the Tower of London, where Prestall remained until 1567. He was finally released after promising to use his alchemy skills to change silver to gold on the Crown's behalf.

Surprisingly, John Prestall appears not to have learned his lesson from his involvement in the Pole plot of 1562: in 1571 he was tried for treason a second time and sentenced to death. Elizabeth, however, had the sentence reduced once again to imprisonment in the Tower of London and the last record of Prestall, dating from the 1590s, has him still practising his magic in London as a free man.

Preston, Jennet *see* PENDLE WITCHES.

pricking The practice of jabbing a suspected witch repeatedly with a sharp implement in order to locate an insensitive area that might be confidently identified as the DEVIL'S MARK. The Devil's mark that every witch was believed to have was supposed to be totally impervious to pain and incapable of bleeding, so WITCHFINDERS throughout Europe developed the 'science' of pricking the carefully shaved bodies of alleged witches as one of the principal means of sub-stantiating allegations of witchcraft. The discovery of the Devil's mark was particularly important evidence in countries where tor-ture was not allowed, although such examinations were also routine elsewhere as useful corroborating evidence of guilt. Fearsome-look-ing pins, bodkins or lancets were used to prod the accused person's naked body all over, sometimes for hours at a time (especially if the victim was a good-looking young female), until one or more sites where the sharp point had no apparent effect was found. The blade itself sometimes penetrated right to the bone.

Expert 'prickers' such as Matthew HOPKINS and his assistants John Stearne and Mary Phillips sometimes exercised various sub-terfuges in order to be sure of getting the desired result. One favourite method involved jabbing the accused with the point of the bodkin and immediately afterwards applying the blunt end of the implement very lightly somewhere else. Inevitably the pain inflicted by the first jab would make many victims fail to register the second much lighter pressure – and the witchfinder would declare the person's guilt confirmed. Other witchfinders were reputed to use bodkins with retractable points. Very rarely did such experts fail to find the Devil's mark that they searched for so diligently; even if this happened the suspect was often handed over to the torturers anyway, on the grounds that theirs was an exceptional case.

In many areas expert prickers were summoned from some dis-tance away as a first step towards the prosecution of a suspected witch. One well-documented illustration of the way in which prick-ing was conducted as part of an official investigation concerned a certain Scottish 'expert' who was called to Newcastle upon Tyne in 1649. For a fee of 20 shillings per witch confirmed, plus travelling expenses, this man plied his bodkin on thirty suspects, all stripped naked for his inspection in the town hall.

After careful examination he declared no fewer than twenty-seven of them to be witches. At this point, one of those present – a Lieutenant-Colonel Hobson – expressed his doubts about the witchfinder's methods and demanded that he test one of the women again, having observed that she did not bleed when jabbed because, through fear and the shock of humiliation, 'all her blood contracted into one part of her body'. The second time the point was applied blood spurted from the wound, and the witchfinder had to concur that she was no witch.

The best efforts of the observant Lieutenant-Colonel were not enough on this occasion, however, to save the lives of fourteen women and one man whose guilt had been proved by pricking. Flushed with his success at Newcastle, the unnamed witchfinder increased his fee to £3 per witch discovered and toured Northumberland for a time until hostility from the locals obliged him to decamp to north of the border. Fittingly enough, he is reported to have ended his days on the gallows himself – but not before he had been responsible, by his own admission, for the deaths of some 220 suspected witches.

Despite the exposure of many fraudulent prickers, the practice remained in use until the very end of the witchcraft hysteria. In 1712 Jane WENHAM, the last person to be tried for witchcraft in England, was subjected to pricking for the Devil's mark – although in her case no such spot was located.

See also SCORING ABOVE THE BREATH; WITCH'S MARK.

prophecy *see* DIVINATION.

protection against witchcraft The almost universal fear of witches and their magic in the post-medieval era created an overwhelming need for reassurance against the perceived threat. It led to the development of a whole mythology of countermeasures designed to protect the innocent, their livestock and their homes from harm.

Some people were lucky enough to be naturally immune from the effects of witchcraft. Among them were those born on a Sunday or on Christmas Day. A 'chime child' (anyone born while the clocks were striking the hour of three, six, nine or twelve noon, when the church bells sounded) was similarly deemed safe from spells, and in some areas it was claimed that all first-born children were immune from witchcraft. In Scotland, midwives once fed a little ash sap to newborn babies as their first drink in the belief that this would give them lifelong protection against witchcraft.

The vast majority of people, however, felt they needed to take positive action beyond living blameless, God-fearing lives. Many people carried AMULETS of various kinds, while others defended their homes from evil by festooning doors and windows with sprigs of magical plants, chalk patterns or a host of objects (including horseshoes) that were believed to block the entrance of evil. A pair of SCISSORS opened and concealed under the doormat, for instance, was widely considered an effective barrier against any witch who attempted to get inside. Other articles placed in the bedchamber prevented a sleeper from being troubled by evil spirits or NIGHTMARES.

Various other measures could be taken. They included placing a bull's heart stuck with thorns or pins up the chimney, burning the heart of a pigeon or a sheep in the fireplace, placing the poker upright against the fender so as to form a cross, making the sign of the cross over oneself or over one's cooking, washing the hands in urine or dew, hammering nails into the bed of a woman during labour or into the walls of the house (preferably in the shape of a cross), wearing the left stocking inside out, adding a little salt to milk, rubbing a cow's udders with 'passion grass' to prevent it being milked by a witch in animal disguise, tying red threads or ribbons to the horns of a cow or in the hair of children, holding tightly on to one's own thumbs, spitting and never lending pins to suspected witches.

In dire straits an innocent person might use his imagination to protect himself. Andrew Forrester of Knocksheen realised he had been discovered when spying on a COVEN meeting at Waterside Hill, Galloway, around 1750. He drew his sword and, using it to scratch a rough line in the grass between himself and the witches who threatened him, uttered the words: 'I draw this score in the name of God Almighty and may nae evil ever pass over it.' The witches were unable to cross the line and Forrester made good his escape (though not before one of the witches managed to snatch his horse's tail off).

Among the many plants, trees and the like that were believed to have protective qualities were ANGELICA, BAY, ELDER, FERN, GARLIC, HAZEL, LILY, MUGWORT, OAK, PUMPKIN, ROSEMARY, ROWAN, STONECROP, STRAW and THORN. Others included the humble houseleek, which was usually planted in thatched roofs to ward off witches and to prevent a house catching fire, and the berries of herb Paris, with its unusual regular cross-pattern, which were also employed against witches. Hanging a garland of bittersweet or woody NIGHTSHADE around a person's neck was reputed to relieve them of any effects suffered through the casting of the EVIL EYE and also to cure them of a variety of illnesses. Flowers with yellow centres, such as the MARIGOLD, were often credited with similar properties, as was seaweed.

If a spell was thought to have been cast already, one remedy was to go secretly to the suspected witch's house and to steal a little of the thatch. This had then to be burned in order to release the victim from the spell. If chased by a witch the best course was to cross running water, in accordance with the popular superstition that no witch could cross it in pursuit.

See also BUTTER-SPOILING; MAGIC CIRCLE; SILVER; WATER.

pumpkin A prominent emblem of modern HALLOWE'EN festivities, the pumpkin was long revered as a symbol of fertility and protection against evil. Today's grotesque hollowed-out pumpkins, lit from within by candles, were originally intended to protect revellers by scaring away any evil spirits abroad on that particular night. Nowadays, this function seems to be increasingly forgotten as popular mythology revels in tales of pumpkin monsters and pumpkin-headed DEMONS, leading successive generations of children into the mistaken belief that the pumpkins themselves represent evil and may be in league with witches, vampires and so forth.

In keeping with the original idea that pumpkins bestowed protection against evil was the old tradition that they were best planted on Good Friday. Once growing, they should never be pointed at: to do so inflicts the power of the EVIL EYE and stunts their further development.

Witchlore suggested that pumpkin seeds could be consumed to calm an excessively passionate nature, and that when mixed into a paste with oil and rubbed on the skin they eradicated freckles.

Putnam, Ann *see* SALEM WITCHES.

Q Quedlinburg *see* GERMANY.

Queen of Heaven *see* GREAT GODDESS.

Queensberry, Marquis of *see* HELL-FIRE CLUB.

R **rabbit** Like the HARE, the rabbit was long considered a favourite disguise of witches and their FAMILIARS, and in former times it was thought ominous if such a creature was seen too close to livestock or to the family home. This link with the forces of darkness may go all the way back to pre-Christian pagan religion, when sightings of rabbits playing in the moonlight led to their identification with the baleful Moon God. As well as adopting the form of a rabbit as a disguise, witches were also reputed to use parts of rabbits in various SPELLS – notably those connected with the making of mischief or with fertility and sex magic, reflecting the animal's remarkable powers of reproduction.

rack *see* LADDER.

Rais, Gilles de 1404–40. French soldier and aristocrat who acquired lasting notoriety for his involvement in black magic during the reign of Charles VII. At his most powerful the richest noble in

Europe, Gilles de Laval, Baron de Rais, served as a Marshal of France and fought with JOAN OF ARC at Orléans and elsewhere before retiring from military service in 1432 and settling at his sumptuous castle at Tiffauges in Brittany. Subsequently, though also admired for his learning and for his knowledge of music and drama, he established a reputation as an alchemist. A succession of famous mountebanks were invited to his home; dark rumours of child sacrifice and other evils began to spread about the arcane rituals that these men were said to perform – rumours probably fuelled by the Church and the INQUISITION, who stood to inherit the aristocrat's wealth if grounds could be found for its confiscation. Gilles's undoing finally came in 1440, when he was arrested by order of the Bishop of Nantes, Jean de Malestroit, on the relatively insignificant charge of mistreating Jean le Ferron, brother of the treasurer of Brittany. Jean le Ferron had been beaten and imprisoned on Gilles's orders, but the fact that Ferron was a priest presented the Bishop with the pretext he needed to start the trial he had secretly planned some time before. A parallel action was begun in the civil courts at the same time. The charges quickly escalated from those relating to Jean le Ferron, and in due course the nobleman stood accused of murdering some 140 children in the course of his occult activities.

The evidence presented against Gilles cast him as a perverted monster who practised all manner of obscenity and cruelty upon his victims before they died. Besides child murder, he was suspected of HERESY, apostasy, the conjuration of DEMONS, sodomy, sacrilege and the keeping of various prohibited books on the black arts. According to the formal charges against him 'he adored and sacrificed to spirits, conjured them and made others conjure them, and wished to make a pact with the said evil spirits, and by their means to have and receive, if he could, knowledge, power, and riches'. The charges relating to the children were especially horrifying, with accusations that the prisoner had 'inhumanly butchered, killed, dismembered, burned and otherwise tortured' scores of boys and girls and had 'foully committed the sin of sodomy with young boys and in other ways lusted against nature after young girls, spurning the natural way of copulation, while both the innocent boys and girls were alive or sometimes dead or even sometimes during their death throes'.

Gilles had allegedly been aided and abetted in his excesses by Francesco Prelati, a Florentine priest and magician. Prelati was said to have raised a demon called Baron, who promised the pair that he would reveal the secret of manufacturing gold if they performed hideous rites and ceremonies in his honour. This promise had its attractions for Gilles, whose extravagant lifestyle had much reduced the vast wealth he had once enjoyed. On the demon's instructions, scores of children were allegedly kidnapped by Gilles's agents – a cousin of his called Gilles de Sille, an impoverished aristocrat named Roger de Briqueville and two women, Etienette Blanchu and one dubbed 'La Meffraye'. These children were then subjected to various sexual abuses, sadistically mutilated and murdered, usually by having their throats cut.

The accused aristocrat initially scorned the judges before whom he was brought, but his confidence was shaken when his associates, including Prelati, La Meffraye and Blanchu, were tortured into giving full accounts of what had transpired at Tiffauges. Under torture himself, Gilles subsequently made a full confession of his crimes, expressing his regrets and begging the forgiveness of the parents of his young victims. Such was the horror of the murders which he described to the court that the judges ordered the crucifix on the courtroom wall to be covered up. Accomplices of the aristocrat attested that they had seen Gilles cut off the heads of children and then ask them which head they thought was the most beautiful.

The Bishop of Nantes expressed the hope that the prisoner could be redeemed by prayer, but the death penalty was inevitable. In the company of two of his accomplices, the condemned man was strangled on 29 October 1440 while a choir sang prayers for his salvation. His body, together with that of the other two, was then placed on a pyre, but his relatives were permitted to remove it before the flames reached it and his remains were interred in a nearby church. In reward for the evidence they had given, Prelati, Blanchu and La Meffraye were set free after serving a short time in prison.

Just how much of the Gilles de Rais story is factual and how much may be attributed to legend is debatable. The highly irregular conduct of the trial, with the admission of much gossip as evidence and with no attempt to allow statements from the aristocrat's own servants, suggests that most, if not all, of the charges laid against Gilles were inventions of those eager to acquire his wealth. Regardless of the justice of it, the main protagonist, Gilles de Rais himself, has long since become confused in the popular imagination with the murderous figure of Bluebeard, a creation of ancient Breton legend.

Randolf, John *see* JOAN OF NAVARRE.

raven In common with other black-coloured birds, the raven was considered a creature of ill omen and was often depicted in the company of witches as they worked their evil spells. According to time-honoured superstition the raven was a favourite disguise of the Devil, and he flew around the countryside in this form carrying disease on his wings. Sightings of the bird were therefore particularly lamented if anyone was ill in the household, as this surely meant that they would die; the call of the bird was interpreted as 'corpse, corpse'.

Redfearne, Anne *see* PENDLE WITCHES.

Remy, Nicolas c.1530–1612. French judge and demonologist who presided over countless witchcraft trials in Lorraine, eastern FRANCE, in the 1580s, sending some nine hundred witches to their deaths. Born into a family of lawyers in Charmes, Lorraine, Remy witnessed witchcraft trials while still a child and soon developed extreme views about the subject. In 1582, indeed, he personally brought charges against a beggar woman whom he blamed for the death of his own son, claiming he had been done to death in revenge for his own refusal to give the woman alms some days before. As a lawyer, he served as one of the Provosts of Nancy from 1576 to 1591 and was then appointed Attorney-General of Lorraine, in which capacity he was able to ensure that the persecution of witches in the region continued with unabated ferocity.

In 1595 Remy recorded the conclusions he had drawn from his experiences of witchcraft trials in what became a highly influential book called *Demonolatreiae*. On the basis of both his writings and his decisions in court, he was firmly convinced of the reality of witchcraft and argued that 'whatever is not normal is due to the Devil'. Witchcraft was in his eyes far more serious than other crimes, and death was the only appropriate punishment.

A sample death warrant signed by Remy read as follows:

> The undersigned Attorney General of Lorraine, who has witnessed the present examination and torture made by Messieurs the Provost and officers of justice of St-Dié upon George de Haut, of Claingotte, held prisoner at the aforementioned St-Dié on charges of witchcraft, of which he was apprized, to discover information about the fact, hearing, etc., and who has witnessed the statements, reading of depositions, confrontations and procès-verbal of the torture given him, holds this person to have been duly arraigned and deemed and judged that he be condemned to be burned alive, that he be bound to a stake expressly erected for the purpose at the appointed place for such executions, so that at least he will feel the flames keenly before being suffocated, his goods to be declared forfeit and confiscate to whom they belong, reasonable expenses for the trial first being deducted. Given at Nancy, May 4, 1596.

Remy was particularly unforgiving of children who were implicated in the crime of witchcraft. Believing that even the very young were capable of perpetrating acts of sorcery, he regularly condemned the children of condemned witches to be thrashed at the scene of their parents' execution and confided in his book that in his opinion this punishment was barely harsh enough, arguing that such criminals should be 'banished and exiled from the boundaries of human nature'. He doubted, however, that witches could change their shape by magic or actually attended the SABBATS that they described – but argued that they were deceived into such delusions by the

Devil. Either way, they were guilty of dealing with the Devil and as part of the evil army threatening Christian civilisation should be hunted down and put to death.

Remy's book was reprinted many times and, alongside the writings of Jean BODIN, his work effectively replaced the aged MALLEUS MALEFICARUM as the most respected authority on the business of witchcraft and witch-hunting.

Renata, Sister Maria d.1749. German nun who was destined to become one of the last victims of the witchcraft hysteria in Germany. The sixty-nine-year-old sub-prioress of a convent at Unterzell, near Würzburg, Sister Maria Renata Sänger von Mossau had served the convent faithfully for some fifty years when she fell foul of accusations of witchcraft levelled at her by some of the other nuns.

The trouble began when Sister Maria opposed the acceptance of Cecilia Pistorini, who suffered from convulsions and hallucinations, as a nun in 1745. Despite these objections Pistorini was confirmed as a nun, but other sisters in the convent now began to exhibit unmistakable signs of demonic POSSESSION, screaming during services, being seized by convulsions and foaming at the mouth.

One of the nuns, on her deathbed, accused Sister Maria of bewitching her and word of the affair spread beyond the convent walls, leading to an investigation. Father Oswald Loschert, abbot of the Oberzell monastery, built up a strong case against Sister Maria, stating that she had been claimed by the Devil 'even in her mother's womb' and that she 'was his slave and a cursed thing'.

Prayers and services of EXORCISM only led to a deterioration in the condition of the afflicted nuns and Father Loschert felt that Sister Maria's guilt was confirmed, calling her a 'foul witch who hid her sorceries beneath the holy habit'. Sister Maria protested her innocence but was kept in close confinement. A search of her cell uncovered various suspicious herbs and ointments as well as the yellow dress which she was alleged to wear at SABBATS. On the strength of this evidence, and with the support of the University of Würzburg, Sister Maria was tortured into a confession of guilt.

According to her own testimony, Sister Maria had been introduced to witchcraft by a grenadier whom she had met in Vienna. This grenadier had taught her the rudiments of black magic and had then taken her to Prague to see SATAN himself. She had renounced her Christian faith and at the age of fourteen had made a PACT WITH THE DEVIL, being renamed by him Ema. She had later had intercourse with various DEMONS before studying the art of witchcraft in earnest. At nineteen she had entered the convent on Satan's express instructions as part of a plot to achieve its destruction, and he had continued to visit her in her cell every Monday in order to have sex with her, causing her 'horrible and most intense pain'. She had also taken advantage of a rule allowing each nun to keep a CAT (to keep the vermin down) by keeping three FAMILIARS disguised as cats, although these had the ability to talk.

Among other details, Sister Maria admitted flying to sabbats in Würzburg nearly every night, mounted on a BROOMSTICK and wearing the yellow robe that her interrogators had found. Her crimes had included inducing sickness in certain enemies, causing six of the nuns to be possessed by devils and desecrating the host on no fewer than seven occasions, the host 'being struck through with nails, from which spots clear water flowed'. With regard to the latter offence her interrogators demanded to know how she had stolen the host without being detected, upon which she described how she had cut her flesh and hidden the wafers in the wound (she was able to show the scars that had been made). On request from her interrogators, Sister Maria provided full details of the sabbats she was alleged to have attended. Meeting in a deep forest or large meadow, she and other witches had honoured the Devil, feasted and danced.

Despite the fact that the witchcraft hysteria had much abated in the German states by the 1740s, Sister Maria's confession was more than sufficient to convince the Church authorities of her culpability and she was found guilty of thirteen charges of sorcery, HERESY and apostasy. She was dismissed from the order and sentenced to death. Accordingly, on 17 June 1749 the condemned woman was taken to Marienberg and beheaded by the public executioner. Her corpse was burned to ashes on a pyre of tar barrels and wood while one of the Jesuit priests in attendance preached a sermon detailing her crimes.

A hundred years before, the exposure of Sister Maria Renata would doubtless have led to further trials and to a full-blown outbreak of witchcraft panic. At this late date, however, news of the execution stirred up considerable controversy and there were no more arrests.

Renfrew Witches *see* BARGARRAN IMPOSTOR.

Reynie, Nicholas de la *see* CHAMBRE ARDENTE AFFAIR.

Rheinbach Witches *see* BUIRMANN, FRANZ.

Ritchie, Isobel *see* ABERDEEN WITCHES.

Robert of Bristol *see* KYTELER, ALICE.

Robey, Isabel *see* PENDLE WITCHES.

Robin *see* SOMERSET WITCHES.

Robinson, Edmund b.1624. English youth whose detailed accusations of witchcraft in 1634 led to a second outbreak of witchcraft hysteria in the Pendle Forest area of Lancashire some twenty years after the sensational trial of the original PENDLE WITCHES. The first Pendle case had depended largely upon the evidence of a girl well below fourteen, the age when evidence from a minor might legally be heard; this time, too, the case stemmed from a minor, the ten-year-old Edmund Robinson. But on this occasion, the judge at Lancaster Assizes showed himself to be altogether more demanding when it came to accepting the testimony of a mere child.

Edmund Robinson was the son of a mason living and working in the Pendle Forest. As such he was doubtless very familiar with the notorious events that had traumatised the whole of Lancashire a few years before his birth. Whatever the inspiration, the boy startled locals when he began to tell odd stories about various neighbours that strongly suggested occult activity. According to the lad, on All Saints' Day 1633 he had encountered two greyhounds and had tried to persuade them to chase a hare. When the dogs had refused to obey him he had beaten them, only for the creatures to be transformed at once into human beings. One of these was a little boy whom he did not know, while the other he identified as a woman called Frances Dicconson. She tried to buy his silence with a shilling, but Edmund declined the money. Dicconson had then transformed the unidentified small boy into a white horse and had made Edmund ride on it to a SABBAT at a barn at Hoarstones.

With encouragement from two lamentably gullible magistrates, Richard Shuttleworth and John Starkie, before whom Edmund Robinson repeated his story, the boy gave a full description of the witches' sabbat he had witnessed. Some sixty men and women were present at the gathering, of whom he was able to recognise nineteen. Some of these already had local reputations as witches; ironically, they included Jannet Device, whose evidence as a child had hanged the witches in the 1612 case. Meat was cooked on the fire and he was invited to taste some food and drink, but after trying a sample he declined the offer. More food was produced for the company by pulling on six ropes suspended from the ceiling. By magically 'milking' these ropes hot meat, milk and butter fell out of thin air. Three of the women, meanwhile, thrust THORNS into three portraits, clearly intending harm to the person depicted. At this point Edmund had run home, terrified out of his wits:

> ... he saw six of them kneeling and pulling, all six of them, six several ropes, which were fastened or tied to the top of the barn. Presently after which pulling, there came into this informer's sight, flesh smoking, butter in lumps, and milk as it were flying from the said ropes ... And during all the time of their several pulling they made such ugly faces as scared this informer, so that he was glad to run out and steal homewards.

With memories of the 1612 episode thoroughly evoked, the magistrates had some thirty people arrested and committed seventeen of them for trial at the Lenten Assizes in Lancaster. All the suspects except one resolutely protested their innocence of all charges – Margaret Johnson broke down and confessed that she was indeed a witch. Under pressure from the court, Johnson explained how she had sold her soul to the Devil in the form of a black-suited man named Mamilion in exchange for the fulfilment of all her wishes (see PACT WITH THE DEVIL). She confirmed that a sabbat had been celebrated at Hoarstones on the date in question although she herself had not attended.

Margaret Johnson's confession, coupled with memories of 1612, had a deep impression upon the jury in the case and the accused were found guilty. The judge, however, was uneasy about the convictions – the sum total of the testimony against one of the accused, Mary Spencer, for instance, was that she would roll her pail down the hill, running before it and calling to it to follow her. Because of his doubts about Edmund Robinson's story he referred the matter to the King in Council. John Bridgeman, the Bishop of Chester, was asked to interrogate some of the prisoners, after which he agreed with the judge that the allegations were the product of Robinson's imagination. Four of the accused – Frances Dicconson, Jennet Hargreaves, Margaret Johnson and Mary Spencer – were despatched to London, where they were questioned further by Dr Harvey, royal physician to Charles I, and others. These eminent authorities discounted the WITCH'S MARKS that had allegedly been located on their bodies, and they too decided that fraud was at play. Charles I himself interrogated Robinson and the four suspects and quickly came to the conclusion that the boy's story was a pack of lies.

Robinson himself eventually admitted the deception, confirming that he had made up the allegations on the basis of what he had heard about the 1612 trial. At the time of the alleged sabbat he had been picking plums. His only motive, he claimed, had been a desire to make mischief. Others, however, suspected that he had been put up to it by enemies of those accused, pointing out that Edmund Robinson's father was known to have quarrelled with Frances Dicconson over the sale of a cow. Like other notable CHILD ACCUSERS, the boy might also have been seduced by the opportunity to enjoy some local celebrity: certainly, before his exposure he seemed to derive some satisfaction from being invited to one parish after another to identify witches who had been present at the notorious sabbat (and he received a fee for each suspect identified).

Whatever the reasons behind the Edmund Robinson hoax, the consequences of it were regrettable. Although the accused were released without charge, not all survived the experience. Three of those charged as witches, one man and two women, died in prison before the case was resolved.

Nothing is known of Robinson's life after his exposure.

See also WEBSTER, JOHN.

Rogie, Helen *see* ABERDEEN WITCHES.

rosemary Like many other herbs, rosemary was alleged to have a range of supernatural properties including the ability to ward off the EVIL EYE. Witchlore suggested that rosemary might also be administered to cure madness, to guard against nausea and NIGHTMARES and to prevent storms. Many people pinned up a sprig of rosemary at the front door or wore it on their person in order to keep witches and disease at bay.

Rosemary was commonly used in LOVE POTIONS and in SPELLS concerned with DIVINATION. Sleeping with a sixpence and a sprig of rosemary under the pillow on HALLOWE'EN, for instance, was said to draw forth visions of a person's future partner. Wearing rosemary in the buttonhole also aided the memory and promoted a person's luck in general.

Ross, Balthasar *see* WITCHFINDER.

rowan Sacred to the Druids and still respected for its protective properties, the rowan or mountain ash was once widely considered a powerful defence against witchcraft and the EVIL EYE and it was therefore frequently planted in gardens and close to houses. In former times, farmers would often fix a bough of rowan wood at the door to the cowshed if they suspected that a witch was stealing milk from the herd by magical means (typically by sucking at the udder after adopting the disguise of a HARE or snake or else by ritually 'milking' a length of rope). Individual animals could be protected from witches by fixing rowan twigs to their tails with lengths of red thread, and witches could be prevented from turning milk sour by slipping a stave of rowan wood into the pail. Driving a flock of sheep or other livestock through an arch of rowan was widely thought to ensure their immunity from the threat of witchcraft. Riders of horses sometimes carried whips made of rowan or wore a few sprigs of rowan in their hats for similar reasons.

Rowan wood was often kept inside the house all year round in order to prevent evil spirits from entering, the wood being ceremonially replaced on 3 May (Holy Rood Day or Rowan-tree Day). In some cases, rowan wood was actually used for the construction of crossbeams and other parts of the house so that its benevolent effects might be enjoyed for as long as the house itself stood. Small pieces of rowan were also carried on the person or attached to the bedstead so as to deter evil, and rowan trees were often planted in graveyards to prevent witches from disturbing the dead.

The power of the rowan was best illustrated by the folk belief that if a witch was touched by a rowan stick he or she would be immediately hauled off to Hell by the Devil himself.

Rule, Margaret b.1674. New England woman, whose apparent POSSESSION by DEMONS became the subject of investigation by the Puritan demonologist Cotton MATHER. Convinced of the reality of witchcraft, Mather was deeply impressed when the seventeen-year-old Margaret Rule threw a shrieking fit in his North Boston church in 1693. He quickly responded by publishing a brief account of her condition, clearly with the aim of recruiting sympathy in the Boston community for his anti-witchcraft crusade in the wake of the sensational trial of the SALEM WITCHES a few months before.

At Mather's invitation, the girl named the witches who were responsible for her torment. To the preacher's evident satisfaction, several of these were already widely rumoured to be witches – further confirmation in his eyes that there really was a witchcraft threat to New England Christian society. The girl had fits and went without food for days at a time, as well as suffering bruises caused by unseen assailants. The demons that troubled her were also allegedly responsible for stealing sermons being prepared by Mather (later found in the street) and for causing the girl to be levitated to the ceiling of her bedroom. With encouragement from Mather, Margaret Rule described the visitations she had received from both black and white spirits as they battled for her soul.

Mather's readiness to accept that Margaret Rule's symptoms could only be explained by demonic possession were not shared in all quarters, however. Robert Calef, who was also at odds with Mather over the Salem case, scorned him for drawing such a conclusion and drew from the preacher an outraged response, together with unrealised threats that he would sue him for libel. Mather attempted to dismiss Calef's views as an 'abominable bundle of lies' inspired by Satan himself.

After several months Margaret Rule's fits ceased, proof to Mather that his prayers on her behalf had had the desired effect.

S **sabbat** A gathering of witches for the purposes of celebrating allegiance to the DEVIL, casting SPELLS, plotting evil and indulging in the abandoned pursuit of feasting, drinking, dancing and orgiastic sex. The notion of the witches' sabbat (or Sabbath, in imitation of Jewish custom) was central to the mythology of witchcraft, and a simple uncorroborated allegation that a suspect had been seen at a sabbat was all too often sufficient to send that person to the gallows or to the stake. The sabbat was first mentioned in the course of a witch trial at Toulouse in 1335, which ended with some eight people being burned.

The concept of the sabbat as it was understood in post-Reformation Europe had an antecedent in the mass night flights that the followers of the pagan goddess DIANA were once said to gather for, flying through the night sky on bewitched animals or men. There were also marked similarities to the activities of the heretical religious sects (see HERESY) that had previously been ear-marked for persecution by the INQUISITION, with their alleged veneration of the Devil, cannibal eating of babies, obscene kissing (see KISS), consorting with DEMONS and anti-Christian rites. Later generations of demonologists elaborated on the idea, possibly incorporating details taken from classical accounts of the outlandish celebrations connected with Bacchus and Priapus. They depicted the sabbat as a ritual event with a predetermined character and set ceremonial conventions, thus strengthening their claims that civilised society was being threatened by a calculatedly malevolent anti-Christian cult rather than by single individuals of a maverick or simply deranged disposition.

According to the experts, sabbats were held at regular intervals on certain propitious dates. These were usually identified as CANDLEMAS (2 February), WALPURGIS NIGHT (30 April), MIDSUMMER'S EVE (the Eve of the Feast of St John the Baptist, 23 June), Lammas Day (1 August), HALLOWE'EN (31 October) and the Feast of St Thomas (21 December). Hallowe'en and Walpurgis Night were sacred to the Druids, while the other four dates formerly marked the changes in the seasons in the pagan calendar. Sabbats could be celebrated on any day of the week, with Mondays, Wednesdays and Fridays particular favourites, although Saturday was allegedly avoided by some witches as it was the day sacred to the Virgin Mary. Less important regular meetings of smaller groups of witches might be held on a weekly basis (*see* ESBAT).

The concept of the sabbat, and thus the witch cult, was more readily accepted in some countries than in others. On the Continent of Europe witches were routinely tortured into confessing their presence at such gatherings, and were encouraged to provide full details of what occurred and who else was present. In England, however, where torture was not allowed, few witches were pressured to provide such details. In consequence there were relatively few mass trials of English witches implicated through their alleged membership of a particular COVEN that met on a regular basis to celebrate and perform their magic.

The earliest accounts of witches' sabbats date from the first half of the fourteenth century. Perhaps the oldest surviving description is that recorded from Anne-Marie de Georgel in Toulouse in 1335. Having encountered the Devil in the form of a tall dark man with fiery eyes and clothes made of skins, she experienced her first sabbat on a Saturday night, arriving there simply by willing it. There she was educated in the ways of evil by a demon in the form of a GOAT. Another French witch from the same era, Catherine Delort, said she visited the sabbat every Saturday after falling into a trance-like sleep. Two inquisitors were rumoured to have infiltrated a sabbat in northern Italy around 1460, but they were discovered and killed before they could give detailed reports. The notorious MALLEUS MALEFICARUM of 1486 had little to say on the subject, but within twenty years the sabbat had become a central feature of witchlore and the basis of countless prosecutions.

Judging by the testimony of convicted witches, certain characteristics were common to sabbats all the way from Scotland and Scandinavia in the north to Spain and Italy in the south (attributable in large part to the fact that interrogators asked much the same sort of questions and inevitably got similar answers). These large gatherings were generally held out of doors in isolated spots that might already have a local reputation as places of evil (including CROSSROADS, stone circles and the summits of mountains, such as the Brocken in Germany), though they might occasionally be held in houses, barns or even churches.

Because these were special occasions and only held infrequently many witches might attend, drawn from all quarters of a region or country. Records exist of sabbats at which several thousand witches were allegedly present. Perhaps the largest on record was one reported from Burgundy in 1440, which some ten thousand witches were said to have attended.

According to the popular imagination sabbats were always held at night, with witches slipping out of their homes some two hours before midnight and flying through the dark sky variously mounted on demons, BROOMSTICKS, bewitched men and animals or other objects (see TRANSVECTION). In fact, many witches told the authorities they walked to their meetings or rode horses in the normal way. In order to escape detection by their husbands, married witches might leave a demon or a broomstick in their place in the bed and bewitch their spouses into thinking they were still present. Others said they could leave their body behind and attend the sabbat in their 'spirit' form. Once there, light for the gathering was provided either by fires or by candles, which were usually made of black wax.

It was customary for the Devil himself (or his representative), possibly accompanied by his 'Queen' (see GREAT GODDESS), to preside over the meeting, sometimes seated upon a throne. This master of ceremonies usually manifested in the guise of an animal, typically a goat or a DOG. Those present would begin proceedings by offering their allegiance to the Devil, kissing his buttocks and renouncing Christ. In keeping with the belief that servants of SATAN tried to do everything in a way contrary to normal Christian practice, it was rumoured that witches would offer their salutes to the Devil in the most bizarre fashion. The demonologist Francesco-Maria GUAZZO reported how witches would sometimes 'bend their knees as suppliants, and sometimes stand with their backs turned, and sometimes kick their legs high up so that their heads are bent back and their chins point to the sky ... they turn their backs and, going backwards like crabs, put out their hands behind them to touch him in supplication'. According to some witches a roll call might be taken of those present, the names having been inscribed in a red book.

The witches would then relate to the Devil the evil they had done in his name since their last meeting. In return the Devil might give instructions for evil to be performed before the next gathering and hand over to his followers certain magic ointments and powders for their use on his behalf. Where necessary, the Devil explained how a certain end might be accomplished, as described by JAMES I in his *Daemonologie* in 1597:

> As to their consultations thereupon, they use them oftest in the churches, where they convene for adoring; at what time their master enquiring of them what they would be at, every one of them proposes unto him what wicked turn they would have done, either for obtaining of riches, or for revenging them upon any whom they have malice at, who granting their demand (as no doubt willingly he will, since it is to do evil), he teacheth them the means, whereby they may do the same.

Initiates might then be presented to the Devil, who might conduct arcane rituals of a purposefully blasphemous nature (*see* BLACK MASS). These were said to include witch weddings and baptisms, as Pierre de LANCRE explained: 'Witches were accustomed to have their children baptised more often at the sabbat than in church, and presented more often to the Devil than to God.' Wedding ceremonies were perfunctory and obscene in deliberate contempt of Christian rituals, the two partners simply bending over to blow on each other's buttocks.

One of the highlights of the conventional sabbat was the feast that the Devil provided for his minions. Some witches described this as sumptuous, though others said the food was deliberately foul and was prepared without SALT. Pierre de Lancre, who offered a full description of the sabbat in his *Tableau de l'Inconstance des Mauvais Anges* in 1612, declared that 'only the meat of corpses, hanged men, hearts of unbaptised children and unclean animals never eaten by Christians, are eaten …'. Nicolas REMY, in his *Demonolatreiae* of 1595, stated that the 'banquets are so foul either in appearance or smell that they would easily cause nausea in the hungriest and greediest stomach'. For drink, Remy suggested that the Devil provided them 'in a dirty little cup wine-like clots of black blood'. By contrast the PENDLE WITCHES feasted on beef, bacon and roast mutton at their meetings (though these hardly qualified as sabbats in the Continental sense), while the SOMERSET WITCHES partook of meat and cakes washed down with wine or beer. Some witches spoke of a magic cake, incorporating black millet and the flesh of unbaptised children, that would be shared at the end of the banquet.

As well as feasting, the sabbat climaxed in singing and 'indecent' DANCING, often with the Devil himself playing the music. Alternatively one of the witches provided the music, as Gilly Duncan did at the gathering of the NORTH BERWICK WITCHES when she played the tune 'Gyllatripes' on her Jew's harp. Again, it was important that everything was done contrary to the usual manner of Christians, with dancers turning their backs on one another and all proceeding in an anticlockwise (WIDDERSHINS) direction.

As the revelry came to a head, sometimes at a signal from the Devil himself, all present finally engaged in promiscuous sex: every-one – including Satan himself – pleased themselves at random and without regard to normal inhibitions or courtesies. Incest was com-monly alleged, as were bestiality, homosexuality and other practices considered unacceptable by the rest of society. According to Madeleine de Demandolx, certain nights of the week were reserved for particular sexual pursuits:

Upon Sundays they pollute themselves by their filthy copulation with the devils that are succubi and incubi; upon Thursdays they contaminate themselves with sodomy; upon Saturdays they do prostitute themselves to abominable bestiality; upon other days they use the ordinary course which nature prompteth unto them.

Opinion varied about whether sex with the Devil, who might manifest as a black man, goat, dog, bull or even stag or bird, was enjoyable or not. The majority of witches complained that coupling with the Devil was painful (suggesting that an artificial phallus was used when the Devil or his representative found his natural sexual reserves exhausted). Jeannette d'Abadie, a French girl who had allegedly copulated with the Devil many times while still only sixteen, claimed that he caused her intense pain with his scaly member, adding that his semen was 'extremely cold' and that because of this she had never been made pregnant by him. Others similarly attested to the iciness of the Devil's genitalia and semen and agreed that his attentions caused them intense pain.

There were others, however, who stubbornly insisted that the Devil was a far abler lover than any mortal man and that he gave them great pleasure, so that they always looked forward to the next sabbat encounter. Contradicting those who said that the Devil's member was always frigid and as thin as a finger, one witch interrogated by de Lancre claimed he 'had a member like a mule's, having chosen to imitate that animal as being best endowed by nature; that it was as long and as thick as an arm'. According to the demonologist Gianfrancesco Pico della Mirandola, writing in early sixteenth-century Italy, 'the devils can even agitate the thing when it is inside, wherefore the women derive more pleasure than they do with men'.

The Devil, according to some, discriminated between partners according to their looks. Pierre de Lancre, repeating the confessions of witches in his *Tableau* of 1612, maintained that the Devil had intercourse with the beautiful women from the front, but with the ugly ones from the rear. In the case of male witches, the Devil – according to the confession of the elderly Frenchman Pierre Vallin, convicted of witchcraft in 1438 – would adopt the form of a girl so that they might copulate with him in that guise.

The notion that witches had sex with demons at their sabbats was widely accepted, but it did pose a problem for theologians and demonologists because demons were essentially spirits with no physical reality. Various theories were advanced to explain this, including the idea that demons took over the bodies of the dead (especially those of recently hanged men) or created bodies out of the elements.

At the end of the meeting, reputedly signalled by the coming of the dawn or by the sound of the first cock crowing, all present would disperse to their homes in the manner in which they had come or else would be instantly returned there by virtue of the Devil's magic. According to the anonymous *Errores Gazariorum* of around 1450 the witches would urinate and evacuate in a cask in final mockery of the Christian Eucharist before taking their leave.

See also PACT WITH THE DEVIL.

St John's wort *see* MIDSUMMER'S EVE.

St Osyth Witches Outbreak of witchcraft hysteria that led to a notorious mass trial staged at the Chelmsford county sessions in 1582. The village of St Osyth, near Brightlingsea, Essex, suffered more than most communities in Essex and East Anglia during the witchcraft hysteria that swept eastern ENGLAND in the late fifteenth century and again in the seventeenth century. Surviving records from the 1582 trial held at the county sessions in Chelmsford indicate that some fourteen women from St Osyth were indicted on charges of witchcraft. Of these, ten were charged with 'bewitching to death', which carried the death penalty.

The trial, presided over by Judge Bryan Darcy, appears to have had its roots in a series of village vendettas which had escalated from trivial quarrels. At the heart of the affair was Ursula Kempe, an impoverished local woman who offered her services as a midwife and nursemaid and who also had a reputation for 'unwitching' those who feared they were under the influence of malevolent magic.

Witnesses attested that Mother Kempe had cured a young boy, Davy Thorlowe, of illness by the use of incantations but had subsequently taken offence when the boy's mother, Grace Thorlowe, had declined to employ her as nursemaid to her infant daughter. When the baby girl fell out of her crib soon afterwards and broke her neck suspicion immediately fell upon Kempe, although no accusations were made openly. Ignoring the rumours, Grace Thorlowe allowed Kempe to suggest a treatment for her arthritis. Kempe recommended a method that she had learned from an old 'Wise Woman', later described by Mrs Thorlowe in court:

> take hog's dung and charnel and put them together and hold them in her left hand, and to take in the other hand a knife, and to prick the medicine three times, and then to cast the same into the fire, and to take the said knife, and to make three pricks under a table, and to let the knife stick there. And after that to take three leaves of sage, and as much of herb John (alias herb grace) and put them into ale, and drink it last at night and first in the morning; and that she taking the same had ease of her lameness.

The patient refused, however, to pay Kempe's fee of 12 pence, upon which her condition worsened.

At this juncture, Grace Thorlowe decided to make a complaint to the authorities and it was agreed that the matter should be presented to the county sessions. At Ursula Kempe's ensuing trial Darcy persuaded the defendant's illegitimate eight-year-old son Thomas Rabbet to elaborate upon his mother's activities as a witch, and then offered the unfortunate woman the chance of clemency if she would admit her guilt. Mother Kempe seized the opportunity and, 'bursting out weeping', confirmed her son's account of her practices.

According to her own testimony, Ursula Kempe had kept four FAMILIARS, which manifested as two male CATS (a grey one called Titty and a black one called Jack), a TOAD named Pigin and a white lamb she knew as Tyffin (in defiance of the tradition that familiar spirits were unable to manifest as lambs). These imps she fed on white bread or cake and beer as well as drops of her own BLOOD, which they sucked from her body at night. The black cat called Jack had caused the death of Kempe's sister-in-law, while the lamb had rocked the infant Thorlowe from her crib. The accused woman then threw herself on the court's mercy, completing her confession by identifying a number of other St Osyth women as witches like herself. It should be noted that at no point did Kempe or anyone else suggest that these women had acted in confederation as an organised COVEN; Kempe knew of her neighbours' activities only by spying through windows and allegedly learning their secrets from her lamb familiar.

When these women – Elizabeth Bennet, Alice Newman, Alice Hunt and her sister Margery Sammon – were brought before Darcy they followed Kempe's example, not only giving full accounts of their familiars but also repeating the allegations against each other and naming yet more accomplices. Alice Hunt confirmed that her own sister was a witch and then implicated one Joan Pechey, while Margery Sammon returned the compliment against her sister and also named Pechey; Alice Newman, meanwhile, gave details of Bennet's guilt. Also implicated were Agnes Glascock and Cicely Celles, both accused of bewitching to death; Joan Turner, charged with employing the EVIL EYE; Elizabeth Ewstace, who had caused harm to a neighbour's animals; Annis Herd (or Heard); and Alice Manfield and Margaret Grevell, who were both indicted on relatively minor charges.

By the time the accusations had died down fourteen women – mostly of deprived and disreputable backgrounds – stood in the dock. The charges against them ranged from damage to property and livestock to the bewitching to death of some twenty-four persons. Less serious complaints against them included accusations that they had prevented beer from brewing, butter from churning and carts from moving. Virtually all were suspected of having kept familiars.

When the sensational proceedings of the court finally came to an end two (including Margery Sammon) were not indicted, two were discharged but held in prison suspected of various felonies, four were acquitted, four (including Alice Newman, who was accused of murdering her husband and four others) were convicted but reprieved and two (Mother Kempe and Elizabeth Bennet) were sentenced to hang.

Bennet – who confessed to owning two familiars, a DOG-like creature called Suckin and a creature like a lion, called Lierd – was executed for killing a farmer named William Byet and his wife and two others (she was alleged to have murdered Byet after he refused to sell her milk and called her an 'old trot, old whore, and other lewd speeches'). Despite the court's guarantees, Kempe herself went to the gallows after confessing to causing three deaths by witchcraft between 1580 and 1582.

Among the luckier ones who were acquitted of witchcraft was Annis Herd, who was charged with causing the death of the wife of a parson called Richard Harrison. As in several of the other cases the trouble stemmed from a trivial falling out, in this instance over some missing ducklings that Annis Herd was rumoured to have stolen. Harrison's wife, evidently a highly strung character, railed against the suspected thief and subsequently decided that the original crime had been compounded by a spell cast upon herself. The parson's wife went into a gradual physical decline and, despite her husband threatening to break every bone in Annis Herd's body if she did not lift her spell, eventually she died. On her deathbed the dying woman made it perfectly clear whom she blamed for her condition, lamenting as she died, 'Oh, Annis Herd, Annis Herd, she hath consumed me.'

Coming between the infamous trial of the CHELMSFORD WITCHES in 1566 and that of the WARBOYS WITCHES in 1593, the St Osyth trial marked a significant stage in the development of the witch-hunting mania that gripped eastern England for many years. The acceptance of some very dubious testimony, in particular that of several children well below the age at which statements were legally admissible, set an ominous precedent for many future trials (including that of the SALEM WITCHES a hundred years later). Wallace Notestein, in his *History of Witchcraft in England from 1558 to 1718* (1911), commented that: 'The use of evidence in this trial would lead one to suppose that in England no rules of evidence were yet in existence. The testimony of children ranging in age from six to nine was eagerly received ... nothing was excluded.'

The shadow cast over St Osyth by the trial persisted for many years, and more alleged witches from the village were among the victims of the witch-hunts presided over by Matthew HOPKINS in the 1640s. Another noteworthy by-product of the trial was the publication of Reginald Scot's *Discoverie of Witchcraft* in 1584, which did much to counter the spread of the witchcraft hysteria in England by exposing the flaws in such belief.

In 1921 a plough furrow exposed two female skeletons at St Osyth. The skeletons, which had been pierced at the knees and elbows with iron rivets in an apparent attempt to prevent the dead from rising, were tentatively identified as those of Ursula Kempe and Elizabeth Bennet (though they may have been two of the witches killed during the Hopkins era). They are now preserved in a museum in Cornwall.

St Thomas, Feast of *see* SABBAT.

Salazar y Frias, Alonzo de fl.1611. Spanish inquisitor, whose conclusions resulting from an investigation into a mass trial of BASQUE WITCHES in 1611 heralded the virtual end of the witchcraft hysteria in Spain. As a high official in the Spanish INQUISITION de Salazar had helped to compile evidence for a report by the Inquisition into a mass trial that was staged by the secular courts in Logrono, Navarre, in November 1610. The action taken by the secular authorities threatened to trespass on territory previously reserved for the Inquisition, and Salazar and two other inquisitors were despatched to look into the charges. Like the civil authorities, this tribunal – overriding Salazar's opposition – agreed that witchcraft was rife in the area in question, with some two hundred and eighty adults and children actively involved in Devil worship. It was suspected that no fewer than twenty major COVENS (or *aquelarres*) were operating in the region.

As a result of this first, rather hasty, investigation the Inquisition arranged a mass burning of the accused in an attempt to stamp out the threat of witchcraft throughout the district, but the event proved an anticlimax. King Philip III did not attend, as had been hoped, and most of the accused recanted their confessions and thus escaped the stake. In the end, just six witches were burned. In the wake of this fiasco, the local judges were arrested and the Inquisition disowned the conclusions of its own men.

In March 1611 the Edict of Grace was promulgated, allowing accused witches to escape punishment by making a full confession within a certain time. Salazar, who had opposed the original findings of the Inquisitorial tribunal, was appointed to see that the Edict was imposed in the Logrono region and began an exhaustive inquiry into the evidence that had been unearthed. Questioning no fewer than 1802 reformed witches (two-thirds of whom were children), he heard numerous recantations of confessions under the protection of the new Edict and revealed much contradictory evidence that undermined the original charges. Women who had reportedly attended SABBATS had alibis proving they were elsewhere at the time; girls who claimed that they had been seduced by DEMONS were proved to be virgins; no one could agree where alleged sabbats had taken place; magical ointments provided by the Devil were discovered to be quite harmless and ineffective.

Salazar further condemned the use of torture to obtain confessions and pointed to an almost total lack of corroborating evidence. In his lengthy report on the trial he had to conclude that 'I have not found even indications from which to infer that a single act of witchcraft has really occurred, whether as to going to *aquelarres*, being present at them, inflicting injuries, or other of the asserted facts.'

The Inquisition sided with Salazar and all further investigations into the witches of Logrono were halted. New instructions for inquisitors looking into witchcraft cases were issued in 1614, and after that date only allegations that were backed by substantial external evidence stood much chance of reaching court. Limited steps were also taken to compensate the families of those executed at Logrono in 1610.

Without Salazar's bold report, the Logrono trial could well have been widely quoted as authority for those seeking to emphasise the reality of a huge network of covens that extended throughout the Basque area and persisted through the generations. Taken at face value, the evidence presented at the trial suggested that practitioners of the black arts were organised into different ranks and had their own complex hierarchy, adding substantially to the impression that in witchcraft Christianity faced a serious and well-established threat. However, through Salazar's efforts the witchcraft mania in Spain was brought to an abrupt and virtually complete end, with only isolated cases being reported in ensuing years: there were no further executions on charges of witchcraft anywhere in Spain after 1611. Unfortunately Salazar's thoughts on the subject of witchcraft did not reach a mass European audience and it was the work of his contemporary Pierre de LANCRE, who was totally committed to the witchcraft myth, that was fated to be the more widely disseminated and read.

Salem Witches   Notorious witch-hunt that scandalised New England society at the end of the seventeenth century, culminating in many deaths and subsequently becoming enshrined as one of the most traumatic episodes in colonial American history. The trials that ensued from the events that took place at the village of Salem in rural Massachusetts in the early 1690s had a lasting effect upon the American consciousness and represented the worst outbreak of the witchcraft hysteria west of the Atlantic.

The tragedy of the Salem Witches began in 1692 when eight girls between the ages of eleven and twenty began to show symptoms of demonic POSSESSION. The girls, it seems, had been deeply impressed by their reading of sensational pamphlets on the subject of witchcraft and may have been further affected by the hair-raising tales that they heard from the local minister's black slave, a West Indian woman named Tituba. First to succumb to the hysteria were eleven-year-old Abigail Williams and her cousin Elizabeth Parris, the nine-year-old daughter of the minister, Samuel Parris. The girls threw fits, screaming and writhing on the ground as though they believed they had been turned into animals. Relatives and neighbours were stunned at the ungodly behaviour of the two girls, which included flinging the Bible across the room, interrupting church services and extravagant displays of unrestrained disobedience towards their parents. Almost at once the word 'witchcraft' was whispered among the shocked adults who witnessed or heard about what was happening.

The hysteria quickly communicated itself to other young girls in the village who started to exhibit similar symptoms, gibbering in indecipherable tongues and throwing fits. Prominent among them were seven girls mostly in their teens – eighteen-year-old Elizabeth Booth, seventeen-year-old Elizabeth Hubbard, nineteen-year-old Mercy Lewis, twelve-year-old Ann Putnam (who testified at all but one of the trials), eighteen-year-old Susan Sheldon, sixteen-year-old Mary Walcott and twenty-year-old Mary Warren. Also affected were twelve-year-old Phoebe Chandler, twenty-year-old Sarah Churchill, twenty-year-old Margaret Reddington, sixteen-year-old Martha Sprague, nineteen-year-old Sarah Trask and thirty-six-year-old Sarah Bibber. Mary Warren, servant in the household of John and Elizabeth Proctor, enjoyed a temporary but significant respite in her symptoms when John Proctor threatened to thrash her if she had any more fits, but the fits resumed once he had left the house.

Faced with this wave of hysteria in the village ministers and the local physician, Dr Griggs, who was unable to find a medical explanation for the fits, agreed that witchcraft must lie at the root of the girls' extraordinary behaviour. The girls were interrogated and asked to identify the witches responsible for their condition. Perhaps realising that in this way they could escape punishment for their highly publicised misdemeanours the girls eagerly provided the names of several women, all of whom were in one way or other obvious choices for suspicion of witchcraft. Tituba, the Parrises' slave, was named as one of the girls' tormentors, and additional evidence against her was supplied through one Mary Sibley, who had asked Tituba's husband John Indian to make a 'witch cake' (of barley water and children's urine) so that she might feed it to a dog and thus cure her ague. The others identified by the girls were Sarah Good, a beggar woman with a weakness for pipe-smoking, Sarah Osborne, a cripple who had been married three times, and Martha Cory, whose half-caste bastard son placed her outside respectable society.

The four women were given a preliminary examination in February 1692 and denied any involvement in witchcraft. The judges, however, were more impressed by the behaviour of their youthful accusers, who repeated their charges in court and for good measure claimed that they were being invisibly beaten, pinched and otherwise abused by the suspects even as they stood there before them. Sometimes they acted in concert, one of the girls throwing a fit after another girl said she could see the accused moving in her spectral form towards her, unseen by all others present. In addition to the original charges the girls made many more accusations, sometimes apparently at the prompting of Mrs Thomas Putnam, mother of Ann Putnam, until some one hundred and fifty persons of all classes and backgrounds had been implicated. Most of these accusations were of a similar kind, alleging that the person named had tormented the accuser by sending their 'appearance' to pinch, choke and otherwise abuse them.

Not all the accused came from Salem Village – some hailed from neighbouring communities, such as Salem Farms and Topsfield, with which the Salem villagers had long-standing quarrels. Ann Pudeator and Mary Parker came from Andover, further afield, and were among forty people from the town to be charged with witchcraft after being subjected to a 'touch test'. This involved suspected witches being ordered to touch Ann Putnam or Mary Walcott while they were having a fit: if the girls went quiet on being touched, the suspects were assuredly guilty. When a Mrs Cary, from Charlestown, learned that she was being accused of witchcraft she came voluntarily to Salem to join the crowd in the court – only when the children eventually learned who she was did they throw the usual fits (Mrs Cary was arrested but later released).

No one was immune to the girls' accusations. When Justice Dudley Bradstreet of Andover refused to sign any more arrest warrants he was accused of witchcraft himself and fled before he could be tried for murdering nine people. His brother John was likewise accused, his crime consisting of bewitching a dog into committing a crime – the dog was tried and hanged. When the girls were moved to Boston their victims included Captain John Alden, a local hero through his exploits in the Indian wars. The girls fell into swoons when he appeared, recovering immediately when he was made to touch them. He was thrown into Boston prison, but succeeded in escaping some four months later.

The accused did have their allies, however. Attempts were made, for instance, to discredit Sarah Bibber as a witness, with several people testifying as to her 'unruly turbulent spirit' and alleging that she was faking her injuries from invisible spirits by scratching herself with pins concealed in her clothing. John Willard, a farmer and deputy constable at Salem who had arrested the initial suspects, came to appreciate that the real villains of the piece were the eight 'witch bitches' who were the source of most of the accusations and suggested that if anyone was to hang it should be them. This outburst was bound to cause trouble and Willard fled the village, only to be captured ten days later and then charged by the girls and Mrs Putnam on seven indictments. He was hanged on 19 August 1692.

Despite these efforts, the court was inclined to accept the charges without question and those accused by the girls were seized and flung into prison to await trial. Anyone who questioned the reality of the charges was liable to be arrested on charges of witchcraft themselves.

Some of the accused were among the most respected people in the district. They included John Proctor, who resolutely refused to believe in witchcraft and thus attracted the enmity of the court; Martha Cory, who was a devout churchgoer; and the Rev. George Burroughs, who had been minister in Salem from 1680 to 1682. Burroughs, it was alleged, had presided over blasphemous parodies of the Puritan communion service, offering other witches 'red bread and red wine like blood', and had used witchcraft to murder his two wives. (His real crime had perhaps been to win the enmity of the Putnam family, with whom he had once lodged). Mercy Lewis described how the apparition of George Burroughs had promised her anything she desired if she would just sign the Devil's book of names (which the minister reportedly kept in his study), while Abigail Hobbs said that he had appeared to her in person to bring her poppets into which she could stick pins. During the trials the girls showed the judges bite marks that they claimed had been inflicted by the apparition of George Burroughs, and these were allegedly found to match the minister's teeth when his mouth was prised open and forcibly inspected. Burroughs himself flatly refused to admit the possibility of such magic, stating: 'There neither are nor ever were witches that having made a compact with the Devil can send a devil to torment other people at a distance.'

Others of the accused already had dubious reputations, as was the case with Bridget Bishop and Susanna Martin, elderly women who had long been suspected of witchcraft. Bridget Bishop had been tried for witchcraft in 1680, accused of causing the death of her first husband through magic, but had been acquitted largely on the testimony of the local minister.

As the possible consequences of the accusations became evident some of the girls showed some sign of wishing to withdraw their wild charges, but only two – the servant-girls Sarah Churchill and Mary Warren – actually admitted they had deceived the court. Sarah Churchill decided to make a clean breast of things when her master, George Jacobs, was arrested and questioned, while Mary Warren had second thoughts when John and Mary Proctor were thrown into prison and the authorities seized their property, leaving Mary to fend for the couple's five children with no food in the house. However, fearing that the court would disregard her denial, Sarah Churchill changed her mind and reaffirmed her original charges. Mary Warren, meanwhile, was threatened by the other girls, who were evidently anxious not to be exposed, and was ultimately accused of being a witch herself by Ann Putnam, Mercy Lewis, Mary Walcott and Abigail Williams. Under pressure from both the girls and the judges, she gave in and confirmed that she had signed the Devil's book and been tormented by John Proctor's apparition.

Now committed to seeing their charges through, the girls did not waver in their accusations, pursuing their quarry in court with calculated and inhuman ruthlessness. Suggestions that those who confessed to being witches would be reprieved by the court persuaded 55 of the 150 accused, including Tituba, to make full confessions. All these escaped the death penalty, although Samuel Wardwell, who confessed but later recanted, was hanged. Those who confessed were generally ignored from then on by the girls, who concentrated on providing incriminating evidence against those who still publicly resisted their allegations.

The substance of most of the confessions was very much in keeping with the conventions of witchcraft as understood in seventeenth-century New England. Mrs Foster, for instance, claimed that she had seen the Devil on a number of occasions after he had adopted the form of a bird and confirmed that she had flown on the BROOMSTICK of time-honoured legend, as recorded by her interrogators:

> She and Martha Carrier did both ride on a stick or pole when they went to the witch meeting at Salem Village, and that the stick broke as they were carried in the air above the tops of the trees, and they fell. But she did hang fast about the neck of Goody Carrier and were presently at the village, that she was then much hurt of her leg.

As well as hearing the accusations of the children, the court gathered evidence of actual MALEFICIA from adult witnesses until it had substantial supporting cases against many of the accused. Bridget Bishop, already suspected of witchcraft by many of her neighbours, was summarily disposed of and was among the first to be hanged. The invalid seventy-one-year-old Rebecca Nurse, meanwhile, was suspected of having used witchcraft to procure the death of Benjamin Holton after an argument resulting from the Holtons' pigs getting into her field – although, as in other cases, it was impossible to prove any real link between the argument and Holton's subsequent death after suffering violent fits and pains.

The girls went out of their way to confirm the guilt of the persons whom they accused. Whenever a suspected witch was brought into their presence they threw fits and complained that they were being tormented by the suspect's invisible self. These convulsions were readily accepted as corroborating evidence by the judges, who showed themselves to be very easily manipulated by Ann Putnam and her cronies and to have no compunction about accepting such bizarre SPECTRAL EVIDENCE. Because of the unique nature of the crimes that were being alleged, the judges seemed to think themselves released from the usual legal restrictions. If persons were accused of witchcraft, they were deemed almost certain to be guilty; if they sent their spectral selves to torment others, they must have made a PACT WITH THE DEVIL. In their determination to secure guilty verdicts the judges heard testimony from children as young as seven, denied lawyers to the accused and framed questions so that the answer was liable to tell against the defendant. When the jury acquitted Rebecca Nurse they ignored all legal requirements and simply overruled the finding. As a result she was hanged alongside Sarah Good, Susanna Martin and three more on 19 July 1692.

Thirty-one of the accused were sentenced to death and nineteen people were actually hanged: Bridget Bishop, George Burroughs (who was also defrocked as a member of the clergy), Martha Carrier, Martha Cory, Mary Esty, Sarah Good, Elizabeth How, George Jacobs, Susanna Martin, Rebecca Nurse, Alice Parker, Mary Parker, John Proctor, Ann Pudeator, Wilmot Reed, Margaret Scott, Samuel Wardwell, Sarah Wilds and John Willard. Also convicted were Mary Bradbury, who managed to escape, and Sarah Cloyce, Rebecca Eames, Dorcas Hoar, Abigail Hobbs and Mary Lacy, who all secured reprieves. Abigail Faulkner and Elizabeth Proctor were found guilty but were spared when it was discovered that they were both pregnant and were eventually reprieved. Ann Foster and Sarah Osborne died in prison, while Giles Cory was pressed to death. Tituba, the black slave who was one of the first suspects arrested, was sentenced to an indefinite term in prison rather than execution because she had made a full voluntary confession right at the start. Ultimately she was taken from the Parris household and subsequently sold in order to help meet the costs of the proceedings. Those who were released were faced with the further indignities of having to pay fees for their reprieves and to reimburse the gaolers for their maintenance while behind bars.

When the Reverend George Burroughs recited the LORD'S PRAYER faultlessly at his execution there was considerable consternation among the large crowd assembled to see him die, for a witch was deemed to be incapable of saying the prayer without making some mistake. Only the insistence of Cotton MATHER, who attended the execution, persuaded the crowd that Burroughs really was a witch and should be hanged as ordered by the court. The sentence was accordingly carried out and the former minister's body was buried on Salem's Gallows Hill.

The death of eighty-year-old Giles Cory was among the most outrageous atrocities that occurred during the Salem panic. Because he refused to plead to the indictment, which meant that his trial could not begin, he was forced to lie naked and unfed in a field next to Salem gaol and, over a period of two days, to have heavy weights piled on his chest until he changed his mind. The old man, apparently aware that his case was hopeless, still declined to cooperate and died when the weight became too much. He thus goes down in history as probably the only person pressed to death in American history – it was, indeed, illegal under the terms of an Act of 1641 that forbade all 'inhumane, barbarous, or cruel' punishments. Robert Calef, a Boston merchant who recorded the incident, reported how 'in pressing, his tongue being pressed out of his mouth, the sheriff with his cane forced it in again'. When, the next day, the court showed signs of concern at the way Cory had been put to death, Ann Putnam's father sought to strengthen their resolve by explaining how the previous night his daughter had been troubled by witches and by the apparition of a man whom Cory had beaten to death some sixteen years before. The ghost claimed that Cory had pressed him to death with his feet and added: 'It must be done to him as he had done to me.'

The outcome of the Salem witch trials provoked great controversy in New England society. The readiness of the court to accept the extraordinary accusations of young girls, and the enthusiasm with which the unlikeliest spectral evidence was approved, worried many observers. Even prominent Puritan leaders such as Increase Mather voiced doubts about such evidence. Mather declared to his congregation that 'it were better that ten suspected witches should escape than that one honest person should be condemned ... I had rather judge a witch to be an honest woman, than judge an honest woman as a witch.'

A respected and influential Bostonian, Thomas Brattle, published a letter in which he made a number of serious criticisms of the way in which the trials had been conducted: he questioned the reliability of witnesses allegedly under Satanic influence and blamed the judges for their unsatisfactory and self-contradictory attitude to the case. Cotton Mather and his witch-hunting associates responded by publishing in 1693 *The Wonders of the Invisible World*, which purported to defend the judges in the Salem trials and demonstrated the authors' blind acceptance of witchcraft as a reality. This text in turn provoked a counter-publication by Robert Calef under the title *More Wonders of the Invisible World* (1700), which once again made scathing comments about the original trials. Mather's camp replied in 1701 with *Some Few Remarks upon a Scandalous Book* and Calef was run out of Boston – but by then the debate had been long overtaken by events.

The speed with which the hysteria in Salem had swept the colony was matched only by the haste with which the local population changed its collective mind about such action. The acceptance of spectral evidence, which had been so crucial in the Salem trials of 1692, was officially discredited early in 1693 and of the remaining fifty-two suspects awaiting trial only three were sentenced to death, alongside five others condemned the previous year (among them Elizabeth Proctor). In answer to the growing public unease and in response to his own wife being accused Sir William Phips, Governor of New England, overruled the court and granted reprieves for all eight. The groundswell of public opinion against the prosecutions effectively precluded any further action against alleged witches in the region, and after the Salem case there were no more executions of convicted witches anywhere in America.

In 1696, by which time the hysteria was well nigh past, the jurors in the original cases made a public 'Confession of Error'. As well as begging the forgiveness of surviving relatives, they admitted that they had allowed themselves to be deceived by the accusations they had heard:

> We confess that we ourselves were not capable to understand, nor able to withstand, the mysterious delusions of the Powers of

Darkness and Prince of the Air; but were, for want of knowledge in ourselves and better information from others, prevailed with to take up such evidence against the accused, as on further consideration and better information we justly fear was insufficient for the touching the lives of any.

As a gesture of remorse for what had happened, a day of fasting was observed throughout the colony on 15 January 1697. Those who had argued strongly in favour of the original prosecutions, like Cotton Mather, now found themselves marginalised as the mass of people questioned whether there had been any witchcraft in the first place. The admission of spectral evidence was subsequently outlawed, and over the ensuing years the record was adjusted to clear those convicted of guilt. Many relatives and descendants of those executed were granted (albeit meagre) financial compensation in 1711. The last attainders relating to the convicted witches were reversed in 1957.

The girls whose accusations had led directly to the deaths of so many of their neighbours were left unpunished by the courts. It seems that they showed few signs of repentance in later life, and only one of them, Ann Putnam, ever ventured to make something resembling a confession. A full fourteen years after the trials she read her 'confession' in Salem church. Although declining to deny that witchcraft had been at work in the community, she humbly recognised that she had been deluded by Satan:

... it was a great delusion of Satan that deceived me in that sad time, whereby I justly fear I have been instrumental, with others, though ignorantly and unwittingly, to bring upon myself and this land the guilt of innocent blood; though what was said or done by me against any person I can truly and uprightly say before God and man, I did it not out of any anger, malice, or ill-will to any person, for I had no such thing against one of them, but what I did was ignorantly, being deluded of Satan.

Authorities who have examined the case of the Salem hysteria have identified a number of possible contributing factors. These included the restless political climate of the early 1690s, a time when the American colonists were feeling increasingly aggrieved at the high level of taxes imposed by their government and when the possibility of greater independence from Britain was being cautiously discussed. The local magistrates, moreover, had recently won a power struggle against regional authority and were only too willing to latch on to accusations of witchcraft as a means of asserting their expanded role. Further tension was created by the war with the French and by the hostile campaigns being waged by the Indians. The winter of 1691 was particularly harsh and, with the added factors of a smallpox epidemic and raids by pirates to deal with, it seems likely that the entire population was only too ready to accept witches as convenient scapegoats on whom to blame their many troubles. By 1691 there had already been several lesser witchcraft scares in the region, notably that arising from the case of the GOODWIN CHILDREN in 1688 (with which the Salem girls were doubtlessly familiar), and the time was ripe for a full-blown outbreak of witch hysteria. In New England, which was governed on strict Puritan principles, few people doubted the existence of the supernatural and it was relatively easy to persuade congregations throughout the region that Satan and his cohorts were active in their midst with the express aim of bringing down the government itself.

Such was the notoriety that attached to Salem following the trials and the subsequent investigations into the affair that the name of Salem still conjures up images of the witchcraft hysteria three hundred years later. The Salem scandal refuses to be forgotten and continues to inspire discussion and analysis (most famously in Arthur Miller's 1953 play *The Crucible*, which drew parallels with McCarthyism).

See also SHORT, MERCY.

Salmesbury Witches Three English countrywomen who were arrested and tried for witchcraft at Lancaster in 1612 on charges brought by a young girl. Fourteen-year-old Grace Sowerbutts used allegations of witchcraft to vent her malice against her grandmother, her aunt and a third woman named Jane Southworth.

According to the girl, the three women were adept at transforming themselves into BLACK DOGS, using an ointment that incorporated as an essential ingredient the bones of the child of Thomas Walshman, which they had murdered. She further accused the three of feasting on the child's flesh and claimed that she had been invited to join in the feast, but had refused and gone instead to the authorities.

The case was heard at the same Assizes that heard the evidence against the PENDLE WITCHES, but in this instance the jury were unconvinced and the charges were dismissed. Grace Sowerbutts broke down and admitted she had been put up to making the charges by a Roman Catholic priest. It transpired that the accusations had arisen out of a family feud that had resulted from the three accused adopting the Protestant faith.

salt According to time-honoured superstition, salt had considerable potency as a defence against witches and evil spirits and was loathed by them because of its association with holiness. Vital to the maintenance of life and, in the eyes of former generations, apparently magical in its properties of food preservation and evaporation, salt was of great value in classical times. In some cultures it was used in sacrifices to the gods, to ratify important agreements and to solemnify other social transactions.

Salt had particular relevance in Christian mythology: Lot's wife, for example, was turned into a pillar of salt when she looked back at the evil city of Sodom and salt was used in such crucial religious ceremonies as baptism and EXORCISM.

If salt was spilled this was considered almost blasphemous and likely to attract the attention of demons. Tossing a pinch of the spilled salt over the left shoulder, however, was reputed to drive away the Devil if he materialised in order to whisper evil into a person's ear. Such was the Devil's detestation of salt and its protective properties that meals served at witches' SABBATS were widely believed to be prepared totally without it. The story was often told of the guest at a sabbat feast who asked for the salt to be passed to him, only to find that the entire company and the meal itself vanished instantly upon his words. Similarly, salt was never included as an ingredient in spells to raise demons or devils.

Because salt was supposed to deter evil spirits and to forestall corruption, it had various uses in circumstances in which a person was held to be vulnerable to evil influences. Bathing newborn children in salty water or giving them a little salt, for instance, was recommended as a sure way to protect them from witchcraft, and women in labour were sometimes given salt to hold in their palm as this was said to be of great benefit at a time when their strength was weakened. If the malevolent influence of a witch was actually thought to be at work one solution was to toss a handful of salt into the fire nine mornings in succession so that any spell would be broken. Similarly, dairymaids sometimes sprinkled a pinch of salt into their pails and into the butter churns to prevent interference by witches. To establish that a particular suspect was a witch, American 'witch-masters' advised placing some salt beneath the person's chair: if the person was indeed a witch, the salt would melt.

Should a witch utter a curse against a person who had angered them one defence was to hurl after them a handful of salt, which would negate the effects of any ill-wishing. If someone died, when they were laid out a saucer of salt mixed with some soil might be placed on their chest so as to keep them secure from evil spirits attracted by the presence of death.

Sampson, Agnes *see* NORTH BERWICK WITCHES.

Samuel, Alice, John and Agnes *see* WARBOYS WITCHES.

Sanders, Alex *see* WICCA.

Sandwich, John Montagu, Fourth Earl of *see* HELL-FIRE CLUB.

Satan One of the personal names by which the DEVIL was identified in the mythology of witchcraft and during the prosecution of witch trials. In Hebrew the name 'Satan' originally simply meant 'adversary'. The biblical Satan was identical with LUCIFER as ruler of the underworld and arch-enemy of the Christian God. According to some demonologists he was allowed to exercise his evil powers on licence from God, who sought in this way to test mankind, but others depicted him as a rival to God with his own native power. In 1589 the demonologist Peter BINSFELD was more specific, assigning to Satan the role of demon of anger.

See also SATANISM.

Satanic mass *see* BLACK MASS.

Satanism The worship of SATAN, the Lord of the Underworld and the personification of evil, in God's place. Witchcraft necessarily implied allegiance to and service of the DEVIL, and for this alone many suspects were put to death, although the degree to which this 'religious' aspect was emphasised varied a good deal. Where the common law was strong, evidence of actual MALEFICIA was some-times also demanded – but the PACT WITH THE DEVIL was always an important factor.

The term 'Satanism' was not heard until the late nineteenth and early twentieth centuries, when various occultists attempted to build into ancient notions of black magic a more consciously reli-gious element, with its own intellectual foundation and justification, as befitted a sophisticated 'modern' cult allegedly descended from paganism. Before the nineteenth century the essence of Devil-worship was simply that it was anti-Christian. This basic premise was elaborated by the theorists so that Satanism evolved as something more than a straightforward negation of Christian principles and as a religion in its own right, with every effort being taken to reverse normal conventional values. The concept of LUCIFER as 'Lord of Light' was developed so that he became a genuinely divine figure, representing the 'virtues' of pride, dominance, passion, pleasure and unfettered enjoyment of sex, power, money and other earthly pastimes. The Seven Deadly Sins and perversion became worthy ambitions, while chastity was loathed as an indefensible denial of self.

Practising Satanists, who included the likes of Aleister CROWLEY, pointed to the biblical passage in which Christ named the Devil rather than God as his father (John, chapter 8, verse 44) and similarly quoted the Bible as support for their contention that the Devil was 'prince of this world' (John, chapter 12, verse 31) and 'god of this world' (2 Corinthians, chapter 4, verse 4). Parallels were also drawn between modern Satanism and ancient Gnostic sects, which rejected God on the grounds that because He had made the world, and the world was palpably evil, it followed that God was evil too. God, for instance, had denied Adam and Eve true knowledge of the world, and it was only through the intervention of the sympathetic serpent that their eyes had been opened to the real nature of their surroundings. It followed from this that all God's laws were evil, including the Ten Commandments, and that the right course was either to practise complete self-denial and so escape pollution by God's wicked world or to act more positively in rejecting His moral rules.

The Cathars and other heretical sects such as the Luciferans, Waldensians and KNIGHTS TEMPLAR adopted varying standpoints on the goodness or otherwise of the Christian God, and were consequently widely persecuted (*see* HERESY). During the witchcraft hysteria of the fourteenth to seventeenth centuries Satanic belief surfaced in various ways, through descriptions of alleged sabbats and so forth, but there was little attempt to formalise such thinking except by the demonologists of the Christian Establishment. It was noticeable, however, that the offences of which the earlier heretics had been guilty were trotted out time and time again against this new breed of witches. Like their predecessors they were routinely accused of desecrating the host, renouncing Christ, worshipping the Devil in the form of an animal, honouring their master with the obscene KISS and indulging in cannibalism, murder, sexual promiscuity and other crimes.

In the spirit of rebellion against conventional bourgeois values that swept western Europe in the early twentieth century, Satanism re-emerged as a new opportunity for those such as Crowley who sought to extol the virtues of individualism and self, freed of the shackles of the established Church. To promulgate this newly redefined 'religion' in the twentieth century, numerous Satanic 'churches' were set up throughout the Western world. The most famous of them included Anton La Vey's Church of Satan in San Francisco, which was founded in 1966 and attracted such notable members as film star Jayne Mansfield. Occasional desecrations of churches and graveyards in recent years testify to the continuing hold of the Satanic ideal on the anti-Christian mind.

According to the tenets of Satanism, Satan will eventually overthrow the Christian God and take his rightful place as ruler of the universe. Under his rule, human beings will be free to dedicate themselves to the pursuit of power and worldly pleasures – hence Crowley's infamous dictum for the use of his disciples:

> There is no Grace, there is no Guilt,
> This is the Law, Do What Thou Wilt.

See also BLACK MASS.

Scandinavia *see* FINLAND; NORWAY; SWEDEN.

Schüler, Johann fl.1663. German miller who was arrested and tortured with his wife as a suspected witch in one of the most appalling cases in the whole history of the witchcraft hysteria in GERMANY. Schüler was a rich and respected citizen of the town of Lindheim in Hesse-Darmstadt, which was effectively under the control of a ruthless former soldier-turned-magistrate named Geiss. This man cynically realised that witch-hunting could produce great profits through the confiscation of property belonging to convicted witches, and accordingly set about stirring up local fears of supernatural interference.

Having appointed four vicious local thugs as his assistants, Geiss began a systematic campaign to have as many suspects as possible arrested, tried and executed. The whole procedure was pushed through as quickly as possible and with terrible cruelty. Many of the victims, who included young children, were manacled some fifteen feet above the floor of Lindheim's Witches' Tower and slowly roasted over a fire.

Geiss's campaign continued its dreadful progress through a confession that he extracted from a local midwife. Frau Schüler had given birth to a stillborn child the previous year, and Geiss tortured the midwife into admitting that the baby had been killed by witchcraft in collaboration with six other people. The six suspects were duly arrested and tortured until they admitted cutting the baby's corpse into small pieces and using these to make a magic ointment. The Schülers countered by having the grave of their child opened, and the body was found to be whole. Geiss, however, suppressed this revelation and had the midwife and her six confederates burned to death, threatening Schüler with torture if he said anything.

Geiss now turned his attention to an old woman by the name of Becker-Margareth, who had been implicated as a witch. In return for being excused torture and allowed Christian burial after her execution, the prisoner provided the magistrate with a detailed confession in which she made allegations against Frau Schüler and another thirteen people. Geiss was known to have designs on the Schülers' property and Frau Schüler was arrested. An old scar was subsequently identified as the DEVIL'S MARK and her fate was sealed. Johann Schüler managed to escape to Würzburg and there petitioned the authorities to intervene to save his wife. In the meantime, Frau Schüler was tortured into making a confession.

When Johann Schüler returned to Lindheim he was thrown into prison and tortured with the utmost savagery into making a full confession. When he recanted, which he did twice, he was returned to the torture chamber. News of the abuses leaked out, however, and the outraged townsfolk started to riot, allowing Schüler and others the opportunity to escape. When the prisoners showed their injuries to the Imperial Supreme Court in Speyer there was widespread indignation. Back in Lindheim, however, Geiss defied the anger of the mob and on 23 February 1664 he burned Frau Schüler alive.

Geiss, who had amassed a fortune from his work, was dismissed from his post shortly afterwards on the insistence of the Supreme Court, although no further action against him was taken (perhaps because some of the proceeds of his activities had been passed to his superiors). In all, he had accounted for the lives of some thirty innocent persons.

Schultheis, Heinrich von fl.1630s. German witch judge and demonologist, who argued firmly for the extermination of all accused witches. As secretary to a succession of witch-hunting bishops in the Rhineland, Schultheis applied his detailed knowledge of the law towards the persecution of witches in what was the bloodiest period of the witch hysteria in GERMANY. He justified his standpoint in a notorious book of 1634 entitled *Detailed Instructions How to Proceed in the Inquisition against the Horrible Vice of Witchcraft*, which was described centuries later as 'the most gruesome in all the gruesome literature of witch persecution'.

In his book Schultheis sanctioned the severest measures against suspected witches, including TORTURE and the abandonment of the usual legal safeguards. Evidence that was deemed unacceptable in other trials should, he argued, be admitted in the trials of witches in view of the seriousness of the alleged offences. If evidence presented to the court was self-contradictory or incredible, that was no reason to dismiss it: the Devil was cunning and tried by these means to confuse God's lawyers and witch-hunters. God himself would not object to the torturing of witches, he declared:

> With the same, in fact with even greater indifference do I regard torturing you than I do bending this reed out of my path with my stick; for by so doing I earn nothing. But when I have you tortured, and by the severe means afforded by the law I bring you to confession, then I perform a work pleasing in God's sight; and it profiteth me.

He reserved particular venom for those who opposed his strict views on witchcraft, warning ominously: 'He who opposes the extermination of the witches with one single word can not expect to remain unscathed.'

Schwägel, Anna Maria d.1775. Bavarian servant-girl who became the last person to be officially executed as a witch in the whole of

GERMANY. Her tragedy began when, in her thirties, she was proposed to by a coachman on condition that she renounce her Catholicism in favour of the Lutheran faith. Accordingly she renounced her faith, but was then seduced and abandoned by the coachman. Deeply affected by this betrayal, she sought solace through consultation with an Augustinian friar – only to find that he too had turned to the Protestant faith. Finally, half mad from despair, she was incarcerated in an asylum at Laneggen, near Kempten, where she was subjected to savage beatings and merciless interrogation by the unhinged matron, Anna Maria Kuhstaller.

Under pressure from Kuhstaller, Schwägel confessed that the coachman must have been the DEVIL himself, upon which she was arrested by the authorities and imprisoned. Although torture was not applied, Schwägel, demented and defenceless against her interrogators, confirmed in court that she had signed a PACT WITH THE DEVIL and had had intercourse with him. She was beheaded as a witch at Kempten on 11 April 1775.

scissors Being made of metal (long considered a magical material) and possessing the power to cut, scissors were once thought to offer some PROTECTION AGAINST WITCHCRAFT and other evils. It was once quite common for householders in rural areas to conceal a pair of scissors under the doormat or under the threshold of their homes, for tradition advised that no witch would be able to get past them into the house. The scissors were usually left open, so that the blades formed the shape of a cross.

scoring above the breath Ancient belief that causing witches to bleed anywhere above the mouth and nose would break any spell that might have been cast by them. The theory, largely confined to England, was that at the sight of the witch's blood the FAMILIAR that was causing someone distress would instantly return to its master or mistress in order to feed on it. Although it was by no means a legal test of witchcraft, there remain scores of reports of suspected witches being attacked by their neighbours or friends of their alleged victims in this way, often with the approval of the local community and sometimes also that of Church and State officials. The same procedure was also used against werewolves.

The practice had a long history. By the end of the sixteenth century it was already established as a time-honoured method of countering witchcraft. In 1599, for instance, Thomas Darling, the so-called BURTON BOY, scratched the face of the alleged witch Alice Gooderidge in a public attempt to destroy her supposed hold over him. The woman surrendered herself to the ordeal with good grace, evidently realising the danger she faced if she did not cooperate and telling the boy: 'Take blood enough, child. God help thee.' Darling retorted with the words: 'Pray for thyself, thy prayer can do me no good.'

Faith in the efficacy of scoring above the breath lasted well into the eighteenth century and, in some areas, beyond. In 1717 Jane Clarke and her son and daughter, accused of witchcraft by neighbours in Great Wigston near Leicester, were subjected to the ancient ordeals of SWIMMING and having their faces scratched until the blood ran (the case, however, was thrown out before it came to court). According to the official record: 'The old woman's skin was so tough that they could get no blood of her by scratching, so they used great pins and such instruments for that purpose.' Over a hundred years later, in 1823, Anne Burges, from Wiveliscombe in Somerset, was assaulted by one Elizabeth Bryant and her two daughters, who used an iron nail to scratch Burges's arm very badly, claiming that she was a witch. None of the crowd of locals who witnessed the attack made any attempt to intervene until one of the accused witch's friends came to her aid. Elizabeth Bryant and her daughters were subsequently tried in Taunton and were imprisoned for four months.

Isolated reports of alleged witches being scored above the breath continued to surface right up to the end of the nineteenth century, although the risk of punishment at the hands of the local justices meant that there were few further instances of such action actually being taken. As late as 1924 *The Times* reported that a smallholder had attempted to shoot a local woman whom he suspected of having bewitched his pigs, after first failing to scratch her with a pin.

See also IZZARD, ANNE; MORGAN, NANNY; NEWBURY WITCH.

Scot, Reginald 1538–99. English author whose celebrated *Discoverie of Witchcraft*, published in 1584, attempted to expose the absurdities of the witchcraft hysteria then threatening to engulf Europe. To Scot, a Kentish squire who had attended Oxford University, the mythology of the SABBAT and FLYING OINTMENTS and so forth was palpable nonsense, invented by the INQUISITION:

> And because it may appear unto the world what treacherous and faithless dealing, what extreme and intolerable tyranny, what gross and fond absurdities, what unnatural and uncivil discourtesy, what cankered and spiteful malice, what outrageous and barbarous cruelty ... what abominable and devilish inventions, and what flat and plain knavery is practised against these old women, I will set down the whole order of the Inquisition, to the everlasting, inexcusable and apparent shame of all witch mongers.

Scot admitted the possibility of supernatural phenomena and the existence of evil spirits, but claimed that many common beliefs about them were the product of either delusion or people's imagination. When it came to claims of flying, witches were probably deluded by the drugged ointments and potions they used. He found the suggestion that witches might kill their enemies by poisoning them plausible (concluding that women were 'more naturally addicted thereunto than men'), but he refuted the notion that they might also employ overtly magical means to the same ends. He allowed that certain stones and magical objects might cure disease, but claimed that many feats of witchcraft were achieved through fraud or juggling tricks.

Scot's highly sceptical book, possibly inspired by the trial of the ST OSYTH WITCHES in 1582, had a profound influence and was later hailed as the most important English publication attacking the witchcraft delusion, but in its time it also encountered fierce opposition. Among the most significant of its opponents was JAMES I, who was outraged by Scot's book and had all copies that could be traced burned by the hangman. In response the King wrote his own *Daemonologie* of 1597, which supported the witch-hunts and became a major authority for those seeking to prosecute alleged witches throughout the British Isles.

It is thought that William Shakespeare consulted Scot's book when he needed information about witchcraft for his play *Macbeth* (as did Thomas Middleton for his play *The Witch*).

Scotland The history of witchcraft in Scotland was unequalled by all European countries exempt GERMANY for the savagery with which suspects were tortured and put to death. Although Scottish witches were never examined by the INQUISITION, the Presbyterian Church took a leading role in the persecution of witches throughout the country. Once charged, there was little chance that a suspect would be acquitted because of the way the secular courts, often in collusion with the Church, were biased against them.

Belief in the power of witchcraft was common to all classes, right up to the royal court. Witches were rumoured to consort with the FAIRIES (or rather goblins, brownies, spunkies, kelpies and moulachs), long feared for their malevolent supernatural skills, and passed their knowledge of magic down through the generations. As time passed, accusations of PACTS WITH THE DEVIL became standard, SATAN himself being known by such names as Auld Clootie, Auld Chiel, Auld Harry, Auld Sandy, Plotcock, the Earl of Hell, the Big Brindled One and (in Gaelic) *Muc Mhor Dhubh* (the Big Black Pig).

As in England the archetypal witch was an unkempt old woman, often living apart from the rest of society and loathed for her repellent ways, her vicious temper and her reputation for evil-doing. She might keep one or more FAMILIARS in the form of domestic animals and could be readily identified by PRICKING for the DEVIL'S MARK that all witches were said to carry. Typical MALEFICIA associated with the Scottish witch ranged from spoiling milk and bewitching cows to sinking ships and committing murder by witchcraft. Allegations that suspects could turn themselves into hares and other animals were commonplace (*see* SHAPE-SHIFTING). According to superstition, the most important dates in the Scottish witch's calendar were CANDLEMAS (1 February), the Spring Equinox (20 March), May Eve (30 April), the Summer Solstice (21 June),

Lammas Day (31 August), the Autumn Equinox (20 September), HALLOWE'EN (31 October) and the Winter Solstice (20 December).

In fact the witchcraft hysteria was relatively slow to develop north of the border. Before the Reformation there were only a few trials and not one single case of a witch being burned at the stake (although as far back as AD 860 Kenneth II had prescribed the death penalty for all who were found guilty of invoking spirits). A high percentage of the victims were of good birth, suggesting that other motives, such as jealousy or financial gain, lay behind the accusations.

One noble who fell foul of accusations of witchcraft in these early years was the notorious William De Soulis, Lord of Liddesdale, who was reputed to have been a pupil of the wizard Michael SCOTT and who worked his magic at Hermitage Castle, Roxburghshire, in the early fourteenth century. Because of the evil he had perpetrated through witchcraft, legend has it that he was boiled to death in a cauldron of molten lead (in fact he was sentenced to perpetual imprisonment in Dumbarton Castle). Other cases appear to have been born chiefly out of political considerations, with allegations of murder by witchcraft being levelled at suspected traitors (as happened in 1479 when the Earl of Mar was charged with plotting the death of his brother, James III). Another noble to perish at the stake was Janet Douglas, Lady Glamis, who was burned on Castlehill, Edinburgh, in 1537 on charges of using charms against James V.

The climate changed significantly when Mary Queen of Scots ascended the throne and introduced sterner anti-witchcraft legislation in 1563. The number of trials and burnings crept up, the accused in these early cases typically being found guilty of dealing in magic with the fairies of Elfame (fairyland), rather than being convicted of pacts with the Devil or on the basis of SPECTRAL EVIDENCE as elsewhere in Europe. By the 1580s, however, the pact was a significant factor and the basis of many charges – in line with what the writer George GIFFORD suggested in 1587 in his *Discourse of the Subtle Practices of Devils by Witchcraft*: 'A witch by the word of God ought to die the death not because she killeth man – for that she cannot, unless it be those witches which kill by poison, which either they receive from the Devil, or he teacheth them to make – but because she dealeth with devils.'

Among the most widely reported trials of this first period were those of Bessie Dunlop of Lyne, Ayrshire, who was burned in 1576 for being a member of a COVEN (the first recorded mention of covens in Scotland) and for having contact with the fairies, and of Allison Peirson of Byre Hills, Fifeshire, who was sent to the stake in 1588 on much the same charges.

The trial of the NORTH BERWICK WITCHES in 1590, presided over by the superstitious James VI (later JAMES I of England), signalled the real start of the witchcraft hysteria in Scotland. The King's *Daemonologie* of 1597 widely disseminated his views on witchcraft and added royal authority to the witch-hunts that then burgeoned – even though James subsequently appears to have moderated his thoughts on the subject. His writings, influenced as they were by his contact with intellectuals on the Continent, provided a model for witchcraft trials over the ensuing century and brought Scottish thinking on the topic into line with the harsh suppression of such activity elsewhere in Europe.

The first major outbreak of the witchcraft panic in Scotland lasted until 1597 (the year of the trial of the ABERDEEN WITCHES) and there were further outbreaks in 1640–4 and 1660–3, all inspired by renewed calls from the Presbyterian Church for witches to be hunted down and destroyed. Suspects were generally hauled before special commissions set up by the Privy Council, each comprising eight of the local gentry. If a case was thought to be serious enough the prisoner was taken before an Assize, with a jury of fifteen men from the locality and one of the commissioners as judge. Charges were often brought to the court by Presbyterian ministers, who enjoyed enormous power in their parishes through the laymen who were appointed by them to seek out suspects in their congregations. Many churches had a 'kist' (chest) into which informants could slip written accusations against their neighbours. In other instances charges arose from the activities of professional witch-hunters or 'prickers', the most feared of whom included John Balfour of Corhouse, John Dick and John Kinaird of Tranent.

Accused witches were, contrary to the practice in other countries, allowed their own lawyer if they could afford one. If convicted, prisoners had to reimburse the courts for the costs of their torture, trial and execution. If they had no money or assets, the costs were borne by the town council and the church sessions.

The Scottish courts laid less emphasis upon obtaining confessions than was usual in Germany and elsewhere, and often considered a reputation for witchcraft hard evidence of guilt. None the less the use of barbaric torture was extensive, with prisoners undergoing a wide range of abuses from solitary confinement and sleep deprivation (*see* WATCHING AND WAKING) to flogging, 'thrawing' (jerking the head violently with ropes), pressing and the application of the THUMBSCREWS (known locally as the 'pilliwinks') and the BOOTS or the so-called 'caspie claws' (vices that crushed the arms). One torture peculiar to Scotland involved putting a hair shirt soaked in vinegar on the prisoner, so that the skin was pulled off. Prisoners might also be hanged by the thumbs, branded or savagely whipped. Condemned witches were generally burned to death.

The most celebrated Scottish witch of them all – leaving aside the 'Three Weird Sisters' of Shakespeare's *Macbeth* – was undoubtedly Isobel GOWDIE, whose confession in 1662 provided a detailed insight into the real or imagined activities and delusions of the archetypal witch at the height of the hysteria. The Gowdie case suggested, more than any other, the possibility that Scottish witches really did form covens and observe SABBATS as on the Continent, flying through the air and turning themselves at will into various animals (although the degree to which her confession was pure invention has been long debated). Whatever the truth of the matter, Gowdie's confession, which was extracted without the use of torture, had a profound impact and undoubtedly contributed to the witch hysteria in Scotland lasting for as long as it did. To the modern reader, it seems self-evident that Gowdie was simply insane. The same was also probably true of Major Thomas WEIR, who made a startling confession of evil perversions eight years later.

The Scottish witch-hunts tailed off after 1700. The last trial on charges of witchcraft took place at Dornoch, Sutherland, in June

1727, ending with Janet Horne being put to death in a burning pitch barrel (her daughter, also charged, was acquitted). Her crime was to ride her daughter as a flying horse and having her shod by the Devil, rendering her permanently lame. The 1604 Witchcraft Act, under which most prosecutions of Scottish witches were staged, was finally repealed in 1736 (although members of the Associated Presbytery declared their continuing belief in witchcraft some forty years later, in 1773).

Witchcraft did not disappear from the courts altogether, however. As late as 1883 the sheriff's court at Inverness heard a case in which the use of IMAGE MAGIC was alleged: a woman had used a four-inch clay poppet (a *carp creagh*) wound with green thread and stuck with pins against an enemy of hers, in the hope that it would bring evil down upon her. In 1947 a deceased man's will was contested in the Scottish Land Court at Stornoway on the grounds that the testator had believed in witchcraft and had used it against his neighbour in order to make his livestock lame; the case was thrown out.

As elsewhere, it is next to impossible to give a definite statistic for the numbers who were executed throughout the witchcraft mania in Scotland. The frequency of executions fluctuated wildly, with none at all in 1651–60, when Scotland was under the rule of Oliver Cromwell, and a total of 120 in a single month in 1661. Estimates of the total dead have been put as high as 17,000 between 1563 and 1603, although a more likely figure is the 4400 burned in the years 1510–1727, as deduced from examination of contemporary records.

See also BARCLAY, MARGARET; BARGARRAN IMPOSTOR; GLENLUCE DEVIL; GRIERSON, ISOBEL; HALDANE, ISOBEL; PITTENWEEM WITCHES.

Scott, Michael *c.*1160– 1238. Scottish wizard who is still remembered for his legendary skills as a sorcerer and occultist. Scott, who hailed from Balweary near Kirkcaldy in Fife, was renowned for his learning: he studied Arabic, astronomy and chemistry at Oxford, mathematics and theology at Paris and the occult at Padua in Italy. His reputation was international, winning him a mention in Dante's *Inferno* and in the poetry of Sir Walter Scott, who dubbed him 'the wondrous Michael Scott, a wizard of such dreadful fame'.

Although relatively little is now remembered of his career, various legendary feats are still attached to Scott's name. Among other achievements, he taught the witches of Glenluce how to plait sand (a trick which they still perform, judging by the curious rope-like patterns that the sands naturally form in Luce Bay), was once transformed by a rival witch into a hare (in which shape he was pursued by his own hounds) and used his magic to cleave the Eildon Hills in two. He is supposed to lie buried in Melrose Abbey.

scratching *see* SCORING ABOVE THE BREATH.

scrying The art of divining the future and discovering secret information by gazing into a MIRROR, a crystal ball or some other reflective surface, such as a brightly polished sword blade. The reflection was considered magical in classical times and according to some theories it was a visible manifestation of a person's soul (thus the tradition sometimes encountered that anyone who has sold their soul to the Devil has no reflection at all). Such reflections, in mirrors or in water, could be asked questions about the future: if they trembled or broke up, the prognosis was generally considered bad.

Some experts employed scrying, also known as catoptromancy or crystal-gazing, to root out witches and thieves, revealing the face of the culprit in their mirror to any enquirer. The method could also be employed to trace lost property or missing persons, or to contact spirits. Only the pure in heart were said to be able to communicate with good spirits, and therefore many young children were employed as scryers.

By medieval times scrying had become very sophisticated and was highly regarded even by royalty. Not everyone could master the art, and those who claimed to have such powers were much sought after. Expert practitioners became famous and mixed with the highest in the land, although they risked being accused by their enemies of dealing with the Devil and might acquire a popular reputation as a witch.

Pre-eminent among these individuals in the Elizabethan and Jacobean ages, when scryers were much respected, was Dr John DEE, who performed such services at the English court and, among other events, foretold the Gunpowder Plot of 1605. Like many others, Dee was unable himself to see anything in the mirror or, in his case, the crystal, and so had to employ someone else to act as an intermediary. His first assistant was the much-respected Barnabas Saul, who passed on Dee's enquiries to the Angel Annael, the spirit with whom Saul had communication. Saul was eventually exposed as a fraud and was replaced by the notorious Edward KELLY, who provided the necessary link between Dee and a number of spirits, variously identified by such names as Madini and the Angel Uriel.

It was widely believed that the crystal ball or mirror used for scrying purposes should never be handled, as this reduced its effectiveness, and that passing the right hand over it several times helped to cause images to appear.

See also DIVINATION.

Selwyn, George *see* HELL-FIRE CLUB.

Shandy Dann *see* BURNING OF WITCHES.

shape-shifting The ability to use magic to change one's physical form, usually to that of an animal, as widely credited to witches throughout Europe over the centuries. Just how such metamorphoses were achieved varied from one part of the world to another. In some regions it was sufficient simply to don an animal skin to assume its characteristics; elsewhere, a witch had to perform an elaborate ritual and to smear his or her body with magic ointment in order to change shape. In some cases, the ability to change shape was unlooked for and was the result of a spell or curse placed on a family. Celtic legend, for instance, had it that certain ancient Scottish and Irish families were descended from seals or wolves or other animals, and that the descendants were obliged to take those forms from time to time.

In keeping with the CANON EPISCOPI, shape-shifting was dismissed as an impossibility by the medieval Church, because God alone could perform such transformations. Anyone who professed to change their shape was therefore suffering from delusions brought on by DEMONS. Nicolas REMY, one of the most respected demonologists of the sixteenth century, wrote: 'The Demon can so confuse the imagination of a man that he believes himself to be changed; and then the man behaves and conducts himself not as a man, but as that beast which he fancies himself to be.' Other authorities, however, argued that with the emergence of a new, more powerful sect of witches such metamorphoses were relatively commonplace. Whether transformations were real or illusory, the theory finally became an accepted feature of witchcraft mythology.

Sometimes the suspects themselves confirmed the allegations that they could change shape, often through the use of magic ointments given to them by the Devil. In the form of wolves or other beasts they savaged livestock and attacked men so as to feast on their flesh. In many other cases, they adopted animal shape in order to spy on their neighbours or to escape pursuit (HARES and CATS were their favourite disguises, though tales were also told of witches who turned into bees, birds and other creatures). Isobel GOWDIE, for instance, gleefully told her interrogators that by repeating the following verse three times she had often turned into a hare so as to evade capture:

> I shall go into a hare,
> With sorrow and sigh and mickle care;
> And I shall go in the Devil's name
> Ay while I come home again.

To return to human form she recited three times:

> Hare, hare, God send thee care.
> I am in a hare's likeness just now,
> But I shall be in a woman's likeness even now.

To assume the form of a cat the CHARM ran as follows:

> I shall go into a cat,
> With sorrow and sigh and a black shot.
> And I shall go in the Devil's name
> Ay while I come home again.

DOGS were another popular disguise. In 1612, a twelve-year-old girl called Grace Sowerbutts claimed before a Lancaster court that her grandmother, her aunt and another woman had smeared themselves with an ointment made from the bones of a murdered child and had been transformed into BLACK DOGS. Fortunately for the three women in this case, dubbed the SALMESBURY WITCHES, the charges were dropped after Grace's allegations were proved to be false.

Rarer, though still occasionally recorded, were the witches who were reputed to be able to change themselves into inanimate objects, especially wheels. An example of this phenomenon was found in Essex tradition with relation to the skilled CANEWDON WITCHES. When a local waggoner found he could not move his cart he whipped his horses, but to no avail. Advised to whip the wheels instead, he was rewarded for his efforts by a scream and the emergence from them of a witch, her face bearing the mark of his whip.

Belief in the power of witches to change shape lasted a long time. Many stories of such metamorphoses described how a witch had narrowly escaped death in her changed form, and how injuries she had suffered while in disguise had been found to be reproduced on her human body. Only by shooting a witch in her animal form with a SILVER bullet could she be killed. As late as 1718 a Caithness woman named Margaret Nin-Gilbert was alleged to have lost an arm after she was wounded by a hatchet while in the guise of a cat. Similar tales were still current over a hundred years later.

See also COX, MRS JULIAN; LYCANTHROPY.

Sharpe, Sarah *see* SWIMMING.

shaving *see* DEVIL'S MARK; TORTURE.

Shaw, Christine *see* BARGARRAN IMPOSTOR.

Shaw, Elinor *see* PHILIPS, MARY.

Sherwood, Grace fl.1698–1706. Alleged witch who was the focus of a series of witchcraft trials that were among the last ever prosecuted in colonial America. In 1698 Grace Sherwood was incensed when her neighbours in the remote Princess Anne County, Virginia, accused her and her husband John of being witches, specifically claiming that Grace had bewitched their pigs. The Sherwoods took their complaint against their neighbours, John and Jane Gisburne, to court but lost the case. A similar trial resulted from allegations made by other neighbours, Anthony and Elizabeth Barnes, to the effect that Grace Sherwood was in the habit of escaping through the key-hole of her house in the form of a black CAT. Once again the Sherwoods lost their suit.

A third trial opened in 1705, with Grace Sherwood accusing Luke Hill and his wife of assault. This time she won damages, but a year later Luke Hill brought his own action against Grace 'on suspicion of being a witch'. Despite the fact that the trial of the SALEM WITCHES some thirteen years earlier had effectively brought the witchcraft hysteria to a standstill in America, the court decided there was a case to answer and Grace Sherwood was searched for WITCH'S MARKS. Two suspicious-looking teats were identified as the sites where she fed her FAMILIARS, and her home was searched for waxen images. When, however, another search for witch's marks was ordered by the court, the jury of women refused to cooperate; they were charged with contempt and replaced.

Next, Grace Sherwood sought to clear her name by volunteering to undergo SWIMMING as a witch. Accordingly she was swum, and was found to float. Another search of her body confirmed the presence of the two witch's marks previously located. In an earlier era the situation would now have been hopeless for Grace Sherwood, but the public appetite for witch trials and executions was jaded and, although she was kept in irons at the local gaol, the case proceeded no further.

Shipton, Mother 1488–c.1560. English fortune-teller who was widely renowned for her skills as a prophet and witch. Mother Shipton was born Ursula Southeil (or Sontheil), the daughter of Agatha Southeil, a sixteen-year-old orphan pauper of Knaresborough in Yorkshire. Legend had it that Agatha had been seduced by the DEVIL in the disguise of a handsome young man, and that during a terrible storm she gave birth to his baby in a cave beside the River Nidd, which runs through the town. The Devil reputedly bestowed upon Agatha various magical powers, which she used in order to attack livestock and to have revenge upon her enemies in the town, but she did not survive childbirth and her daughter had to be brought up on the parish.

Ursula Southeil suffered from various deformities (it is thought she may have been a hunchback) and as a child she was much feared for the powers she was thought to possess. Many stories were told of strange happenings that occurred in her vicinity, with houses being ransacked by invisible hands and a mysterious BLACK DOG manifesting near her at regular intervals as if to confirm that all was well with her. Anyone who taunted her for her deformities was punished by some misfortune or humiliation, all allegedly at Ursula's command.

When she was a young woman Ursula Southeil established her reputation as a soothsayer, delivering numerous prophecies in the form of riddles and rhymes. As her fame grew, the curious flocked to Knaresborough from far afield in order to hear her words and to enquire about their own prospects. This was not without its risks, for many people believed that Ursula would punish those who approached her with wicked motives. When one young man asked her to tell him when his father would die, as he was impatient to inherit, she would not reply – the young man himself died shortly afterwards and was buried in the grave intended for his father.

In 1512, in spite of her physical deformities Ursula married a carpenter, Toby Shipton. Citizens of Knaresborough speculated that she had used a LOVE POTION to win her husband. The name of Mother Shipton now became a household word, but she remained safe from persecution as a witch – if only because she lived before the witchcraft hysteria had really got a hold in England. She died (as she had foretold) at the age of seventy and was buried in unconsecrated ground outside York, but her fame lived on and was much enhanced by the publication of her prophecies in 1641.

Among other things Mother Shipton is supposed to have foretold the death of Cardinal Wolsey, to have given details of the deaths and accessions of future kings and queens of England, to have warned of the Great Plague and the Great Fire of London and to have foreseen various wars and other events of national importance, such as the invention of the motor car and the building of the Crystal Palace. Another rhyme seemed to prophesy the development of modern communications:

> Around the world thoughts shall fly
> In the twinkling of an eye.

Some prophecies, fortunately, failed to come to pass:

> This world to an end shall come
> In eighteen hundred and eighty-one.

The cave where Mother Shipton was born in Knaresborough has long since been developed as a major tourist attraction, and, though she was principally a fortune-teller rather than a witch, she now ranks among the most famous names in English witchcraft. There is even a small British moth named the Mother Shipton, distinguished by wing markings that suggest the shape of the archetypal witch's face.

Shore, Jane *see* WOODVILLE, ELIZABETH.

Short, Mercy fl.1690–3. New England servant-girl whose apparent demonic POSSESSION attracted the interest of colonial America's most respected witch authority, Cotton MATHER. Mercy Short, a maidservant with a Boston family, was diagnosed as being possessed after she began to throw violent fits that could only be subdued with the assistance of several strong men. Witnesses reported how she gave wild shrieks and behaved with a total lack of inhibition, even with complete strangers. She swallowed pins and was also prone, they claimed, to bouts of severe depression, going without food for days at a time.

On interrogation Mercy Short spoke of visions of the DEVIL, which Mather found convincing proof of her possession by DEMONS. He wrote a monograph on the case and traced the root of the trouble to Sarah Good, one of the SALEM WITCHES whom Mercy

Short was said to have taunted when she saw her in Boston gaol – although he failed to compile enough evidence for a trial based on the girl's account.

silver According to the mythology of witchcraft, silver was one of the most potent of all precious metals. Linked with the moon, silver had many uses in occult rites. The metal was valued primarily because it was deemed to be pure and impervious to magical influence, which made it ideal for use in association with some design or object supposed to have inherent magical properties. Silver coins and receptacles were much favoured by the well-heeled magician because they would introduce no corrupting influence, although the more impecunious witch was unlikely to have access to such articles.

Because silver could not be influenced by magic, it was widely believed that a silver bullet was the only sort that could kill a witch or werewolf – ordinary bullets could be warded off by SPELLS (although the case of the NEWBURY WITCH was but one that disproved the theory). This tradition has persisted into modern times in relation to the vampire myth.

skull Conventional depictions of witches, sorcerers, magicians and conjurors frequently included a human skull, reflecting the widely held belief that the skull, the traditional seat of the soul, itself had considerable magical potency. Possession of a human skull was highly desirable to sophisticated sorcerers, as the skull was thought to be a focus of supernatural power and therefore increased the chances of a spell working if the magic was enacted in its vicinity.

Flakes from a human skull had many uses in the realm of folk medicine, and many remedies associated with witchlore included powdered skull as an ingredient. Sprinkled on someone's food, powdered skull was supposed to cure epilepsy, while taking a little of the moss sometimes found on old skulls in the form of snuff was said to cure headaches.

On other occasions, witches were reputed to use skulls for darker ends. In order to work evil magic the Irish witch Alice

KYTELER, for instance, was said to boil up in the skull of a decapitated criminal brews of spiders, black worms, herbs, snake flesh, the brains of unbaptised children and the hair and nails of corpses. Old Chattox, one of the PENDLE WITCHES, meanwhile, was alleged to have dug up three skulls in Pendle churchyard and to have extracted teeth from them so as to bury them with clay images of her enemies, who were thus threatened with death. Another tradition insisted that, when using teeth from old skulls, a witch had to remove them by 'biting' them out of their sockets.

Somers, William *see* DARRELL, JOHN.

Somerset, Robert Carr, Earl of *see* OVERBURY, SIR THOMAS.

Somerset Witches Two alleged witch COVENS that were exposed in the course of official investigations in 1664. The case is particularly significant in the annals of English witchcraft as it was one of the very few times when accused persons admitted to membership of an organised coven.

According to the accusations collected there were two full-scale covens active in the 1660s in the Somerset area, one at Wincanton and the other at Brewham. Both were presided over by the DEVIL, answering to the name Robin, who was described by his minions as a deep-voiced and handsome, though little, man in black.

The investigations into the Wincanton coven culminated in accusations of witchcraft against a total of six women and eight men, at whose head stood Ann Bishop. Other members of the coven included Elizabeth Style and Alice Duke. The Brewham witches comprised ten women and a single man; they included Henry Walter, Margaret Agar, four women called Green and three named Warberton. The man in black, possibly a member of the local gentry, was never identified.

As well as feasting at open-air SABBATS after dark with the man in black, who provided the food, the accused witches – who variously claimed to be present 'in the flesh' or only in spirit – danced to his music and plotted harm to their enemies by sticking pins or thorns into wax images. These poppets were formally baptised by the Devil, with himself and two of the witches standing as the god-parents, and named after the intended victim. A man called Dick Green was supposed to have died as the result of such a spell cast by the Brewham group.

Alice Duke described how she was initiated into the coven through Ann Bishop. She and Bishop had walked backwards three times round the local church. On the first circuit the man in black appeared; on the second a large black TOAD leaped up at them; on the third a rat-like creature ran past them. The man in black then spoke to Ann Bishop and Alice Duke was accepted into the coven shortly afterwards, the Devil pricking the fourth finger of her right hand to make his DEVIL'S MARK. Elizabeth Style, recalling her own INITIATION, said that she had traded her soul for money and twelve years of pleasure on Earth and had signed a pact to this effect in her own blood (*see* PACT WITH THE DEVIL). The Devil had then given her sixpence and disappeared.

Of particular interest was the testimony of the accused about the FLYING OINTMENTS that they used in order to soar through the air to their meetings. According to Elizabeth Style, she and the other witches smeared their foreheads and wrists with a raw-smelling grease that was given to them by their spirit contacts and then, upon reciting the words 'Thout, tout, a tout, tout, throughout and about' they were able to fly wherever they chose. When the time came to fly to the sabbat, they observed the same procedure but recited the words 'Rentum tormentum'. Anne Bishop, meanwhile, described how she was carried off to the sabbat after similarly anointing her forehead with a feather dipped in oil. When the time came to go home from the sabbat they shouted, 'A boy! Merry meet, merry part' and repeated the 'Rentum tormentum' charm, after which they were quickly returned whence they came.

Most of the witches were alleged to keep FAMILIARS. Alice Duke, for instance, had a CAT, which sucked at her right breast, while Christian Green suckled her imp in the form of a HEDGEHOG. Elizabeth Style, meanwhile, claimed that the Devil manifested himself to her in the form of a BLACK DOG and would grant her wishes, which she expressed with the words 'O Sathan, give me thy purpose.'

The trial of the Somerset Witches was pursued with considerable zeal by a local justice, Robert Hunt, until his superiors – responding to changing views of the whole issue of witchcraft – obliged him to desist from further enquiry. Joseph GRANVILL, a former vicar of Frome whose record of the investigation was published in 1681 under the title *Sadducismus Triumphatus*, complained bitterly at this interference, claiming that there were many more covens to be uncovered in the county.

See also COX, MRS JULIAN.

soothsaying *see* DIVINATION.

Southwell, Thomas *see* COBHAM, ELEANOR, DUCHESS OF GLOUCESTER.

Sowthern, Elizabeth *see* PENDLE WITCHES.

sow-thistle *see* INVISIBILITY.

Spain *see* BASQUE WITCHES.

spectral evidence Testimony by witnesses to the effect that they were being tormented by the accused in their otherwise unseen spirit form was accepted in courts throughout Europe, despite the apparent impossibility of the allegation. The need to secure convictions of alleged witches, regardless of proof, often overrode niceties of the law, and the acceptance of so-called 'spectral evidence' epitomised the degree to which judges were prepared to compromise themselves in order to get the desired result. Countless suspects were sent to the stake or gallows on the strength of often hysterical accusations by alleged victims of such psychic interference. Witnesses often threw fits before the court officials, complaining bitterly that the accused person standing before them was at that very moment assaulting them in their invisible spirit form.

Doubts about the reliability of spectral evidence were expressed even during the first witchcraft trials in the fifteenth and sixteenth

centuries, but the demonologists became adept at inventing expla-
nations to counter the arguments that such things were impossible.
If a suspected wife was found to be in her bed at the time when
someone else alleged she was at a SABBAT the explanation was clear:
she had arranged for a demon to impersonate her, or had attended
the sabbat in her spectral form, leaving her physical body behind to
allay suspicion. If critics persisted in their arguments, the demonologists pointed to the numbers of convicted witches who had
confessed to such deceptions (albeit under TORTURE).

Allegations that a particular person had been seen in their spectral form were very dangerous to the accused, for they could not
defend themselves even on the grounds that they had been impersonated by the Devil. The Devil, it was claimed, was forbidden by
God from impersonating the innocent, so his manifestation in the
accused's shape was itself proof of their guilt.

The notion of spectral evidence lasted almost as long as the
witchcraft hysteria itself. As late as 1692, the court in the case of the
SALEM WITCHES was much impressed by the testimony of the young
plaintiffs as they writhed in the courtroom under the blows of
unseen assailants. As before, accusations that DEMONS had tormented the girls in the spectral form of the accused were deemed
sufficient to incriminate the suspects themselves. But the controversy that ensued from the Salem trials meant that the
witch-hunters were driven to acknowledge that the Devil could also
adopt the form of a good and pious person without that person's
consent. This admission undermined the whole case for spectral evidence, and such testimony was disregarded in later trials.

Spee, Friedrich von 1591–1635. German Jesuit priest who was one of
the foremost opponents of the witchcraft persecutions that swept
Europe in the first half of the seventeenth century, when the mania
was at its height. Having studied at the Jesuit College at Cologne and
been made a professor in 1627, Spee witnessed many trials in
Würzburg, acting as confessor to countless accused witches (*see*
WÜRZBURG WITCHES). He was driven by his observation of these cases
to conclude that most of the people indicted were totally innocent of

the charges laid against them. Such was the horror of his experiences, it was said that his hair had turned prematurely grey as a result.

Spee did not question that SPELLS could be cast, and probably were, by a small minority of malevolent witches, but he refused to accept that the majority of suspects whom he met could be guilty of such crimes. He maintained that the number of real witches was very small and therefore brought into question the whole process of the witch-hunt, which thrived on mass accusations.

Spee expressed his scepticism eloquently (though anonymously) in his *Cautio Criminalis*, published in 1631, which attacked among a host of other evils the acceptance of accusations of witchcraft on little evidence and the self-defeating TORTURE of prisoners. In his view the persecution of witches reflected very badly upon the Church, which should realise that most accusations were born out of superstition, envy and petty malice – hardly the province of men of God. He denied the reality of an invasion of the civilised world by a host of witches, claiming that it was the magistrates themselves who through their own gullibility and zealotry had made witches so numerous. His criticisms were blunt and unforgiving and encompassed everyone involved in the persecution, whatever their motives: 'The innocent zealots who encourage witch-hunts should realise that, since the tortured have to denounce some persons, trials will become more and more numerous, until at length accusations will encompass them, and in the end everybody will be burned.'

Spee's attack, which was welcomed by a minority of both Catholics and Protestants, was embarrassing to his superiors in the Church, who took action to prevent him from broadcasting his views in public. A final solution to the threat he posed was found by ordering him to work as confessor to plague victims in Trèves, where he contracted the disease himself and died. On a more positive note, it seems that the publication of Spee's book (subsequently translated into sixteen languages) did dissuade Prince-Bishop Philipp von Schönborn and the Bishop of Brunswick from staging further witchcraft trials.

spells The casting of spells for both good and evil purposes has always been central to the mythology of witchcraft.

Witches might raise DEMONS or employ their FAMILIARS to perform various deeds on their behalf, but the conventional depiction of the European witch had her bent over a bubbling cauldron, muttering weird incantations and cackling hideously at the thought of the consequences of her magic.

According to the demonologists there were various categories of spells, each with distinct aims. These aims reflected the most serious preoccupations of both witches and their clients, with the majority of them pretending to counter physical ills (perhaps themselves the result of witchcraft), to win the love of a desired partner or to inflict harm and even death upon some enemy.

Spells threatening serious physical incapacity or even the death of the intended victim and the destruction of his or her livestock and property inspired the greatest dread among the general population. All manner of means were employed to such ends, ranging from the use of waxen images or poppets (see IMAGE MAGIC) to poisons and 'overlooking' (see EVIL EYE). Among the simplest procedures to ensure the death of someone was burying in an existing grave something belonging to or representing the intended victim. One spell to blight a farmer's fields and to steal his crops involved the assembling of a miniature plough drawn by a team of TOADS (a spell detailed in the confession of Scottish witch Isobel GOWDIE).

Other malevolent spells were of a less serious nature, designed only to bring inconvenience of a more trivial kind to an enemy. Typical of such mischief-making spells was that which, back in 1645, a Suffolk witch named Alicia Warner admitted to casting against two women whom she disliked. By her spell Warner hoped to send evil spirits to the women to infest them with lice, and the court found that the two women were indeed 'lousy according as she confessed'.

Many spells were designed to provoke love in a reluctant partner. As well as preparing LOVE POTIONS at the request of a client – or, indeed, on their own account – witches might also offer other forms of spells to achieve the same end. One of the oldest of these required the making of a poppet of virgin wax mixed with the desired partner's bodily secretions (blood, semen, saliva and so forth). The name of the person was written on the forehead of the image and the name of the aspiring lover on the breast, using blood from the third finger of the LEFT HAND. The figure was then pierced in the back, the head, the heart and the pelvis with four new needles and subsequently laid in a fire after being sprinkled with SALT and mustard seed. The fire had to be kindled using a piece of paper bearing a sample of the handwriting of the desired person. When the fire died down the person's name was inscribed once more in the ashes, to make doubly sure that the magic was directed at the right party.

Other spells were designed to solve the problems that might arise from realised desire – specifically, to procure the abortion of unwanted babies. These spells usually worked by virtue of being so disruptive of the body's system that the pregnant woman would be taken seriously ill and more than likely have a miscarriage (there was also, however, the ever-present risk that she would die). Among the noxious substances that were commonly included in such spells were the poisonous pennyroyal, rye ergot and oil of tansy.

Spells might also be cast for such purposes as reading the future (*see* DIVINATION), spreading the plague by poisoning the air, or influencing the weather (*see* STORM-RAISING). Popular imagination had it that witches could also use their magic to start fires, to make people go mad, to render couples impotent, to spoil butter and beer and to steal milk from cows. To achieve the last-named feat witches were supposed to 'milk' lengths of rope or straws, or the handle of an axe stuck in a wall.

The preparation of spells might be simple or exceedingly complicated, requiring extensive knowledge of the magic arts and access to a GRIMOIRE detailing procedures to follow. The ingredients of witches' brews were likewise many and various. They included herbs, plants, roots, animal organs and parts of human corpses (especially those of babies and hanged men). Tradition insisted that witches derived powerful magic from potions that were enriched by such constituents as deadly NIGHTSHADE, bats' blood, MANDRAKE root, snake's venom and other unlikely ingredients. Typical of the arcane recipes that witchlore advised was a seventeenth-century remedy for the healing of wounds, the ingredients of which included powdered worms and bloodstones, stale boar fat and moss taken from an old human SKULL.

For a spell to work it was important that, together with the right ingredients, a witch forged a link between the magic being made and the intended victim. This was especially necessary when using waxen figures to attack intended victims. The most effective way was to incorporate in the figure or spell physical traces of the person to be bewitched, ranging from purloined samples of nail trimmings, teeth and locks of hair to bodily fluids, garments and even the straw on which the victim slept. Even a footprint could be used against the person who made it; a typical procedure involved banging a nail from an old coffin into the print, causing the victim terrible pain until the nail was removed. The connection could also be made by identifying the person against whom the magic was to be directed by simply repeating their name several times during the preparation of the spell (*see* NORTH BERWICK WITCHES).

Since witches relied on the DEVIL for their magic powers, it was usual for an appeal to be made to the spirit world for assistance in ensuring that a particular spell worked as desired. This was best done from within the safety of a MAGIC CIRCLE, for the spirits raised might easily turn their evil upon the magician responsible for disturbing them. Many witches explained that the Devil and his minions actually showed them how to pursue their magic and provided them with the raw materials they would need.

See also AMULET; ATHAME; BUTTER-SPOILING; CANDLE MAGIC; CHARM; CURSE; FLYING OINTMENT; KILLING OINTMENT; LIGATURE; MALEFICIA; NECROMANCY; POSSESSION; SHAPE-SHIFTING; STORM-RAISING; TRANSVECTION; WAND; WHITE WITCH.

spitting *see* EVIL EYE.

Sprenger, Jakob *see* MALLEUS MALEFICARUM.

squassation Form of TORTURE extensively employed as a last resort against suspected witches on the Continent of Europe. Squassation was an extreme version of STRAPPADO, in which the prisoner was suspended by ropes from the ceiling of the torture chamber. In the process of squassation condemned persons were prepared as for strappado, with their hands tied behind their back. Suspects were then hoisted up to the ceiling by means of ropes tied to their hands, while heavy weights (as much as 660 pounds) were suspended from the limbs to pull them from their sockets. After a period of time in this excruciating position the rope holding the prisoner was suddenly released, so that he or she fell rapidly several feet towards the floor until, at the last moment, the rope was jerked tight. The violence of the arrested fall was sufficient to dislocate virtually every bone in the prisoner's body.

This greatly feared torture represented one of the most savage tests that might be applied to any prisoner. Four applications of squassation were generally considered enough to kill all but the hardiest of victims.

Starkie, Nicholas *see* DARRELL, JOHN; HARTLAY, EDMUND.

Stearne, John *see* HOPKINS, MATTHEW.

Stebbings, Isaac *see* SWIMMING.

stigmata diaboli *see* DEVIL'S MARK.

stonecrop Flowering plant which often grows among rocks or on walls and was once reputed to ward off witches and other evils. Stonecrop was often brought inside the house in order to prevent witches entering and to protect the inhabitants from fire and lightning. Witchlore also recommended extracts of stonecrop for the treatment of ulcers, piles, eye problems, scrofula and ague.

storm-raising Among their other crimes, many alleged witches were accused of raising storms in order to wreck ships, destroy crops and inflict a host of other calamities upon their enemies. Sorcerers of various kinds had been accused of using such magic for many centuries before the witchcraft mania, and it was inevitable that the new breed of witches should be linked with such dubious magical activity. Such was the belief in the power of witches to control the elements, in fact, that whenever a strong wind caused damage in a locality the blame would be laid almost as a matter of course at the door of some elderly and little-loved crone.

Francesco-Maria GUAZZO gave his own account of storm-raising in his classic *Compendium Maleficarum* of 1626:

> Witches have confessed that they made hailstorms at the sabbat, or whenever they wished, to blast the fruits of the earth. To this end, according to their confessions, they beat water with a wand, and then they threw into the air or into the water a certain powder which Satan had given them. By this means, a cloud was raised which afterwards turned to hailstones and fell wherever the witches wished. When water was lacking, they used their urine.

To achieve the same result, other witches threw sacrificial pullets or sea sand into the air, tossed pieces of flint over their left shoulder towards the west, shook wet brooms, poured water or urine into holes in the ground, boiled hog bristles or eggs, laid sticks on a dry river bank, recited charms, boiled babies in cauldrons or buried leaves of sage in the soil to rot. One Scottish variant, described in the trial of the AULDEARN WITCHES in 1662, was to beat a 'cursing stone' with a wet rag in the course of reciting the following spell three times:

> I knock this rag upon this stone,
> To raise the wind in the devil's name,
> It shall not lie until I please again.

To lay the wind once more, the following charm had to be repeated three times:

> We lay the wind in the Devil's name.
> It shall not rise until we wish to raise it again.

Typical of the confessions extracted from suspects accused of such crimes was that of the Frenchman Pierre Vallin in 1438. According to his own testimony Vallin, on the orders of the Devil, flailed the waters of a stream in order to whip up wild and highly damaging tempests. Similarly, in 1493 one Elena Dalok claimed before the Commissary of London that she could summon rain-storms at will. In 1563 the King of Sweden allegedly enlisted four witches in his army when fighting the Danes so that he might influence the weather in his own favour. Among others to confess to controlling the weather for nefarious purposes were Margaret Byx and Ellen Pendleton of Wymondham, Norfolk, who admitted in 1615 to conjuring up a strong wind to fan a fire that they had started with the intention of burning the whole town.

Accusations that witches raised storms in order to sink ships were especially common in SCOTLAND and the seafaring Scandinavian countries. One celebrated instance of alleged storm-raising was the case of the NORTH BERWICK WITCHES, in which the accused admitted to tossing into the sea a CAT bound up with the limbs of a corpse in order to threaten the ship carrying James VI to Denmark (the King's ship survived, but another vessel bound for Leith sank). Two centuries later, in 1645, Elizabeth Harris of Faversham admitted causing John Woodcott's boat to sink by placing a CURSE upon it, and that same year the Reverend John Lowes, an elderly victim of the 1645–6 Matthew HOPKINS witch-hunt, was executed for using magic to sink a ship off Norwich with the loss of fourteen lives (although the sinking of such a vessel was never actually established). As late as 1707 a storm that struck the fleet of Admiral Sir Cloudesley Shovel off the Scilly Isles, resulting in the loss of two thousand lives including that of Shovel himself, was widely blamed upon a curse laid by a sailor unjustly hanged on the Admiral's orders.

Superstition suggested at least a couple of defences that might be tried during violent storms. One was to toss some meal out of the window, in the hope that this would appease the demons whipping up the wind; the other was to ring church BELLS, whose sound was widely reputed to ward off witches and demons.

Not all storms were raised to cause harm, however. The ancient tradition of buying a favourable wind from a witch was popular among seafarers until relatively recent times. The best-known means of purchasing a good wind was to acquire from a witch a length of knotted cord, the KNOTS being untied in order to raise a good breeze whenever a ship was becalmed.

In many parts of Europe it was formerly believed that storms would spring up when a witch died, signifying that the DEVIL was coming to claim his own. In 1642, for instance, the death of a musician named Thomas Holt, who suffered a broken neck during a storm over Coventry, was immediately linked to an old rumour that he had sold his soul to the Devil some years before. Witnesses remembered that on the evening of his demise a handsome stranger was seen entering his house while the gale raged. It was also said that if a storm blew up during an Assizes this was a sure sign that the proceedings would result in many executions.

Belief in the power of witches to raise storms lasted several centuries. As late as 1691, when the witchcraft hysteria was dying down in most areas, the American Presbyterian teacher and author Richard Baxter wrote in his *Certainty of the World of Spirits*: 'The raising of storms by witches is attested by so many, that I think it needless to recite them.'

See also EGG; KNOTS; TREVISARD, ALICE.

Strachan, Isobel *see* ABERDEEN WITCHES.

strappado Extreme form of TORTURE which was widely employed during the interrogation of witches on the Continent of Europe. Among the first mentions of this torture in witchcraft trials was one suggesting that it was used in Piedmont in 1474, when it was known to Italian courts as *tratti di corde*. Subsequently it was adopted as an effective means of extracting information from prisoners in many European countries, including SCOTLAND (though never England).

The procedure was to tie the prisoner's arms behind his or her back and then to hoist the suspect to the ceiling by means of a pulley and a rope attached to the hands. This method had the advantage of dislocating the prisoner's shoulders without leaving obvious marks of physical abuse. Heavy weights suspended from the victims limbs increased the agony.

The torture might be repeated many times if a prisoner refused to answer the interrogators' questions in the desired fashion. Records exist of a twenty-year-old German woman, interrogated in

Tettwang, near Constance, in 1608, being hoisted in strappado eleven times in a single day, with a fifty-pound weight suspended from her legs; she was tortured for a further ten weeks before fears that she would die led to a halt.

A particularly brutal refinement of the practice of strappado was recorded in the CHANNEL ISLANDS, where even after the death sentence had been passed suspects were often tortured to make them disclose the names of accomplices. This involved the rope being tied securely round the condemned person's thumbs (in some cases the prisoner was allowed to drop suddenly, so that the thumbs were torn off).

Other tortures often applied while a prisoner hung in strappado included the THUMBSCREWS and toescrews. The sadistic Balthasar Ross, a German witch judge of the early seventeenth century, pierced women with red-hot skewers as they hung in strappado, while other torturers were reputed to apply balls of flaming brimstone to the prisoners' genitalia.

See also SQUASSATION.

straw Representative of fertility, straw was generally thought of as lucky in rural superstition, but it could also be used for nefarious purposes by witches. Any witch who obtained possession of a little of a person's bedstraw would be able to use it, so tradition had it, to exert magical influence over the person in question. Samples of bedstraw could be used in connection with IMAGE MAGIC to inflict harm on the victim or else to sway his or her feelings in matters of love. Other miscellaneous beliefs connected with straw included one that it was possible to cut the DEVIL in half with a straw, and also that by decking a cow out with straw the animal would be safe from interference by evil spirits.

Style, Elizabeth *see* SOMERSET WITCHES.

succubus Demon, the female equivalent of an INCUBUS, who seduced mortal men while they slept. According to the earliest legends about succubi, they were half human and half demon in appearance and by seducing mortals they gave birth to monsters. Not all offspring of such couplings were DEMONS, though: many notable men in history – including Alexander the Great and Merlin – were rumoured to be the product of these liaisons. Anyone found guilty of having a sexual liaison with a succubus, however, committed the sin of bestiality and was held to be doomed to an eternity in the fires of Hell.

According to the demonologists succubi were organised into their own hierarchy, at the head of which stood Princess Nahemal (otherwise identified as LILITH), queen of all succubi. Tradition had it that succubi commonly manifested in the forms of very beautiful women or even assumed the appearance of wives or lovers so as to 'steal' the semen of the men whom they tempted. Particularly susceptible to assault from succubi were monks and others dedicated to a life of celibacy, which suggests that these demons were invented in order to explain uninvited erotic dreams and NIGHTMARES with sexual overtones. Several early saints, notably St Anthony of Egypt, were tormented by succubi who tempted them with lascivious thoughts and tried to turn them from their sacred way. Another, St Victorinus, was actually overcome by the temptation and had intercourse with a succubus, as did the future Pope Sylvester II as a young man in the tenth century AD when he was tempted by one calling herself Meridiana.

Many men claimed that sex with a succubus was far superior to any pleasure that might be had with a mortal partner. One entrepreneur of the fifteenth century staffed his brothel in Bologna entirely with succubi, to the evident satisfaction of his clients; he himself was put to death in 1468 for his pains. The demonologist Pico della Mirandola, meanwhile, told a story about a man who enjoyed a sexual relationship with a succubus over some forty years and could not be prevailed upon to give her up. There were risks, however: a hermit was reported to have died of exhaustion after just one month of such exchanges. Nevertheless others found the experience less than fulfilling. One man discussed in Nicolas REMY's *Demonolatreiae* in 1595 described sex with a succubus as 'cold and unpleasant' and complained of 'putting his instrument into an ice-cold cavity'.

Sweden In common with the other Scandinavian countries Sweden seemed relatively immune from the witchcraft hysteria for many years, though events were to prove that here too the popular imagination could be easily swayed in a climate of fear and superstition. Trials on witchcraft charges were actually prohibited under the reign of Queen Christina during the Thirty Years' War of 1618–48. In the second half of the seventeenth century, however, the country witnessed an outbreak of witch panic that equalled anything in Europe for its ferocity.

The trigger for this late outburst was the infamous case of the MORA WITCHES in 1669. The accusations which multiplied so quickly in that one area inspired similar outbreaks in neighbouring towns and villages, and prompted the establishment of special commissions in Uppsala and Helsinki to root out those suspected of dealing with the Devil. On the instructions of a royal commission seventy-one people were executed for witchcraft in the parishes of Thorsaker, Ytterlannas and Dahl in the years 1674–5, and a year later Stockholm itself was traumatised by mass accusations. Six women were executed and scores of suspects were flung into gaol. The Church authorities, meanwhile, enjoined their congregations to fast and pray for deliverance, which intensified the hysteria sweeping the city.

Ultimately, it was the tragic case of Magdalen Mattsdotter that led to the return of reason. Mattsdotter was among those convicted, in her case on the strength of evidence supplied by her servants and her own children. After she was burned as a witch, accompanied to the stake by her younger daughter challenging her to confess before it was too late, it was revealed that the charges had been concocted out of jealousy and malice. Charles XI, who had sanctioned the initial royal commissions, was persuaded to take stern action and he banned any more witchcraft trials, thus bringing the panic to an abrupt end.

The death penalty for witchcraft was finally repealed in Sweden in 1779.

swimming The ordeal of casting a suspected witch bound hand and foot into a pond, pool or river to see if she floated (in which case she was guilty) or sank (in which case she was innocent, but risked being drowned anyway). Testing a witch by swimming was not a recognised part of the legal process of examining witches, but was popular as an informal trial that might be undertaken before any decision was made by alleged victims of witchcraft and various friends, relatives and neighbours to take their suspicions to the magistrates. Occasionally such ordeals were sanctioned by the local authorities but more often the test was tried at the whim of an unruly mob, sometimes with the encouragement of a visiting WITCHFINDER.

Having seized the person suspected, the usual procedure was to tie the right thumb to the left big toe and the left thumb to the right big toe and then to throw or lower the alleged witch into the water, or else to pass the victim from one bank to the other by means of ropes tied round the waist. This procedure, customarily repeated three times, was rarely performed without much ill-handling of the accused, who might be elderly, infirm or mentally unbalanced and was all too likely to die from injuries received or simply to succumb to shock (as appears to have happened, for instance, in 1699 in the case of the Widow Comon, the so-called COGGESHALL WITCH).

The custom of swimming suspected criminals was of antique origins, being first practised in testing for sorcery in ancient Babylon and later in pre-Christian northern Europe. It was accepted in Anglo-Saxon England as a wide-ranging legal test of guilt on the grounds that God would surely intervene to ensure that the innocent escaped further punishment and that the guilty were revealed. In order for the ordeal to win God's favour officials would engage in prayer and fasting prior to the test, and both Church and civil authorities would be present during the ritual itself. If the test was performed in an incorrect manner, without the authority of the Church and the law, those responsible were subject to heavy fines.

Henry III banned the water ordeal as a legal test in 1219 in response to pressure from the Church, but the test of swimming retained its hold on the popular imagination for centuries afterwards. As adopted in post-Reformation England, the test was imposed without any member of the clergy necessarily being present, but prestigious support for the theory of swimming was proffered by JAMES I, who approved the procedure warmly in his 1597 text *Daemonologie*. According to James, witches who had renounced the sacred water of baptism would never be received by the water into which they were thrown, and in this way their guilt would be revealed.

English law forbade witchfinders and their confederates from using torture, but local justices tended to cast a blind eye to the swimming of witches and in many cases they actually condoned it as a useful first step in a possible prosecution. The earliest instance of swimming being used as evidence during an actual witchcraft trial in England dates from 1612, when such testimony was accepted in the trial of Arthur Bill and his parents at Northampton. Such formidable witch-hunters as Matthew HOPKINS routinely swam suspects to consolidate the evidence against them, sometimes subjecting their victims to more than one ducking in order to confirm their suspicions in public (although Hopkins protested that he did not introduce the results of swimming as evidence in court). No argument of age or infirmity could save a suspect from such mistreatment – as evidenced by the swimming of eighty-year-old John Lowes on Hopkins's orders in 1645. Swimming of suspects continued even after the practice was expressly forbidden by a Parliamentary Commission that same year. The procedure was also banned as a legal test in France in 1601 and again in 1641, and seems to have been outlawed in Germany around the same time.

Once tossed into the water, most suspects prayed that they would sink, desperately hoping that they would be rescued before they drowned. In the case of Jane Clarke and her children, for example, who were swum at Great Wigston near Leicester in 1717, all three did their best to go under, but were reported to have 'swam like a cork, a piece of paper, or an empty barrel, though they strove all they could to sink'. Fortunately for them, the case never went to trial. Other late examples of swimming included the tragic case of John and Ruth OSBORNE, swum to death in Hertfordshire in 1751, and that of an old man known as DUMMY who was humiliated in this way in the Essex village of Sible Hedingham as late as 1863.

In 1785 Sarah Bradshaw, of Mear's Ashby in Northamptonshire, actually volunteered to be swum as a witch in order to clear herself of local suspicions that she was meddling in the occult (*see also* SHER-WOOD, GRACE). When she sank and had to be rescued from drowning the assembled spectators had no choice but to agree that she was innocent. Four decades later, in 1825, Isaac Stebbings, of Wickham-Skeith in Suffolk, also volunteered to undertake the test of swimming so as to clear himself of suspicion of witchcraft. In his case, suspicions had been aroused when he appeared in the doorway of a neighbour's house while a CHARM was being performed with the aim of identifying the witch alleged to be responsible for various misfortunes that had lately occurred. Stebbings's explanation that he had been calling (at four in the morning) in order to sell the family some mackerel was not accepted, and he was twice swum in Grimmer Pond in front of a large crowd. All Stebbings's attempts to sink were in vain, and not even the assistance of other men thrusting him under could prevent him bobbing back up once more. A date for a second trial by water was arranged, but, to Stebbings's own frustration, the authorities heard of the plan and had it stopped.

As late as 1880 legal proceedings were opened against Charles and Peter Brewster of Dunmow in Essex on charges of attempting to swim a woman named Sarah Sharpe from High Easter. According to the two men, Sharpe was a witch who had cast spells over the Brewster household, causing livestock to die and various poltergeist-like phenomena to occur. The defendants were bound over to keep the peace for six months, and nothing more was heard of the matter.

sword Skilled practitioners of magic sometimes used swords rather than WANDS when casting SPELLS; the sword, plain or decorated with mystic symbols, remains one of the optional accessories of modern-day witches. Laid on the altar during the celebration of various semi-religious ceremonies, the sword was once also used as an alternative to a MIRROR or a crystal ball for the purposes of SCRYING. Some sorcerers relied on their specially blessed swords to defend themselves against particularly hostile spirits raised by their spells.

sympathetic magic *see* IMAGE MAGIC.

Ttalisman *see* AMULET.

Thomasius, Christian 1655–1728. German lawyer who began as an apologist for the persecution of witches but became one of its bitterest opponents. Head of Halle University, which was nicknamed 'Hell University' by his critics, Thomasius was renowned for his nonconformist and liberal views. He first interested himself in the subject of witchcraft when he participated in a review undertaken by the university of the trial of a woman named Barbara Labarenzin. Initially, Thomasius went against public opinion and approved the use of mild TORTURE against the accused, but he later changed his mind, having studied the case of the MORA WITCHES among many others, and came to believe that the whole witchcraft myth was an illusion. The Church obliged him to concur that witches really existed, but he could not be persuaded that any witch had ever signed a PACT WITH THE DEVIL. He also argued strongly against the use of torture. Thomasius published his conclusions about witchcraft in 1701 in *De Crimine Magiae*, which was widely read and helped to counter the efforts of the witch-hunters.

thorn The role of the Crown of Thorns in Christian mythology meant that the thorn was often regarded with mistrust in rural superstition, but, perhaps by virtue of its biblical connections, it was considered a safeguard against witchcraft. In former times boughs of thorn were often nailed up over barn doors to protect livestock from interference by witches and other evil spirits.

See also HAWTHORN.

thumbscrews Widely employed TORTURE device comprising a vice in which the thumbs of suspected witches and other criminals were crushed so as to extract confessions of guilt. The thumbscrews (known in SCOTLAND as the 'pilliwinks' and in FRANCE as the *grésil-lons*) were classed as one of the milder forms of torture available to interrogators, though surviving descriptions of their use are often horrific. Johannes JUNIUS, mercilessly tortured in a German prison in 1628, described how the blood spurted from his shattered thumbs as the screws were steadily tightened. Similar vices were also used on the toes. The thumbscrews were often employed in conjunction with other tortures such as STRAPPADO in order to intensify the agonies to which the accused were exposed.

Tituba *see* SALEM WITCHES.

toad The toad is one of those animals most closely associated with witchcraft in the popular imagination. According to tradition FAMILIARS often appeared as toads, and in central Europe it was alleged that witches themselves might adopt such a disguise. In *Paradise Lost*, John Milton had Satan take the shape of a toad so as to inject poison into Eve's ear, and the heretical Luciferan sect of the Middle Ages venerated the Devil in the shape of a toad.

A fair number of witches admitted to conversing with their familiars in the form of toads, and occasionally the creatures themselves were produced. Dr William Harvey, physician to Charles I, was once shown the toad-familiar of a suspected witch from Newmarket. Ignoring the woman's protests he set about dissecting the luckless animal, only to find that it was in all respects an ordinary toad. Some decades later, during the celebrated trial of the BURY ST EDMUNDS WITCHES in 1665, a Dr Jacob of Yarmouth – who prided himself on his skill in helping bewitched children – gave evidence in court to the effect that he had found a toad in the bedding of one of the children in the case. He told the court that he had realised at once that it must be a familiar or a witch in disguise, and had immediately ordered one of the children to throw it into the fire. It then exploded; corresponding burns were subsequently found on accused witch Amy Duny's arms, suggesting that she had been the creature in disguise.

Toads, or parts of toads, were a standard ingredient of witches' brews. This connection with witchcraft was probably inspired by the creature's reputation for being venomous (it can, in fact, exude acids from glands in the skin if alarmed): witches were reputed to make use of this venom in their SPELLS. The NORTH BERWICK WITCHES, tried in 1591, admitted to attempting to poison James VI of Scotland (later JAMES I of England) by soaking a sample of his clothing in the venom collected from a black toad hung up by its feet for three days. Unfortunately for them, they could not obtain a garment belonging to the King upon which to smear this supposedly deadly concoction. Agnes Sampson, one of those implicated in the plot, claimed that had they been successful the King would have died in great pain 'as if he had been lying upon sharp thorns and ends of needles'. Elsewhere it was said that if a witch made a magic potion out of toad spittle mixed with the sap of sow-thistle, and then used this to mark a crooked cross on her own skin, she was instantly rendered invisible.

In eastern England superstition suggested that certain 'toadmen' could exercise power over horses, fixing them to the spot despite all efforts by others to make them move. They acquired this power through a complicated ritual which involved skinning a toad, pegging the body to an anthill until only the bones were left, then placing the dried bones in a stream at midnight. The bones, it was claimed, would let out a fearful shriek and one of them, which contained great magic, would start off upstream – the aspiring 'toadman' had only to seize this and he would enjoy various occult powers.

Toads were also supposed to carry a precious jewel within their heads, and this was much valued as a means of detecting poison. Nobles fearing assassination often sported rings holding such jewels in the belief that these would warn them of the presence of poison.

Great store was placed by the superstitious in so-called 'toad-stones' (any stone that was reminiscent of a toad by virtue of its shape or colour). These were held to have highly effective curative properties when laid against bites and stings. To test whether a toad-stone had any potency it had only to be placed in front of a real toad: if the toad leaped forward to take it, the stone was genuine.

As a result of its long-standing association with witchcraft the toad has always been considered an unlucky creature, and some people still view the animal with loathing because of the bad luck that comes with it. If livestock fell ill it was once not uncommon for locals to blame the bites of toads for their condition, although they would hesitate before killing a toad for fear of bringing on a rainstorm. Devon tradition insisted that toads should be caught and burned, as witches were on the Continent, in order to destroy their magic. Handling toads was not advised, as this was alleged to cause WARTS.

torture The use of torture was perhaps the worst feature of the witchcraft hysteria, and it was extensively employed in most Continental European countries. The precise extent to which torture was applied is, however, impossible to gauge for certain: only occasionally is it clear from surviving records what means were employed in extracting confessions. Sometimes it is obvious that torture was employed even where the official record states that it was not, as Friedrich von SPEE explained in his *Cautio Criminales* of 1631:

> There is a frequent phrase used by judges, that the accused has confessed without torture and thus is undeniably guilty. I wondered at this and made inquiry and learned that in reality they were tortured, but only in an iron vice with sharp-edged bars over the shins, in which they are pressed like a cake, bringing blood and causing intolerable pain, and this is technically called without torture, deceiving those who do not understand the phrases of the inquisition.

Torture was justified on the grounds that witchcraft was a unique crime against God and not subject to the usual legal safeguards and considerations. Because of the difficulty of obtaining evidence of the crimes, which were none the less so serious that they could not be ignored, the securing of confessions was of paramount importance. In most cases torture was the only realistic way of extracting them – no lawyer pretended that he would be able to persuade the Devil to appear in court against his own disciples. The successful use of torture, it was argued, also had the beneficial side-effect of persuading proven witches to confess their error and thus to appease the wrath of God and perhaps save their immortal souls, compromised though they may have been.

Without the widespread use of torture it is unlikely that the panic would ever have seized Europe as it did. Only through its regular employment were the demonologists able to substantiate their claims regarding what they perceived as the witchcraft threat by pointing to a body of actual confessions. It is significant that when the Margrave of Hesse in Germany forbade torture in 1526 there was not a single execution for witchcraft in that state until 1564.

Long before witchcraft became a central preoccupation of both ecclesiastical and secular courts the INQUISITION had developed the theory and practice of torture with great ruthlessness as part of its campaign against HERESY in all its guises. The Inquisition first occupied itself with wholesale attacks on witches in the fourteenth century, treating mere suspicion of such offences as adequate grounds for arresting suspects and subjecting them to the most savage torture. Kramer and Sprenger, in the highly influential *Malleus Maleficarum*, emphasised the appropriateness of torture in witchcraft investigations, arguing that only confessions made under such physical extremity could be taken as genuine. Their call was heard most clearly throughout Continental Europe, especially in GERMANY, where the most brutal physical abuses were routinely inflicted upon accused persons.

Set procedures governed the use of torture in many regions, making it appear to be something open and legal. Most courts instructed that prior to torture the suspect had to be meticulously shaved, on the grounds that any demon left undetected in the prisoner's body hair might intervene to deaden the agony that the torturers tried to inflict or might seek to influence the answers that the suspect gave. The whole body also had to be carefully examined for any CHARMS secreted about the person that might prevent the prisoner feeling the pain as intended. Some courts insisted that female prisoners were checked by women, but often they were minutely probed by the opposite sex.

The suspect was then subjected to tortures that were categorised according to their severity into two or three 'degrees' (as described by Philip van Limborch in his *History of the Inquisition* of 1612). Others distinguished between an initial stage of questioning, in which relatively mild tortures were employed, and a second, much more rigorous stage, in which the full armoury of the torturer was drawn upon. First-degree tortures, designed to obtain confessions, included stripping suspects, binding them tightly with ropes and flogging them. Prisoners might be fed salty foods and denied any liquid, so that they suffered raging thirst; they might actually be placed on the LADDER (or 'rack') at this stage and stretched by ropes until their muscles tore; or their limbs might be crushed in vices (*see* BOOTS). Other tests employed in this 'Preparatory Torture' – the *question préparatoire* – included giving the prisoner a guided tour of the torture chamber, so that he or she might see what horrors they risked by not admitting at once the full measure of their guilt. If the accused was an attractive woman or girl she risked being raped by the torturer's assistants. Those who confessed at this stage would frequently be reported to have made their statements without being tortured, as these measures were considered relatively mild by many courts.

If a confession was still unforthcoming, the accused person was then subjected to tortures of the second degree, the 'Final Torture' or the *question définitive*. The first stage of this was 'Ordinary Torture', which included the procedure known as STRAPPADO, variously augmented by the application of the THUMBSCREWS or other supplementary torments. Questions would be addressed to the victim throughout the torture, until he or she was ready to sign a full statement of guilt.

The most uncommunicative prisoners moved from the second degree to the third degree, or the second stage of the *question définitive*

– the 'Extraordinary Torture' or *question extraordinaire*, the aim of which was usually to learn the names of a witch's accomplices. Strappado was now succeeded by the even more savage procedure known as SQUASSATION, which might be repeated many times and which all too easily culminated in the suspect's death.

Various other measures used at the different stages included enforced drinking of holy water on an empty stomach, breaking on the wheel and, in Scotland, 'thrawing', which involved the prisoner being jerked violently about by means of ropes fastened round the neck (these were sometimes attached to a spiked collar that tore the victim's flesh as he or she was thrown about). A relatively rare, and exceedingly dangerous, procedure was the water ordeal, which involved the prisoner being forced to swallow large quantities of water together with lengths of knotted cord. These cords were then violently yanked from the prisoner's mouth, a process which usually resulted in disembowelling. Other extreme tortures included the cutting off of hands and ears, immersion in scalding baths laced with lime, and the tearing of flesh with red-hot pincers (a punishment usually reserved for those who had been found guilty of desecrating the host). Some prisoners were forced to wear large leather or metal boots into which boiling water or molten lead was poured.

Recantations of confessions made in the torture chamber only led to the prisoner being returned there directly. Doctors would often be in attendance to stop the torture if it seemed likely that the prisoner would die. The accused person would then be allowed time to recover a little before the torture was recommenced. Prohibition of torture being carried out more than three times unless new evidence came to light was side-stepped by arguments that the latest resumption of torture was but a continuation of the previous sessions (records exist of a woman named Barbara Schwartz being tortured eight times in Bamberg in 1630 – each time to no avail – and other victims were returned to the torturer upwards of fifty times). Similarly, the law that a prisoner who withstood three sessions of torture must be considered innocent was thus circumvented. If a prisoner actually died under torture the court officials usually excused themselves on the grounds that the Devil had intervened, breaking his disciple's neck with the purpose of sparing the victim further physical agony or of preventing them from revealing his diabolic secrets.

Prisoners who fainted during torture were revived by water being thrown in their faces, or else by vinegar being poured into their nostrils. Little consideration was shown to prisoners who were already ill, and even pregnant women might be handed over to the torturer (although some courts tried to postpone examination in such cases).

Some suspects proved more resilient to torture than others. With the Devil's help it was widely believed that accused witches could withstand the most appalling agonies, as illustrated by a tale repeated by Francesco-Maria GUAZZO in the *Compendium Maleficarum* in 1626:

> A woman of fifty endured boiling fat poured over her whole body and severe racking of all her limbs without feeling anything. For she was taken from the rack free from any sense of pain, whole and uninjured, except that her great toe, which had been torn off during the torture, was not restored, but this did not hinder or hurt her in any way.

Other witches, it was claimed, only laughed in the faces of their interrogators as their bodies were subjected to the most savage abuses that could be envisaged. Paulus GRILLANDUS actually cited a Latin charm that was supposed to grant the suspect immunity from the pain of torture: 'In the same way that the milk of the Blessed and glorious Virgin Mary was sweet and pleasing to our Lord Jesus Christ, so may this torture be sweet and pleasing to my arms and limbs.'

Some of the worst atrocities were committed in Germany in the late sixteenth and early seventeenth centuries, when suspects of all ages were subjected to the cruellest torments. In 1614, for instance, during the wholesale slaughter of the BAMBERG WITCHES, a seventy-four-year-old woman died while being tortured up to the third degree. Many towns in Germany boasted their own 'witch prisons' where suspects were interrogated and tortured in large numbers. The instruments of torture were formally blessed by a priest before the proceedings began. Among the hideous tortures used by German courts were roasting suspects on iron chairs, tearing the flesh from their bones with red-hot pincers and crushing arms and legs in vices. Other specialities included the application to the armpits and the groin of burning feathers soaked in sulphur and dipping suspects in scalding baths laced with lime.

The iron torture chair used in the city of Offenburg and elsewhere was among the most effective devices adopted by the German courts. The suspect was strapped into the chair, which was studded with points, and a fire was then lit beneath it – according to the official records, only two people who were put in the chair at Offenburg failed to confess. Both these two, Jakob Linder and Gotter Ness, were forced in 1629 to undergo the torture on a total of three occasions.

The situation in ENGLAND and Wales was somewhat different because, except in very special cases, torture was not permitted under the common law (though it was permitted in Scotland and was employed there with great barbarity). In England, WITCHFIND-ERS such as the notorious Matthew HOPKINS were restricted to relatively mild forms of pressure when it came to extracting confessions, but they showed considerable ingenuity within the confines in which they had to operate. Thus, they argued, the law allowed them to starve prisoners for days at a time, to subject them to the ordeals of PRICKING and SWIMMING, and to keep them without sleep by such devices as forcing them to sit cross-legged on hard stools for hours on end and 'walking' them (in other words, keeping them marching back and forth until they were weak from exhaustion; see WALKING A WITCH). Searches for the DEVIL'S MARK were also conducted with some roughness: the suspects were shaved before their naked bodies were carefully checked, sometimes in full public view. Isolated instances of more overt torture did occur from time to time, even in England. In 1603, for instance, eighty-year-old Agnes Fenn, of Catton in Suffolk, was forced by an unruly mob to sit repeatedly on a stool studded with the points of several knives, while in 1614 one Lyon Gleane was put in the stocks and whipped.

To add insult to very real injury, the victims of torture – or their estates – were often required to reimburse the courts for the costs of their ill treatment. Surviving documents shed an interesting, if disconcerting, light on the financial arrangements made in relation to the testing of suspects. As an illustration of the cold-blooded business aspect of torture, authorities often quote the table of charges that the Archbishopric of Cologne set out in response to escalating demands from torturers in 1757. Alongside other items, it cost five reichsthalers to cut out a suspect's tongue and to burn the mouth with a red-hot iron (with another two reichsthalers for the raw materials required), one reichsthaler to flog someone in gaol and twenty-six albus to apply the thumbscrews. In Scotland, in 1649, the witchfinder John Kincaid charged £6 to prick one Margaret Dunhome, while in 1692 the suspects imprisoned during the trial of the SALEM WITCHES had to pay five shillings for their fetters.

Enlightened attitudes gradually obliged the Church to instruct its representatives to moderate their use of torture in cases of witchcraft. Papal bulls issued in 1623 and 1657 actually admitted that torture had been misapplied in many cases in the past.

See also CONFESSIONS.

touching a corpse *see* BIER RIGHT.

transformation *see* SHAPE-SHIFTING.

transvection The alleged ability of witches to fly through the air, mounted on such vehicles as BROOMSTICKS, animals (including black rams and GOATS), bewitched men and a variety of other objects such as forked sticks, unbroken egg-shells (*see* EGG) and wisps of straw – or even without any such means of support at all. The belief that witches could fly was central to the mythology of witchcraft, and such feats were routinely described as evidence of a suspect's guilt. The notion that certain people, through deals with DEMONS, enjoyed the power of flight was, however, much older. It found expression long before the development of witchcraft proper in the story of the 'night ride' that the followers of DIANA were supposed to perform. The idea that such women could fly through the air was flatly denied at an early stage by the CANON EPISCOPI, but later generations of demonologists learned to side-step this ruling, arguing that witches might indeed *imagine* that they took such flights but in so doing were just as guilty as if they had performed them in reality. In 1529 ten high officials of the Spanish INQUISITION debated the question: six of them concluded that witches really flew, three decided that they imagined they flew, and one was unable to make a choice on the evidence presented.

Among the earliest accounts of transvection by witches was that concerning Alice KYTELER, the famed Irish witch of the early fourteenth century. Kyteler was reputed to own a staff on which 'she ambled through thick and thin, when and in what manner she listed, after having greased it with the ointment which was found in her possession'. Such FLYING OINTMENT, supplied by the Devil or made by the witch herself using various exotic ingredients, was widely thought to be essential for any witch who desired the power of transvection, and samples of it were from time to time actually produced as evidence in court. Some argued that the Devil presented such ointments only to those witches who would otherwise experience difficulty in reaching SABBATS, although many more contended that all witches enjoyed the power of transvection. There was also speculation that the Devil taught his minions to fly as a means of showing his contempt for the powers of flight that the angels enjoyed.

The courts were generally content to accept that, if a witch confessed to flying, she had probably flown through the air exactly as she described or as was alleged by her accusers. Suggestions by certain demonologists that witches flew 'in spirit only' (their physical body being left behind to fool their husbands) or only in their imagination were usually lost on witch judges, who preferred to confirm the popular opinion that witches were carried bodily aloft by their magic. Significantly, many accused witches confessed to flying through the air while in a trance-like state – suggesting that they were dreaming.

The fact that many witches confessed to flying to sabbats after rubbing themselves with ointment has encouraged theories that they only imagined themselves to be in flight through the influence of certain drugs (perhaps absorbed through the skin via the ointment that seemed to play such a crucial part). Other theories pointed to ergot poisoning as a result of eating rye bread, which could easily lead to hallucinations.

Whatever the reason, many witches certainly believed that they were capable of such feats. Back in the fifteenth century a Basque witch called Maria of Ituren described how, after she and her companions had smeared themselves with an ointment containing such ingredients as pulverised toad and water plantain, they were transformed into horses and took to the air. Isobel GOWDIE, who made a voluntary confession in 1662, claimed that she flew on a 'horse' comprising a straw or a beanstalk, which she slipped between her legs with the words 'Horse and hattock in the Devil's name'. Two years later, during the trial of the SOMERSET WITCHES, Mrs Julian Cox calmly related how one evening she had met three people flying on broomsticks some four or five feet above the ground.

Occasionally, independent witnesses claimed to have seen witches in flight. In his *Compendium Maleficarum* of 1626, for instance, Francesco-Maria GUAZZO told the celebrated story of some soldiers at Calais who reported firing their muskets into a cloud when they heard voices coming out of it, with the result that a buxom naked woman wounded in the thigh landed at their feet.

According to some early authorities good witches rode on sticks while bad witches rode on wolves, but broomsticks eventually became the most common form of transport described in confessions. The conventional means of escape from the witch's home was the CHIMNEY.

Once in the air, witches only rarely came to grief. One apparent exception to this was an incident in which a male witch flew a little too close to a church and got his breeches entangled with the steeple – the badly torn breeches were produced in court and accepted as evidence. Otherwise, the only real risk of mishap was if someone happened to ring church BELLS as a witch passed by. The sound of bells was widely believed to arrest any witches within earshot in mid-flight and to cause them to crash to the ground. When a region believed itself to be particularly pestered by witches the authorities would sometimes order all the bells in the area to be rung so as to ward off the threat. Another countermeasure was to scatter scythes and other sharp-edged instruments on the grass so that witches would not be able to land.

Belief in the power of transvection persisted throughout the history of the witchcraft mania. In England, it finally perished at least in the law courts in the latter half of the eighteenth century, when Lord Mansfield refused to take accusations of such a feat seriously. He declared that even if a suspect had flown through the air there was, as far as he was aware, no law of England prohibiting flying and anyone was free to do so, if they could.

Trembles, Mary *see* EXETER WITCHES.

Trèves Witches The German archbishopric of Trèves (modern Trier) in the Rhineland witnessed some of the worst excesses of the witchcraft mania in the late sixteenth century. Panic about the witchcraft threat crossed into Trèves, then part of the Holy Roman Empire, from Lorraine and Luxembourg and developed into full-scale hysteria from 1582, at a time when local people were ready to accept a scapegoat as a result of several failed harvests and other problems.

Prince-Archbishop Johann von Schönenburg signalled the start of a major campaign of persecution in Trèves when he attacked the civil judge Dietrich FLADE for his leniency in witchcraft trials and, with the assistance of Governor Johann Zandt, the notary Peter Ormsdorf and the Suffragan Bishop Peter BINSFELD, had him removed from his post and ultimately executed as a witch himself. An attempt by Father Cornelius Loos to publicise the scandalous disregard of the law involved in the rash of witchcraft trials that followed was ruthlessly quashed by the Church; Loos was banished to Brussels and the campaign proceeded largely unhindered. Some six thousand people were implicated in crimes of witchcraft in the city of Trèves between 1587 and 1594. Johan Linden, a canon at Trèves Cathedral, wrote how 'the whole country rose to exterminate the witches' and very few of those accused escaped TORTURE and punishment. He also noted that many of the victims were among the wealthiest citizens, inferring that they died because they had money that could be confiscated: 'Meanwhile notaries, copyists and innkeepers grew rich. The executioner rode a blooded horse, like a noble of the court, and went clad in gold and silver; his wife vied with noble dames in the richness of her array.'

By the time the hysteria finally abated the city boasted a veritable forest of stakes where condemned witches had been burned. Lack of money to fund further trials, coupled with the cost of war, eventually brought the trials to an end.

trials Courts throughout Europe treated witchcraft as a crime quite separate from the usual run of offences, with its own procedures and legal peculiarities. The seriousness of the crime, which constituted a challenge to the authority of God himself, and the difficulties involved in obtaining hard evidence of PACTS WITH THE DEVIL, SABBATS and so forth, meant that the need to secure convictions often overrode the niceties of normal legal practice. Evidence that would be rejected in other cases was enthusiastically welcomed. Many judges, acutely aware of the public outcry that would follow an acquittal, doubtless looked for incriminating testimony in order to pander to public opinion.

The first trials for witchcraft as it is now recognised were staged in southern FRANCE in the late thirteenth century, while the first trials on charges of heretical sorcery (see HERESY) were presided over by the INQUISITION at Carcassonne in 1320. By the mid-fifteenth century the mythology of witchcraft was well developed, with accusations of intercourse with DEMONS, child murder, STORM-RAISING, desecration of the sacred host, murder by means of KILLING OINTMENTS and flying on BROOMSTICKS (see TRANSVECTION) all fairly commonplace allegations. Suspects were also searched for the DEVIL'S MARK, one of the few physical proofs that were available to the courts.

In the early years cases were generally investigated and tried by the ecclesiastical courts, with condemned prisoners being handed over to the secular authorities for punishment. The first secular trial on charges of witchcraft was staged in Paris in 1390 and later the two systems often ran in parallel, although the civil authorities often insisted on allegations of actual harm done by witchcraft and were reluctant to prosecute on the grounds of ideas alone.

In many countries, both Catholic and Protestant, the pattern of procedure was modelled on that laid down by the Inquisition. Defendants, who were automatically presumed to be guilty, were hauled before the judges often on circumstantial evidence alone and were usually disbarred from having their own lawyer. Witnesses for the defence were routinely prohibited from entering the court (as was true in all heresy trials), while witnesses for the prosecution might remain unidentified, so that the accused had little hope of challenging them effectively. The testimony of very young children, accomplices, perjurers and excommunicated people was frequently accepted, and judges adopted all manner of ploys to deceive the accused (including sending spies into gaols to listen to the gossip between prisoners). Of particular interest to the prosecutors were confessions of guilt and the names of accomplices. If a suspect had to be acquitted (an unlikely occurrence) the courts reserved the right to reopen the case at their own discretion. Several books were published offering guidelines on how to prosecute witches successfully, the most famous of these being the notorious MALLEUS MALEFICARUM by Heinrich Kramer and Jakob Sprenger, and recourse was also made to university law faculties when difficult legal issues were raised.

Most trials on the Continent of Europe, of which only partial records survive as a rule, hinged on confessions extracted during TORTURE. These were highly standardised, with interrogators following a set sequence of questions so well known that they were often signified in the court records by a number rather than being written out in full. In some regards these formulaic confessions were comparable with records relating to the trials of demon-worshippers as early as the fourth century AD. Once a confession had been obtained the court proceedings were largely irrelevant, with little further debate about a person's innocence or guilt.

Unsupported confessions were, however, inadmissible as evidence in law courts in England and Wales, where the prosecution rested instead on the substantiation of MALEFICIA and on the physical proofs revealed by PRICKING. In English courts, the identification of a witch's FAMILIAR and discovery of potions or other incriminating evidence at a suspect's lodgings were consequently invaluable as relatively hard evidence of guilt – as was requiring a suspect to recite the LORD'S PRAYER without making any mistakes (if the suspect stumbled over the words in any way he or she was clearly guilty). English judges were, however, liable to bend the law in order to hear the evidence of children below the legal age at which they were deemed to be acceptable witnesses and, like judges elsewhere, were all too easily influenced by the fact that the accused had a previous reputation as a witch, regardless of the facts of the evidence in the case itself.

See also CONFESSIONS; EXECUTIONS; SPECTRAL EVIDENCE; SWIMMING; TORTURE.

Turner, Anne *see* OVERBURY, SIR THOMAS.

UUnited States of America Witchcraft came to the Americas with the first settlers, who took with them a wealth of European superstition and witchlore, but it remained confined for the most part to New England (originally colonised by the English). Some areas remained clear of the contagion at all times, largely because (as was the case with New York) most of the early inhabitants hailed from countries such as Holland where the witchcraft hysteria had never ignited.

Conscious of the threat, at an early date several of the pioneer states passed legislation prohibiting a range of witchcraft practices, warning anyone who entered into a PACT WITH THE DEVIL that they would be put to death if detected. The first execution for witchcraft was that of Alice Young, who was hanged in Connecticut on 26 May 1647 (*see* CONNECTICUT WITCHES).

A steady trickle of witchcraft trials continued through the 1650s, chiefly in New England, and in 1662 Connecticut once again became the focus of popular interest when a COVEN of twelve witches was allegedly exposed and put on trial in Hartford; several people were convicted and hanged as a result. In 1671 Elizabeth Knap, of Groton, Long Island, created another stir when she confessed (without TOR-TURE) to consorting with the Devil and was hanged.

After a lengthy lull, fear of witchcraft suddenly intensified throughout the eastern states in the late 1680s (by which time the hysteria was much abated in Europe) and – after further panic was whipped up by the case of the GOODWIN CHILDREN in 1688 and by the inflammatory writings of Cotton MATHER and others – the stage was set for the most infamous witch-hunt of them all, that of the SALEM WITCHES in 1692. The ferocity of the persecution at Salem, and the number of victims who lost their lives on the unlikeliest testimony of hysterical children, traumatised colonial American society and provoked a strong response from the opponents of the concept of witchcraft. Even before the trials were over the climate of opinion had reversed dramatically and within a year or two the panic subsided, obliging the original jury to make a public apology. Even Cotton Mather was forced to acknowledge that mistakes had been made.

There were no further official executions for witchcraft in America following the Salem tragedy, which brought the total of people executed for witchcraft in colonial America to thirty-six (as a result of some fifty trials). Isolated outbreaks of witch mania continued for some time, however. In 1706 Grace SHERWOOD of Virginia had to go to court in an attempt to clear her name after neighbours accused her of being a witch, and in 1712 several people in a neighbouring state narrowly escaped being murdered by a mob who believed that they were members of a coven.

Witchlore did not die out completely with the end of the trials in the Americas, however. Various witchcraft beliefs surfaced from time to time in certain areas, especially in Missouri, Arkansas, Kansas and the Ozark Mountains, with many locals fearing the malevolence of the EVIL EYE and taking care to protect their livestock and homes through time-honoured CHARMS of various kinds. As in Europe, householders nervous of witchcraft protected their homes and outbuildings by such devices as HORSESHOES nailed up on doors or carried protective AMULETS of one kind or another.

American witchlore included many variations on well-established European ideas. Although American witches seemed bent on the same sort of misdemeanours as their European cousins (their offences ranging from flying to SABBATS and roaming the countryside in the guise of domestic animals to bewitching cattle and using IMAGE MAGIC to cause illness) they had their own versions of the methods to be employed. One local spell to secure the death of an enemy, for instance, involved mixing some dirt from a grave (gathered by the left forefinger at the hour of midnight) with the blood of a raven or some other black bird, wrapping it all up in a rag that had been in contact with a corpse, and then burying it beneath the doorstep of the intended victim – who was sure to die within a few days.

Stories of thriving covens in various backwoods regions of North America were rife well into modern times, and for many years people continued to consult so-called 'witch-masters' who could advise on countermeasures to the threat of witchcraft and were also reputed to be able to identify the witch responsible for casting a particular spell. The legacy has been demonstrated in quite recent times: in 1956, for instance, over the border at Ojinaga in Mexico, Josephina Arista was burned at the stake by a mob of locals who believed she was a Devil-worshipper responsible for bewitching their cattle.

Urban VIII, Pope *see* ITALY.

urine Because of its intimate connection with the body, urine was often cited as a favoured ingredient in alchemy and SPELLS. Urine retained its supernatural link with the body and could therefore be used in magic to gain influence over the person concerned. To prevent this happening, superstition advised potential victims to spit into their own urine in order to spoil it for the purposes of witchcraft, or to wash their hands in it. Sprinkling urine over the doorposts of the family home was recommended as a way to prevent witches and evil spirits entering the house, and shaking drops of it over the family similarly bestowed protection.

In cases where witchcraft was already suspected, the best remedy was said to be baking some urine in a cake or boiling some nails in the urine of the bewitched party. In both cases the witch who cast the spell would be obliged to reveal her identity by being suddenly taken ill. German witchlore, meanwhile, suggested that a girl might capture a man's heart by the simple ruse of urinating in his shoe.

See also WITCH BOTTLE.

V

Vecchia, La *see* ITALY.

Voisin, La *see* CHAMBRE ARDENTE AFFAIR.

Volta, La *see* DANCING.

vomiting *see* POSSESSION.

Voss, Balthasar *see* WITCHFINDER.

W

waking a witch *see* WATCHING AND WAKING.

walking a witch Relatively mild but effective form of TORTURE in which a suspect was obliged to walk continually back and forth until exhaustion forced a confession. Such mistreatment was not considered a true torture as such and was therefore much employed by WITCHFINDERS in England, who were forbidden to use sterner measures against suspects. Matthew HOPKINS was one of those who found walking a witch a useful method of interrogation; among his victims was the aged Reverend John Lowes, who confessed to being a witch after being obliged to walk back and forth for several days and nights without rest. Hopkins justified the procedure on the grounds that as soon as alleged witches were allowed to sit down and rest their FAMILIARS would appear to feed from them, frightening those whose job it was to attend and question the suspect.

walnut In common with many other species of tree the walnut was reputed to have the power to ward off witches, though it was also claimed that some COVENS arranged to meet under walnut trees in foul weather (perhaps because the tree was supposed to be immune from lightning). Superstition had it that by placing a few walnuts under a chair any witch who sat in it would be immediately deprived of all power of movement.

Walnuts had various uses in witchlore and folk remedies. Stewed walnuts were reputed to improve fertility in ancient times; in later centuries it was claimed that, if a person walked three times round a walnut tree at midnight on HALLOWE'EN and then looked up into the branches and asked for some nuts, the face of their true love would appear among the leaves. It was deemed dangerous, however, to fall asleep under a walnut tree, as the person concerned might fall into a sleep from which there was no awakening.

Walpurgis Night The evening of 30 April, which was long considered one of the two nights in the year when evil held sway (the other being HALLOWE'EN). As a result of this belief, Walpurgis Night was allegedly much favoured as an auspicious time for the holding of SABBATS and the working of magic. The most famous sabbat held on Walpurgis Night was the traditional annual meeting of German witches that was supposed to take place on the summit of the Brocken in the Harz Mountains in Germany.

Walton, Charles 1871–1945. English agricultural labourer whose murder near the village of Lower Quinton, Warwickshire, appears to have resulted from his local reputation as a witch. That belief in the power of witchcraft survived well into modern times in certain rural areas is amply illustrated by the Walton case, which was never solved despite the best efforts of Scotland Yard under the celebrated detective Robert Fabian.

Charles Walton was an eccentric character who was well known for his odd ways. Among other things, he was reputed to be able to converse with birds, to exercise influence over dogs and other animals and to breed large natterjack TOADS in his garden. (Local tradition had it that he harnessed the toads to a miniature plough in order to steal crops for the Devil, just as Isobel GOWDIE confessed to doing three centuries before.) Introverted and somewhat reclusive, he was reputed to have been deeply affected by his encounter with a phantom BLACK DOG on nearby Meon Hill three nights in succession when he was just a boy: immediately after the third sighting, his sister had died. Local gossip claimed that he often visited a nearby megalithic stone circle called the Rollright Stones, where witches' COVENS were reputed to meet, in order to watch the witches DANCING.

Walton was murdered on 14 February 1945, his body being found at the foot of a willow tree in the field where he had been working. He had been killed and pinned to the ground by the pitchfork he had been using – its prongs had been thrust through his neck. A rough cross had been hacked on his throat and chest with his billhook, which had then been plunged deep into his chest.

The official investigation into the murder met with a wall of silence in the village and its surroundings, and suggestions were soon being voiced that Walton's death was a witchcraft killing. After exhaustive enquiries Fabian concurred that witchcraft probably was at the bottom of the incident, although he was unable to furnish enough evidence to bring charges against any individual.

Some speculated that the murder was the unintentional result of an attempt to break a spell thought to have been cast by Walton by the ritual of SCORING ABOVE THE BREATH. Others drew parallels with a strikingly similar murder that had taken place in the neighbouring village of Long Compton in 1875, when a suspected witch named Ann Tenant had been killed by the mentally retarded John Haywood. In this earlier case, Haywood too had pinned the 'witch' to the ground with a pitchfork and then slashed her throat in the form of a cross with a billhook. A last theory referred to the pagan custom of human sacrifice that required the blood of a dead man or woman to be allowed to drain into the soil to promote its fertility for the coming harvest.

wand The supposedly magical rod that was an indispensable tool of the aspiring sorcerer and many a witch, as still used by stage conjurors today. The rods of biblical prophets may have inspired the notion that a wand should be used in the pursuit of magic. Certainly many sorcerers were supposed to invest much faith in the properties of a properly made magic wand, claiming that by pointing the wand in a certain direction they ensured that their magic was projected as desired.

The earliest references to the use of wands in witchcraft date from the fifteenth century. In the anonymous *Errores Gazariorum*, for instance, it was claimed that witches were given a wand when they were initiated by the DEVIL (*see* INITIATION). Such sticks or rods were commonly used for the purposes of TRANSVECTION or DIVINATION, but they could also be used to detect buried treasure and so forth. Wands could additionally be employed to test virginity and to identify thieves and murderers. By pointing a wand at an animal, those practised in such magic were reputed to be able to rob it of the power of movement, making its capture a straightforward affair. Wands were also useful in healing, and doctors continued to carry walking sticks as a symbol of their profession well into the eighteenth century.

Wands came in different shapes and sizes, with some sorcerers variously favouring iron wands or using unsheathed SWORDS in their stead. Wands made of cypress wood – connected with death – were thought to be best in the business of NECROMANCY and in contacting SATAN. According to John FIAN, during the investigation into the NORTH BERWICK WITCHES the Devil himself had materialised in his cell carrying a white wand as his staff of office; when the Devil broke the wand he vanished. To arouse the spirit of a suicide the magician touched the corpse nine times with his wand of cypress, upon which the ghost would manifest itself in order to answer any questions demanded of it. Wands made of HAZEL or WILLOW were more usual in other contexts.

Occasionally very strict rules governed the type of wand to be used in certain rituals. Some authorities, for instance, claimed that to draw a MAGIC CIRCLE correctly a witch or sorcerer had to use a switch of hazel, exactly 19½ inches long, which had to have been cut at sunrise with the magician's bloodstained ATHAME. Other rituals that had to be performed over a new wand in order to ensure its latent magic was awakened included the saying of prayers and the reciting of NAMES OF POWER. Some magicians fitted magnetised caps over the end of their wand in order to intensify its properties and carefully purified and consecrated the wand before each use.

See also CHARM WAND.

Wapping Witch Joan Peterson, a self-confessed WHITE WITCH, who was tried and executed for witchcraft in London on 12 April 1652. Her case is remembered chiefly for the disgraceful way in which evidence was rigged or disallowed in order to secure a conviction. Witnesses wishing to testify on Peterson's behalf were frightened into staying away from the court, while others were bribed not to voice their support for the accused, whom many credited with being able to relieve headaches, unwitch cows and so forth.

The prosecution's account of Joan Peterson's activities suggested that her magic was much more malevolent. According to her enemies, among other nefarious doings she had cast a spell over a child and had kept a FAMILIAR in the unusual guise of a squirrel. The magistrates included Sir John Danvers, a confidant of Oliver Cromwell, and it was he who ensured – for unclear reasons – that the accused was duly found guilty and hanged at Tyburn.

Warboys Witches Three alleged witches – Alice, John and Agnes Samuel – whose trial at Huntingdon in 1593 attracted huge popular interest. The trial of the 'Witches of Warboys' was one of the most important ever staged in ENGLAND and it became the most widely reported episode of witchcraft in England prior to 1600, providing a model for a whole series of similar cases. One reason for the degree of interest shown in the case was the untypically high social standing of those involved.

According to the charges brought against them, the Samuels were responsible for bewitching the five daughters of a wealthy country squire, Robert Throckmorton of Warboys in Huntingdonshire, and for the murder by witchcraft of Lady Cromwell, grandmother of the man destined to govern England as Oliver Cromwell, Lord Protector. At the heart of the case of the Witches of Warboys was the hysteria of the Throckmorton girls, which began with a series of fits (probably epileptic) suffered by ten-year-old Jane Throckmorton in 1589. The girl had no doubt that seventy-six-year-old Alice Samuel, a neighbour of the Throckmortons who happened to call while Jane was having a seizure, was responsible for her suffering. Her claims were quickly backed up by her four sisters, aged between nine and fifteen, who were subsequently thrown into similar spasms.

Examination by a doctor specially brought in from Cambridge failed to reveal any medical cause for the girls' condition and witchcraft was strongly suspected. Robert Throckmorton and his wife attempted to discount the idea and clearly bore no malice towards Mrs Samuel, refusing to take further action for some time. Eventually, with no relief from the symptoms of POSSESSION, they were persuaded to confront the woman – upon which the girls threw even more violent fits and attempted to scratch her. Others who began to suffer similar seizures included seven of the servants and the children's aunt, Mrs John Pickering. When the girls' fits started to happen only when Mrs Samuel was absent, the hapless woman was ordered to move into the Throckmorton household.

The children took every opportunity to heap further accusations on the house guest, as contemporary reports related:

> Many times also as she sat talking with these children, being in their fits by the fire side, they would say unto her: Look you here, Mother Samuel, do you not see this thing that sitteth here by us? She would answer no, not she. Why, they would say again, I marvell that you do not see it. Look how it leapeth, skippeth, and playeth up and down, pointing at it with their fingers here and there as it leaped.

When Lady Cromwell, the wife of the Throckmortons' landlord Sir Henry Cromwell, came to call at the house she tried to destroy the hold that Mrs Samuel was reputed to have over the girls by cutting off some of the woman's hair and ordering it to be burned to break any spell she had cast. The attempt failed, however, and shortly afterwards Lady Cromwell was taken ill after a nightmare in which she was tormented, she claimed, by Mrs Samuel and her CAT. Some fifteen months later, when Lady Cromwell died, it was recalled that when she was attacked Mrs Samuel had complained with the rather ominous words, 'Madam, why do you use me thus? I never did you any harm as yet' – which seemed in retrospect to sound like a threat for the future.

Later in 1592, in a desperate effort to stop the nonsense, Mrs Samuel ordered the girls to desist from their fits, upon which the seizures immediately ceased. Thoroughly confused, Mrs Samuel began to doubt her own innocence and confessed to the local parson that she must indeed be a witch. The girls' fits recommenced when Mrs Samuel subsequently retracted her confession, thus furnishing the authorities with further 'proof' that the woman did indeed have magical influence over the Throckmorton children.

The case was presented to two local justices of the peace and Mrs Samuel was taken before William Wickham, Bishop of Lincoln. Under pressure from these dignitaries, she broke down once more and admitted her guilt. This time she gave more detail of her activities as a witch, describing for good measure her three FAMILIARS, Pluck, Catch and White, which manifested to her as chickens.

Alice Samuel, along with her husband and daughter, was tried for witchcraft at the Huntingdon Assizes on 5 April 1593, by which time the Throckmorton girls had elaborated on their original accusations to claim that the accused were also responsible for the death of Lady Cromwell. Other locals added further charges relating to illness and death among their livestock. The trial culminated in all three defendants being found guilty and in the abject Alice Samuel confessing to intercourse with the Devil. Agnes Samuel refused to admit any guilt and also declined to plead pregnancy as a possible way out of her dilemma, arguing resolutely: 'Nay, that I will not do: it shall never be said that I was both a witch and a whore.'

All three condemned witches were hanged and their property, worth some £40, was forfeited to Henry Cromwell, who used it to set up a fund for an annual sermon against witchcraft to be preached at Huntingdon. The last was given as late as 1814, although by then the preachers of the sermon generally used the opportunity to attack belief in witchcraft rather than to warn against it. The Throckmorton girls, finally released from their fits, apparently returned to their normal lives.

The case remains one of the best-known witchcraft trials in English history and amply demonstrates the degree to which the fear of witches had gripped the public imagination by the year 1600. Many later authorities lamented the court's gullibility in accepting the wild accusations of young girls, but to contemporaries their allegations only confirmed their innermost fears, preparing the way for the 1604 Witchcraft Act, which imposed the death penalty for all convicted witches.

Waring, Paul *see* KELLY, EDWARD.

wart Many a depiction of the archetypal witch, a hag with crooked nose and evil features, included a large wart or mole, and these were once likely to be identified as quintessential WITCH'S MARKS. Undoubtedly many of the 'teats' and other suspicious marks and protuberances exposed during minute examination of suspected witches were in reality warts or other natural flaws.

Because of the link with witchcraft it was highly desirable to be free of warts, and many were the 'wart-charming' treatments offered by local witches and 'Wise Women' to rid a person of such imperfections. Most cures fell back on magic and herbalistic theory. More straightforward treatments included washing warts in HOLY WATER, in the water that collected in a stump or in the blood of cats, eels, moles or pigs. Encircling a wart with a horse hair or a thread of silk was supposed to make it vanish, as would rubbing it with the inside of a broad bean pod, blowing on it nine times in the light of a full moon, spitting on it every morning or making faces at one's own reflection at the hour of midnight for three nights in a row.

Among the more bizarre ways of getting rid of incriminating warts was the contention that a wart would disappear if it was surreptitiously rubbed against a known adulterer who had fathered a child out of wedlock. It was also thought possible to use magic to transfer unwanted warts to others, either by 'selling' them to a friend or by wishing them upon a corpse as a funeral procession passed by. A wart could be transferred to an enemy by rubbing it with a coin or pebble and then ensuring that it came into the possession of the person concerned.

One cruel remedy was to carry a TOAD in a little bag around the neck until the creature died, while another required rubbing a live frog or snail on the wart and then impaling the animal on a thorn.

In order to avoid contracting warts in the first place and thus being exposed to accusations of witchcraft, people in former times were warned against handling toads. They were also, somewhat curiously, advised never to wash their hands in water in which eggs had been boiled.

watching and waking Form of duress that was applied to suspected witches in an attempt to enforce a confession through sleep deprivation. One method of 'waking a witch' involved fitting the suspect with an iron bridle which was then attached to the wall by a chain so short that the prisoner was unable to lie down to rest (*see* WITCH BRIDLE). If the suspect showed any sign of falling asleep the men guarding the prisoner would intervene to keep the man or woman awake. Alternatively the suspect could be placed crosslegged on a stool or table and kept there for up to twenty-four hours, tightly bound. Bishop Francis HUTCHINSON, in his *Historical Essay Concerning Witchcraft* of 1720, was among those to condemn the practice:

> Do but imagine a poor old creature, under all the weakness and infirmities of old age, set like a fool in the middle of a room, with a rabble of ten towns round about her house; then her legs tied cross, that all the weight of her body might rest upon her seat. By that means, after some hours, that the circulation of the blood would be much stopped, her sitting would be as painful as the wooden horse. Then she must continue in her pain four and

twenty hours, without either sleep or meat, and since this was their ungodly way of trials, what wonder was it, if when they were weary of their lives, they confessed any tales that would please them, and many times they knew not what.

Sleep deprivation was often employed by English WITCHFINDERS, who under the common law were barred from using more overt TORTURE. Matthew HOPKINS adopted it as a most useful means of applying pressure to confess, although he claimed that he ceased using it after the early stages of his campaign following complaints from magistrates. It was, however, sometimes used even in countries where more severe tests were allowed, including GERMANY. One advantage of the procedure was that it left no trace of physical abuse upon the victim; it could also be prolonged indefinitely.

Waking witches continued to be practised into the later history of the witch panic. One of the last instances of its use in England was in 1693, when an old woman named Widow Chambers was tested in this way at Beccles in Suffolk. The case never reached court, however, as the suspect died in prison.

See also WALKING A WITCH.

water One of the most widely held beliefs relating to witches was that they could not cross running water. The origins of this superstition are obscure, although people have long believed running water to be supernaturally potent, thus creating a magical barrier that evil spirits and witches might not cross.

Many tales were told of victims being pursued by witches, ghosts or demons and saving themselves by crossing bridges or jumping over streams. By extension the bodies of suicides, executed criminals and vampires were sometimes buried under running water to prevent their ghosts from walking.

In witchlore it was said that applications of water from fast-flowing streams would cure WARTS, sciatica, thrush and a host of other ailments, and in some cases stones taken from the bed of a stream would be rubbed against the patient's skin to achieve the same curative effect. Witches were also reputed to bring on rainstorms by dipping twigs in water and then shaking them in the air.

It was once thought unlucky to take boiled water into a bedroom. Boiled water, it was explained, was anathema to the Devil, who would cause trouble in any household where this convention was disregarded. Similarly it was deemed unwise to toss water out of the house after dark, because the presence of water helped to ward off evil spirits.

See also HOLY WATER; SWIMMING.

water ordeal *see* SWIMMING; TORTURE.

Waterhouse, Agnes *see* CHELMSFORD WITCHES.

waxen images *see* IMAGE MAGIC.

weasel In many countries the weasel was traditionally considered an ill-omened creature closely associated with witchcraft. Witches were said to favour the form of a weasel as one of their disguises and therefore any encounter with the animal, either inside or outside the house, was supposed to bode ill. In order to protect oneself from the threat of evil implied in seeing a weasel or hearing its cry, the best procedure was reputed to be throwing three small stones in front of oneself and then making the sign of the cross seven times.

Anyone wishing to acquire the gift of DIVINATION was advised that such powers could be enjoyed for a whole year by the simple measure of eating a weasel's heart while it was still beating.

weather magic *see* STORM-RAISING.

Webster, John 1610–82. English evangelical preacher and physician who was the author of a notable book criticising the witchcraft mania of his time. Although he wrote many other books on a wide range of subjects, Webster's *The Displaying of Supposed Witchcraft* of 1677 was perhaps the most significant in that it did much to hasten the final demise of the witch-hunt in ENGLAND. Webster, who claimed to have witnessed some of the trials he described in his text, attributed belief in witchcraft in the main to 'melancholy and fancy' and utterly refuted the entire mythology of PACTS WITH THE DEVIL, FAMILIARS, SHAPE-SHIFTING, STORM-RAISING and SPELLS.

He admitted the possibility of there being persons who thought themselves witches and conceded that such people might very well attempt harm against their neighbours, but he denied that in so doing they had any access to supernatural powers: 'I do not thereby deny either the Being of Witches, nor other properties that they may have, for which they might be so called; no more than if I deny that a dog hath rugibility (which is proper only to a Lion), doth it follow that I deny the being of a Dog, or that it hath latrability.'

Among other famous cases, Webster personally involved himself in that of Edmund ROBINSON in 1634. He managed to get an interview with the boy at the centre of the hoax after Robinson appeared in his church, accompanied by two confederates, in order to identify witches in the congregation. The first that Webster knew of the boy's presence was a disturbance during one of his services:

> ... after prayers, I enquiring what the matter was, the people told me that it was the boy that discovered witches. Upon which, I went to the house where he was to stay all night, where I found him, and two very unlikely persons that did conduct him and manage the business. I desired to have some discourse with the boy in private, but that they utterly refused. Then in the presence of a great many people, I took the boy near me and said, 'Good boy, tell me truly, and in earnest, did thou see and hear such strange things of the meeting of witches as is reported by many that thou dost relate? Or did not some person teach thee to say such things of thyself?' But the two men, not giving the boy leave to answer, did pluck him from me, and said he had been examined by two able justices of the peace, and they did never ask him such a question. To whom I replied, 'The persons accused had therefore the more wrong.'

weighing against the Bible Traditional method of testing the guilt of a suspected witch, by which the accused person was weighed against the BIBLE in the local church to see which was the heavier. In accordance with the age-old theory that witches were unnaturally light, if the witch proved heavier than the book he or she was innocent, but if the Bible weighed more the suspect was clearly guilty as charged and a trial should be pursued.

It seems that in most cases suspected witches managed to outweigh the Bible and were set free, albeit reluctantly, by the mobs who usually instigated such informal tests of witchcraft. The practice continued well into the eighteenth century: in 1759, for instance, Susannah Haynokes of Wingrave in Buckinghamshire was subjected to the test after being accused of bewitching a neighbour's spinning-wheel – she proved heavier than the Bible and was released. In 1780 two more witches were similarly acquitted after they were suspected of witchcraft at Bexhill in Sussex.

Weir, Major Thomas c.1600–70. Scottish soldier and evangelist who came under suspicion of witchcraft as a result of his increasingly eccentric behaviour, and was eventually tried and executed for his alleged crimes. The case is illuminating in that it demonstrated how obvious insanity could be misinterpreted as evidence of diabolical magic.

Weir seems to have been born into a relatively well-connected Lanarkshire family, and in 1641 distinguished himself as a Parliamentarian soldier in the suppression of Irish papists. In 1649 he was appointed commander of the Edinburgh city guard. A strict Presbyterian who lived quietly with his sister, Jane Weir, he was much admired for the intensity of his praying and was among the senior figures in the Presbyterian Church in Edinburgh. Contemporaries spoke of him being considered 'more angel than man' and reported that others referred to him as 'Angelical Thomas'.

As he grew older Weir's behaviour became more erratic and eventually, at the age of seventy, he startled all those who knew him by making a voluntary confession of witchcraft. At first this confession met only with scepticism and the Major was examined by physicians sent to establish the state of his sanity. The doctors, however, concluded that he was sane and the Provost of Edinburgh had no choice but to arrest both Weir and his sister, who was implicated by her brother's confession. Among the crimes to which Weir confessed were fornication, incest and sodomy, as well as numerous acts of sorcery.

The couple were brought to trial on 9 April 1670, although all mention of witchcraft was deleted from the charges by those who were embarrassed by such a well-known Presbyterian figure being implicated in the diabolic. Instead Weir was accused of incest with his sister and his stepdaughter Margaret, adultery with her servant-girl and bestiality with horses and cattle. Jane Weir was accused of incest and sorcery. On questioning, Jane Weir, whose mental state was even more dubious than that of her brother, described how she had sold her soul to the Devil and how she kept a FAMILIAR spirit that, among other favours, enabled her to spin yarn at three or four times the rate of other women. She also explained to the appalled interrogators that her brother worked his magic through the use of the carved thornwood staff that he was never seen without.

The court found both the accused guilty of incest and bestiality and they were condemned to death. Accordingly, on 11 April 1670 Thomas was strangled and burned on Edinburgh's Gallowhill and his body was burned to ashes, while Jane Weir was hanged in the Grassmarket the following day.

Long after his execution, Thomas Weir was being cited as one of SCOTLAND'S most famous witches. Strange tales continued to be told of his former, long untenanted, house at the Head of the Bow in Edinburgh, as reported by Robert Chambers in his *Traditions of Edinburgh*, written in 1825:

> His house, though known to be deserted by everything human, was sometimes observed at midnight to be full of lights, and heard to emit strange sounds, as of dancing, howling, and, what is strangest of all, spinning. Some people occasionally saw the Major issue from the low close at midnight, mounted on a black horse without a head, and gallop off in a whirlwind of flame.

When one couple finally dared to move in after the house had been empty for some hundred years they vacated it the following morning, complaining that they had been woken during the night to find a spectral calf staring at them as they lay in bed. After a further fifty years in which the building remained unoccupied it was demolished.

Wenham, Jane d.1730. English countrywoman, nicknamed the 'Wise Woman of Walkerne', who was the last person to be sentenced to death for witchcraft by an English court. Wenham, of Walkerne in Hertfordshire, had long had a local reputation as a witch although she did not take at all kindly to such accusations. When a local farmer repeated the allegation she complained to the magistrates, but they refused to take the case any further (they did, however, fine the farmer one shilling for the insult).

More serious legal proceedings began in 1712 when Wenham was again accused of witchcraft practices, this time by Anne Thorne, servant-girl to a local minister. The girl complained that Wenham had used magic to afflict her with fits and with hallucinations of cat-like demons, and had also caused her to vomit pins. On one occasion the girl had been forced by the witch's magic to run for half a mile, despite the fact that she had recently injured her leg in an accident. The allegations were corroborated in part by a number of people including one James Burville, who claimed that he had seen numerous cats at Anne Thorne's door, one of them bearing a face just like Jane Wenham's.

On the strength of these accusations, backed up by her reputation, Jane Wenham was arrested and carefully searched for the DEVIL'S MARK in the time-honoured fashion, pins being plunged deep into her arm numerous times to see if the blood flowed freely and to ascertain whether she felt any pain. No insensitive spots were located but the prisoner made a full confession, admitting that she was a witch just as everyone claimed she was, but protesting that she practised only 'white magic (*see* WHITE WITCH).

Notwithstanding the confession made by the old woman (who appears to have genuinely believed she had a witch's powers), her accusers satisfied themselves with bringing a charge of 'conversing familiarly with the Devil in the shape of a cat'. Corroborating evidence was produced in court in the form of 'cakes' of feathers and a suspicious ointment that had been found under the woman's pillow. According to the prosecution the ointment was made of human fat, rendered down. The court, very much against the judge's wishes, found the woman guilty of this charge and she was sentenced to death. However, the judge, Sir John Powell, delayed the execution and subsequently secured a royal pardon for her – to the fury of many of the locals.

The case generated intense interest on a national scale and helped to polarise opinion about witchcraft: large numbers of tracts and pamphlets about the affair were published. After the verdict Jane Wenham found it impossible to return to her home village, such was the intensity of feeling towards her, and a local gentleman who was sympathetic towards her plight provided her with a small cottage at Hartingfordbury, where she lived quietly until her death in 1730. Anne Thorne, who had furnished the original charges against Wenham, was advised by her doctors to wash her hands and face twice a day and a young man was appointed to watch over her while she recovered from her hysteria. The treatment proved a success in more ways than one – Anne Thorne going on to marry the young man sent to watch her.

werewolf *see* LYCANTHROPY.

West, Rebecca *see* HOPKINS, MATTHEW.

Weyer, Johan 1515–88. German physician who was among the first outspoken critics of the witchcraft hysteria. A pupil of Cornelius AGRIPPA, he served as a tutor to the French royal family and subsequently accepted a post in Cleves, where he wrote several works on the subject of witchcraft. With his experience in the medical field, in such important books as *De Praestigiis Daemonum* (1563) Weyer was able to explain that many of the symptoms associated with demonic POSSESSION and witchcraft were the result of various psychological conditions. Certain people were deceived into thinking that they could work magic, but such claims, he argued, were the product of delusion. The Devil might do actual evil but witches had no supernatural powers. He dismissed the concept of the SABBAT as pure fiction and refuted the idea that all unexplained diseases were attributable to witchcraft – although he did not discount all supernatural phenomena as inventions (he recounted, for instance, how he personally had rescued a young virgin from being carried off by the Devil).

As a Protestant, Weyer laid much of the blame for the witchcraft panic at the door of the Catholic Church, accusing priests of assuming witchcraft to be the origin of all manner of symptoms that had a simple medical or psychological cause. He also condemned the use of torture to extract confessions and attempted to differentiate between black and white magic, although in this regard his views appear to have had relatively little influence on his contemporaries. To the witch-hunters of his time he issued a dire warning:

> But when the great searcher of hearts, from whom nothing is hidden, shall appear, your wicked deeds shall be revealed, you tyrants, sanguinary judges, butchers, torturers and ferocious robbers, who have thrown out humanity and do not know mercy. So I summon you before the tribunal of the Great Judge, who shall decide between us, where the truth you have trampled under foot and buried shall arise and condemn you, demanding vengeance for your inhumanities.

Through Weyer's writings the Duchy of Cleves and Juliers-Berg, where he acted as physician to Duke William, adopted a fairly lenient line on witchcraft and as a result the region was spared the worst excesses that traumatised other parts of Europe. This was not to say that there was not much outspoken opposition to Weyer's views: only the support of Duke William saved him from being burned as a witch-lover.

Whitehead, Paul *see* HELL-FIRE CLUB.

white witch A witch who drew on his or her magical powers solely for the purpose of doing good. Herbalists and local 'Wise Men' and 'Wise Women' (sometimes called 'Cunning Men' and 'Cunning Women') specialised in such beneficial magic centuries before the development of witchcraft as such, and the boundaries between folk magic of this kind and witchcraft proper are indistinct. Unfortunately, although sorcery for beneficial purposes was often tolerated by the authorities in the Middle Ages, during the witch-craft hysteria of the post-medieval era no such distinction was made. To acquire magical powers for any purpose a person must have signed a PACT WITH THE DEVIL and a so-called white witch was therefore, in the eyes of many courts, just as guilty as someone who had used their supernatural powers for more obviously nefar-ious ends.

The first legal moves against 'white' witchcraft were made as early as the tenth century, when excommunication (along with various lesser punishments) was threatened against anyone found guilty of such activity. Over the next five centuries opinions gradu-ally hardened against white witches along with the darker variety. Some authorities came to the conclusion that they were even more dangerous than the more obviously evil type, because their magic appeared to be good when it came in fact from the same source as the blackest sort – Satan himself. William PERKINS, writing in 1608, concluded:

> Though the witch were in many respects profitable, and did not hurt, but procured much good, yet because he hath renounced God, his king and governor, and hath bound himself by other laws to the service of the enemies of God and his Church, death is his portion justly assigned him by God: he may not live.

The general population, however, tended to view white witches with some sympathy, turning to them in times of need and even risking their own lives by so doing. Some authorities actually attempted a theoretical justification of 'white' witchcraft. According to Francesco-Maria GUAZZO, for instance, powers to perform such beneficial magic came from God rather than from the Devil and were therefore no cause for instituting legal proceedings (many white witches, in fact, invoked the name of God while casting their spells). More often, however, the demonologists viewed magic of any kind with a jaundiced eye and regarded all sorcerers and practitioners of magic – and those who consulted them – as necessarily evil. Many a white witch who professed to use magic only for good ended up on the gallows or at the stake because he or she was accused of also using their magic for evil ends.

White witches were generally 'born' rather than self-appointed, although many denied that they could pass their powers to their offspring purely by virtue of their birth. Some claimed to have received their powers from supernatural sources. One Yorkshire witch interviewed by John WEBSTER in 1653 explained how he had been befriended by some FAIRIES while on his way home one night, full of sorrow that he did not have the means to feed his family. The fairies provided the man with a white powder with which he could make a living curing the sick. The man was tried as a witch on the strength of such claims, but since no one could prove that he had done any evil through his powers he was acquitted.

Some people, not strictly witches, did not necessarily practise magic but were in themselves 'magical'. They included anyone who was the seventh son of a seventh son (in which case they were supposed to have great healing powers), women whose maiden names and married names were the same, and those with particularly significant names (couples named Mary and Joseph were often consulted for their advice in such matters). Blacksmiths were also reputed to have special powers and were believed to have possession of the highly valued and highly secret 'Horseman's Word' that, when uttered, calmed even the wildest horse. Another class of healers sometimes confused with white witches were the 'charmers', who usually specialised in the treatment of a specific ailment. These skills were often passed down through the generations in a single family, which might enjoy considerable local renown for its expertise in treating diseases of the blood, of the eyes or some other speciality.

White witches proper offered a variety of services, ranging

from countermeasures to malevolent spells and LOVE POTIONS to treatments for sick animals and magic remedies for bodily ills. They could protect households from lightning strikes, could trace lost or stolen property, could promote the growth of crops by conjuring rain, could prevent witches from 'hag-riding' livestock to their SAB- BATS and, among a thousand other things, could divine the future, sell fair winds to sailors and detect thieves. In identifying the evil witch who had cast a particular spell they usually declined to give precise names, but rather instructed the petitioner how they might find out the person's identity, typically advising them to be at a certain place at a certain time and to wait to see who arrived. Some white witches were also prepared to work spells designed to cause great pain to the person who was guilty of bewitching their client. If an animal had perished as a result of a spell, for instance, a white witch might advise burning the creature's heart – the culprit would be irresistibly drawn to the fire and so be identified (*see also* WITCH BOTTLE).

Experienced white witches boasted a huge repertoire of treat- ments for illnesses, and they were often consulted when appeals to conventional physicians had failed to produce a satisfactory treat- ment. In some cases they attempted to 'transfer' the ailment to another person, an animal or a tree. In others they used the magic of 'association', linking the ailment with a bean pod or a piece of meat or something similar and dictating that, as the object rotted, so the disease would fade. A third method involved the magic of sacrifice, with some small animal being ritually killed to placate the spirits causing the ailment in the first place.

As well as claiming skill at 'WART-charming' white witches treated such commonplace ailments as rheumatism (for which willow bark was a favoured ingredient), headaches and impotence as well as much more serious conditions of all kinds. Sometimes these apparent skills brought a particular Wise Man or Wise Woman con- siderable fame. Among the most celebrated was Bridget Bostock, who attracted many patients to her home in Church Coppenhall, Cheshire, in the mid-eighteenth century, as recorded in the *Gentleman's Magazine* of 1748:

She cures the blind, the lame of all sorts, the rheumatic, King's evil, histeric fits, falling fits, shortness of breath, dropsy, palsy, leprosy, cancers and, in short, almost every thing, except the French disease which she will not meddle with, and all the means she uses for cure is, only stroking with her fasting spittle, and praying for them ... the poor come in cart loads ... so many people of fashion now come to her, that several of the poor country people make a comfortable subsistence by holding their horses. In short, the poor, the rich, the lame, the blind and the deaf, all pray for her and bless her, but the doctors curse her.

Many of the herbal remedies recommended by white witches had soporific or narcotic properties and turned out to be the forerunners of modern drugs. Among the ingredients of their recipes were MANDRAKE, FOXGLOVE (the source of digitalis), poppy (from which they extracted opium), deadly NIGHTSHADE (the berries of which are the source of belladonna) and rye fungus (which developed into ergot). Both belladonna and ergot were likely to bring on hallucinations when absorbed through the skin. Less potent ingredients included soot and grease.

Herbalism was only one of many forms of action that a white witch might take to benefit a client. Methods, too, varied from one region to another. White witches in Germany and parts of the USA, for instance, often whispered or sang their patients back to health, while those in Italy tied KNOTS in lengths of thread and buried these in cemeteries in order to relieve their clients of bodily ills.

As was the case with black magic, a white witch might employ IMAGE MAGIC to achieve results, making wax figures of the client so as to cure them of their ailments and other problems. One procedure to lay a GHOST, for example, involved the witch preparing an effigy of the dead person and then ceremonially burying it and washing in water the person who had seen the ghost.

Tales of black witchcraft are in the main historical and belong to previous centuries, but there are still many people who claim skills as more socially acceptable white witches. A fair number of these work for no reward, claiming that to accept payment would oblige them to compromise their magic according to the patient's needs and desires.

See also PROTECTION AGAINST WITCHCRAFT; WICCA; WRIGHTSON, JOHN.

Whittle, Anne *see* PENDLE WITCHES.

whooping cough Witchlore offered a number of possible treatments for those afflicted with whooping cough, one of the most distressing and dangerous childhood illnesses. These ranged from relatively innocuous remedies to others that were quite outlandish. Among the more revolting cures were feeding the patient owl soup, a roast mouse or the slime of a snail mixed with sugar; suspending a hairy caterpillar in a bag around the sufferer's neck until it died; hanging a live frog in the chimney; coating the patient's feet with chopped garlic and lard; and feeding a dog a few strands of the patient's hair in bread and butter. Those whose mothers died in giving birth to them were reputed to have special powers of healing, and could cure whooping cough and thrush by simply breathing into the sufferer's mouth.

Wicca The name for the modern witchcraft movement which has gathered some momentum since the middle of the twentieth century. Members of the Wicca cult, which evolved from the writings of the historian Margaret MURRAY and Gerald GARDNER among other modern occultists, claim that their magic is devoted purely to the purposes of good, with the aim of benefiting health, countering evil and so forth. The accent is firmly on the ceremonial aspects of witchcraft, with elaborate procedures and a strong quasi-religious element, although the fact that participants are usually naked and sometimes engage in sexual rites has occasioned much scandalised comment.

The connection is frequently made between modern Wicca and post-medieval witchcraft, and then all the way back to pre-Christian pagan religion. The link between pagan worship and post-medieval witchcraft is tenuous in the extreme, however, and it is equally arguable that the link between the modern movement and historical witchcraft is little more than artificial. None the less, attempts to get a national centre for Wicca activities built in Milton Keynes, Buckinghamshire, in the early 1990s aroused much controversy in the locality, in part reminiscent of the response that witchcraft engendered in former times.

Prominent among proponents of Wicca belief since Gardner have been such figures as Alex Sanders, the self-styled 'King of Witches', who steered modern witchcraft in a more ceremonial direction, and Sybil Leek, a US witch who made a good living from the media through her pronouncements on television. The original movement has split many times over the years, with various offshoots pursuing their own interpretation of Wicca beliefs, some practising what is in essence a fertility religion and others concentrating on the sexual content.

widdershins Anticlockwise, the direction opposite to the path of the sun through the heavens, which was often stipulated as the correct movement to make in raising the Devil and in the execution of various ill-intentioned spells. To do something 'widdershins' or 'withershins' (from Anglo-Saxon *wither sith* – to 'walk against') implied a deliberate rejection of the 'normal', Christian way of doing things and was likely to attract the favour of the Devil and evil spirits, thus increasing the spell's chances of success.

Witches were widely reputed to stir their magic brews in a widdershins direction if evil was to be done. MAGIC CIRCLES, however, were drawn in a clockwise – 'sunwise' – direction in order to establish an effective barrier to evil spirits. Witches would customarily take an anticlockwise route in moving from one point to another or when approaching the Devil; many people claimed that, by simply walking 'the wrong way' three times round a church, a witch could raise ghosts and demons. According to both participants and independent witnesses SABBAT dances were always performed in a widdershins direction, and attempts were similarly made to oppose the conventions of the Christian world by saying prayers backwards and by reversing the symbols of the Christian Church.

Wier, Johan *see* WEYER, JOHAN.

Willies, John *see* HELL-FIRE CLUB.

Williams, Abigail *see* SALEM WITCHES.

willow The willow was associated in superstition with sorrow and lost love, but it also had some significance in witchlore. Although many people claimed it was unlucky to bring willow catkins into the house or to burn willow wood on the domestic hearth, it was agreed that certain varieties would ward off witches and the threat of the EVIL EYE. Those particularly nervous of interference by witches were advised to carry a 'sally rod', a switch made of the great sallow (or goat willow), which was reputed to be immune to enchantment and was therefore a deterrent to evil. It was, however, unwise to thrash children with willow sticks as this would stunt their growth.

Willow was much favoured by sorcerers and witches as a wood for the making of magic WANDS as it promoted success in the casting of SPELLS. In folk medicine, infusions of willow were reputed to be beneficial in the treatment of ague and against rheumatism (modern aspirin is based on salicylic acid, after *Salix*, the Latin name for the willow genus). Children suffering from rickets and other ailments were sometimes passed through a fork in a willow tree to effect a cure.

Wilson, Bessie and Margaret *see* AULDEARN WITCHES.

Wincanton Witches *see* SOMERSET WITCHES.

wind-raising *see* KNOTS; STORM-RAISING.

Wise Man/Woman *see* WHITE WITCH.

Wishart, Janet *see* ABERDEEN WITCHES.

witch The quintessential witch of popular imagination was an old hag, bent upon evil and deriving pleasure from inflicting pain and misfortune upon others in the name of her diabolical master. Dressed in black rags with a tall peaked HAT, and accompanied by a FAMILIAR in the form of a CAT, a bird or some other animal, she was irredeemably malevolent and contemptuous of those who sought to condemn her. Indeed, a time-honoured tradition held that witches were so indifferent to normal human emotions and sympathies that they were unable to weep (records of TRIALS and EXECUTIONS, however, suggest otherwise).

The terminology varied, some authorities preferring to distinguish male witches as wizards or warlocks, although historically the term 'witch' was understood to include both sexes. The fact that the majority of witches were women was readily explained by generations of demonologists: women were said to be more talkative, quicker to share their secrets than men, more gullible and more impressionable. Women were also deemed to be more likely to suffer from hallucinations than men. The term 'witch' was not technically synonymous with 'sorcerer', however – despite the fact that a sorcerer might similarly call on DEMONS to assist him in his magic, he did not intend that magic to be directed primarily at the destruction of Christianity as true witches were alleged to do.

Demonologists built up a detailed mythology of witchcraft and often agreed on the physical qualities of the average witch, who was depicted as aged, evil and unappealing. Typical was the depiction of the quintessential witch offered by Samuel Harsnett, Archbishop of York, in his *Declaration of Popish Impostures* in 1599:

> ... an old, weather-beaten crone, having the chin and her knees meeting for age, walking like a bow, leaning on a staff; hollow-eyed, untoothed, furrowed on her face, having her limbs trembling with the palsy, going mumbling in the streets; one that hath forgotten her paternoster, and yet hath a shrewd tongue to call a drab a drab.

A description of a witch in an English Christmas book of 1700, *Round About Our Coal Fire*, showed how little this popular image had changed in the intervening hundred years, which witnessed the worst excesses of the witchcraft hysteria: 'A witch must be a hagged old woman, living in a little rotten cottage, under a hill, by a wood-side, and must be frequently spinning at the door; she must have a black cat, two or three broomsticks, an imp or two, and two or three diabolical teats to suckle her imps.'

In many cases the popular image of the archetypal witch was mirrored in reality. WITCHFINDERS looked for easy targets during their witch-hunts and showed a marked preference for ignorant elderly women who tended to live as outcasts from the local community. It was usually no difficult matter to persuade neighbours to furnish accusations against such suspects, whose odd ways and unfriendly behaviour might have acquired them many enemies and an evil reputation over the years. Anyone with a squint, with eyebrows that joined in the middle or with a generally unattractive appearance was a natural candidate for such attention, and the discovery of WARTS or scars, reinterpreted as the DEVIL'S MARK or WITCH'S MARKS, would quickly confirm suspicion. According to the Scottish, anyone who had a 'mole above the breath' (in other words, above the mouth) could safely be assumed to be a witch. Other grounds included accident of birth: if a person's mother had been a witch the chances were that the child had inherited her powers and had followed her into the same manner of life (long-established tradition had it that a witch could not die until he or she had passed on their powers to someone else).

The historian Sir Charles Oman divided English witches into four classes: deliberate charlatans, those who believed that they really had power to harm their enemies, lunatics and victims of TORTURE or duress. Analysis of the surviving English records in the hundred years following the trial of the ST OSYTH WITCHES in 1566 suggests that over ninety per cent of convicted English witches were women, while eighty-five per cent of them were over the age of fifty and forty per cent were widows. Almost without exception they hailed from the lowest classes of society (many were beggars).

It was not uncommon, however, for young and beautiful women to be singled out as likely witches, especially on the

Continent – possibly because lusting magistrates wished to enjoy the power they could exert over them. Such accusations were not encouraged by the Church, which clearly feared that depictions of witches as young and sexually desirable would encourage more people to succumb to such heresy.

The stereotype that was accepted in ENGLAND held generally less well on the Continent of Europe. Although a good many suspicious elderly women were convicted as witches, as in England, the majority of them came from a quite different mould. The involvement of the INQUISITION from the very earliest beginnings of the witch-hunting hysteria meant that witch-hunters and judges alike had an eye to securing the conviction of rather better-heeled witches, whose wealth could be confiscated to reimburse costs and to line the pockets of both court officials and inquisitors. Among the victims of the hysteria in GERMANY, for instance, were senior members of universities, respected merchants and their families, and even the occasional mayor. Anyone who inspired envy through their wealth, popularity, learning or good looks was liable to be denounced as a witch by their enemies. To those who protested at the selection of such victims came the answer that the Devil was more than cunning enough to disguise his minions as the most worthy, the most honourable and the most pure people on Earth. There seemed to be no restriction on ages either: everyone from young children to aged grandparents was subjected to hideous torture and burning.

According to the European demonologists witches could be categorised in different ways. Sister Madeleine de Demandolx, one of the AIX-EN-PROVENCE NUNS, attempted her own version of the hierarchy as she perceived it at the SABBATS she witnessed:

> ... the hags and witches, who are people of a sordid and base condition, and whose trade and custom is to murder infants, and to bring them to the sabbat, after they have been buried in their grave, are the first that come to adore the Prince of the Synagogue ... in the second place come the sorcerers and sorceresses, who are people of a middle condition, whose office is to bewitch and spread abroad charms ... in the third place come the magicians

who are gentlemen and people of a higher rank; their office is to blaspheme God as much as they can.

Others attempted to subdivide witches by type according to the magic they worked. John Wycliffe, for instance, split them up into soothsayers, diviners (of which there were several species), enchantresses, fortune-tellers and various lesser classes. The Reverend John Gaule, tried as a witch in 1646, listed eight types: diviners, astrologers, witches who used the magic of signs and numbers, poisoning witches, exorcist or conjuring witches, gastronomic witches, magical witches and necromancers.

Once identified, all manner of MALEFICIA would be laid at the suspected witch's door, from illness in livestock and failure of crops to plagues, storms and murders. Typical charges laid against witches included SHAPE-SHIFTING, sexual intercourse with the DEVIL, flying on BROOMSTICKS, desecration of the sacred host and the keeping of familiars. However, not all witches professed to evil intentions (*see* WHITE WITCH).

witch ball Reflective MIRROR ball, once a popular domestic ornament. Formerly such balls were used by some sorcerers for purposes of DIVINATION, but they could also be used to deflect the power of the EVIL EYE.

Witch of Berkeley *see* BERKELEY, WITCH OF.

witch bottle A glass or iron bottle containing URINE and horseshoe nails that in former times was heated on a fire in order to counter any malevolent spell that might have been cast, sometimes with the intention of bringing about the death of the person responsible. The use of witch bottles was first recorded in the Netherlands, from where the idea was introduced to England. The ceremony, in the early years at least, was fairly complex, with participants being required to recite the LORD'S PRAYER backwards while the bottle heated up. If successful, the magic in the original spell would be turned back on the witch who had made it.

It was said that only the urine of a person untainted by witch-craft should be put in the bottle: if that of a witch was used, the bottle would explode (although some people held that this meant the witch would die). The usual practice was to put in the bottle the HAIR, nail parings, BLOOD and urine of the victim of the spell in question and to boil these up on the hearth at midnight. This would draw the culprit to the scene so as to be identified, or cause him or her so much agony that he or she was obliged to lift the spell.

The employment of witch bottles was still known in parts of East Anglia into the 1870s and possibly beyond, although at this late date the ritual had been much simplified and a humble jam jar of urine was usually placed on the fire.

Witch of Brandon *see* BRANDON, WITCH OF.

witch bridle Form of iron gag that was sometimes fitted to con-demned witches during TORTURE or on their way to execution. Many people feared that proven witches would expend their last breath placing CURSES upon those who had brought about their downfall, so they were anxious to deprive them of the power of speech. The bridle worked by holding down the tongue, making such utterances impossible.

A surviving example of a witch's bridle, preserved at Forfar Museum in Scotland, was used at the execution of several witches in the 1660s. One of these known by name was Helen Guthrie, a much-feared witch who was put to death in 1661.

See also WAKING A WITCH.

Witch of Eye *see* COBHAM, ELEANOR, DUCHESS OF GLOUCESTER.

witch hazel *see* HAZEL.

Witch of Newbury *see* NEWBURY, WITCH OF.

witch's mark Mark, protuberance or imperfection on the skin of an accused person, which was once considered physical proof of witchcraft. The theory of witch's marks was that every witch who kept a FAMILIAR fed it with drops of blood from his or her own body. These imps fed at special teats, and locating them furnished courts with proof of guilt. Evidence of witch's marks was especially welcomed in TRIALS staged in ENGLAND and SCOTLAND – and consequently also in New England.

Critics who questioned whether the Devil's minions had need of such physical sustenance were answered by Henry Hallywell in his *Melampronoea* of 1681 with the claim that DEMONS needed a supply of nutrients in order to maintain their immoral lifestyles:

> ... being so mightily debauched [they] wear away by a continual deflux of particles, and therefore require some nutriment to supply the place of the fugacious atoms, which is done by sucking the blood and spirits of these forlorn wretches ... And no doubt but these impure devils take as much pleasure in sucking the warm blood of men or beasts, as a cheerful and healthy constitution in drawing in the refreshing gales of pure and sincere air!

Witch's marks could be located virtually anywhere on the body, although they were usually found in relatively secret places and had to be carefully searched for. Sometimes the teat would be found near the fingers, sometimes it would be discovered on the head, under the tongue or near the genitals. It varied considerably in size. Elizabeth Sawyer, the Witch of Edmonton, who was tried in 1621, had 'a thing like a teat the bigness of the little finger, and the length of half a finger, which was branched at the top like a teat, and seemed as though one had sucked it'. Bridget Bishop, one of the SALEM WITCHES, on the other hand, was reported on first examination to have a smaller teat, which had disappeared altogether when a second search was made. John Bell, a Scottish clergyman who wrote on the subject in the eighteenth century, described witches' marks as being 'sometimes like a little spot, or a little teat, or red spots like flea-biting, sometimes also the flesh is sunk into a hollow'.

Many witches were found to have several witch's marks in different places on their bodies. When Amy Duny, one of the BURY

ST EDMUNDS WITCHES tried in 1662, was examined the experts identified no fewer than four such teats:

> They began at her head, and so stripped her naked, and in the lower part of her belly they found a thing like a teat of an inch long. They questioned her about it, and she said that she had got a strain by carrying of water which caused that excrescence. But upon narrower search, they found in her privy parts three more excrescences or teats, but smaller than the former. This deponent further saith that in the long teat at the end thereof there was little hole, and it appeared unto them as if it had been lately sucked, and upon the straining of it there issued out some white milky matter.

Witch's marks were quite distinct, it should be noted, from the DEVIL'S MARK, the insensitive visible blemish or invisible point that betrayed where the Devil had marked a suspected witch as one of his own. However, some WITCHFINDERS – including the notorious Matthew HOPKINS – claimed that both the Devil's mark and witch's marks were impervious to pain and made no distinction between them, routinely searching for them both at the same time in the process of PRICKING victims.

In answer to complaints from critics that there was no way to tell the difference between a witch's mark and a natural blemish or growth, Hopkins explained in *The Discovery of Witches* that there were three significant clues. The first two were the unusual position of the teat, far removed from the normal site, and the insensitivity of such areas. The third proof was what happened to a barely detectable mark if a suspected witch was prevented from feeding her familiars for some twenty-four hours:

> ... keep her 24 hours with a diligent eye, that none of her spirits come in any visible shape to suck her; the women have seen the next after her teats extended out to their former filling length, full of corruption ready to burst, and leaving her alone then one quarter of an hour, and let the women go up again, and she will have them drawn by her imps close again.

Such was the faith placed by people in the witch's mark as a proof of guilt that in 1593 the newly hanged body of Alice Samuel, one of the WARBOYS WITCHES, was stripped naked so that all present could see the 'little lump of flesh, in manner sticking out as if it had been a teat, to the length of half an inch' that so clearly demonstrated her culpability. Among the last authorities to espouse the theory of the witch's mark was the American demonologist Cotton MATHER, who defended his position with indignant resolution: 'I add, why should not witch marks be searched for? The properties, the qualities of those marks are described by diverse weighty writers. I never saw any of those marks, but it is doubtless not impossible for a surgeon, when he sees them, to say what are magical.'

Witchcraft Acts *see* ENGLAND.

witchfinder An official of the court, or, more usually, an independent individual who made it his business to root out witches in a local community. The typical witchfinder, claiming an intimate knowledge of the mythology of witchcraft, was motivated by the prospect of achieving monetary gain, personal prestige and power and, in some cases, the extermination of the Devil's followers on Earth. Loathed and feared throughout Europe, witchfinders fed on local gossip and trivial quarrels, preying on irrational fears of the supernatural and providing scapegoats for communities that might be hard-pressed by economic problems, disease and other difficulties beyond human control.

Taking it upon themselves to furnish the initial evidence for a case to be pursued by the authorities, from whom they usually received generous fees, they were certainly not above faking evidence to secure convictions (*see* PRICKING) and often adopted the most brutal methods available to them under local law to extract confessions. Most witchfinders, however, found pricking and SWIMMING sufficient to provide the evidence they required. Having made their allegations to the authorities, they collected their reward and in most cases left the village or town long before the actual TRIALS got under way.

Witchfinders travelled from town to town at the invitation of local authorities anxious about rumours of witchcraft in their midst. The fact that they were generally paid per witch identified was an obvious encouragement to the witchfinders to incriminate as many suspects as possible without antagonising local susceptibilities by naming people who were too popular or well placed enough to be able to defend themselves. Some of the witchfinders amassed substantial fortunes from their activities. Among the most infamous was Matthew HOPKINS, the self-styled 'Witchfinder-General', who terrorised East Anglia and neighbouring areas of England for a couple of years in the mid-1640s. Others active in the British Isles included Samuel Cocwra, who operated in the north-west Midlands under a licence granted by the Privy Council in 1579, and Scotsman Alexander Chisholm, who interrogated and tortured suspects in the comfort of his own home in Commer in the 1660s.

Professional witchfinders were a particular threat in the German states in the early seventeenth century. Among the most notorious of these corrupt investigators were Jakob Bithner, who identified witches on payment from the authorities in Styria, and a man named Geiss, who instituted a reign of terror in Lindenheim. Here he concentrated mainly on the richer members of the community, whose wealth was confiscated for the benefit of Church and town officials, but after overstepping the mark he was eventually driven from the town by the outraged citizens. Equally murderous were the attentions of Count Balthasar Voss (or Noss), who claimed to have secured the conviction of nearly a thousand witches over a fifteen-year period before the Supreme Court of the Holy Roman Empire curtailed his activities in 1603. Other zealous witchfinders included Jörg Abriel, who identified many witches in the Schongau area, and a man known as Nagogeorgus, who instituted a reign of terror at Esslingen near Stuttgart.

Particularly remarkable was the case of a German witchfinder named Kothmann, whose mother had been executed as a witch in the town of Lemgo. Kothmann subsequently rose, by nefarious means, to become mayor of Lemgo and then set about the systematic persecution of the families of those who had presided over his mother's death. By the time of his own demise in 1684 he had secured the execution of ninety people on charges of witchcraft.

As popular belief in witchcraft fell off after the mid-seventeenth century the witchfinders quickly disappeared from the scene. Most escaped punishment for their crimes and wisely withdrew from the public eye.

witch-stone *see* HAGSTONE.

withershins *see* WIDDERSHINS.

wolf Among the favourite disguises of the DEVIL was the wolf, a creature long feared in the annals of European superstition. Sightings of wolves were greeted with dismay in many regions and were widely regarded as portents of evil. The mere sight of a wolf could render a man dumb if the wolf saw the man first, and even saying the word 'wolf' was likely to conjure one up.

Welsh legend claimed that the wolf was created by the Devil rather than by God, and that the creature had remained faithful to its creator ever since. In German legend the Devil squatted between the creature's eyes. Some witches talked of assuming the form of wolves so as to terrorise local communities (*see* LYCANTHROPY) and the mythology of the 'werewolf' included the casting of various spells to achieve the transformation. Sometimes it was described how victims of spells had been transformed into wolves. In one old story witches turned a clergyman into a wolf, in which form he was identifiable only by his white collar.

On a more positive note, witchlore advised that the wolf had certain uses in folk medicine. Wrapping sufferers from epilepsy in a wolf's skin prevented them from having fits, and similar action could save the life of anyone who had contracted rabies. Hanging a wolfskin in the house kept flies away, it was claimed, and rubbing wolves' teeth against the gums was said to relieve the pain of toothache in the young, according to the French. Furthermore, a person who ate some wolf meat would be immune from seeing ghosts, and one who slept with a wolf's head under the pillow would be safe from nightmares. Those suffering from the colic, meanwhile, were recommended to smear wolf dung on their limbs.

Woodville, Elizabeth c.1437–92. English queen whose secret marriage to Edward IV in 1464 brought about sensational accusations of witchcraft. The eldest daughter of Sir Richard Woodville, First Earl Rivers, and Jacquetta, Duchess of Bedford, Elizabeth Woodville was first married to Sir John Grey. After he was killed in battle in 1461 she won the heart of Edward IV after meeting him for the first time under an oak tree in Whittlebury Forest. When news of the secret marriage (solemnised at Grafton, near Stony Stratford in Buckinghamshire) leaked out there was a furore, as the marriage was not deemed suitable for various political reasons.

The rumour spread that, with the assistance of her mother, the Duchess of Bedford, Elizabeth Woodville had used witchcraft to ensnare the King. The accusations were finally given full rein in 1469 when, during an uprising, Edward was imprisoned by the Earl of Warwick. A man called Thomas Wake took the opportunity to make formal charges against the Duchess of Bedford in an attempt to get the royal marriage invalidated. As evidence he produced a lead figure of a knight tied round with wire which had, he claimed, been fashioned for the Duchess for the purposes of IMAGE MAGIC. John Daunger, parish clerk at Stoke Bruerne in Northamptonshire, supported the claim that two more figures had been made, one to represent Edward and the other his intended bride.

The case came to court early in 1470, but by then Edward was free once more and Daunger retracted his statement, denying that the Duchess of Bedford had ever been involved in witchcraft. The Duchess was acquitted, but the rumours persisted and when Edward died in 1483 the allegations were revived (at least, according to Tudor propagandists, though historians refute it) by the King's brother, Richard of Gloucester, who hoped to usurp the throne from the young Edward V. If the marriage could be invalidated even at this late stage, Edward V's claim to the throne could be challenged.

Accordingly, Elizabeth Woodville and the deceased King's

mistress Jane Shore were accused by Richard of wasting his body through magic. Richard presented his withered arm as proof of their interference (his arm had in fact been withered since birth, but no one dared to point this out). Shore was thrown into the Tower of London and her property seized; she was forced to do penance in the streets of the capital, walking barefoot and clad only in a smock. Elizabeth Woodville, meanwhile, fled for the safety of Westminster with her youngest son. With the stage cleared, the usurper had himself crowned King Richard III. Not long afterwards he had both sons of Edward IV imprisoned in the Tower, where in due course they met mysterious deaths.

Elizabeth Woodville was restored to her rights as dowager queen on the accession of Henry VII in 1485, and died in retirement at the abbey of Bermondsey.

Wright, Elizabeth *see* BURTON BOY.

Wrightson, John fl.1800. English witch, known as the 'Wise Man of Stokesley', who was widely considered the most gifted WHITE WITCH of his generation. Wrightson was renowned throughout north Yorkshire and south Durham for his great wisdom, although many people also feared the strength of his powers. The seventh son of a seventh daughter, he claimed that his magic only worked when he was fasting. He was able to help in a wide range of circumstances, using his magic to trace lost or stolen property, to restore sick animals to health and to see great distances. Such was his reputation that men and women came from far and wide to consult him.

On one occasion, a miller realised that a set of valuable weights had been stolen and asked for help. Wrightson prophesised that the weights would soon be restored to him, covered in manure, and advised that when they did turn up the miller should take no further action. Sure enough, the weights reappeared exactly as foretold and the miller, suitably impressed, took the case no further. In all probability, the news that the famed witch was investigating the matter had been more than enough to persuade the thief to return the goods in the manner prescribed.

In another celebrated tale, two young lads, thinking to make fun of the old witch, called at his house on some pretext of needing his assistance. Wrightson sat them in front of a roaring fire, but when the pair tried to move their chairs further away from the blazing heat they found they could not budge. At length the old man relented and lifted the spell, allowing his thoroughly chastened guests to make good their escape.

Würzburg Witches The bishopric of Würzburg witnessed some of the worst atrocities committed in GERMANY during the witchcraft hysteria of the early seventeenth century. Comparable with what was happening at Bamberg, the witch-hunts in Würzburg claimed hundreds of lives, including those of many of the most distinguished and respected citizens. During the reign of Prince-Bishop Philipp Adolf von Ehrenberg between 1623 and 1633 some nine hundred witches were put to death throughout Würzburg in a holocaust that was instituted and largely maintained by the Jesuits.

The Chancellor of Würzburg, writing to an unidentified friend in 1629, gave a graphic account of the horror that had gripped the bishopric:

> The woe and misery of it! There are still four hundred of both sexes in the city, of high and low estate, even clergy, so strongly accused that they may be arrested at any minute ... In one word, a third of the city is surely implicated. The richest, most attractive, most prominent of the clergy are already executed. A week ago, a girl of nineteen was burned, of whom it is said everywhere that she was the fairest in the whole city, and universally regarded as a girl of exceptional modesty and purity. In seven or eight days, she will be followed by others of the best and most attractive persons ... To conclude this horrible matter, there are three hundred children of three or four years, who are said to have had intercourse with the devil. I have seen children of seven put to death, and brave little scholars of ten, twelve, fourteen and fifteen years of age ...

At the same time that he noted these tragedies, the Chancellor also represented the opinion of the times, however, when he added in a postscript details of the latest rumours of huge SABBATS of eight thousand witches being held in the locality.

He reported that the names of the guilty were all recorded at the sabbat by a notary, now arrested, and that he hoped the book would be found – 'everybody is diligently searching for it'.

The panic in Würzburg only subsided after the Prince-Bishop's sole heir, Ernest von Ehrenberg, was accused of witchcraft by the Jesuits and executed after a secret trial and sentencing (secret even to the defendant). The first the young man knew of his plight was on the morning of the execution, when he was led directly to the torture chamber and, after a brief struggle, put to death. The Prince-Bishop, who had resisted last-minute calls for clemency, subsequently appears to have regretted his decision and the climate of opinion began to change under his now moderating influence (although the name Ehrenberg remains one of the blackest in the whole history of the witchcraft mania). The approach of an invading Swedish army finally distracted the authorities from persevering with their witch-hunts with the fervour they had previously espoused.

wych elm Otherwise called the 'witch elm', this tree was supposed to have various magical properties. The tree was widely regarded as lucky, and carrying a stick of wych elm was reputed to ward off all manner of evil. In order to prevent witches interfering with the churning of butter, a favourite misdemeanour (*see* BUTTER-SPOILING), one defence was to slip a twig of wych elm into the churn.

Y **yarrow** Herb that was once highly valued for its alleged magical properties, which included an ability to deter witches. Variously known as soldiers' woundwort, nose bleed, milfoil, devil's plaything, thousand weed and bad man's plaything, yarrow was widely believed to be a protective against evil, probably because in Christian legend it was the first herb held in the hand of the infant Jesus. Consequently, anyone who carried a little of it on their person was presumed safe from witchcraft.

Witchlore suggested that anyone who slept with a little yarrow beneath their pillow would enjoy visions of their future partner in love, providing they first intoned the following rhyme:

> Good night, fair yarrow,
> Thrice good night to thee,
> I hope before tomorrow's dawn
> My true love I shall see.

Yarrow taken from the grave of a young man was held to be the most magically potent. It was also believed to be useful in the treatment of nosebleeds and stomach upsets.

yew Evergreen tree long associated with life after death and therefore also with the supernatural in general. Often planted in graveyards, the yew, with its poisonous leaves and dense timber, was believed to provide PROTECTION AGAINST WITCHCRAFT and to keep people safe from GHOSTS – the reason why it was also frequently planted close to houses. It has even been suggested that many churches were originally built in spots where they would be close to an existing yew tree, to enjoy the benefits it offered. Because of such notions it was thought unlucky to cut down a yew tree – as it was to bring any of its foliage into the house, for evil spirits might enter with it. Yew wood was formerly much favoured for the making of dowsing rods and magic WANDS, although the fact that it was used for weapons of various kinds increased its reputation as an essentially malign tree.

Young girls consulting witches to obtain a glimpse of a future partner in love were sometimes advised to sleep with a sprig of yew under their pillow, with the proviso that the girl picked the sprig herself from a graveyard that she had never before visited.

Youghal Witch *see* NEWTON, FLORENCE.

Young, Alice *see* CONNECTICUT WITCHES.